D0401444

Also by Donald Keene

BOOKS

The Battles of Coxinga

The Japanese Discovery of Europe

Japanese Literature: An Introduction for the Western Reader

Living Japan

Bunraku: The Art of Japanese Puppet Theatre

Nō: The Classical Theatre of Japan

Landscapes and Portraits

World Within Walls: Japanese Literature of the Pre-Modern Era, 1600–1867

Dawn to the West: Japanese Literature of the Modern Era (Volumes I and II)

Some Japanese Portraits

The Pleasures of Japanese Literature

Travelers of a Hundred Ages: The Japanese as Revealed Through 1,000 Years of Diaries

Seeds in the Heart: Japanese Literature from Earliest Times to the Late Sixteenth Century

On Familiar Terms: A Journey Across Cultures

TRANSLATIONS

The Setting Sun (by Osamu Dazai)

No Longer Human (by Osamu Dazai)

Five Modern Nō Plays (by Yukio Mishima)

Major Plays of Chikamatsu

The Old Woman, the Wife, and the Archer (by Shichiro Fukasawa, Chiyo Uno, and Jun Ishikawa)

After the Banquet (by Yukio Mishima)

Essays in Idleness (by Yoshida Kenkō)

Chūshingura (by Takeda Izumo, Miyoshi Shōraku, and Namiki Sōsuke)

Madame de Sade (by Yukio Mishima)

Friends (by Kobo Abe)

Twenty Plays of the Nō Theatre (edited and translated)

The Man Who Turned into a Stick (by Kobo Abe)

Three Plays by Kobo Abe

ANTHOLOGIES

Anthology of Japanese Literature

Modern Japanese Literature

Modern Japanese Diaries

The Japanese
at Home and Abroad
as Revealed Through
Their Diaries

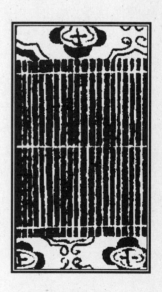

Donald Keene

Henry Holt and Company
New York

Dedicated to Sam Houston Brock, Jr.

Henry Holt and Company, Inc.
Publishers since 1866
115 West 18th Street
New York, New York 10011

Henry Holt® is a registered
trademark of Henry Holt and Company, Inc.

Copyright © 1995 by Donald Keene
All rights reserved.
Published in Canada by Fitzhenry & Whiteside Ltd.,
195 Allstate Parkway, Markham, Ontario L3R 4T8.

Library of Congress Cataloging-in-Publication Data
Keene, Donald.
Modern Japanese diaries : the Japanese at home and abroad as
revealed through their diaries / Donald Keene. — 1st ed.
p.   cm.
1. Japanese diaries—Meiji period, 1868–1912—History and criticism.   2. Japanese diaries—
Taisho period, 1912–1926—History and criticism.   I. Title.
PL741.6.K43   1995
895.6'840309—dc20   94-33827
                                                                                                     CIP

ISBN 0-8050-2055-1
ISBN 0-8050-4665-8 (An Owl Book: pbk)

Henry Holt books are available for special promotions and
premiums. For details contact: Director, Special Markets.

First published in hardcover in 1995 by Henry Holt and Company, Inc.

First Owl Book Edition—1996

Designed by Betty Lew

Printed in the United States of America
All first editions are printed on acid-free paper. ∞

10   9   8   7   6   5   4   3   2   1
10   9   8   7   6   5   4   3   2   1 (pbk.)

Contents

PREFACE   ix

INTRODUCTION   1

The Early Missions to Foreign Countries

    Diary of a Voyage to America   9

    Journey to America in His Excellency's Service   31

    Leisurely Journey of a Fly on a Horse's Tail   43

    Diary of a Journey to Europe   57

    Journey to the West   64

    Journey to France and England   73

    Voyage to the West   77

    True Account of a Tour of America and Europe   90

    Journal of a Voyage to the West   119

Travelers in Asia

    Bridges in the Clouds, Rain in the Gorges   135

    Travels in the North   148

    Exploration of the Southern Islands   164

Writers Abroad

The Diaries of Mori Ōgai *189*

The European Diary of Natsume Sōseki *213*

The Diaries of Niijima Jō *225*

Diaries by Politicians

The Diary of Kido Takayoshi *249*

The Diary of Ueki Emori *254*

Diaries by Women

Koume's Diary *269*

The Diary of Higuchi Ichiyō *284*

The Diary of Tsuda Umeko *304*

Mineko's Diary *313*

The Diary of Shimomura Toku *321*

Poets and Novelists

An Undeceitful Record *329*

The Diaries of Masaoka Shiki *355*

The Diaries of Ishikawa Takuboku *377*

The Early Twentieth Century

Record of Impressions *403*

The Diary of Kōtoku Shūsui *436*

The Diary of Tokutomi Roka *447*

The Diaries of Kinoshita Mokutarō *470*

The Diaries of Nagai Kafū *488*

CONCLUSION *507*

INDEX *511*

Preface

The essays on Japanese diaries contained in this book originally appeared in the *Asahi Shimbun* four or five times a week for somewhat over a year. The pace of publication was hectic and, inevitably, errors crept into my text. In preparing the English version, I have taken advantage of the opportunity to correct those that I spotted.

The text is essentially the same as the one which appeared in Japanese, though I have not hesitated to add information that I thought might be helpful to readers unfamiliar with Japan and the Japanese. My account of any one of the diaries can be read independently, but various themes (such as travel abroad) link the different diaries and impart, I believe, a certain unity to personal accounts by men and women who wrote under strikingly different circumstances.

I have followed throughout the Japanese practice of calling people by their surnames followed by their personal names, rather than in normal Western order; but there is unfortunately a problem involved in this usage. Many writers were known by their literary names (*gō*), rather than by either their surnames or the names by which their mothers called them. I have referred to writers in the way followed by Japanese today, rather than attempt to impose uniformity. Thus, Natsume Sōseki and Mori Ōgai are called Sōseki and Ōgai (Natsume and Mori alone would be unintelligible); but Kume Kunitake and Iwakura Tomomi, who were not literary men (and therefore lacked well-known *gō*), are called by their surnames. I have also followed Japanese practice in referring to women who did not have a *gō* by their personal names, rather than their surnames. All this is confusing, I realize, but I believe it is preferable to follow Japanese usage, rather than impose alien ideas of order.

Introduction

I have used the word "modern" in this book to describe the diaries written by Japanese between, roughly, 1860 and 1920. Diaries of this period tend to cluster into groups written under similar circumstances. The journeys to America and Europe of various Japanese during the 1860s, the last years of the shogun's rule, are very similar, regardless of how greatly the personalities of the diarists differed. Several diaries even have identical titles such as *Kōsai Nikki* (Diary of a Voyage to the West). Other diaries cluster around such events as the Sino-Japanese War of 1894–95, the Russo-Japanese War of 1904–5, or the Pacific War of 1941–45. Still others relate to the settlement of Hokkaidō or the assertion of Japanese control over the Ryūkyū Islands. All the diaries share a feature not true of many diaries of earlier times: because they were faithfully kept day-to-day, they rarely falsify the facts for literary reasons.

Even a diary that is intended to be no more than a truthful account may, however, contain fiction. Nothing prevents a diarist from changing an entry after the fact, or adding material with hopes of making the diary more easily publishable. For example, the principal diaries by Masaoka Shiki were published serially in a newspaper, and he no doubt felt obliged to maintain a constant level of interest, even if this involved some fabrication. Again, various authorities doubt that the diary of Nagai Kafū, published after the conclusion of the Pacific War, was what he actually wrote in 1941–45; it would have been easy for him, if he so chose, to add expressions of hatred for the military once militarism had been rejected by the mass of Japanese.

It is hard for a person with literary gifts to keep from improving on the truth even when relating something that happened that day, and the temptation to embellish is all the greater when he describes the events in his diary. He may relate events that never really occurred, simply because life is generally not as artistic as the artist might desire. But even if we can demonstrate that certain diary entries must be untruthful, they may nevertheless reveal much about the diarist: as products of his imagination, they are certainly more important than the weather and other more mundane aspects of everyday life.

During the eleventh and twelfth centuries the ladies of the Japanese court kept diaries, often because they had no friend in whom they could confide. They were also, whether they realized it or not, addressing readers of future times, and lending immortality to events that would otherwise have disappeared without a trace. Courtiers of the time kept diaries for quite a different reason, to record events at court with a view to providing their descendants with information about precedents and other important matters. By the nineteenth century, however, the writing of diaries had become so common a feature of Japanese life as to require no special explanation. Most people kept diaries simply in order not to forget what they did on a certain day, perhaps with the vague expectation that in old age they would reread the diaries and enjoy the experiences afresh. Ishikawa Takuboku, the author of several of the most remarkable diaries of the modern period, declared in one of them, "Writing a diary is extremely interesting. It is interesting when one is actually writing it, but when one reads it again years later the interest is all the greater."

Takuboku had at least two other reasons for keeping diaries. The first was that he needed someone to talk to, and the diary served as a kind of audience for his perceptions. He grew up in a remote village in the north of Japan. The education he received there was surprisingly good, but as his intellectual interests deepened, he felt a distance separating him from the other inhabitants of Shibutami village, and this made him lonely. He wrote, "Shibutami is an out-of-the-way village, with not even a hundred houses, in the wilds of Michinoku. It is an extremely backward place where there is almost no one with whom to talk about poetry, a haunt of country bumpkins without one redeeming feature apart from its splendid natural scenery."[1]

Unable to discuss poetry and other matters that absorbed him with his friends in Shibutami, Takuboku turned to his diary for company. In general, the greater the alienation he felt from his surroundings, the more moving his diary becomes. But it took time, perhaps several hours on some days, to write his extensive diary entries, and in later years Takuboku was (consciously or not) faced with the choice of whether to express his emotions fully in his diary or to write poetry instead. In his last years, when he chose poetry, his diary was neglected, and the entries were no longer very interesting.

Takuboku had another reason for keeping a diary. As a modern man, living in an age when literature had increasingly become a commodity, he sometimes thought of his diary as raw material from which he would someday fashion works of literature. This use of the diary or journal is familiar in Europe, but I cannot recall an earlier Japanese example. Takuboku in fact wrote several stories in which he employed materials from his diary. In every instance the stories are less affecting than the diary.

Finally, on occasion Takuboku attempted to publish sections of his diary either as originally written or after giving the text some literary embellishments. This use of the diary was also new, but it soon became common in Japan, especially among writers of naturalist fiction. In this way the diary acquired new functions which it still retains.

It is harder to understand why many nonliterary people of Takuboku's time also kept extensive diaries. A few important statesmen recorded in their diaries private information that they could not openly disclose. They seem to have expected that historians would read their diaries; but many other diarists of the late nineteenth and early twentieth centuries recorded almost nothing more exciting than descriptions of the weather, or names of visitors and of people from whom they received letters. Only a scholar who was desperately searching for clues into the life of a particular person would find interest in these diaries. Why, we are likely to wonder, should busy men have spent hours each day writing down facts that might just as well have been forgotten?

The impetus to keep diaries went back to old Japanese traditions. It was as natural for these people to keep diaries as it is for Japanese today to take group photographs as souvenirs of an occasion. Wherever I travel in Japan I know in advance that such photographs will be taken, and sooner or later I will receive copies. They are occasionally useful when I try to recall the faces of people who have been helpful to me during a lecture tour, but what is one to do with all the photographs that accumulate in thirty years? And how is one to keep one's attention focused on a diary that covers thirty years if it is written in the factual style favored by most diarists? As I read such diaries, I always entertain hopes of making a discovery, and it sometimes does happen: after wading through page after page of boring details of daily life, each page as unmemorable as a group photograph of strangers, I will suddenly encounter something of exceptional literary or human interest. Those are the unpredictable moments that make the reading of diaries particularly exciting and exceptionally interesting.

My greatest pleasure in the diaries I have selected for consideration in this book has been the individual voice of the diarist. I have tried always to detect something that comes from the writer's heart, some statement that (even if inartistically expressed) makes me feel I know the author and could recognize him or her even in a group photograph; and knowing one person well can sometimes make it possible also to know the world he or she lived in.

Notes

1. Diary entry for March 4, 1906.

The Early Missions to Foreign Countries

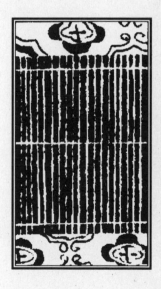

Diary of a Voyage to America

The most important event of modern Japanese history, it goes without saying, was the opening of the country after more than two hundred years of isolation. This event is often discussed in terms of the arrival of foreigners in Japan, either as diplomats or merchants living in concessions in Nagasaki, Yokohama, and elsewhere. But even more important in terms of Japanese history is the fact that some people were given permission to go abroad, as members of diplomatic missions or as students of foreign learning.

A small number of Japanese had gone abroad even during the period of isolation. Most of them went involuntarily: they were fishermen whose ships were caught in a storm and driven to the corners of the Pacific. A few of the shipwrecked men were found by the Russians in Kamchatka and the Aleutian Islands and taken to Siberia. The Russians, eager for trade with Japan, had established a Japanese language school in Irkutsk at the beginning of the eighteenth century, and the school depended on Japanese castaways for teachers. On several occasions the Russians attempted to "open" the country by returning castaways to Japan, but without success. The most famous of these castaways, Kōdayū, who had been shipwrecked on the island of Amchitka in 1783, was taken back to Japan by the Russians in 1792. He was allowed to proceed from the port of Nemuro in Hokkaidō to Edo, where he was closely examined by officials of the shogunate.

Kōdayū was an intelligent man and an excellent observer of European customs, as we know from the transcripts of the interrogations to which he was subjected, but neither he nor any other of the shipwrecked fishermen kept extensive diaries. Most were illiterate, and even the educated ones were not of a class that normally kept diaries. Kōdayū, John Manjirō, Joseph Heco, and various others in later life wrote absorbing accounts of their life abroad, and the few men who intentionally left the Japanese islands, such as the explorers of the north, Mamiya Rinzō and Mogami Tokunai, described their travels in the form of reports. The first diary to describe in detail travel abroad was probably the one kept by Muragaki Norimasa (1813–1880), the governor of Awaji.[1] His diary, *Kōkai Nikki* (Diary of a Voyage), describes his journey in 1860 as a member of the embassy sent to the United States to ratify the treaty of amity and commerce concluded in 1857. The diary is of exceptional interest, not only because of the descriptions of everything Muragaki saw, but because of the highly personal, even literary style. The literary aspect is underlined by the inclusion, in the traditional manner, of the poems composed by the diarist on every occasion of interest. Muragaki had the same prejudices about foreigners shared by most Japanese of his day, which accounts for his unfriendly comments, but it is hard not to feel affection for a man who recounted his impressions and sentiments with such honesty.

Muragaki was born in Edo (the present Tokyo), the son of a shogunate official. In 1854 he was placed in charge of the sea defenses of Ezo (Hokkaidō), and later that year, when the Russian admiral E. V. Putiatin's fleet called at Shimoda, he was sent to receive the visitors. He spent the following year supervising the construction of fortifications along Edo Bay, and the year after he was appointed magistrate (*bugyō*) of Hakodate in Ezo. In 1859 he was named second-in-charge of the embassy sent to Washington to exchange documents signifying the ratification of the treaty with the United States.

Muragaki's diary opens with an entry written during the ninth moon of 1859. That day he reported for duty at the castle in Edo as usual, but was informed that he should go at once in a linen *kamishimo*[2] to the Hibiscus Chamber. In the presence of Ii Naosuke, the virtual dictator at the time, and various other officials, Muragaki and two other men were informed of their mission and commanded to make suitable preparations. That night, when Muragaki returned home, he discovered that a moon-viewing party was to be held, but his mind was too full of his new responsibility to think about the moon. He wrote in his diary, "When I told them that, to my great surprise, I had been chosen as an envoy on an unprecedented mission to a distant country, my wife and children, not saying a word about the great honor, looked much distressed, and moaned, 'What shall we do? What shall we do?'"[3]

Muragaki tried to comfort his family by emphasizing what an honor this appointment was, but even as he spoke he felt uncertain of his capability in carrying out this great mission:

> I humored them by telling them of the unprecedented responsibility I had been given, and of the possibility of gaining such celebrity in all five continents that it would truly make it worthwhile to have been born a man, but after much careful consideration, I felt terrible pangs in my heart at the thought that someone as incapable as myself had been commanded to accompany the first Japanese mission sent abroad since the creation of heaven and earth; if I should fail my lord by bungling this commission, what a disgrace it would be to the Land of the Gods![4]

But that night the moon was brightly shining so, in the traditional manner, Muragaki exchanged cups of sake with his men and composed this poem:

ima yori wa	From today forward
kotokunibito mo	Even men of other lands
aoguran	Will look up to see
wa ga Akitsushima	The light of the moon shining
tsuki no hikari wo	On our Akitsushima.

No doubt Muragaki was apprehensive about crossing the sea to an unknown land, but he took comfort from thinking of the respect for Akitsushima—a poetic name for Japan—that would be stirred even among foreigners. This consolation remained with him even during the worst days of the journey.

Muragaki crossed the Pacific aboard the American warship *Powhattan*. The *Kanrin Maru*, a ship purchased from the Dutch by the Japanese government, was to accompany the *Powhattan* as training for its crew. The captain of the *Kanrin Maru* was the noted Katsu Kaishū (1823–1899), who had studied in Holland, but some shipwrecked American officers and sailors had been given passage aboard the ship, and they guided it on its course while Katsu was incapacitated by seasickness.

Before the departure of the two ships many parties were held at which Muragaki and his associates composed innumerable poems. Muragaki did not actually go aboard ship until three months after he had first been informed of his commission. When shogunate officials arrived at his house on the morning of the eighteenth day of the first moon of 1860 to inform him of the imminent departure of his ship, he felt that, despite his apprehensions, he had to act nonchalant before his family. He wrote in his diary, "If I hadn't put on as big a show of heroism as I could muster, my children would probably have been very downcast." He composed this farewell poem:

tama no o wa	Entrusting the thread
kami to kimi to ni	Of my life both to the gods
makasetsutsu	And to my liege lord,
shiranu kuni ni mo	I shall leave behind a name
na wo ya nokosan	Even in unknown countries.

Muragaki's first taste of the sea occurred when he went by small boat to the *Powhattan*, then anchored in Edo Bay. The wind was high and the waves so rough that some in Muragaki's party were already seasick, even before leaving Japan, a foretaste of the weeks of misery awaiting them.

As soon as the Japanese set foot on the deck of the *Powhattan*, they were greeted by what Muragaki called *kogaku* (barbarian music). He never became accustomed to the sounds of Western music, and constantly complained in his diary about the earsplitting noises to which he was subjected. But he noted with approval that the party was greeted by a seventeen-gun salute, evidence of the respect the Americans accorded to the Japanese embassy. Once the formalities had been completed, there ensued a scene of enormous confusion as the two or three interpreters valiantly attempted to cope with sorting and sending the baggage of eighty-one Japanese to the right quarters.

The *Powhattan* set sail from Edo on the twenty-first day of the first month. Muragaki calmed his fears by composing a tanka:

maho agete	With its sails raised high
shinato no kaze ni	May the ship run speedily
toku hase yo	In the cleansing wind,
kami no mikuni no	For ours is a departure
funade nariseba[5]	From the country of the gods.

The next day Muragaki reported in his diary, "Every last man seems to be seasick. Some are in great agony, others not quite so bad. Seasickness is one malady that strikes regardless of a person's strength or weakness."[6] The Japanese were unable to rinse their mouths in the morning, let alone eat, and spent their days lying help-lessly in their bunks.

Even during the worst of his seasickness, Muragaki did not ne-glect his diary.[7] The sea was unusually rough: the commodore said that it was the worst storm he had encountered in his twenty-eight years before the mast. There was a constant sound of breaking dishes and glassware, and it was hard to keep one's footing while emerging from one's bunk. Before leaving Japan the Japanese had worried about the difficulties they were likely to encounter abroad, but they had not expected to experience such torment even before reaching a foreign country.

On the third day of the second month Muragaki wrote in his diary, "It is already ten days since we set sail, and at some point we seemed to have become accustomed to the motions of the ship. First one man then another got up, apparently cured of his sickness, and since yesterday there have been quite a few on deck."[8] But as the Japanese recovered from their seasickness, other things began to annoy them: "The barbarian music, played morning and evening, is absolutely deafening."

On the fourteenth the Hawaiian Islands were sighted. It had originally been expected that the ship would sail directly from Edo to San Francisco, the course that the *Kanrin Maru* in fact followed, but because of the damage suffered during the storm the *Powhattan* had turned south to Honolulu for repairs. Muragaki was delighted to see land again:

hatsuka amari	Twenty days and more
nami no ukifushi	Of repeated tossing in
kasanete wa	The raging billows:
sasuga ni ureshi	No need to say with what joy
oki no shima yama[9]	We saw the island mountains.

Even the sickest Japanese aboard the *Powhattan* was revived at the sight of land. Muragaki wrote, "Every last one of us looked like an invalid, exhausted by the days at sea, but the sight of land was like rain after a terrible drought." In Honolulu the Japanese had their first experience of attracting crowds. Of course, the crowds in Honolulu were modest in size and no match for the unprecedented turnouts that welcomed the Japanese at the major American cities, but they made the Japanese realize for the first time that they would be as great a curiosity to the foreigners as the foreigners were to them.

After they reached their hotel they obtained some local fish that they cut up into sashimi. Muragaki wrote that the taste was incomparably delicious, but he added a note (perhaps when putting the diary into final shape) that after a day or two the local fish began to taste like mud. The yearning for Japanese food is a constant motif throughout the diary. Although the members of the embassy had brought along large quantities of miso, soy sauce, pickles, and so on, these supplies dwindled rapidly. One of the memorable pages of Muragaki's diary describes the joy of the Japanese when rice in a bowl with a lid was served to them in Philadelphia. However, the rice had been cooked in butter, to their dismay. They sent the rice back to the kitchen, asking that it be cooked without butter, only for it to reappear cooked with sugar. The disappointed Japanese ate bread instead.[10] Muragaki commented, "In general, customs relating to food are the same throughout the world, but our country's are unique. For this reason, it is impossible to describe adequately in words the hardships we suffer when we travel abroad."[11]

Muragaki and the others went sightseeing in Honolulu. The royal palace did not impress them much: "The fence is broken, and it looks like some deserted mountain temple. Only two structures might be called main buildings."[12] The people in the streets were unusual, but nothing in the shops surprised Muragaki because, he says, he had already seen similar wares in Yokohama. Two days later an invitation came to visit the palace. Muragaki noted, "Although he is called a king, he is no more than the chieftain of an island, so we decided to go in our traveling clothes."[13]

Muragaki was not impressed with Kamehameha IV: "He was

dressed in a black serge suit with narrow sleeves, exactly like an American, but he wore something like a sash draped around his shoulders."[14] He was more favorably impressed by Queen Emma: "She is twenty-five or -six. Her face is extremely dark, but she does have a certain dignity appropriate to her station. She wore a thin robe that left both shoulders exposed but concealed her breasts. From the waist down, she wore a garment that looked like a *hakama*[15] of some beautiful brocade. She wore a necklace of beads and looked for all the world like a living Amida Buddha." The royal couple inspired Muragaki to compose a comic poem:

goteishu wa	The master of the house
tasuki kake nari	Wears a sash round his middle,
okusan wa	The lady of the house,
ōhada nugite	Her shoulders fully exposed,
chinkaku ni au[16]	Meets visitors from afar.

Nothing pleased Muragaki in Honolulu. He complained there was nothing to buy that would make souvenirs. When a child sang a Hawaiian song for him, he sourly commented, "The voice was like a dog howling late at night." But when he gave the child a present, the child was just as happy as a Japanese child would be. The discovery that, despite appearances and customs, people everywhere are basically the same, is a frequent comment in the diary. Despite his prejudices, Muragaki could not help but admit that he was learning much from his journey: "When I carefully reflect on what happened today, I realize that all I had previously known about conditions abroad had been derived from the notes on the reports of men shipwrecked abroad that I happened to have read. To have been treated with such courtesy by a king and his queen made me feel as if I were in dreamland."[17]

The *Powhattan* sailed from Honolulu on the twenty-seventh day of the second month. The voyage to San Francisco was smooth, and the Japanese were not troubled with seasickness. The ship entered

San Francisco Bay ten days later. Muragaki had already learned by *teregarafu* (telegraph) that the men aboard the *Kanrin Maru*, which had reached San Francisco while the *Powhattan* was still in Honolulu, were impatiently waiting to see them. After the joyful reunion, Muragaki noted in his diary, "To meet in a foreign country people from our own land was so unlike similar experiences during an ordinary journey that I felt extremely nostalgic, and for a moment was incapable of words."[18]

When Muragaki and the others reached their hotel, "At the entrance to the place there were many attractive-looking women. We were not accustomed to this and were suspicious, but later we learned that this was true everywhere abroad. It is an example of the difference in national customs."[19] Muragaki never really got used to the presence of women at state gatherings, and when, after his return to Japan, he and the other principal figures in the embassy were invited by the captain of the American warship to visit the ship with their wives and children, Muragaki commented, "It is because he still does not know the customs of our country that he, in conformance with his own customs, should have made such a suggestion."[20]

On the thirteenth day of the third month the Japanese were invited to a dinner given in their honor by the mayor of San Francisco. This was the first time they had attended a Western-style banquet, and they were bewildered—not by the cutlery or the food but by the complete absence of formality. Muragaki's description is humorous and captures the atmosphere of a dinner party attended by the high society of a town that was still in the Wild West. (The gold rush had taken place only twelve years earlier.) Muragaki wrote,

> After a while the mayor stood and banged on a plate. Another man, standing off in the distance, catching the signal, also banged on a plate. When the barbarian music stopped and the place became quiet, the mayor talked about something in a loud voice and at extremely great length. When he finished, everybody stood up and shouted three times in a loud voice,

ippinwā,[21] and everybody drained his glass and applauded or else beat on a plate. The barbarian music started again, and the sound of people's voices was such as to make one want to cover his ears.[22]

The interpreter later informed Muragaki that the gist of the mayor's speech was his pleasure that the Japanese delegation had visited his city and his best wishes for the health of the shogun. The American commodore, replying for the Japanese, had offered a toast to the health of the president of the United States. It seemed to Muragaki that the speeches would go on forever. He noted that the most admired speeches were greeted with applause, and the next best ones by banging on plates. The popping of champagne corks sounded to him like cannon fire. When the Japanese could endure no more they asked an American officer to make their excuses to the mayor, who at once banged on a plate and announced that the dinner was over.

After returning to their hotel that night, the Japanese discussed the party in these terms: "Considered as an expression of goodwill, it no doubt was sincere, but less indulgently considered, it much resembled the drinking party of coolies after they have completed a building in Edo."[23] This sober appraisal of the party was accurate, and the lack of etiquette that so distressed him in San Francisco would characterize more civilized parts of the United States as well. To a shogunate official, whose deportment was always controlled by etiquette, this new country seemed barbarous indeed.

The *Powhattan* sailed on the eighteenth from San Francisco to Panama. The transcontinental railway was not yet completed, and the easiest way to get from San Francisco to Washington was by sea to Panama, across the isthmus by train, and then by another ship to a port near Washington. The voyage to Panama was uneventful and took a little more than two weeks. When the Japanese said goodbye to the captain and crew of the *Powhattan* they shook hands in the Western manner. Muragaki commented, "Although we are foreigners on our first voyage overseas, they shared the hardships we have experienced ever since leaving our country; and when I recalled the great care and kindness they had bestowed on us and their sincerity, I felt as if we were taking leave of fellow Japanese, and kept wanting to turn back." He composed this poem:

sugata mireba	If one examines
kotonaru hito to	Their appearance one would think
omoedomo	They are foreigners,
sono magokoro wa	But in terms of sincerity
kawarazarikeri[24]	They are just the same as us.

These sentiments do not often occur in Muragaki's diary, but they would be typical of many Japanese who later traveled abroad.

The train journey, the first for any Japanese, proved to be boring, once the initial excitement had faded. The train made so much noise they could not hear one another speak, and the villages they passed were so dreary they reminded Muragaki of Ainu settlements in Hokkaidō.[25] At the Atlantic side of the isthmus, they boarded another American warship. The captain of this ship had been with Commodore Perry in Japan. Muragaki noted, "Adams, who was the second-in-command after Perry, is the captain of a patrol vessel in this port. When he visited our ship and told stories about his experiences, he acted as if he were very familiar with our country. The look of pride on his face convinced me he was a hateful person."[26] Adams was evidently an early member of a familiar species, the foreigner who thinks he knows more about Japan than the Japanese, and Muragaki's words *nikuki jimbutsu* (hateful person) reveal his distaste for the type.

On the *Roanoke*, as it headed for New York, two American sailors died, and Muragaki described their burial at sea. He felt sorry for ordinary seamen who have no grave but the sea—unlike the officers, whose remains would be carried to dry land for burial—but he remarked, "When we Japanese saw that even the commodore was present to send off to their graves some ordinary seamen, it made us think that he did so because his country is governed without etiquette or distinction between high and low; people act solely by exhibiting their true feelings." Muragaki considered the attendance of the commodore at the funeral of ordinary sailors another instance of the lack of *reigi* (etiquette) in America, but he may also have been impressed by this display of *shinjitsu* (true feelings).

When the Japanese were about to disembark from the *Roanoke* and board a steam launch that would take them into the city of Washington, Muragaki noted, "They played barbarian music, and the *Roanoke* fired a salute of seventeen guns. The sailors of one accord climbed up the many masts and, at the sound of a cannon, they let out a great shout. I was informed that this was the highest mark of respect they show when bidding farewell."[27] Later, when they passed George Washington's tomb at Mount Vernon, Muragaki observed another instance of American etiquette: "At this place they always make it their practice before they pass to stop the boat and play music, and each person aboard then takes off his hat and bows in worship. The fact that they do this in a barbarous country without decorum must reflect natural principles."[28]

Muragaki and the other samurai were not much impressed by the American military men they saw. He estimated that not more than twelve or thirteen men aboard the *Roanoke* were professional military personnel; the rest were mainly foreign hirelings who knew nothing about weapons. He concluded, "It would be an easy matter with the heroism of our country to reduce them in one blow to smidgeons."[29] Needless to say, some of the Europeans and Americans who visited Japan arrived at similar conclusions with respect to the capabilities of the Japanese military.[30]

The Japanese were the objects of unbounded attention in Washington. Muragaki wrote in his diary, "On shore men and women swarmed inside and outside the houses, some even climbed up on the roofs to get a look at us . . . There were so many sightseers filling the streets that the streets disappeared from sight. Among the onlookers were what they call newspaper men who ran around taking notes of some kind. I heard later that the newspapers were quickly printed and put on sale the same day. I also heard that they had set up their cameras in second-story windows and taken pictures of us landing."[31] Church bells were rung in honor of the Japanese, and women threw bouquets of flowers into their carriages. Muragaki wrote, "The thoroughfares and houses were jammed with people, like Edo on the day of a festival. I was told that never before in the history of Washington had so many sightseers assembled."[32]

Muragaki had no trouble in guessing why the Japanese were so popular. When embassies from other countries came to Washington, the members did not differ in appearance from Americans, and usually only one or two foreigners arrived at one time. But in the case of the Japanese, "our country has long been closed, it is our first trip abroad, and our customs and government are different. Moreover, there are eighty of us. No wonder people have found us unusual."[33] Muragaki nowhere expressed pleasure over the reception given to the Japanese wherever they went, but he could hardly have failed to be at least a little moved.

When the Japanese arrived at their hotel rooms in Washington, the first thing they did was to get rid of the chairs. "There were chairs, but we disposed of them and spread mattresses on the floor and sat informally. Then, after taking precautions so that none of *them* could enter, we clustered in various groups to tell stories about our journey today. Everything we had seen was so strange that at times we could hardly restrain our laughter." Sitting on chairs was evidently a strain for the Japanese: Muragaki related after his return to Japan that "Sitting on a tatami crosslegged for the first time since sailing from Japan, I felt resuscitated."[34]

The Americans tried to please the Japanese with a display of unaffected friendliness, but their informality sometimes surprised or even shocked their guests. After they had visited the secretary of state, Muragaki wrote, "There was not the slightest display of courtesy toward a foreign embassy on first meeting. They acted as if old friends they met every day had arrived, and they did not bother to the end to serve even tea. I thought it really would be difficult for them to escape being called a barbarian country."[35]

The Japanese never forgot their sense of decorum even in a country that seemed to lack this virtue. The day before they were to meet the president, they asked an American about the etiquette to be observed. He answered in a typical American manner, "Do as in your own country." They decided to follow the decorum observed by Townsend Harris when he had an audience with the shogun, but because they attached such importance to performing the ceremony correctly, they wanted to have a rehearsal at the White House the next morning. They were informed that if they wanted a rehearsal it would have to be that night, but the Japanese refused, saying they made it their policy never to go out at night.

On May 17, 1860, the day the Japanese were to deliver to President Buchanan the documents of treaty ratification, the senior members of the delegation, splendidly attired in formal clothes and hats, traveled from their hotel to the White House in a procession of carriages. Along the way crowds strained to catch glimpses of the Japanese in their finery. Muragaki reflected, "I felt as if I had gone to this barbarian country and made the light of the Imperial Country shine. Forgetting my limitations as a foolish person, I allowed a look of pride to cross my face—how silly of me!"[36] For a moment Muragaki was able to see himself with humor.

The Japanese arrived at the White House and proceeded to the room where the president, along with civil and military officials and many women, was awaiting them. Shimmi Masaoki (1822–1869), the governor of Buzen, the head of the mission, delivered the documents to the president. The Japanese supposed that this marked the end of the ceremony, but they were called back, and the president, shaking Shimmi's hand, declared (according to Muragaki's diary) that "not only he, the president, but the people of the entire country were overjoyed that the Japanese had concluded their first treaty of amity since entering into seclusion, and had set an embassy to the United States before any other country; and he expressed his special appreciation for the contents of the gracious messages that had been vouchsafed from the Imperial Country."[37]

Back at their hotel, the Japanese discussed the president's appearance: "He has white hair, is amiable, and has dignity, but he dresses exactly like a merchant in black serge with narrow sleeves and tight trousers. He wears no decoration whatsoever, and not even a sword."[38] The high-ranking American officials looked undistinguished and, strangest of all, a large number of fancily dressed women were permitted to be present on this important occasion. In such a country, Muragaki concluded, "there is no distinction between high and low and absolutely no decorum, and for us to have worn formal court costume had served no useful purpose." However, Shimmi was pleased to think that his picture, showing him in his finery, would appear in the newspapers.

Muragaki was happy for another reason: "I was absolutely overjoyed to think that we on this first embassy ever sent to a foreign country should have transmitted without mishap the message from our lord; it really was worth having been born a man for this occasion." He added the tanka:

emishira mo	Barbarians too,
aogite zo miyo	Look up and behold on high
higashi naru	Far off to the east
wa ga hi no moto no	The light emanating from
kuni no hikari wo[39]	Our land of the rising sun.

Muragaki was skeptical about American democracy. He had heard that the president was elected every four years by ballots from the entire people, but he suspected that the elections were rigged. He had heard that the next president had already been secretly chosen, and that he was a relative of Buchanan's. He predicted, "It is unlikely that the laws created at the founding of the country will long continue."[40] It is hard to imagine the source of this rumor: the next president was Lincoln, who was definitely not a relative of Buchanan's. Muragaki also expressed skepticism about the rule that gifts offered to the president and other high officers must be turned over to a museum. He wrote, "I gather that any kind of present, as long as it is specified that it is for a man's wife, becomes his possession."[41] Muragaki's cynicism reflects his distrust of a society that was so unlike his own.

The Japanese broke their rule about never going out at night when they were invited a few days later to attend a dance party. Muragaki recorded, "Men and women in pairs line up, and then, in keeping with the rhythm of the music, circle the room like dancing mice, without the least elegance or skill. Any number of pairs come circling by, and it is amusing to see how the hems of the women's skirts, catching the wind, spread out all the more. This they call *dansu*, which must mean dance."[42] Twenty years later, Japanese ladies would be dancing in similar fashion at the Rokumeikan Ballroom in Tokyo, but naturally Muragaki could not foresee this.

Again and again Muragaki complained of the uncouthness of the Americans that permitted what for him were shocking displays of discourtesy to foreign guests:

> I was so appalled by the sight of hundreds of men and women, after first taking their fill of food and drink at table, coming to this place to participate in the dancing, all night long I was told, that I could not be sure whether I was seeing a dream or reality ... We said goodbye to our host and returned to the hotel. In general, this is a country without decorum, and if one were to tax the prime minister (*saishō*) for discourtesy in the reception given to an embassy from a foreign country, there would be no end to it. I decided to let it go as an affair that

showed they have no decorum, no integrity, nothing more than kindliness."[43]

The Japanese envoys were given special permission, never before accorded to foreigners, to attend a session of Congress. Muragaki was not favorably impressed by this glimpse of democracy in action. He observed a meeting of the Senate at which "some forty or fifty men sat in rows. One of them got up and started to rant in a loud voice, flailing with his hands like a madman. When he had finished saying something, another man got up and acted in the same way."[44]

Most of the other sights of Washington upset Muragaki. The marble busts of the presidents displayed in the Capitol reminded him of severed heads at an execution place in Japan, and the locks of hair of the successive presidents, kept in a glass case, seemed even more disgraceful: "One can tell from this one thing, that they possess no sense of decorum."[45] He was sure that unless the Americans learned to pay greater respect to the people of the past "they will be unable to escape the reputation of being savages."[46]

When the Japanese attended one large party at the White House they were deafened by the "barbarian music" and annoyed especially not to be offered tea or tobacco. When they asked to go to the toilet, they were told to endure the need because there were no toilets in the building, and when they persisted, they were led through deserted halls, making them wonder if they were being tricked by foxes and badgers, the traditional bewitchers of Japanese fairy tales. But when it was explained to them that the purpose of the party was to enable people from all over the country to see the Japanese envoys, Muragaki commented, "This is proof that it really is no more than a collection of states."

The silly questions the Japanese were asked also annoyed them. The president's niece, for example, asked how many court ladies the shogun had in his palace. Muragaki squirmed out of that question only to be asked whether Japanese or American women were more beautiful. He answered diplomatically, "American women are better because their complexions are fair."[47] The answer pleased the lady. Muragaki commented in his diary, "Her character must be one of simple honesty." But one gets the impression, despite his constant complaints, that Muragaki, the object of attention of so many persons of high rank, was beginning to enjoy his stay in America.

After leaving Washington the Japanese made brief visits to Baltimore and Philadelphia before proceeding to New York where they were to board an American warship for the journey back to Japan. The Americans urged the Japanese to see more of the country, but the latter refused to go even as far as Niagara Falls, believing that it was improper to linger in America now that their mission had been accomplished.

Their arrival in New York was greeted by crowds even bigger than those in Washington. Muragaki noted, "Not a foot or an inch of land was left vacant by the sightseers, men and women."[48] Muragaki, looking out from his room on the fifth floor of a hotel, surveyed the sprawling city. He does not reveal whether it impressed him, contenting himself with the remark that New York was about one-third the size of Edo.[49] Philadelphia had pleased the Japanese with its quiet dignity, but New York seemed ungracious: "The people are cold-hearted, and the things on sale are expensive and of inferior quality."[50]

The Japanese visited the widow of Commodore Perry, an impressive, dignified old lady. Muragaki wrote in his diary, "Perry is highly respected for his great accomplishment in having opened our closed country and having brought the two countries into friendly relation, but I heard that he died three years ago. When I mentioned that the visit of the embassy on this occasion was also being credited to his achievement, and said that having unexpectedly come to this house, I could only wish that he were still in this world, the old lady's eyes filled with tears and she could not speak."[51] This was probably the closest human contact between the Japanese and the Americans they met on this journey.

The Japanese naturally were unaware that the visit to New York was commemorated by Walt Whitman in a long poem that begins,

> *Over sea, hither from Niphon,*
> *Courteous, the Princes of Asia, swart-cheeked princes,*
> *First-comers, guests, two-sworded princes,*
> *Lesson-giving princes, leaning back in their open barouches*
> *bare-headed, impassive,*
> *This day they ride through Manhattan.*

Whitman contrasted the impetuous spirit of freedom of New York with "the venerable Asia, the all-mother," and urged New Yorkers: "Bend your proud neck to the long-off mother, now sending messages over the archipelagoes to you." Undoubtedly the people of New York were impressed by the Japanese, and some may have felt for a moment ashamed of their brash, indecorous ways. The reception in New York brought an auspicious close to the visit of the Japanese envoys.

The return voyage to Japan was by way of the Cape of Good Hope and the Indian Ocean. The Japanese passengers did not suffer from seasickness this time, but they were often short of water and the heat in the tropics was oppressive. Their joy upon seeing Japan again can only be imagined.

Only at the very end of his diary does Muragaki state why he kept it. "I have put together this volume of tedious length, not because I have ever intended to show it to anyone, but because I thought it would be unfortunate if I were to forget completely how, when I traveled abroad, I came to realize the sacred nature of the Land of the Gods or if I forget how other countries and peoples differ or, for that matter, the hardships I endured at sea. For this reason

I kept a diary at the time and thought I should like to show to my descendants this awe-inspiring instance of divine favor."[52]

Muragaki had written the first important Japanese diary of the modern era, an unforgettable chronicle of the meeting of two civilizations.

Notes

1. High-ranking officers of the shogunate often had such old-fashioned titles as "governor of Awaji" or "governor of Settsu," but this did not involve residence in their supposed posts.
2. The *kamishimo* is a semiformal costume, the most distinguishing feature of which is a hempen jacket with wide shoulder boards. It is still used at many festivals as well as by Kabuki actors and Bunraku performers.
3. Muragaki Norimasa, *Kembeishi Nikki,* p. 1.
4. *Ibid.*, p. 2.
5. *Ibid.*, p. 15. *Shinato no kaze* is a wind that purifies all taint or sin, but the emphasis here is not on its power to cleanse but on its origins in the holy, pure land of Japan.
6. *Ibid.*, p. 17.
7. It should be noted, however, that the diary was not put into its present form until Muragaki's return to Hakodate after his voyage.
8. Muragaki, *Kembeishi Nikki,* p. 22.
9. *Ibid.*, p. 27.
10. *Ibid.*, p. 159.
11. *Ibid.*
12. *Ibid.*, p. 32.
13. *Ibid.*, p. 35.
14. *Ibid.*, p. 36. The word translated as "sash" is *tasuki,* a cord worn around shoulders to hold back the hanging sleeves of a kimono.
15. Divided skirts of a formal Japanese costume.
16. Muragaki, *Kembeishi Nikki,* p. 39.
17. *Ibid.*, p. 38.
18. *Ibid.*, p. 52.

19. *Ibid.*, p. 57.
20. *Ibid.*, p. 237.
21. Hip-hip-hooray?
22. Muragaki, *Kembeishi Nikki*, p. 61.
23. *Ibid.*, p. 63.
24. *Ibid.*, p. 74.
25. *Ibid.*, p. 78.
26. *Ibid.*, p. 82.
27. *Ibid.*, p. 95.
28. *Ibid.*, p. 97.
29. *Ibid.*, p. 96.
30. For example, the celebrated novelist Ivan Alexandrovich Goncharov, who visited Japan with the Russian fleet in 1854, made fun in his *Voyage of the Frigate Pallada* of the appearance of the Japanese and expressed scorn for their martial prowess.
31. Muragaki, *Kembeishi Nikki*, pp. 98–99.
32. *Ibid.*, p. 100.
33. *Ibid.*
34. *Ibid.*, p. 242.
35. *Ibid.*, p. 104.
36. *Ibid.*, p. 106.
37. *Ibid.*, p. 108.
38. *Ibid.*, p. 109.
39. *Ibid.*, p. 110.
40. *Ibid.*
41. *Ibid.*, p. 112.
42. *Ibid.*, p. 113.
43. *Ibid.*, p. 114.
44. *Ibid.*, p. 128.
45. *Ibid.*, p. 146.
46. *Ibid.*, p. 147.
47. *Ibid.*, p. 137.
48. *Ibid.*, p. 164.
49. *Ibid.*, pp. 166–67.
50. *Ibid.*, p. 167.
51. *Ibid.*, p. 174.
52. *Ibid.*, p. 254.

Bibliography

Miyoshi, Masao. *As We Saw Them: The First Japanese Embassy to the United States (1860)*. Berkeley: University of California Press, 1979.

Muragaki Awaji-no-kami. *Kōkai Nikki: The Diary of the First Japanese Embassy to the United States of America*, trans. Helen M. Uno. Tokyo: Foreign Affairs Association of Japan, 1958.

Muragaki Norimasa. *Kembeishi Nikki*, in Nihon Shiseki Kyōkai (ed.), Kengai Shisetsu Nikki Sanshū series, I. Tokyo: Tōkyō Daigaku Shuppankai, 1971.

Journey to America
in His Excellency's Service

As we have seen, it was originally planned to have the *Kanrin Maru* accompany the *Powhattan* to San Francisco and from there to Panama. These plans had to be abandoned when the damaged *Powhattan* put in at Honolulu for repairs. The *Kanrin Maru* traveled on to San Francisco alone, but it too had been damaged in the Pacific storms, and could not accompany the *Powhattan* to Panama. Instead, it put into dry dock at San Francisco for repairs and later returned to Japan.

The *Kanrin Maru*, a steamship purchased from Holland in 1857, was the first ship of the new Japanese navy. It was also the first Japanese ship to travel abroad with official permission since early in the seventeenth century. The captain, Katsu Kaishū, had received naval training under Dutch instructors in Nagasaki, and is generally regarded as the founder of the Japanese navy, but the commanding officer was Kimura Yoshitake (1830–1901), the governor of Settsu and commissioner for warships (*gunkan bugyō*) in the shogun's government. Kimura's diary, *Hōshi Meriken Kikō* (Journey to America in His Excellency's Service), describes the voyage of the *Kanrin Maru*. Although it lacks the idiosyncrasies and prejudices that make Muragaki's diary such entertaining reading, it is not only of historical value but also a document of unusual human interest.

Kimura states in the opening words of the diary why it had been decided to send him aboard the *Kanrin Maru* to San Francisco and beyond, even though he was not charged with any special mission:

> The reason I was commanded to travel to America was, first of all, in order to escort during its voyage the first embassy we have ever sent to a foreign country. This grand and unprecedented undertaking of sending ships abroad for the first time since antiquity would also mark a beginning in our relations with other countries. This was my long-cherished desire, and since I was occupying the appropriate office, I could not at this point decline on the grounds that I was incompetent.[1]

Kimura was excited by the prospect of opening a new era in Japanese history, but he realized that although some members of the crew of the *Kanrin Maru* had been trained in navigation, they lacked the experience to make the voyage unaided. He related,

> Our navy was created only a year or two ago, and the various items of discipline have not been uniformly mastered. The fact is, when it comes to the arts of navigation, nobody on the face of the globe is the equal of the Europeans, and even we Japanese have no choice but to take them as our teachers in the arts in which they excel. However, it would be difficult to put into practice overnight foreign ways of doing things in our country. This factor was the most difficult aspect of the voyage and the one that worried me from the very beginning."[2]

The solution that occurred to Kimura was to arrange for some experienced Americans to assist the captain and crew of the *Kanrin Maru*: "I requested the government to have some Americans who were familiar with the sea routes accompany us on the forthcoming voyage, and permission was speedily granted. Fortunately, I was informed by the American minister that a Lieutenant Brooke[3] of the same country was residing in the city of Yokohama, and he accepted without reservations."[4] Kimura later wrote of Brooke, "He is an extremely amiable man, and is thoroughly familiar with the art of navigation. To have this man participate in our operation was for me the greatest good fortune."[5]

Fukuzawa Yukichi, who would emerge as one of the major figures in Japanese history of the late nineteenth century, was also aboard the *Kanrin Maru* on its epoch-making voyage. Probably in order to emphasize the achievement of the Japanese crew, he played down the importance of Brooke and the other Americans. He wrote in his autobiography, "As I have shown, the Japanese officers were to receive no aid from Captain Brooke throughout the voyage. Even in taking observations, our officers and the Americans made them independently of one another. Sometimes they compared their results, but we were never in the least dependent on the Americans."[6] But there was no need to distort the truth for patriotic reasons. Captain Kimura and the other Japanese of the *Kanrin Maru*, even though they received American help, performed an extraordinary feat. They served aboard a ship that crossed the Pacific during the winter storms and reached their destination safely. On the return voyage they managed to do without American aid.

Preparations for the voyage of the *Kanrin Maru* were extensive. The officers, from Katsu Kaishū on down, were all known to Kimura, who had personally selected them for the mission. He wrote, "These men were all my close friends, and being well acquainted with their devotion and outstanding abilities, I recommended them to the government, and they were chosen for the crew on this occasion."[7] Perhaps it was Kimura's friendship for Katsu that induced him to neglect to mention the fact that Katsu was running a fever even before the ship sailed, and was so seasick that he was unable to leave his cabin during most of the voyage; his commands could not have been very effective.

The preparations included storing immense quantities of food. Kimura wrote, "We took aboard large amounts of the food that makes up the normal diet for people of our country—rice, soy sauce, salted fish, seaweed, and so on, especially rice, which is the most essential item, and because we feared that after a long period the rice might rot, we also laid in a large supply of dried rice."[8] The terror inspired among Japanese at the thought of not being able to obtain Japanese food while abroad continues to this day. At the beginning of the century, the American dancer Loie Fuller, the backer of the European tour of the celebrated actress Sada Yacco and her company, wrote, "These thirty cost me more than ninety of another nationality might have done; for apart from everything I was obliged to do to entertain them, I had constantly to go down on my knees to secure permission to attach to each train that carried them an enormous car laden with Japanese delicacies, rice, salted fish, mushrooms and preserved turnips."[9] Kimura, like Muragaki, seems to have been convinced that "food and customs are in general the same everywhere in the world. Only our country is different."

Kimura was fortified before his departure by a promotion granted by the shogun. He wrote in his diary,

> On the twenty-eighth day of the tenth month he bestowed a special promotion to the lower junior fifth rank, appointed me as governor of Settsu, and increased my stipend by two thousand *koku*.[10] On the following day, the twenty-ninth, I was also given leave to carry out my mission in America, and I had the honor of an audience with the shogun himself. At the conclusion he bestowed on me ten pieces of gold and two costumes, to which he added an overcoat. At these repeated marks of his favor and gracious generosity I could not restrain tears of gratitude.[11]

On the twelfth day of the first month Kimura visited the shogun's palace and formally took leave of the shogun and the other senior officials. Afterward, he returned home and drank parting cups of sake with his relatives and friends. That evening he bade farewell to his father, wife, and children, and went by small boat to the *Kanrin Maru*, then anchored off Shinagawa. The ship did not set out for America until the nineteenth, and in the meantime it called at various nearby ports. On the fifteenth, for example, it put in at Uraga to load firewood, water, vegetables, and fish. Members of the crew who came from Uraga were given special permission to go ashore and say goodbye to their families. A local official named Sashida Rinzō visited the ship along with the son of one of the ship's officers. Kimura and he had known each other from childhood but had not met in almost ten years. Kimura was surprised to see that Sashida's hair was already gray. Such small, intimate details give this diary far more appeal than the usual official reports. It is easy to feel that one has made a friend in Kimura, the governor of Settsu.

Hardly had the *Kanrin Maru* left Uraga than it was buffeted by strong adverse winds. On the twenty-third Kimura noted in his diary, "Ever since yesterday a fierce wind has been blowing. We have been unable to eat cooked food anywhere on the ship. The sailors are exhausted, and most of them are unable to leave their bunks." Kimura's assistant, Saitō Tomezō, wrote in his diary that a bare four or five of the ninety-six Japanese aboard were able to go out on deck to do their work. "At this time we have received help from the Americans in taking in, paying out, raising, or lowering the sails and all such work. Even when they encounter a storm like this, not one of them is afraid, and they perform their tasks in a manner hardly different from ordinary."[12] It must have been galling for the Japanese, confident in their ability as sailors because of the training they had received from the Dutch at their station in Nagasaki, to see the Americans going about their work, indifferent to the storm, and eating three square meals, while they could not even crawl from their bunks.

On the seventh day of the second month a major event in the history of the Japanese navy occurred. A three-masted ship was sighted. It raised the 4910 signal flag, asking the nationality of the *Kanrin Maru*, to which the signal flag 5472 was raised, signifying it was a warship of the Japanese navy. This was probably the first time a Japanese ship had raised this flag.

California was not sighted until the twenty-sixth day of the second month, over a month after leaving Japan. That afternoon the *Kanrin Maru* dropped anchor in San Francisco Harbor. Kimura recorded, "It was such a truly rare event for a Japanese ship to come here that the people of the city turned out in crowds, and the crowds gazing at us from a distance looked like ants."[13] When the Japanese boarded the horse carriages that would take them to their official reception, mobs of people, old and young, swarmed around, hoping for a look at them. At the hotel various American officials presented their compliments. "Many women also came to see us. I was surprised at this and asked who they were. I was informed that they were all the wives and daughters of officials and had come to welcome the distinguished visitors."[14] Perhaps Kimura (like Muragaki) at first supposed the women had been charged with quite other duties!

From the next day on Kimura and the other officers were frequently invited to receptions offered by the prominent people of San Francisco. He showed a great deal more appreciation of the entertainment than Muragaki had. He described the banquet on the twenty-ninth in these terms: "The reception was extremely friendly, and the food and drink were of the finest quality." He was also more tolerant of Western music than Muragaki, as he indicated in this account of a military band: "The sounds are heroic, quite unlike the music of our country. I was told that in Europe, America, and elsewhere this music is used at all naval and army events. The instruments consist of flutes and bugles made of brass as well as drums. The fourteen musicians all wore the same caps and uniforms and made an extremely impressive sight."[15]

It is noteworthy that even in these early encounters between Japanese and Americans, the reactions of the Japanese were by no means the same. Kimura, though no less of a shogunate official than Muragaki, responded far more positively to unfamiliar customs, dress, food, and music. The same two varieties of Japanese travelers are still to be found in every corner of the world, some ordering the most exotic dishes on the menus of local restaurants, others eating their instant *ramen* noodles in their rooms.

Muragaki could express no more than grudging admiration for the Americans he met, but Kimura was able to think of some of them as friends. I wonder if this was not the first time a Japanese used the word "friend" for a Western person. When Captain Brooke informed Kimura that he was about to leave San Francisco and return home (he would before long join the Confederate Navy[16]), Kimura decided to offer a farewell dinner for him:

> I arranged for a small farewell party to be held at the hotel. On that occasion Captain Mackey attended, along with his wife, the children of the commodore, and various other officers, making for a festive gathering. I felt his friendship and kindness during the voyage, of course, but from the time I first arrived on the ship he took care of many things for me, and when the ship was in for repairs, he exerted himself to the utmost, remaining in the shipyard for days at a time, and arranging things as he thought best. The fact that the repairs were completed in a short time, as I had hoped, was truly thanks to his ability. I frequently thanked him for his efforts, but he always replied that he did it to repay even by one ten-thousandth the extraordinary kindness he was shown by the government while he was in Japan; at the same time, he believed that the formation of friendly ties between the two countries represented service to the president. I was more and more impressed by his greatness.[17]

Words like these make one believe in the possibility of friendships being formed by people of different countries and even by the countries themselves. Kimura mentions also having been taken by Brooke to the house of a friend. The friend's wife played the *fūsō* (a harmonium?) to entertain Kimura. Perhaps Kimura did not really appreciate the Western music, but he recognized without difficulty the meaning of the wife's gesture.[18]

Kimura was not content to accept passively the respect and friendship offered by the Americans. On one occasion a disaster occurred: on the eleventh day of the third month, when the *Kanrin Maru* was about to leave San Francisco Harbor, a shell fired by the *Powhattan* as part of a salute struck Commodore Cunningham, who was walking on the dock. It was a blank shell, but it nevertheless caused severe burns and deprived him of his sight in one eye. Kimura could not sleep well that night, worrying about Cunningham. Early the next morning he visited the commodore, to see his condition for himself. He wrote in his diary, "His face is swollen and bandaged, but his speech was unimpaired. He seemed particularly glad that I had visited him so soon."[19]

Clearly, Kimura did not think that Cunningham was simply a barbarian whose illness was of no interest to a Japanese, and the commodore in turn was grateful for Kimura's visit. During Cunningham's recuperation, Captain Mackey took personal charge of the repairs to the *Kanrin Maru*, working every day from seven in the morning until six at night. Kimura commented, "He is extremely capable and reliable. It was because of this captain that the repairs to our ship were completed so quickly."[20]

When the work was more or less finished, Kimura wrote the commodore a letter expressing his wish to pay for the repairs. The next day he received a reply stating that the expenses would all be met by the American president as a gesture of goodwill to the Japanese emperor.[21] Kimura, overwhelmed by this generosity, answered that he would discuss the matter further with the American minister in Japan. The United States was a young and inexperienced country, but such examples of impetuous generosity affected the Japanese more than the protocol of the old nations of Europe.

Just before his departure Kimura attended a party given by Captain Mackey at his house. Muragaki no doubt would have refused the invitation on the grounds that his orders did not authorize him to attend parties given by individuals, but Kimura interpreted his instructions more freely, knowing how much pleasure his presence would give to Mackey. He wrote in his diary,

> Accepting his earnest invitation, I went to his house at dusk, taking with me the other officers. The officers of this locality attended without exception. The captain's wife and the children of officers of the neighborhood came in beautiful clothes with flowers in their hair, and they danced. Mackey and all the other American officers also danced ... We also heard a song sung by a little girl. Her voice was pure and rather tragic. Everyone seemed to be deeply affected. I enjoyed myself extremely, but it was getting late, so I thanked the captain and returned to the hotel.[22]

Muragaki found American social dancing totally lacking in grace, and all Western music was for him an abomination, but Kimura unquestionably enjoyed the evening at Mackey's house. Summing up the fifty days he spent in San Francisco while the *Kanrin Maru* was being repaired, Kimura wrote, "It is already fifty days since we anchored here, but we have had not the slightest unpleasant incident with the people of this country. We owe this to the authority of our country and the conscientiousness of our officers. I consider it to be my great good fortune."[23] Kimura neglected to say how much his own character accounted for the affection the Japanese inspired among the Americans.

While in San Francisco, Kimura made friends with various American naval officers and their families, and when the *Kanrin Maru* was about to set sail for Japan, these friends came to see him off. Just at this time a ship passed the *Kanrin Maru* and Kimura noticed: "Somebody took out a white cloth and waved it at our ship. When I looked carefully I saw that it was Mr. Sawyer,[24] and beside him was an old lady who was also waving a white cloth. Later, facing me, she did a little dance."[25] It is touching to think of this old woman (who was, in fact, the commodore's wife) waving her handkerchief and performing a dance as a farewell gesture to the Japanese.

When the *Kanrin Maru* left the harbor it was given a thirteen-gun salute. Kimura responded with a twenty-one gun salute for the American president, and this was acknowledged in turn with a twenty-one gun salute, presumably for the shogun. After the ship had left port, Kimura reflected, "This voyage was a great and unprecedented enterprise for our country, and people were all apprehensive. I myself was uneasy, but it has ended without the slightest hitch. This is truly thanks to the authority of our empire and the diligence of our officers."[26]

The *Kanrin Maru* anchored in Uraga Bay on the fifth day of the fifth month. The long voyage was over. The Japanese had demonstrated by the return trip that they were capable of sailing a ship unaided across the Pacific. More important, perhaps, there were some Japanese who proved that, despite over two hundred years of seclusion, they could move easily and effectively among people in foreign countries and make friends with them.

Notes

1. Kimura Yoshitake, *Hōshi Meriken Kikō*, p. 1.
2. *Ibid.*
3. John Mercer Brooke (1826–1906), a graduate of the U.S. Naval Academy and the inventor of a deep-sea sounding apparatus. His schooner, the *Fenimore Cooper*, was shipwrecked while surveying the sea floor of the North Pacific, and he remained in Japan until asked to accompany the crew of the *Kanrin Maru*. He kept a journal that provides conclusive evidence of the

importance to the voyage of the help rendered by himself and the other Americans. See George M. Brooke, Jr., *John M. Brooke's Pacific Cruise and Japanese Adventure, 1858–1860.*

4. Kimura, *Hōshi*, p. 3.
5. *Ibid.*, p. 4.
6. Eiichi Kiyooka (trans.), *The Autobiography of Yukichi Fukuzawa*, p. 110.
7. Kimura, *Hōshi*, p. 2.
8. *Ibid.*, p. 3.
9. Loie Fuller, *Fifteen Years of a Dancer's Life*, p. 207.
10. A *koku* was somewhat more than five bushels of rice. The stipends of samurai were calculated in terms of the number of *koku* they were granted.
11. Kimura, *Hōshi*, p. 3.
12. Shinohara Hiroshi, *Kaigun Sōritsu Shi*, p. 68.
13. Kimura, *Hōshi*, p. 19.
14. *Ibid.*
15. *Ibid.*, p. 23.
16. Brooke designed and built the ironclad ship *Merrimac.*
17. Kimura, *Hōshi*, 26–27.
18. *Ibid.*, p. 27.
19. *Ibid.*, p. 30.
20. *Ibid.*, p. 31.
21. *Ibid.*, p. 32.
22. *Ibid.*, p. 33.
23. *Ibid.*, p. 34.
24. A guess. Kimura's text gives Sōe.
25. Kimura, *Hōshi*, p. 36.
26. *Ibid.*, p. 38.

Bibliography

Brooke, George M., Jr. *John M. Brooke's Pacific Cruise and Japanese Adventure, 1858–1860.* Honolulu: University of Hawaii Press, 1986.

Doi Ryōzō. *Gunkan Bugyō Kimura Settsu no Kami.* Tokyo: Chūō Kōron Sha, 1994.

Fuller, Loie. *Fifteen Years of a Dancer's Life.* Boston: Small, Maynard, 1913.

Kimura Yoshitake. *Hōshi Meriken Kikō*, in Nihon Shiseki Kyōkai (ed.), Kengai

Shisetsu Nikki Sanshū series, II. Tokyo: Tōkyō Daigaku Shuppankai, 1971.

Kiyooka, Eiichi (trans.). *The Autobiography of Yukichi Fukuzawa*. New York: Columbia University Press, 1966.

Shinohara Hiroshi. *Kaigun Sōritsu Shi*. Tokyo: Riburopōto, 1986.

Leisurely Journey of a Fly on a Horse's Tail

The second embassy sent by a shogunate to the West sailed from Japan about two years after the first, on the thirteenth day of the twelfth month of 1862. Unlike the first embassy, whose only specific task was the exchange of letters of ratification of the treaty between Japan and the United States, this one had both official and unofficial duties of great magnitude. The shogunate was anxious to persuade the five European countries to which it had promised to open the ports of Niigata, Hyōgo, Osaka, and Edo to consent to a postponement because of the likelihood that opening the ports at this time would lead to disorder. While in Russia, moreover, the embassy was to discuss setting the degree of longitude at which the frontier between Japan and Russia would be created on the island of Sakhalin. The main task of the mission, however, and the one for which the members of the embassy were particularly selected, was the observation of hospitals, shipyards, prisons, and other state facilities in Europe that the Japanese would have to duplicate if they were to be considered a modern nation.

The British and French were eager to have the Japanese visit their countries, apparently because they feared that American influence had become excessive ever since the visit of the Japanese embassy to Washington in 1860. The Japanese, for their part, were pleased with the successful voyage of the *Kanrin Maru* across the Pacific, and hoped to send the new embassy aboard a Japanese warship, at least as far as Suez. This plan was eventually abandoned, and it was agreed that the embassy would travel to Europe aboard a British warship and return aboard a French one.

The Japanese mission consisted of thirty-eight men[1] headed by the ambassador Takenouchi Yasunori, the governor of Shimozuke. Six of the Japanese had previously traveled abroad, either on the *Kanrin Maru* or the *Powhattan*. The membership quality of the embassy was probably superior to that of the previous one.

Several members of the embassy kept diaries. These diaries naturally all describe the same cities and often the same events, whether they are details of the welcome in some foreign capital or impressions of an evening at the theater. This tends to reduce the importance of any one diary as a source of historical information, but because the diaries treat the same materials, one can more easily distinguish the characteristics of the individual diarists than if they had described totally different experiences. It is disappointing that the diary of Fukuzawa Yukichi, the best-known member of the embassy, was not more personal; but his unwavering absorption with practical matters and administrative details indirectly suggests the limitations of this admirable man. The diaries of the less-celebrated members of the embassy often provide more vivid descriptions of what they saw.

Ichikawa Wataru was thirty-eight years old when he traveled to Europe as the retainer of Minister Plenipotentiary Matsudaira Yasunao, the governor of Iwami. The curious title of Ichikawa's diary *Biyō Ōkō Manroku* (Leisurely Account of the Journey to Europe of a Fly on a Horse's Tail)[2] indicated the very humble capacity in which he accompanied the mission. He was not at liberty to do anything except by his master's command. Again and again in the course of the diary he expressed disappointment over not being permitted to accompany the minister on a particular day. For example, when others in the embassy went to inspect the armory and fortifications at Kronstadt in Russia, Ichikawa wrote, "I couldn't go. Most lamentable."[3] It was particularly disappointing to a samurai not to be able to view military equipment, but Ichikawa was also disappointed not to be asked to accompany Matsudaira when he went to the theater, a botanical garden, or a zoo.

Ichikawa was the most observant diarist of the 1862 mission. Fukuzawa probably did not bother to describe the hotel rooms in which he stayed while in Europe because he had already seen similar ones in America, and other diarists may have felt that it was beneath their dignity to notice how their rooms were furnished; but Ichikawa never failed to describe the hotels in which he stayed, beginning in Hong Kong where he noted that the bed had two blankets as well as mosquito netting, and that there was a lock on the door.[4] The Hôtel du Louvre in Paris inspired this description: "The floor of each room is covered with an extremely beautiful carpet in brilliant colors. A carved fretwork cornice goes around the ceiling. In the center of the room there is a round painting in the shape of a flower inlaid in gold. From the center a wire hangs down and from this is suspended a lamp shaped like a glass amaryllis."[5]

The interest of such passages lies not in the objects described—a carpet and a chandelier—but in what in the room caught Ichikawa's attention. They tell us what it was like for a samurai, who was probably familiar with the elegance of a daimyo's mansion, to visit Europe at the height of its glory. Ichikawa's hotel room in Paris was much like those one can still see in Europe today, but few Japanese visitors would now exhibit Ichikawa's surprise over the furnishings. He was impressed even by the most humble facilities: "Under the bed there is a cabinet, and inside it is a clean porcelain chamber pot."[6]

Elsewhere in the diary Ichikawa related his first encounter with a Western bathtub, a toilet, and running hot and cold water. His account of the streets of Paris shifts without transition from a description of a *vespasienne* (street urinal) to a lyrical evocation of the elegantly attired men and women promenading along the boulevards. He commented, "Truly one can say of this place that it is a supreme paradise, unparalleled in the world."[7] Ichikawa was one of the first Japanese to see Paris, and like many since then, he had fallen under its spell.

The diary abounds in references to the extraordinary welcomes that the Japanese received wherever they went in Europe. There were no parades of the kind that marked the visit to America by the first mission, but they were all the same acclaimed by friendly crowds. In Marseilles the crowds were so big they had to be held back by the police. "We left our hotel in horse carriages. The streets swarmed with spectators. Some thirty mounted police and about five hundred soldiers armed with rifles maintained order in the streets."[8] In Paris, Ichikawa reported, "Mobs of old and young, men and women, choked the streets in the attempt to get a glimpse of us Japanese. I have no idea how many thousands, or tens of thousands, were there."[9]

The most frenzied welcome was in England. When the Japanese landed at Dover, "From the midst of the crowd a man about fifty years in age came forward, and weeping and leaping, cried in a loud voice, '*Yappanīsu, Yappanīsu, Yappanīsu,*' which means Japanese."[10] Another Englishman, who had served as a consul in Hakodate, was so delighted over the safe arrival of the Japanese that he stepped forth from the crowd and, removing his hat, raised his arms and shouted, "*Peppepe hōrei.*"[11] Ichikawa solemnly noted, "The meaning is unclear but it is probably an expression of welcome." The surrounding crowd again and again raised the same felicitous cry. Everywhere in England that the Japanese went they saw Japanese flags and were met by surging crowds. In Birmingham, "Tens of thousands of spectators swarmed in the courtyard of our hotel until one couldn't fit another person in. The crowd all called out in welcome, '*Hōrei, hōrei.*'"[12]

In The Hague a crowd estimated at no less then ten thousand massed before the hotel in which the Japanese were staying and serenaded them.[13] In Berlin, "While we Japanese were staying there, spectators gathered in throngs, filling half the main square, and they did not disperse even at night."[14] When they were about to leave Germany for Russia, they were besieged by crowds who begged for their calling cards. Ichikawa commented, "They could not have been noisier."[15]

Ichikawa (unlike Muragaki, the governor of Awaji) expressed no theories as to why the Japanese were so enthusiastically welcomed. Certainly it was not because of the admiration of the masses for Japanese culture, which was extremely little known in Europe at the time, and it probably was not out of hopes of making money from trade with Japan. The style of the welcomes at various places suggests that the Japanese appeared to the Europeans like men from Mars. It is true that in Holland and elsewhere the Japanese met a few people who had actually visited Japan, but for the majority of Europeans it was the most remote country in the entire world, particularly intriguing because of its long seclusion. Curiosity about the appearance of Japanese must have been mingled with the pleasure of welcoming them back into the world.

Ichikawa generally confined himself to recording the size of the crowds and their degree of boisterousness, but he could not have remained unmoved by these demonstrations of affection. No doubt, however, he felt along with the pleasure a certain distaste for the undignified behavior of the Europeans. He heard from someone who had attended the reception of the three chief Japanese envoys in St. Petersburg that "Some three hundred court ladies lined up to see the Japanese, but they made no commotion. One must say that, compared to the other countries, they behaved with courtesy and deference."[16] But perhaps Ichikawa, when directly or implicitly criticizing the noisy reception the Japanese received, was reflecting on how differently a delegation of Europeans would probably be received in Japan.

Ichikawa had little prior knowledge of foreign countries when he set out on his journey, and regardless of what he may have read, he was not prepared for the contrasting landscapes he saw. The first glimpse of Hong Kong from the ship inspired him to write the most poetic prose of his diary:

> At night, when I went out on deck and gazed at the scene, the light of lamps shining through the glass windows of the houses built on the sides of the mountain and the tens of thousands of lamps on the ships tied up in the harbor, reflecting one another, were like the scattered points of light of fireflies on an autumn evening. Just then I saw the thin sliver of the moon emerge from behind the thin pale of clouds over the harbor. The view at night is magnificent.[17]

Later on, the French countryside, observed from a train window on the journey from Marseilles to Paris, moved him with its beauty: "The waves of wheat were freshly green, and here and there peach, plum, cherry, and pear trees were in full bloom, creating spring scenery of sufficient beauty to comfort me somewhat in my homesickness."[18] The English landscapes were also lovely: "At places along the roads the green shade seemed to drip from the trees. Saxifrage and forsythia blossoms were at the height of their blossoming. The shapes of the flowers and leaves resembled those of *hagi* in our country. There were trees with yellow flowers in full bloom. I also saw several pastures for cattle, horses, and sheep."[19] Much later, when passing through Belgium on the way back from Russia, Ichikawa was pleased to see landscapes that reminded him of Japan: "Alongside the road was a river some sixty or seventy feet wide. Fishing boats and steamboats were floating there. I have never seen such scenery before in Europe. The place is a magical world of its own."[20]

Ichikawa was not always favorably impressed by the places he visited. His initial reactions to the ports at which his ship called tended to be colored with contempt for the natives who swarmed in their boats around the ship, shouting and trying to sell local produce. At Singapore, for example, the Japanese were pestered by people who wanted them to buy bananas, coconuts, shells, coral, straw mats, and so on. He commented, "Their chattering was unbearably irritating."[21] Again, when the ship stopped at Aden on the outward journey, Ichikawa noted the baskets woven of palm leaves, the ostrich eggs and dates for sale. But his entry for Aden made on the homeward journey is mainly devoted to the boys who dived for coins thrown into the sea by passengers. He declared, "They appear and disappear at will in the sea exactly like fish or sea turtles. I once saw a picture of black people in the sea gathering coral, and I wondered how it was possible there could be such different kinds of human beings."[22]

In contrast to the admiration he often expressed for Europeans, Ichikawa generally looked down on non-European foreigners. In Hong Kong he contrasted the imposing houses in which the Europeans lived with the flimsy wooden dwellings of the Chinese. One might suppose that the contrast would have made Ichikawa sympathize with the Chinese, but he interpreted the appearance and crude decorations of their houses as proof of their inferiority: "These people are all crude and cunning by nature. As soon as they catch sight of a Japanese they come up to him, surround him, then deafen him with their jabbering. They have not the slightest knowledge of courtesy or deference. They are often greedy and cruel, and sometimes they snatch travelers' baggage and run away. They have only themselves to blame that the people of a great country are now being whipped, driven, and treated as slaves by the English barbarians."[23]

Ichikawa was even more scathing in his comments on the Egyptians. The people of Cairo, he declared, were ignorant, untrustworthy, and lazy, and the city itself was filthy: "Everything combines to make the place unendurable. The streets are always filled with ordures and foul smells, and bluebottle flies bounce off one's face."[24] At times he criticized the Europeans, but he had to admit that the Japanese had something to learn from them; he was sure that the Chinese and Egyptians could teach them nothing.

While in Hong Kong Ichikawa visited the famous Yinghua (Anglo-Chinese) College where, by good fortune, he met the outstanding European authority on the Chinese classics, James Legge

(1815–1897),[25] together with two Chinese scholars. Ichikawa related, "I took out a notebook I was carrying with me and asked him to write something. He firmly refused again and again." But Legge finally yielded and inscribed a properly Confucian sentiment in Ichikawa's notebook: "All under heaven is one family; all within the four seas are brothers." The two Chinese also gave samples of their calligraphy. Ichikawa commented, "Although the power behind their brushes was feeble, and the writing itself clumsy and hardly worthy of a second glance, I took it out occasionally and it helped to relieve the fatigue of the journey." It was typical of the independence and self-confidence of the man; most Japanese would readily have admitted that they were no match for the Chinese when it came to writing Chinese characters.

During his stay in Europe, Ichikawa occasionally met Europeans who had studied Japanese. In Paris, for example, he was visited by the German scholar Johann Joseph Hoffmann (1805–1878), who in 1855 had become the first professor of Japanese at the University of Leiden.[26] He wrote in his diary, "This man has studied the Chinese classics and understands Japanese extremely well. For this reason I was able to converse with him with the brush[27] and had a few conversations with him. I couldn't help thinking of trying to scratch an itchy foot through one's shoe,[28] but it too helped a little to divert me from the tedium of travel."[29] He met a Frenchman who had lived in Japan and understood Japanese. This man brought with him an album in which he asked Ichikawa to write a poem in Chinese or Japanese together with an explanation in Japanese.[30] He also met Jan Hendrik Donker Curtius (1813–1879), the last director of the Dutch trading station in Deshima,[31] and Sir Rutherford Alcock (1809–1897), who had served as British consul and later as minister to Japan between 1859 and 1864.

Other Europeans, usually without the assistance of Japanese teachers or reliable textbooks, were beginning to study Japanese at the time. The visit of the Japanese mission seems to have inspired scholarly as well as commercial interest in Japan. The teaching of the

Japanese language in Paris began in 1863, the year after the visit. The first instructor was Léon de Rosny, whom some members of the mission (notably Fukuzawa Yukichi) met in Paris.[32] In other countries the study of Japan was beginning with the acquisition of Japanese books and works of art.

The seclusion of Japan had only recently ended, but already Japanese wares were beginning to appear in Europe. Ichikawa attended in London an exhibition of products from around the world and discovered, "They had assembled merchandise of all kinds from our country, including martial equipment, armor fittings, chains, bows and arrows, swords and spears, and so on. There were also books and maps, men and women's clothes, and firemen's suits ... Also, displays of pottery, lacquerware, and articles of copper and iron. In addition, there were many miscellaneous small articles, too numerous to mention."[33]

Japanese lacquer was so highly esteemed at the time in Europe that the word *japan* was used to designate any kind of lacquerware. Japanese swords were also prized. When the Japanese envoys had an audience with the king of Prussia, Ichikawa noted that the king wore a Japanese sword.[34] In Holland Ichikawa discovered that the moxa[35] he had brought from Japan had been soaked by salt water during a storm at sea; but he was able (to his surprise) to buy Japanese moxa at a Dutch shop, though at an elevated price. He commented, "It seems that they sell this because the Dutch also practice moxa treatment."[36]

Ichikawa was pleased by this interest in his country, but he was also the forerunner of many Japanese in his embarrassment over the way Japanese culture tended to be presented in the West. In Cologne he was shown some pictures of Japan. He wrote, "When I examined them, it was apparent that the customs, features, and so on of the people portrayed had been skillfully drawn. However, people of our lower classes, depicted naked, were shown with their faces concealed with cloths ... Before I knew it, I had let forth a deep sigh. Ah, I had not seen one naked person since coming to the lands of the barbarians, but in these pictures, Japanese were depicted in so disgraceful a state. Could I help but blush over this?"[37] Like many Japanese of the Meiji era, Ichikawa was desperately concerned lest Europeans, seeing scantily clad Japanese, consider the whole population backward and laugh at them.

It may be wondered what Ichikawa learned during the course of his journey. Most of his experiences abroad were unfamiliar, and he therefore recorded them with precision. His account of a visit to a Turkish bath in Alexandria—to cite one instance—is unusually detailed. But Ichikawa was interested less in the oddity of foreign institutions and customs than in their potential usefulness to Japan. He was impressed by the museums, botanical gardens, and zoos he visited in the various capitals of Europe, and noted that even "woodcutters and hunters" benefited by them. "I believe that they have created these facilities in order to obtain such benefits as enabling the lower classes to share in their pleasures and increasing the knowledge of natural history."[38]

Ichikawa seems to have felt obliged to balance his praise for some aspect of European civilization with harsh remarks about another. After expressing his admiration for European museums, he added this caution, "However, they make every visitor pay something by way of entrance fee. This is an example of the barbarians' contemptible practice of making a profit out of everything. Ah, each virtue has an accompanying defect. I earnestly hope that we shall adopt the things worthy of being adopted and reject the things that should be rejected."[39] Despite his reservations, the museums he visited in Europe produced such a powerful effect that when, after the Meiji Restoration, Ichikawa entered the Ministry of Education, he devoted his efforts chiefly to establishing a Japanese National Library and National Museum.

Ichikawa's admiration for Western newspapers was similarly tinged with suspicions of the publishers. He related how the manager of the hotel in which the Japanese stayed in Ceylon showed them a newspaper article describing their visit. Ichikawa was impressed that the newspaper reported the event the same day it occurred, but he felt obliged to make this warning: "Because [newspapers] are made by people who think of nothing but making money, they are written in frivolous language and, consisting for the most part of hearsay and gossip, are not worth looking at; but, all the same, their speed is astonishing."[40] He wrote in a similarly ambivalent vein about Paris, the most splendid city of Europe, where thieves stole the belongings of Japanese.

During his visits to museums Ichikawa saw Western art for the first time. He noted the photographic realism of some paintings in London and commented, "It is probably because foreigners esteem pictures only to the extent that they exactly resemble the things portrayed that, apart from the resemblances, the pictures lack any grace or spirituality. Ah, what a pity!"[41] He was equally unimpressed with Western music or dance, which struck him as being boring if not downright barbarous.[42]

Ichikawa witnessed Christian services every Sunday aboard the English and French ships, but he expressed no feelings about this religion, at the time strictly forbidden in Japan. However, he was annoyed to discover in his hotel room in London a copy of the Chinese translation of the New Testament. He wrote, "I had heard about this before. This book is the book of the Western religion. Their craftiness [in leaving this book for us to see] is to be hated and loathed."[43]

For all his criticism of the West, Ichikawa learned much. One trivial experience affected him particularly. An Italian woman with her daughter of six was staying in the same hotel in Paris as the Japanese. Ichikawa was charmed by the pretty, intelligent little girl, and she in turn was so impressed by the Japanese that she politely bowed whenever they passed. One day the girl brought a playmate to the hotel. Ichikawa thought that the other girl must be her sister, but his little friend informed him that the other girl was Spanish. "I sighed without realizing it. Ah, for this little Western girl even a country a thousand miles away was nevertheless like a neighbor. I could see now why the foreign barbarians constantly sail the seas and think nothing of it."[44] Ichikawa realized from this experience that friendly relations could exist even between people of different nationalities. Perhaps he even forgot for a moment that he was a Japanese in an alien land.

Notes

1. Originally, only thirty-six, but two members joined the mission a few weeks later on. See below, p. 66.
2. There is a translation of this diary under the title of "Diary of a Member of the Japanese Embassy to Europe in 1862–63," made by Ernest M. Satow. Most of this translation appeared in *The Chinese and Japanese Repository*, beginning with vol. 3, no. 24, but the periodical ceased publication before the whole translation could be issued. Parts of the remainder of the translation appeared in *The Japan Times* in the issues from December 29, 1865, to March 9, 1866, but the promised book containing the full text seems not to have appeared. The translation is fairly literal.
3. Ichikawa Wataru, *Biyō Ōkō Manroku*, p. 481.
4. *Ibid.*, p. 277. In a Japanese inn there would not have been a lock on the door.
5. *Ibid.*, p. 327.
6. *Ibid.*
7. *Ibid.*, p. 331.
8. *Ibid.*, p. 323.
9. *Ibid.*, p. 340.
10. *Ibid.*, p. 349.
11. Probably Hip-hip-hooray.
12. Ichikawa, *Biyō*, pp. 375–76.
13. *Ibid.*, p. 411.
14. *Ibid.*, p. 424.
15. *Ibid.*, p. 446.
16. *Ibid.*, p. 458.
17. *Ibid.*, pp. 376–77.
18. *Ibid.*, p. 326.
19. *Ibid.*, p. 370. Grazing domestic animals are still so unfamiliar a sight in Japan as to draw tourists from other parts of the country.
20. *Ibid.*, p. 492.
21. *Ibid.*, pp. 287–88.

22. *Ibid.*, p. 533.

23. *Ibid.*, p. 282.

24. *Ibid.*, p. 307.

25. Legge, a full-time missionary, somehow found the time to translate the Four Books of Confucianism, plus the Book of History, the Book of Poetry, and various other classical works. His translations are still valuable for the traditional interpretations of Chinese scholars that he incorporated in his work. He also compiled a textbook of English for Chinese, published in 1856, that was subsequently used in Japan too, where it was modified (by omitting the Christian references). Various words in the modern Japanese language (such as *ginkō*, bank) first appeared in this work, which was known by various titles.

26. Hoffmann, after a brief career as an opera singer, took employment with Philipp Franz von Siebold in 1830, and assisted him in writing his monumental *Nippon*. He also produced textbooks of Japanese, both literary and practical. See Numata Jirō et al. (eds.), *Yōgakushi Jiten*, p. 660.

27. *Hitsudan* (conversing with the brush) refers to the practice, common when Chinese, Japanese, or Koreans can read but not speak one another's language, of writing Chinese characters, which are intelligible to scholars of all three countries.

28. A proverbial expression suggesting the frustration of being unable (in this case) to communicate one's thoughts fully because of problems in language.

29. Ichikawa, *Biyō*, p. 352.

30. *Ibid.*, p. 497.

31. For further information on Donker Curtius, see Numata, *Yōgakushi*, pp. 509–10.

32. For a good account of Rosny, see Haga Tōru, *Taikun no Shisetsu*, pp. 89–94. Rosny became a professor at the École des Langues Orientales in 1868.

33. Ichikawa, *Biyō*, p. 359.

34. *Ibid.*, p. 427.

35. A plant, pellets of which are burned on a patient's skin for therapeutic effect. The treatment was known from the late sixteenth century in Europe, where its name derived from the Japanese *mogusa*.

36. Ichikawa, *Biyō*, p. 416.

37. *Ibid.*, p. 422.

38. *Ibid.*, p. 365.

39. *Ibid.*, pp. 365–66. The translation by Satow, typical of his literalness, is worth quoting: "Wherefore I think these places are made in order to please

the common people, and, at the same time, to profit them by increasing the knowledge of universal things. But from every spectator they take a little sight-money, according to the barbarous custom of always trying to make a profit, which we should think very mean. Ah! ah! If they gain by it, they also lose. To adopt what is proper, and to reject that which is bad, how fine a thing this is." (From *The Chinese and Japanese Repository* 3:29, Dec. 1, 1865, p. 569.)

40. Ichikawa, *Biyō*, p. 296.
41. *Ibid.*, p. 281.
42. *Ibid.*
43. *Ibid.*, p. 350.
44. *Ibid.*, p. 346.

Bibliography

Haga Tōru. *Taikun no Shisetsu*. Tokyo: Chūō Kōron Sha, 1968.

Ichikawa Wataru. *Biyō Ōkō Manroku*, in Nihon Shiseki Kyōkai (ed.), Kengai Shisetsu Nikki Sanshū series, II. Tokyo: Tōkyō Daigaku Shuppankai, 1971.

Numata Jirō et al. (eds.). *Yōgakushi Jiten*. Tokyo: Yūshōdō, 1984.

Diary of a Journey
to Europe

The most artistic of the diaries that describe the 1862 mission to Europe was *Ōkō Nikki* (Diary of a Journey to Europe) kept by Fuchibe Tokuzō. He related at the outset of the diary how he had suddenly received word that he was to proceed in two days' time to England. His reaction to this quite unexpected news was "a moment of surprise and a moment of joy."[1] Not until the next day did he learn why he was to leave so unexpectedly: the British minister, Sir Rutherford Alcock, was returning to his country, and the shogunate had decided to send Fuchibe and the interpreter Moriyama Takichirō (1820–1871) with him. The three men left Japan about two months after the main body of the embassy and traveled to Europe by way of Shanghai, Hong Kong, Ceylon, and Suez. Eventually, Fuchibe and Moriyama joined the other Japanese in England, and from then on they traveled with the main party.

Fuchibe was a gifted painter, and made himself popular aboard ship by drawing pictures of the people around him. He wrote in his diary, "During the voyage I have been drawing pictures on fans and giving them to my fellow passengers. I have been drawing pictures of Western people. The pictures are extremely clumsy, but one must pass the time somehow. I dash off pictures of flowers, birds, human beings, whatever my hands feel like painting, and the other people, when they see how quickly it is done, sigh with admiration."[2] Painting was a useful distraction during the long ocean voyage, and Fuchibe was glad to divert the other passengers. He noted, however, that when he drew a picture of a European man on a fan, the man always said he would give it to his wife because European men do not carry fans.

Fuchibe's most impressive displays of his art were three paintings executed later in the journey while in Russia. He presented them to the czarina. He wrote, "One picture showed Mount Fuji, the second the scenery of the Neva River before our hotel, and the third an eagle, executed in ink. I drew the last one because the eagle is the symbol for Russia."[3]

Fuchibe, no doubt because he was an amateur painter, expressed greater pleasure in the landscapes of the journey than other diarists of the embassy, and he described in considerable detail paintings in the museums and palaces of Europe. He was also more tolerant of Western music than the other diarists. He described a dance party aboard ship in these terms: "Black musicians made barbarian music. There were violins,[4] drums, long and short flutes. The tunes were extremely lively and made those who heard them want to dance."[5] Other diarists (notably Muragaki) had complained of the noisy music and had found Western dancing unbearably monotonous, but Fuchibe recognized that dancing was a pleasant shipboard activity: "They played music on deck, and all the men and women danced. They do this in order to divert themselves from the tedium of the long sea voyage."[6]

Fuchibe was unusually ready to change his opinions in response to new experiences. At Versailles he was so impressed by the architecture and the gardens that he wrote, "I strolled through the gardens. They must be several *ri* across. Here and there are ponds, woods, hills, gardens. All are clean-swept and elegant. There are also small pavilions and other buildings of great refinement. I had previously supposed that Western people liked only gaudy things but to my surprise they showed in their gardens that they have a taste for elegance."[7]

Fuchibe was the first diarist to discover that foreigners sometimes have good taste. This discovery unfortunately seems to have had little effect on later Japanese purveyors who remained convinced of the importance of gaudiness to foreign customers.

More by temperament than by special training, Fuchibe was able to adapt more easily to European life than other Japanese of the mission. The day before he sailed from Yokohama he called at the Dutch Legation to offer his respects, probably because he would be traveling on a Dutch warship for the first stage of the journey. While having lunch at the legation, probably his first experience of European food, it occurred to him that once the ship sailed it was unlikely he would eat Japanese food again until he returned. Perhaps, like others in the embassy, he felt apprehension at the thought of being deprived of soy sauce and miso, but his diary is in fact filled with references to delicious Western food, and he never says anything to suggest that he missed Japanese food.

His first taste of exotic food was a banana he ate in Hong Kong: "I ate the fruit of the plantain tree. The taste was sweet and appealing."[8] In Singapore he ate with pleasure pineapples and mangosteens. He wrote of a lunch in Ceylon, "The fresh fish and the vegetables all tasted delicious."[9] He enjoyed other meals (presumably quite different in content) in Cairo, Paris, The Hague, Berlin, and St. Petersburg. He was especially fond of Atlantic Ocean lobster and ice cream. He was ready to try any kind of food. One wishes that his diary gave some explanation of how he became so cosmopolitan.

Fuchibe obviously enjoyed his stay in Europe, especially in Paris. He not only went sightseeing but also enjoyed the amenities of life there: "On the way back to the hotel we relaxed for a while at a café. We drank a bottle of wine among the three of us and ate some appetizers before we went back."[10] There is something heartwarming in the ease with which Fuchibe and his friends adapted themselves to the rhythm of Parisian life. What an enormous contrast their little gathering makes with the Japanese of 1860 who refused to go out after dark! Other places in Europe also pleased Fuchibe, but when he returned to Paris after having visited London, Berlin, St. Petersburg, and elsewhere, he wrote, "Coming back here after have seen various countries, I realized just how thriving this place is."[11]

He had surprisingly little to say about the enthusiastic receptions given to the Japanese in Europe, perhaps because (until he reached England) he traveled in a small group. However, he described with warmth the reception the Japanese received in Berlin, where their carriages were filled with bouquets thrown to them by the crowds: "The flowers were so fragrant that our clothes were impregnated with the sweet smells. I wondered if I had not entered the realm of immortals in a dream."[12] He also wrote a poem in Chinese in which he predicted that never again would he have such an experience; he anticipated telling people in Japan about it, just as soon as he returned.

Perhaps the reception that affected him most deeply was at the house of Donker Curtius in Delft. The whole family turned out to meet the Japanese, and Fuchibe felt as if he were in the house of old friends. He wrote in his diary, "The house is not especially grand, but it is not poor either. It is extremely clean and is furnished with many Japanese objects."[13] He seems to have realized that being invited into the house of someone of another country is what makes a journey memorable. No doubt that is why he wrote of Holland, "Here, unlike France, England, and the other countries, I felt as if I had returned to my old home."[14] For two hundred years the Dutch trading station on the island of Deshima in Nagasaki Harbor was the only Japanese window on Europe. The ties, though largely sentimental now, had not been forgotten.

Fuchibe's travels in Europe inevitably made him reflect on the shogunate's policy of seclusion. Of course, criticism of this policy was implicit each time he expressed admiration for some aspect of European civilization, whether parliamentary democracy or education of the blind and deaf, but it was particularly evident whenever he saw an exhibition of Japanese products. When, for example, he saw the display in London arranged by Sir Rutherford Alcock (the same one that Ichikawa saw), he felt ashamed that Japan seemed to have nothing better to show the world than samples of different kinds of paper and wood. He wrote, "In addition, there were many objects that had been sent by merchants residing in Yokohama who were trying to attract customers. These included women's secondhand clothes, swords of crude workmanship, and such items as bows and arrows, armor, lacquerware, pottery and—worst of all—paper lanterns, clogs, bowls, wooden pillows, and so on, a collection of odds and ends that looked exactly like a junk shop. They didn't bear looking at."[15] Fuchibe contrasted the practice of the European nations of sending abroad samples of their country's finest products with the Japanese indifference to trade: "In Japan the importance of trade is still not understood. That is why the Japanese, reluctant to sell their products to other countries, send abroad only badly made items like those on display. This, too, is because they have no contact whatsoever with the rest of the world."[16] The last sentence clearly reflected his dissatisfaction with the policy of seclusion.

The Japanese were invited while in Holland to visit the palace of the queen mother, the widow of King Willem II who in 1844 had sent a letter to the shogun warning of the danger of British aggression. Fuchibe interpreted the courtesy shown the Japanese ambassadors by the queen mother in these terms: "We regretted that when the late king sent a warning intended to benefit Japan nothing was done about it, but instead relations were opened with America; at the same time, we were overcome with joy to think that Her Majesty would grant the embassy an audience today, even though there had been no response during his lifetime to the sincere attempt of the late king to open relations between his country and Japan."[17]

Fuchibe implied that the policy of seclusion had prevented Japan from behaving like a civilized country. Elsewhere, his diary is full of memorable passages describing such varied topics as veiled women in the streets of Cairo, kangaroos at the Paris Zoo, and Buddhist art in European collections. He related how Minister Alcock boasted of the superiority of England to France in the speed of its trains, the quality of its horses, and the excellence of its cuisine.[18] He also gave affecting vignettes, such as the one of a Dutch girl, unable to take her eyes off the Japanese, who continued her knitting without interruption.[19] He was moved when he visited a school for the deaf in Holland where the children displayed their knowledge of the geography of Japan.[20]

Toward the end of their European stay, the embassy learned from the Dutch minister to Russia that the London newspapers had reported an attack on the British Legation in Japan and the deaths of some of the British personnel.[21] There was no way to verify this report; but Fuchibe also heard that people in Japan believed that the infuriated Europeans had massacred the members of the embassy in revenge.[22] He *knew* this was untrue, and it put him on guard against future rumors.

The last thing Fuchibe did in Europe was to buy some old Chinese pottery in Lisbon. It is rather disappointing that he was not more sensitive to the beauty of Lisbon. He wrote instead, "The city looks filthy, and there is nothing worth seeing."[23] Despite his artistic temperament, he was a samurai and in his travels he sought not the picturesque charm of Lisbon but guidance in how to make Japan a modern country.

Notes

1. Fuchibe Tokuzō, *Ōkō Nikki*, p. 1.
2. *Ibid.,* p. 16.
3. *Ibid.*, pp. 96–97.
4. He actually uses the word *kokyū*, the name of a stringed instrument still played in Japan. Although it resembles certain Chinese instruments, it has been traced back to the Portuguese rebec, presumably introduced in the sixteenth century.
5. Fuchibe, *Ōkō Nikki*, p. 9.

6. *Ibid.*, p. 24.
7. *Ibid.*
8. *Ibid.*, p. 14.
9. *Ibid.*, p. 25.
10. *Ibid.*, p. 47.
11. *Ibid.*, p. 114.
12. *Ibid.*, p. 84.
13. *Ibid.*, p. 68.
14. *Ibid.*, p. 58.
15. *Ibid.*, pp. 49–50.
16. *Ibid.*, p. 50.
17. *Ibid.*, p. 74.
18. *Ibid.*, p. 48.
19. *Ibid.*, p. 59.
20. *Ibid.*, p. 62.
21. *Ibid.*, p. 108.
22. *Ibid.*, p. 116.
23. *Ibid.*, p. 120.

Bibliography

Fuchibe Tokuzō. *Ōkō Nikki*, in Nihon Shiseki Kyōkai (ed.), Kengai Shisetsu Nikki Sanshū series, III. Tokyo: Tōkyō Daigaku Shuppankai, 1971.

Journey to the West

Fukuzawa Yukichi (1835–1901), who was only twenty-seven at the time of the first embassy to Europe, is today its best-known member. He had the humble status of an interpreter, the same as when he visited America two years earlier. He had written a brief report describing his visit to Hawaii and America, but it is of minor interest, of significance chiefly because it indicates that Fukuzawa not only observed people abroad but tried to understand something about them.

Fukuzawa's account of his journey to Europe, *Seikōki* (Journey to the West), is fuller and contains valuable materials, but it is nevertheless disappointing to readers who hope to learn something about Fukuzawa's personality or understand how his first glimpse of European civilization affected a man who stood at the forefront of the Enlightenment that would soon sweep over Japan.

Fukuzawa had virtually nothing to say about the departure from Japan or the visit to Hong Kong. For that matter, he did not indicate whether he was surprised or pleased that the British had taken great trouble to make the quarters of the Japanese aboard the warship *Odin* as comfortable as possible. Tatami had been laid on the deck, Japanese wallpaper pasted over the bulkheads, and sliding doors installed. Perhaps the Japanese took these preparations for granted, but more likely their thoughts were so much on the mission ahead of them that they did not think it worth describing the details of their daily lives.

The first incident of the journey to Europe that Fukuzawa treated at any length was the visit to his hotel in Singapore by a Japanese named Otokichi. He wrote in his diary, "Otokichi is a sailor from Onomura in the Tsuta area of Bishū. In the third year of Tempō [1832] he and seventeen companions, shipwrecked, drifted ashore in California on the western coast of North America. Later, he went to England, and, after acquiring British citizenship, then lived in Shanghai. He married a native of Singapore and had three children by her."[1] Fukuzawa was interested in Otokichi mainly because of the rumors he purveyed of the unsuccessful Taiping Rebellion, against the Manchu régime, that had torn China from 1850 to 1864. He did not ask many other questions about events during the thirty years Otokichi had spent abroad. It seems not to have occurred to him that Otokichi might be useful as an interpreter or as a go-between in negotiations with the Europeans. Despite his advocacy of enlightenment, he probably thought of Otokichi as no more than an illiterate sailor with whom there was no point in wasting time.

A month later, Fukuzawa's ship reached Egypt. He and the others of the embassy were probably the first Japanese to come into contact with Muslim civilization, but he was unimpressed by Cairo: "Population is 500,000. Many poor people. City not prosperous. People backward and lazy, do not work at any occupation. The laws are also extremely strict."[2] He related that the local men disliked military service so much that they tried to avoid being called up by deliberately injuring their eyes or cutting off fingers. It is not difficult to imagine the scorn a samurai would feel for such people.

We also catch a glimpse in the diary of the youthful Fukuzawa Yukichi who, while in San Francisco two years earlier, had surprised his shipmates by having his photograph taken alongside the photographer's beautiful daughter. He related, "Many of the natives drive camels and donkeys. I also spent one day riding a donkey and took in the sights at different places. The donkey was obedient and lovable."[3]

Fukuzawa was observant enough to be able to tell from surviving monuments that Cairo, despite its present squalor, had at one time been a magnificent city. He went to see the Pyramids, though he got no closer than three *ri*.[4] However, the ruins of the past inspired no romantic reveries in this highly practical man. As far as he was concerned, the old monuments "are now all fallen into ruin and not worth seeing."[5] Fukuzawa probably would not have lingered long over the remains of Egyptian antiquity even if the mission of the Japanese had not been specifically intended to acquire modern European technology.

He wrote little about the train journey from Cairo to Alexandria, where the Japanese boarded another British vessel. He recorded exactly how long the train stopped at each station, and noted that the scenery consisted entirely of desert wastes, but his diary reveals not even momentary excitement over the train journey itself. The Japanese of two years earlier had been excited to cross the isthmus of Panama by train, but trains were no longer a novelty to the Japanese.

On the fifth day of the third month the ship bearing the Japanese reached Marseilles. The party traveled in easy stages by train to Paris, which they reached on the tenth. Fukuzawa was mildly interested in how the land he saw from the train windows was cultivated, but unlike other diarists in his party, who were enchanted by the French scenery, all he had written was, "The land is uncultivated and largely covered with woodland, but is mainly scrub, and I did not see any big trees."[6] However, at one place the sight of peach, apricot, pear, and cherry blossoms, all in full bloom, moved even this highly unsentimental man to comment, "The scenery along the road was extremely lovely."

The Hôtel du Louvre, where the Japanese stayed in Paris, was the finest in the city and perhaps in the entire world, but Fukuzawa had no words to spare about the beautiful decoration of the room. His interests were confined almost exclusively to the staffing of the hotel: "More than five hundred servants, as well as tailors, laundresses, and repair men belong to this building, and everything necessary for daily living can be arranged within the hotel. In every part of the hotel there are rooms for the servants. These rooms are connected by telegraph with each guest room, and when one wishes to summon a servant from a guest room, one pulls the end of the telegraph wire and gives a signal."[7]

Fukuzawa visited several hospitals in Paris and inquired not only about their facilities but also about where they got the money they needed. He learned while in Paris about the building of the Suez Canal, and expressed curiosity as to how so huge a project was financed. He was impressed by his visit to the Chambre des Députés (which he called "the House of Commons") and admired the French system of elections: "A deputy is elected not because of his wealth but because of his popularity, and this means that when the man expresses his views, these are the views of his constituency and not those of a functionary of the state."[8] Fukuzawa's praise is subdued, but it is clear that *this* is what he had been hoping to observe in France, not magnificent hotels, nor works of art in the museums, nor even beautiful landscapes.

Fukuzawa was fortunate to have made a useful French acquaintance, Léon de Rosny (1837–1916), who had been studying Japanese. Rosny was eager to practice the language, and he frequently visited the hotel where the embassy was staying. On occasion he took Fukuzawa to such places as the Jardin des Plantes, where he admired not only plants but also animals from all over the world. Rosny followed the Japanese to various parts of Europe, partly at the request of the French government, but perhaps also because he feared he might never have another chance to speak Japanese.

The embassy left Paris for London on the first day of the fourth month. In London Fukuzawa visited an exhibition of world products. One corner was devoted to miscellaneous Japanese wares—lacquer, swords, pottery, paper, small handicrafts. Fuchibe Tokuzō[9] had scathingly commented on the inadequacy of the display. Fukuzawa was also disappointed, but he was far less interested in teaching the West about Japan than in learning what in the West could make Japan stronger.[10] His most affecting experience in England occurred when he visited a school for the deaf and dumb. He tried out his English on a little girl who had been trained in lipreading. "How do you do?" he asked, to which the girl replied, "Very well, thank you."[11] Such moments of personal intimacy are rare in Fukuzawa's diaries.

The stay in England included visits to Birmingham and Liverpool. The sovereigns of the other European countries visited by the Japanese mission gladly gave them an audience, but Queen Victoria, still in mourning for her beloved husband, Prince Albert, who had died the previous year, declined to see anyone.[12] Even if she had granted an audience to the Japanese, Fukuzawa was of so lowly a rank he could not have hoped to be presented.

We can conjecture that the visit to Holland was the part of the European journey that Fukuzawa anticipated with the most pleasure. He had studied Dutch assiduously at the school of Ogata Kōan (1810–1863) in Osaka, and he undoubtedly felt a special attachment to the language that had opened Western learning to him. As usual, however, he was reticent about expressing personal feelings in his diary, and he confined his writing to objective notations on what he saw and heard.

As soon as the ship from England bearing the Japanese embassy arrived in Rotterdam, Fukuzawa noticed in every direction innumerable crossed Japanese and Dutch flags. Their hotel in The Hague was decorated not only with the flags of the two countries but also with the crests of the three highest-ranking Japanese dignitaries and a pennant in Japanese stating "The capital of Holland respectfully welcomes its honored guests from Japan."[13] Fukuzawa's diary disappointingly contains very little on the whole month he stayed in Holland. Not until the embassy reached Utrecht on the nineteenth day of the sixth month did he note something that should have been obvious long before: "Everybody remembers that Japan has long been a friendly nation and the reception has been extremely warm."[14]

The Japanese traveled from Holland to Berlin and from there to St. Petersburg. Arriving at their hotel, they discovered, "The furnishings inside the building are entirely in Japanese style. In the guest rooms there are sword stands, Japanese pillows, and tobacco, and the washrooms are equipped with rice-bran bags and similar things.[15] The food is entirely Japanese and served with chopsticks, rice bowls, and so on, exactly as in Japan."[16] The excitement over finding himself once again in Japanese surroundings, complete with Japanese food, seems to have prompted Fukuzawa to compose a poem in classical Chinese. The total lack of literary pretension is typical of the man:

> We get up and go to the table; when dinner is over, we sleep.
> Food is plentiful, we sleep soundly; in this way we spend a year.
> If by chance in the future an acquaintance should ask,
> The sky in Europe is no different from the sky at home.

The Japanese furnishings and provisions were apparently the work of Tachibana Kōsai (1820–1885), who had secretly left Japan for Russia in 1855 with Putiatin's fleet, and who would in 1870 become the first teacher of Japanese at the University of St. Petersburg.

Fukuzawa had little to say about St. Petersburg or anywhere else he visited in Russia except for a school he visited: "I went to a school. This school is called Gymnasium Commercial. It is a place where students learn physical education and commerce."[17] He seems to have confused the English meaning of gymnasium with the German one (a school where the student is prepared for an academic degree), and was impressed that physical education was given such attention. Of course, physical education formed a part of even the Russian (or German) gymnasium, and Fukuzawa, seeing a gym class, supposed it was the principal activity of the school: "The teaching of exercise is invariably a part of the school curriculum. The students climb ladders or squirm their way up poles or do stunts with ropes; all of these are exercises to strengthen the students' muscles. This instruction is carried out in all of the countries of Europe." Perhaps he was already thinking of creating a similar school in Japan.

The return from St. Petersburg to Berlin and from Berlin to Paris went unnoticed in the diary. Not until the embassy was back in Paris did Fukuzawa evince much interest in his surroundings. Rosny took him to the Bibliothèque Nationale and the Institut de France, but the French government by this time seemed to have lost interest in Japan. The treatment of the Japanese visitors became conspicuously colder. They were sent by night train to Rochefort, and as soon as they arrived, exhausted by a sleepless night, they were marched ten *chō* (somewhat less than a mile) to the ship. It seemed a bad omen for the voyage ahead.

The French ship aboard which the Japanese traveled to Alexandria was not the splendid new warship that Napoleon III had promised but a battered old troop transport. The weather from the first day was bad, and the crowded quarters made life aboard ship most uncomfortable. When the Japanese reached Lisbon, the last stop of their European journey, they were relieved to set foot on land again.

Fukuzawa wrote little about the beauty of the city. Instead, he expressed his awareness, walking through the shabby streets, that the glory of Portugal had faded. He wrote with a touch of bitter humor: "The Portuguese go to other countries to learn how to make things. They are skillful in what they make, but they have so few new inventions of their own they are like Japan or China."

The French ship that awaited the Japanese after they had crossed the isthmus of Suez by train was even worse than the previous old tub, but they could at least take comfort from the thought that they were getting closer to home. When the ship put in at Ceylon, Fukuzawa bought a Hong Kong newspaper, which reported that daimyo and their families were leaving Edo and selling their possessions. He commented, "The fact that the daimyo are leaving Edo is not simply an internal change; there must also be a change from the past in our intercourse with foreign countries. At present the feeling of Japanese toward foreigners is not exactly one of challenging them to fight, but it cannot be supposed that it is without belligerence."[18] This astute appraisal was the closest thing to a political statement in his diary.

In addition to the diary, Fukuzawa wrote down various facts and observations in a memorandum book he bought in Paris. It is full of such useful information as: "The cost of building one mile (an English mile) of railroad is 650,000 francs. In places that are perfectly flat the cost varies between 90,000 and 95,000 francs."[19] Occasionally, Fukuzawa asked a European to write his name, and sometimes the man also wrote a statement on a matter about which Fukuzawa had inquired. (For example, there is an account by an American of the causes of the Civil War.) But the memorandum book provides no more clues to the personality of Fukuzawa Yukichi than does his diary.

Fukuzawa obviously did not consider his diary the place to record his emotions. As a young man of twenty-seven he surely must have felt attracted to some of the women he saw, but it was beneath his dignity as a samurai to discuss such matters. In this respect he was typical of the entire embassy. The diaries kept by the various members indicate what the Japanese wanted to learn from the West, but usually not much more. There is rarely even a personal observation. Nobody commented on the extraordinary mustache of Napoleon III or the beauty of the Empress Eugénie. Nobody expressed homesickness for Japan or for their families, and although Muragaki had mentioned in his diary his yearning for Japanese food, none of the diarists who went to Europe seemed to be greatly interested in what they ate. It is hard to decide whether or not the Japanese enjoyed their stay in Europe. Probably they never asked themselves the question; they were conscious of fulfilling a mission, and their only desire was to serve their country. This was a noble attitude, but it kept their diaries from possessing the literary interest that more personal expressions would have created.

Notes

1. *Fukuzawa Yukichi Zenshū* (henceforth abbreviated *FYZ*), XIX, p. 11.
2. *Ibid.*, p. 16.
3. *Ibid.*
4. A Japanese *ri* is 2.44 miles. It is hard to believe he could have formed much of an impression of the Pyramids from a distance of seven and a half miles. Perhaps he was thinking in terms of a Chinese *li*, which was about one-third of a mile.
5. *FYZ*, XIX, p. 16.
6. *Ibid.*, p. 20.
7. *Ibid.*
8. *Ibid.*, p. 25.
9. See p. 66 for Fuchibe's *Ōkō Nikki* (Diary of a Journey to Europe).
10. *FYZ*, p. 28.
11. *Ibid.*, p. 30.
12. *Ibid.*, p. 27.
13. *Ibid.*, p. 35.
14. *Ibid.*, p. 37.
15. "Rice-bran bags" (*nukabukuro*) were used to scrub the body.
16. *FYZ, XIX*, p. 42.
17. *Ibid.*, p. 47.
18. *Ibid.*, p. 59.
19. *Ibid.*, p. 69.

Bibliography

Fukuzawa Yukichi Zenshū, XIX. Tokyo: Iwanami Shoten, 1964.

Journey to France and England

The fourth embassy sent abroad by the shogunate was unusual in that its mission was not diplomatic; it was to lay the groundwork for the establishment of a steel mill in Yokosuka. The embassy was headed by Shibata Takenaka (1823–1877), an official of the shogunate, who traveled for this purpose to France and England. Most of his time was spent in France, a reflection of the closeness of the ties that the shogunate had formed with that country. Shibata's diary "Futsueikō" (Journey to France and England), a section of a much longer diary that covers much of his life, describes what happened in between the time the embassy set sail from Yokohama on June 27, 1865, and its return to Japan on March 12, 1866. Of the various diaries kept by members of embassies, this is the least enjoyable for a modern reader and Shibata the least appealing diarist.

Shibata was highly conscious of his mission at all times, and nothing he saw or heard interested him unless it directly concerned the mission. He was meticulous in his accounts. No other diarist recorded with such painstaking care every last centime spent on food or lodgings and every tip given to a servant. He had visited France and England once before, as the fourth most senior member of the embassy of 1862. For this reason, wherever he went in France or England this time he was likely to comment sourly that he had already seen the place and nothing had changed. He seemed totally uninterested in the Frenchmen and Englishmen he met, though occasionally someone did something so irritating that he felt obliged to record it in his diary. For example, while in Plymouth inspecting the Navy Yard, he noted, "The ship's captain I invited last night came along with his wife. The person called Kington did the same. Their only conceivable purpose was to get a look at our party. Hateful."[1]

Of course, it must have been irritating to be subjected to the stares of Europeans who had never seen a Japanese before, but even Muragaki, the governor of Awaji, despite his irascibility, recognized that the Japanese in their exotic costumes were such rarities to foreigners that it was natural to stare, and he seems not to have been offended; but Shibata had no patience with the barbarians with whom, because of his mission, he had no choice but to associate.

Similarly, at his hotel in London, he recorded, "A certain Englishman who is staying at the same hotel as myself, who is interested in productology,[2] has, he says, made a collection of Japanese goods. For this reason he comes and goes into our quarters, accompanied by the hotel keeper. He suddenly asked if he might be present when I meet various people for dinner tomorrow night. The height of stupidity."[3]

Nothing a European did made a favorable impression. When his French servant, Charles, gave him a New Year's present, Shibata noted in his diary, "I was given a leather wallet and a calendar by my foreign servant[4] Charles. I suppose it was intended to convey New Year's greetings."[5] Naturally, he was neither touched nor pleased by the gift.

Shibata had received an excellent Confucian education at the celebrated Shōheikō school in Edo, and this permitted him to compose one or more poems in Chinese each day. They are uniformly cheerless. He seems to have resented the time he was obliged to spend away from Japan, and to have had only contempt for Europeans, as the following poem will suggest:

> Blue-eyed, heavy-bearded, they brazenly stride across the floor.
> Like wolves or hyenas in the fierceness of their mien.
> With their shrike tongues they will learn to sing like nightingales:
> In the gentle warmth of the light of the Land of the Gods.[6]

Some of his poems, in a more appealing vein, described his loneliness. No doubt Shibata missed his friends and family, and it was exasperating to deal with foreigners through inadequate interpreters. His dislike of Europeans remained with him even after leaving Europe: when he stopped in Ceylon on the return journey, he wrote of the people, "In their simplicity, honesty, and kindness they are unlike the Europeans."[7] Shibata's xenophobia did not prevent him from doing business with the Europeans, and it is reported that he was much esteemed by the junior members of the embassies.[8]

Notes

1. Shibata Takenaka, "Futsueikō," p. 415.
2. The word Shibata uses is *bussangaku*, a term coined about this time (but no longer used) to denote studies that combine zoology, botany, and mineralogy.
3. Shibata, "Futsueikō,", p. 415.
4. Shibata used the word *yōdo*, a clearly derogatory term.
5. Shibata, "Futsueikō," p. 419.
6. *Ibid.*, p. 314.
7. *Ibid.*, p. 455.
8. See Haga Tōru, *Taikun no Shisetsu*, p. 21.

Bibliography

Haga Tōru. *Taikun no Shisetsu.* Tokyo: Chūō Kōron Sha, 1968.

Shibata Takenaka. "Futsueikō," in Numata Jirō and Matsuzawa Hiroaki, *Seiyō Kembun Shū*, in Nihon Shisō Taikei series. Tokyo: Iwanami Shoten, 1974.

Voyage to the West

The shogunate sent altogether six official missions to the West, the last in 1867 at the request of the French government. A great exposition was held in Paris that year, and many distinguished persons, including reigning monarchs, attended. It was natural that the French, who had become increasingly close to the shogunate, should have wanted a suitable Japanese representative to attend the exposition. The mission was accordingly organized around Tokugawa Akitake, then fourteen years old, the younger brother of the last shogun, Tokugawa Yoshinobu. He was accompanied by a party of more than thirty officials including Shibusawa Eiichi (1840–1931) who, though of humble origins, had won recognition as an expert in financial matters.

Only seven years had elapsed since the first mission had traveled abroad, but the conditions of travel had totally changed. Shibusawa's *Kōsai Nikki* (Voyage to the West)[1] opens with an account of life aboard the passenger liner that took the Japanese from Yokohama to Hong Kong. Earlier Japanese visitors to the West had endured spartan accommodations aboard warships, but this mission traveled in comfort. The passengers seem to have spent their time mainly eating.

In the morning, after completing their ablutions, they went to the dining room where tea with sugar (a novelty for Shibusawa) and cakes were served. He mentions also *buta no shiozuke* (pig pickled in salt), which may have been bacon, and says that he liked the taste of "coagulated cow's milk spread on bread" (presumably meaning butter). This collation was only a preliminary to breakfast, served about ten. Shibusawa noted with approval the silverware. Fruit, including tangerines, grapes, pears, and loquats, was arranged on a dish from which everyone helped himself. The beverage was wine mixed with water. Various kinds of fish and meat were served with slices of bread, and finally coffee appeared.[2] About one in the afternoon another meal, similar to breakfast, was served along with bouillon, whose ingredients Shibusawa carefully explained. In the tropics they drank ice water, a novelty to the Japanese. At five or six in the afternoon dinner was served, a long series of courses that began with soup and ended with ice cream.

There is nothing remarkable about Shibusawa's descriptions of life aboard an ocean liner, but, so far as I am aware, no Japanese diarist had previously supplied such detailed information on what he ate. The earlier diarists were samurai, who probably felt it was beneath their dignity to discuss food, but Shibusawa explained, "To describe these trivial things is a waste of words, I know, but I was greatly impressed by the attention to details, the courtesy, and the care given to fostering the quality of life. That is why I have recorded here the general outlines."[3] The description of unimportant matters is what gives this diary its particular interest. The manner tells us much about Shibusawa who, not having been born a samurai, could mention such details without fear of ridicule.

The first port of call for the embassy headed by Prince Akitake was Shanghai. Shibusawa recalled mentions in Chinese poetry of the place and of its fish, which had been a prized delicacy, but there was little in the city to evoke its appearance of a thousand years earlier.

From this time on, the decline of China from its glorious past would be a frequent theme in Japanese writings, including diaries. Shibu-sawa found a quite different attraction in Shanghai than its historical associations: it seemed more modern to him than any city in Japan with its gas lights, telegraph wires, and rows of trees along the paved streets.[4] Not far from the European concessions, however, was the old, Chinese quarter of the city, where the influence of the West was still hardly felt: "The streets of the [old] city are narrow. The shops are two stories high, but the eaves are low, and the gates are narrow. They put up advertisement placards of every description, or in some cases they string banners over the streets. There are food shops of every kind—beef, pork, chicken, duck—and because they cook and sell these in the front of the shops, a mixture of smells assaults one's nose. The streets are paved with stones, but the pools of refuse water that collect on both sides of the streets never have a chance to dry."[5] This description, resembling those made by Japanese visitors to China sixty years later, suggests the simultaneous attraction and re-vulsion that Chinese cities aroused in the Japanese.

Shibusawa found places in Shanghai that interested him, such as the antique dealers, but he noted that the paintings on sale were nothing exceptional. He bought brushes and some Chinese ink and was given a towel that had been soaked in hot water. "They give this to you, as much as to say, 'Wipe your face with it!' It must be their way of receiving guests, instead of offering them tea."[6] The o-shibori that is now a Japanese custom in restaurants (or in airplanes) seems to have had its origins at this time.

Shibusawa was struck by the great disparity between the rich and the poor. The former traveled in sedan chairs, but most of the poor people "wear filthy rags and give off foul odors."[7] Like Fuchibe in Hong Kong, he was shocked by the way the Europeans treated the Chinese—"they drive them away exactly as they might drive away cattle or horses." But he felt less pity than contempt for the Chinese. "When I strolled through the streets the natives swarmed around and blocked traffic. Each of them was jabbering away noisily, but when the English and French military police came to drive them away, they withdrew like the tide, only to assemble again immediately. Their ignorance is hateful."[8]

It was astonishing to Shibusawa that an ancient and celebrated country, with vast territory and a large population, fertile soil, and a great abundance of products, should have fallen under the domination of European countries that were basically no match for China. He suggested reasons for this tragedy to have occurred: "The Chinese have fallen behind the progress of other countries of the world. They act as if their own country was the only one, and customarily behave with haughtiness and self-importance."[9] He saw no sign of progress in China; only fear of foreign military powers. "Still clinging to their old system, they fall each day into greater and greater poverty."[10] Shibusawa was referring to China, but surely he was also thinking of Japan where *kaika* (progress) was even at that moment being bitterly attacked by supporters of tradition.

Although Shibusawa deplored the servility of the Chinese and was repelled by the dirt and foul smells of Shanghai, he was also captivated. He went to the Chinese quarter situated behind the hotel where he stayed. He wrote, "There are houses of prostitution and theaters here. There are also women who resemble our geishas, and one hears the sounds of the music they play. Elegance exists."[11] On Sunday he reported, "Today is a holiday here. Europeans and Chinese, little children, boys and girls, all dressed up, go about singing and dancing. At night the view is extremely beautiful, with the pure light of the moon shining on the surface of the sea, which is like a mirror. Taking advantage of the moonlight, I continued my stroll."[12]

He was impressed when he saw French priests attired in Chinese robes who had founded a school for teaching sinology. He wrote, "I have been told that all the Europeans who study orientalism (*tōyōgaku*) are priests, and that the expenses of their study are supplied from a reserve fund set aside for this purpose, with the intention of investigating the origins of the religion of the country in which they reside and, with this historical evidence to assist them, of propagating their own teachings."[13]

The ship proceeded from Shanghai to Hong Kong. Shibusawa gave credit to the British for having transformed a desolate island, inhabited only by fishermen, into a thriving commercial center. He was impressed by the mint, the newspaper offices, public halls, and hospitals—all small-scale replicas of European buildings. He was particularly struck by the number of books published in Hong Kong in both English and Chinese.[14] Shibusawa was impressed by the diligence of the British in studying Chinese. He wrote,

> They assiduously pursue their studies not only in the history of the successive dynasties, the classics of government, and the codes of law, but in the literary styles of everyday life. They translate these books and publish their explanations. There is no scarcity of people to carry out this major undertaking; they consider that devotion to studies that are cultural in character and permeated by the human spirit constitute the glory of a nation, and they are fully capable of investigating in detail the researches of the geniuses of human intellect.[15]

Shibusawa's interest extended to the weekly newspapers published in Hong Kong. He even gave their subscription prices, the kind of information not found in diaries kept by samurai. He also offered practical advice on where to change money, a problem that earlier Japanese travelers to Europe must have faced but never described: "It is advisable when traveling to Europe to change the silver coins one has obtained in Yokohama for English pounds, to be used during the voyage."[16]

From Hong Kong the French ship traveled to Saigon. Shibusawa noted that native resistance to the French occupation had impeded progress and prosperity, but there were agreeable aspects to the city despite its look of neglect: "There are theaters and houses of pleasure, just as in China."[17] He and his companions hired a guide and went to a grove of coconut palms where they saw elephants perform various stunts. Finally, they visited Cholon, the Chinese section of Saigon, where they admired the biggest temple in the city. A plaque in Chinese characters gave its name, Sheng-mu-tien, Hall of the Holy Mother. Shibusawa guessed that it was dedicated to the god of the sea, but perhaps it was a Christian church.[18]

Singapore was the next port of call. Once again, Shibusawa expressed his admiration for the guidance of the British. It is true that the natives went about barefoot, and the streets resembled those in Saigon, but there were also modern facilities: "All these seemed to be achievements brought about by human skill alone, and they were sufficiently numerous to permit one to perceive the bold manner with which England has implemented its ideals in the Orient."[19] On the wharfs moneychangers dealt in the currencies of many countries, but Shibusawa warned that some of the money they gave was counterfeit. Boys in the harbor dived for coins, but only for silver ones because copper coins were hard to detect in the water. Shibusawa wrote exactly like a European traveler on his first visit to the gorgeous East.

The ship carrying the Japanese embassy traveled from Singapore to Galle in Ceylon. Naturally, the members stayed at the best hotel, but this did not prevent Shibusawa from exploring other parts of the town. His description of the natives indicates that he found them completely alien: "The natives are poverty-stricken, but (unlike the Chinese) they are rather well behaved and seem to work hard. This is probably because they have for many years been pressed into the service of the Europeans. Their bodies are hairy. They go about barefoot, and their only garment is a length of printed cotton they twist around the loins. Their color is brownish black. Their eyes are deep set. Their teeth are black and their lips red."[20]

Shibusawa visited a Buddhist temple. The main building was locked, but he persuaded a priest to open it. Inside was a recumbent image made of ceramics showing Shakyamuni Buddha about to enter nirvana. Shibusawa describes the statue, the appearance of the priests, the sound of their prayers, and a relic of the Buddha, but he gives not the slightest hint that he was moved to be in a temple in a land that was closely associated with the Buddha. Instead, he informs us, "From the crest of the mountain one gets a splendid view. There is a little pavilion there where they sell champagne."[21]

It is clear that Shibusawa was repelled by the poverty and nakedness of the people of Ceylon. At the next port of call, Aden, he found the people rather better built than the natives of Ceylon, but they seemed to be of base character. The land was desolate; not one tree was to be seen. Shibusawa paid tribute to the British who had established their rule in Aden: "The British gave unstintingly of their strength, and expended their wealth to erect their flag over this barren, remote wasteland. Ever since they extended their rule, trade in the Orient has prospered, as one can tell from the scale of their territories linking China and India."[22]

On the basis of his observations during the journey, Shibusawa decided that the industriousness of a people was in inverse proportion to the fertility of the soil. In a country with a naturally fertile soil, the people become lazy and give themselves to pleasure; but people who live in countries with poor soil are "thrifty, diligent, and strong. If something requires it, they are ready to go to war at a moment's notice. In other words, they provide the roots for a prosperous and strong country."[23]

When the Japanese reached Suez they heard about the building of the canal, and this inspired Shibusawa to a fresh outburst of praise for the West, an extraordinary change in a man who until a very few years before had been an advocate of *jōi*—the expulsion from Japan of the barbarians. He wrote, "They say that one cannot calculate how many times more convenient this will be than in the past. When people of the West plan an undertaking, they do not think solely of the benefits to their own countries alone, but usually they plan for the great benefits that will accrue to all countries. One can only marvel at the grandeur of the scale, the magnificence of their goals."[24]

The diary contains another, quite different expression of admiration for the West, written just before the Japanese left Egypt, the last of the East. Shibusawa contrasted the monogamy of the West where "from the sovereign down to the lowliest commoner, each man has only one wife; there are no such things as concubines," and the East, where the "barbarous" Turkish sultans had more than 480 concubines.[25] This situation led Shibusawa to pass this judgment on Egypt: "This country is the closest to the West, but unless it changes its ignorant ways, one will have to say that it is hamstrung by old conventions, and has fallen behind in progress." Considering that the diary in its present form was composed several years after Shibusawa's return to Japan from Europe, it is surprising that his residence abroad had not disillusioned him concerning the morality of the European monarchs.

The sections of *Voyage to the West* that describe the Japanese mission's stay in Europe are somewhat less interesting than Shibusawa's amusing if unsympathetic condemnation of the backwardness of the Asian countries, but a new element is added, his reporting of contemporary events. When, for example, his ship entered port in Sicily, he recalled the achievements of Garibaldi in these terms: "Six or seven years ago Garibaldi rose to prominence from a speck of land.[26] He declared that the religious laws were insincere, and advocated anti-Buddhism. He resolutely raised an army, displayed his authority to the Western world, and advanced with an impetus so powerful as to sweep over the whole of Italy in no time . . ."[27] One would suppose that the conservative Shibusawa would have disliked the revolutionary Garibaldi and his "anti-Buddhism," but he declared that Garibaldi's fame had not diminished even after he was sent back following defeat to his little island of Caprera, where "he is enjoying his remaining years in quiet retirement. His heroic qualities are still capable of inspiring reverent admiration."[28]

The sight of Corsica evoked reflections on Napoleon, whose nephew now ruled France. Soon after reaching France, Shibusawa attended a service for the French soldiers who had distinguished themselves during fighting in Cambodia. Far from being upset by this example of European imperialism directed at an Asian country, Shibusawa wrote, "There can be no doubting that these soldiers deserve praise, and it is appropriate to encourage them in their achievements."[29] After his arrival in Paris, he described in detail the attempted assassination of Czar Alexander II by a Polish nationalist. Later, he mentioned the death of Emperor Maximilian at the hands of Mexican patriots. He seems to have read the newspapers carefully while in Europe.

Even more than the awareness of developments in other parts of the world recorded in Shibusawa's diary, his account of everyday experiences in Paris is likely to be of interest to the modern reader. The contrast between his life and the life led by the members of the first mission to visit Europe, only five years earlier, is particularly striking. When the first mission stopped in Hong Kong some members bought shoes there, only to be severely reprimanded for having abandoned traditional Japanese dress in favor of foreign clothes. But five years later Shibusawa took the first opportunity after his arrival in Paris to order a suit, and this became the usual dress of all future Japanese embassies.

While in Paris Shibusawa often attended the theater to see plays, operas, and ballets. He explained that attending the theater was an indispensable part of a formal visit to a foreign country. The preservation of Nō, whose very existence was threatened after the Meiji Restoration because of its long associations with the discredited shogunate, owed much to the same discovery of the importance of the theater by the statesman Iwakura Tomomi: Nō was saved in order that the government might have a suitably dignified entertainment to offer foreign guests.

Naturally, Shibusawa visited the Paris Exposition many times. He was pleased with the Japanese teahouse, and noted that its waitresses were the first oriental women ever to travel to the West.[30] He described these ladies: "In the private rooms three women of tender age—Kane, Sumi, and Sato—sit gracefully and display themselves."[31] Fuchibe had felt ashamed when he saw the Japanese wares displayed in London, but Shibusawa was quite pleased with the Japanese pavilion at the Exposition. He wrote, "Of all Asia, the country with the most complete and brilliant display of products was, of course, Japan."[32] The "of course" would have surprised Fuchibe.

Voyage to the West was probably the first Japanese diary to describe the typical tourist attractions—the Arc de Triomphe, Nôtre-Dame, the Tuileries, the Louvre, the Champs Elysées, and the parks. It is strange that not even the artistically gifted Fuchibe mentioned these places, which he must have known, but perhaps his reticence as a samurai made him reluctant to portray himself as a tourist.

Shibusawa also mentioned meeting various distinguished Europeans—not merely interpreters or persons who had visited Japan in some capacity, but members of the salons of Paris. He was invited to the house of Princess Mathilde, whose salon was especially brilliant. He attended a dance party that lasted until dawn. He went to the horse races at the Bois de Boulogne the same day as did the emperor of France, the czar of Russia, the king of Belgium, and the crown prince of Prussia. He was presented to Queen Victoria.

He also enjoyed popular entertainments. He attended a performance of acrobatics given by visiting Japanese. (The very first Japanese to be issued with passports were members of a troupe of acrobats, and for the next forty or fifty years Japanese acrobats performed all over Europe.) These acrobats were so skillful that the spectators feared they might fall to their deaths during their spectacular acts. As Shibusawa watched the acrobats, a small child behind him asked its mother what would happen if they should fall. The mother answered, "They'll break in pieces." Shibusawa commented, "She seemed to think that Japanese were more or less the same as articles of pottery or lacquer."[33]

On occasion Shibusawa left off his descriptions of life in Paris to consider a newspaper article or to refute the views of Japan published by some foreigner. He wrote, "When foreigners discuss Japanese customs, they say that the Japanese normally have no recourse to activi-

ties of the mind, but are solely addicted to pleasures of the flesh."
He blamed this misapprehension on the existence of "teahouses"
(*chamise*), noting that when Sir Rutherford Alcock traveled in the interior of Japan, the only places to stay were these teahouses, where
women were offered to travelers. An American missionary stationed
in China had declared at a conference that "the Japanese are so lazy,
so promiscuous, and so given to immorality that their natures grow
worse by the day and the population decreases by the year."[34] Shibusawa sprang to the defense of Japanese manhood. He insisted that,
far from decreasing, the population of Japan was rapidly increasing.
Perhaps there was a grain of truth in the missionary's remarks, but
"As everyone who has chosen to live in Japan says, Japanese men are
physically robust, and perform their duties well. Their wives are
healthy, full of vigor, and beautiful."[35]

Both the journey through Asia and the Exposition confirmed
Shibusawa's high opinion of the Japanese. Even in the entertainments offered at the different pavilions of the Exposition, there was
an immense difference between the polished performances of the
Japanese and the crudities offered by other Asians and Africans. But
he must have been perturbed to learn while the embassy was still in
Paris that the shogun had returned his powers to the emperor and
the shogunate, first established at the beginning of the seventeenth
century, no longer existed.

Tokugawa Akitake did not return at once to Japan, but remained in Paris for another year, studying under French tutors.
Shibusawa remained with him. His diary *Pari Gozaikan Nikki* (Diary
of His Excellency's Stay in Paris), which covers this period, is of some
historical interest, but lacks the verve that makes *Voyage to the West*
such a delight to read.

Notes

1. The diary was written several years after the events it describes, in 1870, at
   the suggestion of Date Munenari (1818–1892). It was based on the notes

Shibusawa took on his journey, but he had the literary assistance of Sugiura Aizō. It is unclear which man was responsible for individual sections of the diary, but for convenience' sake, I have written as if Shibusawa were the sole author. For translations of other excerpts from the diary, see Teruko Craig, *The Autobiography of Shibusawa Eiichi*, pp. 152–71.

2. *Shibusawa Eiichi Denki Shiryō*, I, p. 463.

3. *Ibid.*

4. *Ibid.*, p. 464.

5. *Ibid.*

6. *Ibid.*

7. *Ibid.*

8. *Ibid.*

9. *Ibid.*, p. 465.

10. *Ibid.*

11. *Ibid.*, p. 464.

12. *Ibid.*, p. 465.

13. *Ibid.*, p. 464. His comment that all the Europeans who studied "orientalism" in Shanghai were priests contrasts with his praise of the British (clearly not priests) in Hong Kong who studied Chinese for entirely secular purposes.

14. This contradicts Fuchibe's flat statement, "There is nothing special unless one goes to Canton." (Fuchibe Tokuzō, *Ōkō Nikki*, p. 13.)

15. *Shibusawa*, I, p. 466.

16. *Ibid.*

17. *Ibid.*, p. 467.

18. *Ibid.* Shibusawa would not have seen a Christian church in Japan, and probably a Catholic church in Saigon would have looked far more elaborate than any church he might have seen in Hong Kong. However, *sheng-mu* is also found in Confucian and Buddhist texts with the meaning of the mother of a holy person (*sheng-jen*).

19. *Ibid.*, p. 468.

20. *Ibid.*, p. 469. Mention of the redness of the lips probably refers to the effects of chewing betel.

21. *Ibid.*, pp. 469–70.

22. *Ibid.*, p. 470.

23. *Ibid.*, p. 471. The term rendered here as "prosperous and strong country" (*fukoku kyōhei*) was one of the watchwords of the early Meiji era.

24. *Ibid.*, p. 472.

25. *Ibid.*, p. 473.
26. Presumably refers to the island of Caprera, lying between Corsica and Sardinia, rather than to Garibaldi's birthplace, Nice.
27. *Shibusawa*, I, p. 474. It is not clear what the "religious laws" (*kyōhō*) refer to, but presumably "anti-Buddhism" (*haibutsu*) refers to Garibaldi's expedition against Rome, the seat of the "Buddha."
28. *Ibid.* The "retirement" of Garibaldi seems to refer to his activities in 1867. After his unsuccessful expedition against Rome he was arrested and sent back to Caprera. Later in the same year he escaped and led his men against the papal and French troops. He was defeated and once again taken back to his island.
29. *Ibid.*, p. 475.
30. *Ibid.*, p. 512.
31. *Ibid.*, p. 522.
32. *Ibid.*, p. 519.
33. *Ibid.*, p. 521.
34. *Ibid.*
35. *Ibid.*, p. 522.

Bibliography

Craig, Teruko. *The Autobiography of Shibusawa Eiichi*. Tokyo: University of Tokyo Press, 1994.

Shibusawa Eiichi Denki Shiryō, I. Tokyo: Shibusawa Eiichi Denki Shiryō Kankōkai, 1955.

True Account of a Tour of America and Europe

The first mission sent abroad by the new Meiji government that succeeded the shogunate was especially brilliant. It consisted of forty-eight men, headed by the chief ambassador, Iwakura Tomomi (1825–1883), and included three of the chief figures in Japanese politics of the early Meiji era—Kido Takayoshi, Ōkubo Toshimichi, and Itō Hirobumi—as vice-ambassadors. So many important political figures were included in the mission that it was said, in jest, that all that was left in Tokyo (the new name for Edo) was a "caretaker government."

The members of the mission, along with a party of students bound for various countries, boarded the U.S. steamship *America* which sailed from Yokohama on December 23, 1871. The voyage to San Francisco, the first port abroad for the mission, took twenty-two days. Kume Kunitake (1839–1931), the author of *Beiō Kairan Jikki* (True Account of a Tour of America and Europe),[1] does not mention the seasickness that was so prominent a feature of other accounts of Japanese crossing the Pacific, but we know from other sources that many in the mission were indeed seasick. Presumably Kume decided, in view of the official nature of the diary, not to mention such personal matters.

Kume, a thirty-three-year-old samurai from Saga, Kyūshū, was chosen as the scribe of the mission, not because he possessed any special knowledge of the West, but because he was a Confucian scholar, and it was hoped that his account would not be an unqualified panegyric, but would (with Confucian regard for tradition) point out the defects as well as the merits of the different countries of the West.

The plan of compiling an official record of the journey seems to have originated with the American missionary Guido Verbeck (1830–1898). Verbeck had been sent in 1859 to Nagasaki by the Dutch Reformed Church, and had taught many brilliant young statesmen, including two of the vice-ambassadors of the mission, Kido and Ōkubo. He moved to Tokyo in 1869, and became a trusted adviser of the Meiji government, especially in the fields of education and law. In the same year he submitted a memorandum to his former student Ōkuma Shigenobu (1838–1922), now minister of finance, urging that a mission be sent to America and Europe. Members of the mission would be encouraged to record in detail what they had seen and heard abroad. These reports would eventually be published for the enlightenment of the general public.[2]

True Account, as an official record, contains precise information on the many sites the mission visited, ranging from naval dockyards to biscuit factories. However, the special appeal of the diary for contemporary readers lies less in such information than in the essays by Kume scattered through the work. For example, even before the ship arrived in San Francisco, he presented a general account of *Meriken Gasshūkoku* (the United States of America), in which he described not only the geography, natural resources, climate, industries, and history of America but an analysis of the American character. He wrote with surprising insight and with infinitely more information than any previous Japanese observer of the West.

For example, after an account of why the Americans hate kings "like poisonous snakes," he declared that George Washington was chosen as the first president because there was no fear that he might betray the antimonarchical sentiments of the people. He continued,

> Therefore, the people of this country all grow up in a climate of democracy, and possess the sentiments of universal brotherhood. In dealing with other people they are sincere and easy to like, and in other matters they are not shackled by conventions. They are indeed citizens of the entire world. Their faults are that they are careless about official authority, and lose their energy in face of prohibitions. Each man insists on his own rights, and bribes are publicly practiced. They cannot help but suffer from the friction of their political parties. However, Americans have long been imbued with these ways, and their country is a realm of pure democracy.[3]

Kume's admiration for American democracy contrasts with the sardonic comments he makes on the aristocracies of the European countries he was to visit, but it was tempered by the fear that absolute egalitarianism might lead to disorder. In the end, no doubt thinking of Japan, he expressed a preference for a constitutional monarchy to a republic, despite the disadvantages: "In Europe, ever since they arranged to have constitutional governments, these have safeguarded the peace of the world."[4]

There was not much to relieve the tedium of shipboard life during the three weeks at sea between Yokohama and San Francisco. Kume's annotations on wind conditions and the daily position of the ship are enlivened by only two events. The first was the celebration of New Year's Eve by the solar calendar (or the twenty-first day of the eleventh month of the lunar calendar). The Japanese joined the Europeans and Americans in the celebration by drinking punch made of champagne, brandy, and various other exotic liquors. The

second event was the party the Japanese gave in honor of the Great
Food Offering Ritual (*daijōe*) performed by Emperor Meiji as one of
the enthronement rites. The ambassador, Iwakura Tomomi, dressed
for the occasion in a *hitatare* (formal court robe), delivered a speech to
the foreign passengers explaining the ritual. The interpreter was the
American minister Charles E. De Long, who accompanied the Japanese across the Pacific.

Kume noted, "In English they call the recitation of fancy language *supīchi*. At meetings and banquets they all express their feelings in this form. It is especially popular in America and England.
The *supīchi* this day was the first the mission heard on its journey."[5]
During the course of the next year and ten months, until their return
to Japan, the members of the mission would hear many speeches,
most of them boring, and would reply in equally dull terms. This
may mark the beginning of the deplorable practice of "greetings"
(*goaisatsu*), still the bane of every gathering in Japan.

When the ship bearing the mission entered San Francisco Bay
and passed by Alcatraz Island, it was greeted with a fifteen-gun
salute. The Japanese seem to have been somewhat disappointed in
the number of shots fired, but Kume explained, "America is a demo-
cratic country and practices simplicity with respect to the level of politeness and etiquette displayed. For this reason, they normally fire
only fifteen-gun salutes, and do not observe the English system."[6]

After landing in San Francisco the Japanese proceeded to the
Grand Hotel. One misses in Kume's diary the descriptions of wildly
cheering crowds that one finds in older accounts of the arrival of
Japanese embassies. The San Franciscans had evidently become too
blasé to pay much attention to Japanese visitors.

Although the members of the Japanese mission were to stay at far
more luxurious hotels during the course of their journey, probably
none impressed them so much as the first. The Grand Hotel was still
fairly new, and the carpets and chairs that decorated each room were
of dazzling beauty. The ground floor was paved with marble that
was so well waxed that the Japanese all but slid along. The hotel had

baths, a barber shop, and a billiard room. Kume does not say so in this diary, but we know from his memoirs, written many years later, how surprised he was when a porter led him into a small room in which several American men and women were standing. "I was shocked when it suddenly started to move and we were pulled upward," he wrote of his first experience in an elevator.

His hotel room delighted him: "Each guest room is provided with a large sitting room (called *salon* in French), a bedroom, a bathroom, and a water closet. The big mirror is like water, and the carpet like flowers. Gas lights are suspended from above. During the day the pieces of cut glass [in the chandelier] bewitch the eyes with seven colors and exchange light with the gilding. At night when one loosens a screw and sets the gas afire, the planets and stars circle above one as light glows inside white jade [globes]. There are lace curtains on the windows that make one think one is looking at flowers through mist."[7] He examined the bed and discovered there were springs under the mattress. When he twisted the handle of the faucet "pure water leaped forth." He noted also, "There is an electric wire for summoning the servants. A bare touch of the finger and a bell rings a hundred paces away."[8] There was a desk for reading and writing, a mirror in which to examine oneself. Each room was provided with "soap, towels, matches, a wash basin, a stove, a water jug, and a toilet." One envies Kume the sharpness of his vision as he examined the marvels of a modern hotel room.

The first days spent by the Japanese mission in San Francisco were not devoted solely to inspecting factories and fortifications (as one might expect), but included visits to the zoo, the botanical gardens, and a museum. These facilities, intended for the instruction and pleasure of the public, inspired Kume to write an interesting essay in which he described the differences between orientals and occidentals. It opens:

The customs and characteristics of East and West are invariably different, and seem to originate in diametrically opposed sources. The occidental enjoys associating with strangers. The oriental refrains from doing this. This is not solely a lingering effect of the seclusion of the country. It is because [the oriental] pays scant attention to material wealth, and considers that foreign trade is not a pressing concern. The occidental enjoys going out to divert himself. This is why even small villages always have public parks. The oriental enjoys being lazy in his own house. That is why every house has a garden.[9]

It should be noted that when Kume used the word "oriental" (*tōyōjin*) he almost always referred to a Japanese, and not to, say, a Chinese or a Korean. He tended also to write about the Japanese in terms of the samurai class, his own; otherwise, it would be hard to understand why he characterized the Japanese as being indifferent to money matters—not at all the attitude of the merchant class. His insistence that Japanese prefer to loll at home rather than go outside for pleasure also seems to ignore the licensed quarters and theaters that were a part of every city, probably because they were meant chiefly for commoners, rather than samurai. But, even if one cannot accept Kume's generalizations in entirety, it is clear that he had noticed a real difference between the West and Japan. The absence of public places, such as the Roman forum or the parks of modern Europe, was probably not due solely to an oriental love of the solitary pleasures of a private garden, but the difference was there.

Kume ascribed this difference to the Western preference for physical science (*yūkei no rigaku*), as opposed to the Japanese preference for nonphysical science (*mukei no rigaku*).[10] He wrote,

Every Western city has its botanical gardens and zoos, just as we have plant and animal shows. At first glance the two phenomena seem to be similar (leaving aside the question of their size), but the purpose behind creating them is fundamentally contrary. In the West these institutions attract people's attention, and they really study them. In this way, they advance their professions and extend the dimensions of learning. They have never regretted the huge expenses because of the great profits they otherwise reap . . . The profits serve as intermediaries in the advancement of the physical sciences, in discovering what is of material benefit to farmers, artisans, and merchants, and in promoting the prosperity of rich and poor. Those who practice the oriental nonphysical science laugh at those who study one blade of grass or one tree, or they place an exaggerated value on some curiosity, and furtively take whatever profits present themselves, but this is a confusion that does not merit being discussed.[11]

The differences between East and West surely did not arise solely because of the Western compulsion to obtain material benefits, as Kume himself recognized. He suggested elsewhere in the same essay (and at many places later in the diary) that people who live in a country whose soil is fertile tend to be lazy, but those who live in countries with stony soil have no choice but to be industrious. This is the same argument found in Shibusawa Eiichi's diary, and indicates that Kume prepared for his journey by meeting Japanese who had already been abroad. He applied the argument specifically to Japan: the fertile soil permitted the Japanese to be lazy, but in the West, where the soil was not so fertile, commerce had become more important than agriculture. The botanical gardens, zoos, and museums of the West were not mere displays of curiosities, as they would be in Japan, but served to promote knowledge and thereby help people to earn a decent living. This was obviously an oversimplification, but it was typical of Kume not to content himself with merely observing but always to attempt to understand underlying causes.

❖ ❖ ❖

Kume was sensitive to the beauty of the scenery wherever he went, from his first port of call in San Francisco on, and his prose rose to poetic heights when he described sights he admired. After leaving San Francisco the embassy proceeded to Sacramento, where Kume climbed to the top of the state capitol. "When I climbed up there and gazed around me, Sacramento spread out at my feet like a huge chessboard, with the broad Sacramento River to the north. To the east, south, and west the California plains stretched into the hazy distance, and I could see among them a marsh that threw off light like a mirror. Poets of the T'ang dynasty, after climbing the pagoda of the Tz'u-ên Temple, once joined in composing poems about the scenery, but I doubt it had the grandeur of the view here."[12]

Two days later Kume was even more impressed by the scenery of the Sierra Nevada. He wrote,

> Last evening at Summit, the railway station at the crest of the Sierra Nevada, they attached a snowplow to the train. Then we entered a long tunnel, dark as eternal night, and the day came to a close while we were still in the tunnel. The steam whistle, sounding choked, mingled with the echoes from the wheels as the train slid along the tracks. While I was asleep the train emerged from sheer cliffs, and as the train sped on we had behind us "lofty peaks that might be taken for devils' work." Li T'ai-po, in his poem "Hard Road to Shu," spoke of "Earth crumbles, mountains break, brave men die;/ Afterward, ladders to heaven, stone bridges over abysses go on." But I am sure the scenery was no more impressive than it is here.[13]

Kume's descriptions of scenery, whether of America, the Highlands of Scotland, Switzerland, or other places in Europe and Asia that especially impressed him, are beautifully written and account for the literary quality in a diary that was clearly not intended to be a work of literature. Kume's vocabulary owed much to his readings in Chinese literature, and quotations (such as the one from Li T'ai-po above) are evidence that scenery, wherever viewed, made him recall Chinese poetry. But this does not completely explain the literary appeal of his writing. One of my favorite passages describes, in distinctly un-Chinese terms, the coast of Ceylon in the region of Galle, as it appeared to him when he was on the return voyage to Japan:

> The headland to the southwest is curved like an elephant's trunk, and at the point of its tusk they have built a lighthouse that soars fifty feet into the sky. Before the lighthouse, in a place that faces the sea, shore reefs rise up in disarray, some sinking into the submerged reefs, others rising as precipitous rocks to form a chain of islands big and small. The waves of the sea approach the shore like white horses racing in tandem, and dash twenty or thirty feet until they hit the rocks where they are shattered, and here and there snow flowers fly up to strike against the sky. The swollen, roaring surface of the sea, perpetually white, makes one think a thousand whales were fighting, and makes a magnificent spectacle.[14]

Although Kume was by no means begrudging of his praise when he described the scenery in America and Europe, one senses his relief when he reached Ceylon on his way back to Japan: "In the countries of the tropics the mountains are green and the water is blue. Plants abound, the earth is fertile, the air is clean, and the scenery is beautiful. When, having arrived from Europe, I look at this scenery, I feel as if this is truly a paradise for human beings."[15] The chimneys of Europe pouring forth smoke impressed Kume, and he realized that this was the path Japan would have to walk if it was to be recognized as a powerful nation; but it was with great relief that he breathed pure air and gazed at the undefiled scenery of the tropics. Ceylon had not yet attained "culture and progress," but it was "a paradise for human beings."

Kume's style is not easy to follow. He used many rare kanji that give a forbidding look to each page, but this was not mere display; he was taking advantage of the possibility of expressing nuances of meaning that could not be adequately conveyed with simpler Japanese vocabulary. The richness of language at times requires the reader to turn to a dictionary to catch the full meaning, and stylistic complications are likely to slow the reading even more, but anyone who persists and reads to the end the more than two thousand pages of this diary will be amply rewarded, both by the insights of a perceptive observer and by the beauty of passages that reveal Kume's literary skill.

The aspect of American society that puzzled Kume the most was the treatment accorded to women. He described early in the diary a visit to a school in San Francisco where the average male teacher earned a monthly salary of $125, but a female teacher received a starting salary of only $50 that rose, after years of service, to a maximum of $100.[16] Such examples of discrimination did not in the least bother Kume, but he found the courtesies shown to women utterly baffling. He wrote, after visiting Washington,

> Women are not prohibited from entering official buildings in America. Women gather even in the military and naval academies to watch the drill, and when it is over, men and women go hand-in-hand to the dance floor where they dance and enjoy themselves to the full. This is the custom of a republican government . . . Ever since our party boarded the American ship in Yokohama, we have been in a world where different customs prevail. In the same way that our every movement has been observed by them, their actions have baffled us. I cannot list them all in detail, but the thing that has

puzzled us most is the relations between men and women. In Japan the wife serves her husband's parents, a child serves its father and mother, but here it is the practice for the husband to serve the wife. He gets a lamp for her, he fetches her shoes, he offers her food, he brushes her clothes. When she sits down he helps her, when she gets up, he helps her. When she wants to sit, he offers a chair, and when she is about to go out, he offers her what she needs. If he should incur the least anger from his wife, he shows affection, he shows respect, he begs her pardon on bended knees. If she still won't listen to him, he is obliged to leave the room, and it sometimes happens that he does not get anything to eat.[17]

No doubt Kume exaggerated the deference American men showed their wives, but there is enough truth in his words to make us smile. After he completed his journey, however, he realized that the American attitude toward women was not typical of all Western countries. He wrote, "This is true in general of the West, but it is particularly extreme in America and England. This tendency has been intensified in England because it is ruled by a queen, and in America where, because there is a republican government, the idea of equality between the sexes has become rampant."[18] He cited the shocking example of the woman doctor in Washington who went around wearing a silk hat and trousers. But in Japan, where the "oriental" teachings still prevailed, "wives stay inside the house and do not work outside. It is logical for a distinction to be made between men and women."[19]

Not until the Japanese embassy reached Prussia did they find Europeans who shared their views on women. Kume, after describing ways in which the Germans differed from the peoples of other countries, wrote, "There are many other respects in which German customs differ greatly from those in England and America, but the most conspicuous is the scant respect they show women. In Berlin even the women laugh at the servility displayed by the English and

Americans toward women, and consider it a most peculiar custom. Wherever one goes on the European continent, the customs always differ from those of America and England."[20]

But Kume had other criticism to direct at European women: "In general, in Europe formal dress for women leaves exposed everything above the breasts. This is by custom. Piercing the ears and taking in the waist is also by custom. They consider that slender feet are beautiful, and cram their feet into shoes, still another custom. With respect to health, none of these is to be commended."[21] No doubt he was correct in this last observation!

Even as one reads these remarks by Kume on the subject of women, a question is likely to arise that Kume failed to answer: did not this group of Japanese, whose average age was about thirty, yearn for and finally obtain the company of women? Kume noted with tacit disapproval the prostitutes in London, the licensed quarter in Hamburg where prostitutes openly solicited customers, and the people selling pornographic photographs in the streets of Berlin, but he did not indicate whether or not the Japanese responded to such enticements. Years later, when Kume, at the time a distinguished professor of history at Tokyo University, discussed a section of the medieval history *Taiheiki* (Record of Great Peace) in which scantily clad women wait on some conspirators, he wrote, "It was exactly like a brothel in Paris, and the obscenity of the naked women, lined up and dressed in lace like the whores in Paris, made me want to shut the book after one reading."[22] This strongly suggests that Kume on at least one occasion yielded to temptations of the flesh, but there was no likelihood of his reporting experiences of this kind in his diary. In such matters he was a samurai first and a diarist second.

The leaders of the embassy, recognizing that the West could not be understood solely in terms of its industrial output, did not confine visits in America and Britain to places of obviously utilitarian significance. Museums were of special interest, if only because there were no museums in Japan. Even if one had access to some private collection, its treasures were never displayed in entirety, but only in the appropriate seasons. When the Japanese visited a duke's castle in England, they were greatly surprised to see all of his possessions on display: "In the West they do not shut up their treasures in boxes. They display them all in their house, and consider it an honor to show them to guests."[23]

Kume was particularly impressed by the sense of history that the exhibits in the British Museum provided. Observing the ancient artifacts unearthed in Scandinavia, Egypt, and Babylon, he commented, "These are the works that experts thoroughly acquainted with antiquity have most admired. There are a great many objects from ancient Greece and Rome, some in perfect condition, others broken, others copies."[24] The appeal for Kume of these objects was sometimes aesthetic, but he was even more impressed by what they told of the past:

> When one sees them in a museum, they naturally transmit to the eyes and mind of the beholder a feeling of the order of the steps a country has taken in the process of becoming civilized. If one looks into the history of the founding of any country, one is likely to discover that it did not occur all at once. There has always been an order of things. Those who first gain knowledge transmit it to later generations, the predecessors inform those who come afterward. This process of gradual advancement is what we call progress (*shimpo*).

A Briton could not help but become aware of the development of civilization in Britain by walking through the British Museum, far more vividly than from reading a history book. Kume noted, later in his travels in England, "Western people seek progress, but they also think about the past and love old things, which they keep and do not throw away. This invariable practice merits being called civilized."[25]

Kume was an advocate of progress, but he feared that if the

Japanese adopted the more advanced ways of the West they might, out of eagerness to be abreast of the world, forget their own heritage. He wrote, after describing the treasures of the British Museum, "Progress is not simply a matter of discarding the old and seeking the new." Unlike the British, however, the Japanese felt no hesitation about abandoning their past:

> Ever since the Western theory of constant change and progress was transmitted to Japan, frivolous and shortsighted people have discarded the old as soon as they could and vied for the new. Even though they have not yet necessarily obtained the so-called new, they have destroyed so many old things worthy of preservation as to leave nothing. Ah, is this what is meant by constant change? Is this the meaning of progress?[26]

The fears that Kume expressed, so soon after the beginning of the era of *bummei kaika* (civilization and progress), demonstrated his acute vision. The Japanese past was likely to disappear in face of the demands of the advocates of progress, and there were no museums preserving the material objects of the past for the edification of future generations. The Japanese might even have to travel to museums in foreign countries in order to see what their ancestors had created. Kume discovered that Japanese books of the Christian century— from the middle of the sixteenth to the middle of the seventeenth century—though lost and unknown in Japan, were preserved in the great libraries of Europe. Indeed, the Japanese could learn much about their culture as a whole in the European museums. "Whenever I see the libraries and museums of the West, I am amazed by the solidity of their preparations, and how they have collected and catalogued things even from our distant part of the world, the Orient, not begrudging the great expense, nor avoiding the difficulties. That is why when people from our country are shown these exhibits, they are often astonished by things they never knew themselves. In fact, the explanations they hear may enable them to learn all about their own country."[27]

When Kume saw the ruins of Pompeii, he sensed their organic connection with modern Italy, and was moved to the strongest expression of his fears: "In recent years many in our country have approved of the West, and found its ways convenient. They have discarded our traditional ways, even those that were rather advanced, and call this *kaika*, enlightenment, or *bummei*, civilization. Do they not realize that they are actually turning their backs on civilization?"[28]

Visiting the museums and art galleries of Europe made Kume realize that the artistic traditions of the West remained unbroken for centuries. It may seem strange that a man coming from a country whose artistic traditions had been miraculously preserved should have felt envious of the West, but he was struck by the conscious preservation of traditions that he encountered everywhere in Europe.

Kume noted, for example, young artists copying the masterpieces of the past displayed in the galleries of Europe. He wrote about the Uffizi in Florence, "It is a gallery famous all over the world where men and women artists gather each day and crowd its rooms copying the works of art."[29] He insisted that the copying of works of art from the past was essential to the transmission of traditions. Of course, the purpose of this copying was not to produce forgeries, a practice familiar enough in Japan, but to train the young artist by following in the footsteps of past masters. In Japan artists could copy only works of art that they themselves owned or which were in collections accessible to them because of some personal relationship with the possessor, whereas in Europe anyone could go to museums and acquire familiarity with masterpieces.

The ability to create splendid works of art is, in itself, practical. The artistic talents of the French, displayed at various expositions held in the nineteenth century, had quite put the British to shame, and induced them to devote special efforts to encouraging the production of wares of aesthetic appeal. French artistry was admired throughout Europe, enhancing the prestige of the nation. The French government, aware of this, protected the arts: "Sèvres porcelain and Gobelin tapestries, called the twin glories of Paris, are magnificent artistic products. In order to produce such wares in a country that has flourishing literary and artistic traditions, there really must be protection from the government."[30] Without protection, the arts can easily degenerate. Kume noted that Japanese pottery, lacquer, cloisonné, and raised pictures (kirekomi) were highly prized in Europe, but he feared that as industrialization proceeded and profits became the chief consideration, the necessary but time-consuming artistic skills would be lost. France should be congratulated for having wisely avoided this danger.

Kume observed how Japanese works of art, especially ceramics, were treasured in every part of Europe. On seeing some Ko-Imari ware in England, for example, he commented, "Ko-Imari ceramics have long been treasured in Europe, and the collections of major patrons always include one or two examples. Some of them have been repaired before being exhibited. It occurs to me that superior examples of this ware are preserved in Europe, but there are probably not many left in Japan."[31] He discovered that British potters were imitating Japanese motifs in their work, and this convinced him of the necessity of preserving Japanese traditions: "I have been told that Western painters despair of ever being able to achieve, even in their dreams, the Japanese artist's skill of composition. They throw their full energies into copying, but they never succeed in resembling the originals."[32]

European imitations of Japanese art were not confined to ceramics. Kume saw at the Vienna Exposition examples of Dutch lacquerware and commented, "They have copied Japanese lacquers."[33] He saw at the royal palace in Sweden examples of Chinese and Japanese paintings along with Swedish copies of them. "These copies were probably made in Sweden. That is why the brushwork has no vigor and some of the characters are drawn inside out."[34] On the other hand, Kume saw French copies of Japanese inlaying that impressed him as being better than the originals.[35]

Unlike some Japanese today, who deplore the fact that masterpieces of Japanese art have left the country, Kume was pleased to see superior works of Japanese art at the museum in Leiden in Holland, and he praised Philipp Franz von Siebold for having brought these works to Europe.[36] He preferred that Japanese art be represented abroad by its finest examples rather than by the curios purchased in Japan by tourists.

Kume's visits to museums in Europe fostered an appreciation of Western art. He did not specifically identify which paintings or sculptures he most admired, but his tone grew noticeably warmer as he became increasingly familiar with the kind of works he saw. He was dazzled by the collections of the Hermitage, the Uffizi, and the Munich Pinakothek. He wrote of a gallery in the latter, "In the interior there is a room designated as a place for visitors to rest. There are twenty-four landscape paintings along the walls. They depict places in Europe and Africa and display to perfection the different aspects of nature—shade, sunlight, morning, evening, rainbows, halos around the moon, smoke, fog, break of day, the crescent moon. The whole room creates an impression of extreme clarity, and the more time one takes in one's appreciation, the greater the flavor emerges."[37]

Kume believed that the main characteristic of European painting was realism. Even when it came to Japanese art, the Europeans preferred the most realistic examples. In Paris he saw two volumes of Japanese drawings of birds and beasts that were used as models by artists in a cloisonné factory. The illustrations consisted of copies of works of famous painters of the past and included also some drawings of the exotic foreign birds the Americans brought to Japan in 1853. Kume thought that the Japanese copyist was not particularly skillful, and his brushwork very poor, but the French treasured the book and used it as a model because it was so realistic. Kume's conclusion was, "Western people, in any case, admire realism in paintings."[38] He himself, as a practical man, also preferred realism to the more usual Japanese or Chinese representation of the "spirit" of the objects portrayed.

Toward the end of their stay in Europe, the Japanese visited Vienna. After seeing the paintings on display at the Exposition, Kume divided European paintings into five categories, depending on the techniques used—pencil drawing, pen drawing, lithography, engraving, and oil painting.[39] Common to all categories was this love of realism. Kume was impressed not only by the accurate depiction of objects, the principal aim of Western artists, but by the skill with which they conveyed the inner feelings of the people whose portraits they painted. "Nothing of the people they paint—the physique, the dignity, the mental state, the spirit, the prospects—is missing. The great artists take the most pains over this."[40] Kume asserted that, in contrast to the realism of Western artists, whether in landscapes or portraits, Japanese painters did not really attempt to depict Japanese scenes faithfully but copied the mountains from Chinese paintings, changing only the details—"putting a Cantonese man on a Satsuma horse."[41] He insisted that even the clouds in different countries were not the same, let alone people or vegetation. "Unless a painter's knowledge is based on wide research and deep insights, he will probably be laughed at."[42]

Kume was not impressed by everything he saw of European art. In Berlin he saw an example of what he described as pornographic art (shunga). This was not the first time he had seen such works in Europe. "I had only once before seen anything this extreme. Those were some old Italian paintings that tried to outdo one another in their skill in portraying human flesh, often to the point that it becomes ugly. Many were highly injurious to public morals."[43] It is hard to believe that an explicitly pornographic picture would have been displayed publicly in a European museum of the nineteenth century. Perhaps Kume was shocked by nothing more sensational than the painting of a nude.

He disliked Christian art even more than pornography. It is easy to imagine the effect produced on a Japanese on seeing a painting of Christ on the Cross, blood streaming from His wounds. The novelist Yokomitsu Riichi in his *Ryojō* (Travel Sadness, 1937–46) vividly evoked his feelings of horror when he saw, in a dimly lit French church, a realistic statue of the crucified Christ; the shock must have been even greater for a Japanese of sixty years earlier. Kume noticed as soon as he reached France the difference between this Catholic country and the two Protestant countries (America and England) he had previously visited: "When one enters a Catholic country, towers pierce the sky and great churches loom over the city streets. Everywhere one goes one sees displayed in the shops pictures of Mary and of the Crucifixion. I came almost to hate them."[44]

No matter how greatly Kume admired other aspects of European civilization, he never surmounted his dislike for Christianity. As a samurai and Confucianist, he disliked even Buddhism, though he tolerated it as part of Japanese tradition. Christianity (especially Russian Orthodox Christianity) seemed to resemble Buddhism, at least on the surface, and this was not in its favor. Above all, he was repelled by the violence he detected in the Christian art of Europe.

The members of the mission had numerous opportunities to visit churches, and they did not hesitate to enter, even though the prohibition on Christianity was still in effect in Japan. In Scotland, Kume noted, it was the custom to invite strangers from distant countries to join in worship.[45] As yet there was no Japanese translation of the Bible,[46] but when the mission visited the Bible Society in New York each man was presented with a copy of the Chinese translation.[47] Kume learned, to his great surprise, that almost every household and, indeed, every person in Europe and America owned a copy of the Bible, and that many people carried their Bible wherever they went, even on long journeys.[48] He explained the significance of the Bible in these terms:

The Bible is the scripture of the West and the basis of the moral behavior of the people. If one were to compare it to something in the Orient, it is like the Four Books [of Confucianism] in the way it has permeated people's hearts, and it is like the Buddhist classics in the way it is revered by men and women alike. Nothing in the Orient can be compared to its extraordinary popularity among the people of Europe and America who worship it.[49]

Kume's readings in the Bible did not convert him to Christianity.

On examination, it proved to consist partly of absurd tales—a voice speaking from heaven or a dead criminal coming back to life. One might best take these tales as the ramblings of a lunatic. They consider that the man who was fastened to a cross for having advocated a heresy was the true son of the emperor of heaven, and they weep and kneel in reverence before him. I wonder what inspires their tears. In every city of Europe and America, in every place, pictures on the walls of churches or in the corners of rooms depict the dead criminal being taken down from the cross, red blood dripping from him. They make us feel as if we are going by a graveyard or spending the night in the execution grounds. If this is not peculiar, I wonder what can be called peculiar?"[50]

Kume's observations, made from the viewpoint of a Confucian rationalist who had no use for religion, are dismissive, but even he had to admit in the end that the religious fervor he observed in the West was not only genuine but had also inspired hard work and progress. People in the West could not understand why the Japanese refused to believe in Christianity, but Kume never doubted that Confucianism was superior. He was confident that he could reduce Christians to silence by sharp questioning of the weird tenets of their religion; but with respect to the practice of the religion, he could not question Christian zeal.[51] He was aware that Christians were so devoted to their religion that they were ready to suffer hardships and even torture rather than abandon it. Some people might dismiss this as mere obstinacy, but for Kume it was the most admirable aspect of Christianity.[52] On the other hand, there was no escaping the fact that the Japanese were far less zealous in their religious observances than people in the West. He wrote,

> The Four Books and the Six Classics have been known in Japan for two thousand years,[53] but no more than a segment of the samurai class reads and understands them. The rest take the contents on faith and use them to justify the governmental policies that they propagate to the ordinary citizens. All this amounts to is that they have made known in even the remote corners of the country the words loyalty, filial piety, benevolence, and righteousness.[54]

With respect to Buddhism, Kume averred that not more than two or three priests out of a hundred understand its doctrines.

Despite his admiration for Christian fervor, Kume felt repugnance and even indignation whenever he visited the great churches of Europe. He contrasted the poverty of Italy with the splendor of the churches, and declared that it was only by extorting money from the poor that the churches and their treasures came into being.[55] Kume recalled how Garibaldi had resisted the pope, perhaps hoping that this historical fact would make Japanese readers realize that not all Europeans had put religion before the welfare of the people. He feared especially that the Japanese, observing the piety of the Christians, might abandon their own religions in favor of a foreign one.[56] Even in Europe the Protestants had adopted a form of religion more suited to a civilized country than was Catholicism. If the Japanese were to adopt a religion that the Europeans themselves had rejected, that would indeed be ironic. Kume sighed,

Ah, if we abandon [Confucianism?] and they adopt and practice it, and we adopt and wallow in what they have rejected,
after a couple of dozen years the fine flower of the East will
have been completely exported to the West, and the dregs
from the West will accumulate in the East. This is something
to which informed people must give earnest consideration.[57]

Many aspects of Western society displeased Kume almost as much as
Christianity. He expressed his fundamental dislike of the ways of the
West in a succinct passage relating to czarist Russia: "Here we have
sufficient evidence to prove that the races of the Occident, out of
their unbounded greed for material things, are accustomed to op-
press the lower classes, a situation absolutely contrary to that in countries where Oriental morality prevails."[58] He recalled how, when
British and French troops captured Peking in 1860, they were astonished at the vast amount of treasure they found.[59] He commented,

The races of the Orient, having few material cravings, obey
the moral guidance of the state. The ruler with thrift and diligence ministers to the people of the country in extremities,
and the great amount of treasure that accumulates over many
years [for this purpose] will certainly dazzle the foreigner. The
races of the Occident are highly prone to greed, and slow to
mend their character and conduct. Their rulers, basing their
rule on wealth, extort money in taxes from the people of their
territories to pay for their extravagances. It is no great exaggeration to say that their greed is all but unbounded. This is
the reason the peoples of Europe seethe with arguments in
favor of freedom, of paring the powers of the ruler, and of giving full powers to the people. The races of East and West are
almost exact opposites in their natures.[60]

It is normal today to admire people who demand freedom, and
parts of Kume's diary make the reader think he shares this view,

but here, faced with the contradiction between the opulence of the czars and the terrible poverty of his subjects, he seems to be saying that the greed of Occidental rulers has inspired a desire for freedom not shared by people of the Orient who have lived under clement rulers.

The mission boarded ship at Marseilles for the return journey from Europe to Japan. The behavior of the Europeans on board shocked Kume. Although, like most other Japanese visitors to Hong Kong and Singapore, he admired the efficiency and cleanliness that the British had introduced, he had had little contact with the colonizers; not until he observed them aboard ship did he apprehend the nature of their mentality:

> The flesh of the weak is the food of the strong. Ever since the Europeans began to travel to distant places, the weak countries of the tropics have all been fought over and devoured, and their abundant products have been taken in by the home country. At first three countries—Spain, Portugal, and Holland— monopolized the profits. They treated the natives with arrogance and cruelty, taking whatever they could get. There were frequent insurrections, and they lost what they had possessed. The English for this reason avoided their mistakes, and adopted a policy of generosity. They took the lead in bringing education, and adopted the policy of persuasion and gentle pacification that has brought about the present prosperity. My observations of the European passengers aboard this ship now have persuaded me that the English are extremely friendly to natives.[61] The Spaniards, Portuguese, and Dutch are on the whole arrogant. This perpetuation of the customs of former days has now become habitual, and they should be denounced for not having got rid [of this attitude]. It is hard for us even to imagine how natives in the colonies are being oppressed by despotic regimes. In short, although we discovered when we boarded ship at Marseilles that the other passengers were all

pale-complexioned and red-haired, the atmosphere was not like that in Europe itself. Their behavior was rude, their language insulting, and they laughed boisterously, were familiar with women, got angry over trifles, and spent half their time spewing forth abuse. Such behavior in their home countries would be considered shameful, the mark of inferior people . . . The people who go to the Orient or the South Seas to make a living are for the most part people who have been rejected in their own countries because of their outrageous behavior.[62]

Kume's judgment was correct. Perhaps he was somewhat too indulgent toward the British, the only exceptions to the colonialists whom he denounced. We know from other writers (mainly British) how badly the British at times behaved in India and elsewhere. Colonialism was a poison, but Kume could not have foreseen that Japan would also become a colonial power and that some Japanese would behave as arrogantly toward governed peoples as the Spanish and Dutch he observed aboard ship.

For all his generalizations about Westerners, Kume was keenly aware of the differences among the nations of the West. He noticed, for example, differences between the Americans and the English: "America and England are brother nations, similar in speech and customs. To schematize the differences: an American on first meeting is kind and full of friendly affection. People in the streets act like old friends. But after some time has gone by, mutual dislike cannot be avoided. The English are just the opposite. On first meeting they are extremely pompous (this is habitual in an empire), but gradually one feels their friendliness, and after one has met them two or three times, they open their hearts to you in all sincerity."[63] This strikes me as a perceptive description of one difference between the Americans and the English, and confirms my high opinion of Kume's powers of observation.

Kume said of some people he saw in Europe that they looked

like Japanese, including Brazilians (whom he saw in Manchester[64]) and Ceylonese,[65] but the only people who seemed to him spiritually like the Japanese were the French. He made this comparison not on the basis of some analogy between the artistic temperaments of the two peoples but in terms of their strengths and weaknesses.

"The Frenchman is physically not very big. He has a ringing voice and a lively manner, and he abounds in energy. His temperament is the opposite of that of the Englishman or German. His faults are that he tends to be passionate and quick-tempered, is short of persistence and diligence, and always tries to win by his wits. The French temperament is more or less the same as the Japanese."[66]

More often, Kume contrasted the Japanese with Occidentals, sometimes to the advantage of one, sometimes to that of the other. Whether or not one concurs in his evaluations, one has to admire his objectivity. Unlike earlier diarists, he saw Japan without sentimentality and without categorizing its people and customs as either superior or inferior. He saw the brashness but also the kindness of the Americans, the wealth of the British but also the poverty in England exemplified by the London slums and the numerous prostitutes, the beauty of Paris and the influence of the church (which he deplored) on the schools. Of all the places he visited abroad he loved Paris most, and he communicated in his diary his delight in the cafés, the chairs under the trees, the theaters, the restaurants.[67] He also admired small countries such as Belgium and Denmark that had doggedly preserved their independence, mainly by their diligence, and believed they had more to teach the Japanese than the three major countries of Europe.[68]

Among the "major countries" he thought there was more for Japan to gain from Germany than from either Britain or France, if only because Germany had only just become an empire, even more recently than the Meiji Restoration of 1868. With respect to Russia, he declared that the Japanese dread of that country, going back to the depredations of Russian sailors early in the nineteenth century, was exaggerated. Russia was still too backward, too underpopulated to constitute a menace to Japan. But, he added in a flash of intuition, the other European countries had already attained full bloom, and only Russia was still in the bud, and a much more powerful—perhaps even frightening—nature was sure to emerge in the future.[69]

The above analysis of Kume's diary does not do justice to its political aspects. In part, this is because the diary itself does not mention the negotiations for the end of the unequal treaties with the foreign powers and other matters of particular importance at the time, but mainly because I have been looking for Kume Kunitake, the man, and not for information that is easily found in history books. I have ended by finding him not only an exceptionally acute observer but an estimable man, and his diary is one of the monuments of early Meiji literature.

Notes

1. The full title of the work, sometimes employed, was *Tokumei Zenken Taishi Beiō Kairan Jikki* (True Account of the Tour of America and Europe of the Ambassador Extraordinary and Plenipotentiary).

2. See Tanaka Akira, "Kaisetsu," in Kume Kunitake, *Beiō Kairan Jikki*, I, p. 411.

3. *Ibid.*, p. 52.

4. *Ibid.*, p. 53.

5. *Ibid.*, p. 50.

6. *Ibid.*, p. 77.

7. *Ibid.*, pp. 79–80.

8. *Ibid.*, p. 80.

9. *Ibid.*, p. 82.

10. The word *rigaku* was used in the early Meiji period with contradictory meanings: it was used to translate the English word *philosophy*, before *tetsugaku* was definitively adopted, but also for physics, before *butsurigaku* came to be normal.

11. Kume, *Beiō*, I, 82–83.

12. *Ibid.*, pp. 117–18. The Tz'u-ên Temple was built near the city of Hsi-an early in the seventh century. The pagoda survives.

13. *Ibid.,* p. 129.
14. *Ibid.,* V, p. 282.
15. *Ibid.,* p. 283.
16. *Ibid.,* I, p. 89.
17. *Ibid.,* pp. 247–48.
18. *Ibid.,* p. 248.
19. *Ibid.*
20. *Ibid.,* III, pp. 285–86.
21. *Ibid.,* IV, p. 203.
22. Quoted by Uwayokote Masataka, "Rekishisho toshite no *Taiheiki,*" in Nagazumi Yasuaki et al., *Taiheiki no Sekai,* p. 57.
23. Kume, *Beiō,* II, p. 312.
24. *Ibid.,* p. 114.
25. *Ibid.,* p. 331.
26. *Ibid.,* III, pp. 70–71.
27. *Ibid.,* pp. 71–72.
28. *Ibid.,* IV, p. 329.
29. *Ibid.,* p. 276.
30. *Ibid.,* III, p. 136.
31. *Ibid.,* II, p. 312.
32. *Ibid.,* p. 356.
33. *Ibid.,* V, p. 36.
34. *Ibid.,* IV, p. 181.
35. *Ibid.,* III, p. 151.
36. *Ibid.,* p. 249. P. F. von Siebold (1796–1866) resided in Japan from 1823 to 1829 as the physician of the Dutch trading station on Deshima. The collection of Japanese art and ethnographic materials was bought by the Dutch government in 1837 and preserved in the museum at Leiden.
37. *Ibid.,* IV, p. 247.
38. *Ibid.,* III, p. 151.
39. *Ibid.,* V, p. 44.
40. *Ibid.,* p. 46.
41. *Ibid.,* p. 47.
42. *Ibid.*
43. *Ibid.,* III, p. 358.
44. *Ibid.,* p. 53.
45. *Ibid.,* II, p. 250.
46. The first translation of the Bible into Japanese was made in 1873. Earlier, a

crude version of the New Testament had been prepared by a German missionary and some Japanese castaways in Macao. See my *Dawn to the West,* I, pp. 61–62.

47. Kume, *Beiō,* I, p. 341.
48. *Ibid.,* p. 341.
49. *Ibid.,* p. 342.
50. *Ibid.*
51. *Ibid.,* p. 344.
52. *Ibid.*
53. A considerable exaggeration. Somewhat more than a thousand years would be closer to the facts.
54. Kume, *Beiō,* I, p. 343.
55. *Ibid.,* IV, p. 273.
56. *Ibid.,* I, p. 345.
57. *Ibid.*
58. *Ibid.,* IV, p. 42.
59. *Ibid.,* pp. 68–70.
60. *Ibid.,* p. 70.
61. In view of Kume's statement that the passengers were all Europeans, *ijin* (natives) probably referred to members of the ship's crew.
62. Kume, *Beiō,* V, pp. 307–8.
63. *Ibid.,* I, p. 329.
64. *Ibid.,* II, p. 164.
65. *Ibid.,* V, p. 291.
66. *Ibid.,* III, p. 35.
67. *Ibid.,* pp. 51–52.
68. *Ibid.,* p. 165.
69. *Ibid.,* V, p. 42.

Bibliography

Kume Kunitake. *Beiō Kairan Jikki,* 5 vols., in Iwanami Bunko series. Tokyo: Iwanami Shoten, 1977–82.

Mayo, Marlene J. "The Western Education of Kume Kunitake, 1871–76," *Monumenta Nipponica* 28:1, 1973.

Nagazumi Yasuaki, Uwayokote Masataka, and Sakurai Yoshirō. *Taiheiki no Sekai.* Tokyo: Nihon Hōsō Shuppan Kyōkai, 1987.

Ōkubo Toshiaki. *Iwakura Shisetsu no Kenkyū*. Tokyo: Munetaka Shobō, 1976.

Soviak, Eugene. "On the Nature of Western Progress: The Journal of the Iwakura Embassy," in Donald H. Shively (ed.), *Tradition and Modernization in Japanese Culture*. Princeton, N.J.: Princeton University Press, 1971.

Tanaka Akira. *Iwakura Shisetsu Dan*, in Kōdansha Gendai Shinsho series. Tokyo: Kōdansha, 1977.

Tanaka Akira and Takada Seiji (eds.). *Beiō Kairan Jikki no Gakusaiteki Kenkyū*. Sapporo: Hokkaidō Daigaku Shuppankai, 1993.

Journal of a Voyage
to the West

The diaries kept by the members of the various missions sometimes contain passages of literary appeal, especially when they describe the landscapes of Europe and America, but the writers were not primarily literary men. That is why the diary of Narushima Ryūhoku (1837–1884) seems so strikingly unlike its predecessors: we realize from the first page that the diarist was an accomplished writer, and this impression is maintained throughout.

Ryūhoku, the son of a shogunate official, early demonstrated his literary talent. In 1854, when he was only seventeen, he was appointed to succeed his father (who had died in the previous year) as a tutor to the shogun. In the same year he was also named as one of the compilers of the *Tokugawa Jikki* (True Record of the Tokugawas), presumably because of the elegance of his written Chinese. He continued to serve as an official for the next nine years, even though much of his time was spent (in the manner of the *bunjin*[1] of the past) in the pleasure quarter of Yanagibashi in Edo. In 1859 Ryūhoku wrote *Ryūkō Shinshi* (New Account of Yanagibashi),[2] though he did not publish it at that time.

In 1863 Ryūhoku was dismissed from his post and confined to

his domicile, apparently because a *kyōshi* (comic poem in Chinese) he had written was interpreted as being disrespectful to the government. He took advantage of this enforced leisure to study Dutch and later English. Ryūhoku was released in 1865 when it became clear that the shogunate desperately needed men who knew about the West, and he was appointed as *gaikoku bugyō* (commissioner for foreign affairs) in the first month of 1868. Ryūhoku resigned this post three months later, on the day before Edo Castle was surrendered to the forces of Emperor Meiji, and he subsequently refused to "serve a second master."

In 1871 Ryūhoku was appointed as a teacher of history and economics at the school founded at the Sensō-ji, the great Buddhist temple in Asakusa. In the following year, when Gennyo, the abbot of the temple, traveled to Europe to study religious institutions, he asked Ryūhoku to accompany him, no doubt because of Ryūhoku's knowledge of foreign languages and his acquaintance with the institutions of the West. Ryūhoku's diary *Kōsei Nichijō* (Journal of a Voyage to the West) would describe his travels and his experiences abroad. It concludes with an account of crossing the Atlantic and arriving in New York. There is reason to think that the diary went on to describe his travels in America, but that part of the diary was lost. Ryūhoku kept the diary in classical Chinese, but later made a version into Japanese (*yomikudashi*), which he published serially.

The diary opens with an explanation of how his travels to Europe came about. This is followed by the account of boarding a French ship in Yokohama that left port on the fourteenth day of the ninth month of 1872. Hardly had the ship got under way than it was assaulted by fierce waves. Ryūhoku described his feelings in a *kanshi* (poem in Chinese), one of seventy-seven included in the diary. It opens:

> *What is tossing my bed up into the sky?*
> *Now I am lifted to heaven, now thrown to the ground.*[3]

Ryūhoku's various *kanshi*, more artistic than any composed by previous Japanese who had traveled abroad, are of interest not only in terms of content—the foreign people and foreign places he observed—but also because of their expression. Sometimes the images are surprising, as in a *kanshi* that described the roughness of the sea:

> *Where is Mount Ararat?*
> *The blue of surging waves permeates the sky.*
> *The ship carries oxen, sheep, and pigs,*
> *Bringing to mind Noah's ark of long ago.*[4]

The sight of the various animals aboard the ship, destined to be slaughtered and eaten by the passengers, recalled to Ryūhoku the biblical account of Noah's ark and its landing atop Mount Ararat when the deluge subsided. Ryūhoku wondered when his Ararat would be sighted, ending the terrible waves. The biblical imagery is unexpected from a *bunjin*, and contrasts with Kume Kunitake's openly voiced dislike for the sacred book of a forbidden religion.

The first foreign port visited by Ryūhoku was Hong Kong. Characteristically, he headed at once for a hotel to have a drink. Nothing in his diary suggests that he was tense because he was in a foreign country; he behaved exactly as he would have in Japan. He did not spend the night in Hong Kong because passengers had been warned that the city was full of thieves, but he returned the next day and visited the famous Yinghua College. On emerging from the bookshop, he noticed a theater and unhesitantly went in. The presentation impressed him favorably, but the voices of the actors were unpleasantly shrill, and he could not be sure he knew what was going on.[5]

Ryūhoku afterward joined some shipboard friends in going to a Chinese restaurant for a meal. He was far more adventurous than earlier Japanese travelers when it came to food. Much later in the journey, while in Rome, he insisted on having Italian food, rather than the French food served in the restaurant of his hotel, apparently following the dictum that when in Rome one should do as the Romans do.

Ryūhoku's life aboard ship was also more interesting than anything recorded in the diaries of previous Japanese travelers, probably because he spoke some English. But that was not the only reason: he made the effort to be friendly with foreigners, rather than decide in advance that communication was impossible. He revealed in a *kanshi* that he had learned the names of the English and French passengers:

> *Businessmen from Paris, women from London,*
> *All fresh acquaintances, and I know their names!*[6]

He played quoits with one Dutchman, and went ashore in Ceylon with another. He began to collect foreign coins, an unusual hobby for a Japanese of the time, and mentions in his diary trading coins with another passenger.

It is not clear how much English (or Dutch) Ryūhoku knew. He was largely self-taught, but while he was living in Paris he had private lessons in both English and French, as he noted almost every day in his diary. He may have become fairly fluent in French by the time he left Paris, as we can gather from a remark in the diary that when he reached Florence in his Italian tour, he was disappointed that people in the hotel did not speak French.[7]

Ryūhoku's success in making friends with foreigners was not due solely to his ability in speaking foreign languages. He also had the self-confidence needed to undertake a conversation with foreigners, even at the risk of exposing himself to ridicule by his mistakes. This self-confidence may have stemmed from his literary talents, but it may also have represented the "playfulness" (*asobi*) of the *bunjin* that he displayed in his writings and in his life.

Ryūhoku's most endearing feature is his openness to new experiences. The members of the various embassies had dutifully and carefully observed the different aspects of European life, but they rarely expressed pleasure in their experiences. Perhaps they thought it was unseemly for persons on an official mission to express private feelings; but Ryūhoku, not being associated with a mission, was under no such constraint. When he left Hong Kong, for example, he wrote in his diary, "Today, when I am about to leave, I feel immense attachment to the place."[8] This expression is likely to surprise the reader because it follows closely on his description of the filthy toilet at the restaurant where he ate, and his mention of the many thieves that made the city unsafe. But Ryūhoku had the ability, not possessed by every traveler, to forget such annoyances and to savor the beauty and excitement of an unfamiliar place.

In Saigon, the next port of call after Hong Kong, the temperature was ninety-four degrees,[9] but this did not prevent Ryūhoku from enjoying his first glimpse of a palm grove. At night he was bothered by the mosquitoes, but he also admired the fireflies. He wrote a *kanshi* comparing Saigon and Japan in the autumn. Most Japanese would have unfavorably contrasted the heat of Saigon with the invigorating cool of a Japanese autumn day, but Ryūhoku's pleasure in the fireflies is unmistakable:

> *Nights in the tropics it is hard to sleep and dreams are easily broken;*
> *White sand and green grass extend to the water's edge.*
> *Back in Japan this is the season when the frost falls;*
> *I see to my surprise foreign fireflies, big as stars.*[10]

Ryūhoku's ability to converse with Europeans and become their friend did not carry over to the Asians he encountered. In Hong Kong he was upset by the Chinese who clustered around the Japanese, jabbering unintelligibly. In Singapore natives came to the pier and tried to sell parrots and monkeys. Ryūhoku declared in a *kanshi*:

> *How many barbarian rascals have clustered on the pier!*
> *They spread the local produce and chatter noisily.*

Their hair is curly, their faces black, their legs red;
I roared with laughter: the monkey sellers looked like monkeys![11]

In Ceylon, after praising the flowers as being far more beautiful than the Japanese "Seven Grasses of Autumn," he expressed dislike for the people: "The natives are sly and without shame. They are as annoying as mosquitoes in the way they come up to people and hawk their wares."[12] Such a statement may recall Shibata Takenaka, but it is not quite so distasteful because Ryūhoku was interested in these foreigners; it was their noisiness, not their being foreign, that irritated him. In the end, irritated or not, he bought some of their wares, as he mentions in the diary.

Sometimes his comments on foreigners are sardonic. In Singapore he met an old priest who claimed to know Japanese. Ryūhoku wrote, "I tried asking him something in Japanese. He didn't understand a word."[13]

While in Europe Ryūhoku visited many churches. This, in fact, was the main purpose of the abbot Gennyo's journey to Europe, and Ryūhoku naturally accompanied him. At no point does Ryūhoku suggest (in the manner of other Japanese diarists of the time) a dislike for Christianity. In Paris he was astonished by the magnificence of Nôtre-Dame. In Italy he visited the cathedrals of Milan, Venice, Florence, and Rome, and was duly appreciative. He knew something of the Old Testament (as he demonstrated in his poem on Noah's ark) as well as the New. When his ship reached the Red Sea he recalled that the waters had parted for Moses but drowned the Egyptians. But Ryūhoku, no less of a rationalist than Kume Kunitake, did not take the Bible too seriously: he opined that the name Red Sea probably came from reflections of the desert in its waters, not from it actually being red.

Churches were not the only buildings in Europe that interested him. He was fascinated by the ruins of antiquity in Rome, and described them in greater detail than any previous Japanese visitor. Wherever he went in Europe he looked especially for ancient art. In Marseilles, the first European city he visited, he went at once to the museum to inspect the Egyptian antiquities.

Unlike earlier Japanese travelers in Europe, he openly expressed the excitement and pleasure of being in foreign places. The first night in Marseilles, he left his hotel to have a look at the city. He declared in his diary, "The gas lamps are as bright as day. This really is a paradise."[14]

Soon after his arrival in Paris from Marseilles he composed a *kanshi* that conveys his joy over being there:

> In the evening we sit around a table, elbows touching elbows;
> I meet people from Shin and Etsu, and we're all friends.
> When people get drunk they give good imitations of the great poet;
> Into a glass sparkling in lamplight I pour the wine.[15]

Ryūhoku's pleasure in drinking at a café, rubbing elbows with people from different countries (he used Shin and Etsu, the names of two ancient Chinese states, to stand for all foreign countries), is clear.

While in Paris, Ryūhoku went drinking and dining almost every evening, and he was not fussy about where he went. On one occasion, as he records in his diary, he and a friend went into a restaurant that he describes as being very low class. But eating in such a place, rather than in the hotel dining room, was part of the pleasure of travel. Ryūhoku's delight in Paris was not confined to eating and drinking. Soon after he arrived, he had a suit of clothes made. He wrote in his diary, "The clothes I had been wearing ever since I left Japan are so out-of-date that not even coachmen or grooms wear them in Paris."[16] It is easy to imagine how a man who was known in Edo for his elegance felt at the thought that people in Paris might be laughing at his clothes.

Ryūhoku enjoyed strolling in the parks in Paris, especially the Bois de Boulogne. This is how he described his first visit, on November 8. "Today I went with Andō and Ikeda to the *Boa do Buron*.

There is a waterfall, and the place is extremely refreshing and delightful. We drank at the Café des Anglais.[17] The food was excellent.
On the way back we were feeling a little drunk and stopped by at a
brothel in the Rue d'Amboise."[18] Ryūhoku does not state in his diary
whether or not he went back to the brothel. Perhaps the experience
seemed unimportant or not very different from similar places in
Japan. His only comment on the brothel was that it provided a
quickly forgotten pleasure.

Ryūhoku visited Versailles and described the treasures that had
belonged to the kings of France. One inner garden reminded him of
the garden of the shogun's palace at Fukiage. He remained faithful to
the memory of the shogunate, and was moved by this unexpected reminder of the old days. He also visited the Petit Trianon and wrote,
recalling how Marie Antoinette had played at being a milkmaid, "In
the garden there is a thatch-covered cottage. It was built in a countri-
fied style in order that Louis XVI's queen might milk cows."[19]

Another of Ryūhoku's pleasures in Paris was attending the theater. Unlike earlier Japanese visitors who were taken to the theater,
he was not bored, probably because he understood enough French to
follow the plots. His summary of *La Dame aux camélias* is reasonably
accurate. He attended performances at the Palais Royal, the Folies
Bergère, and other places that catered to tourists, and had dinner at
the Grand Véfour. He attended a performance at the Opéra, and
was impressed both by the grandeur of the building and the elegant
attire of the spectators. He does not mention which opera he saw, but
he compared it to the Nō drama, probably the first to make the comparison.

Ryūhoku was surprised at the number of Japanese he saw in Paris.
When he first arrived, he stayed at the Grand Hotel, the finest in the
city, but he found it too expensive for his purse and moved to the
Hotel de Lord Byron. There were already five Japanese staying
there. Ryūhoku was delighted to meet compatriots so far from home.

A few days later he met an old friend, Andō Tarō, who had arrived in Paris from London in advance of the main body of the Iwakura mission. About a week later Iwakura himself arrived, along with Kido, Ōkubo, and the others, but Ryūhoku discovered that members of the mission were not eager to meet him, perhaps because of his connections with the fallen shogunate. He is not mentioned in the diary of Kume Kunitake.

Ryūhoku also met in Paris several Frenchmen he had known in Edo, notably Charles Chanoine (1835–1915), who had arrived in Japan in 1866 and given training in western warfare to the shogunate army until the collapse of the shogunate two years later. Ryūhoku visited Chanoine's home and was astonished to see there not only the sword he had given Chanoine but also a photograph of himself and his wife pasted in the family album. A Japanese visiting Europe today would be pleased but not greatly surprised to see his photograph in a friend's album, but this happened in 1873, and Ryūhoku was profoundly moved. He commented that the Frenchman he had known in Japan was still his friend, but his old Japanese friends who were now serving with the mission treated him like a stranger. When Ryūhoku, along with three members of the mission, was invited to dinner at Chanoine's house, he was seated in the place of honor.[20]

Ryūhoku's life in Paris was full of distractions. He climbed to the top of the Arc de Triomphe to admire the view. He went to the circus. He saw a magician perform. He bought a new pair of shoes. When he complained that the left shoe was too tight, the man in the shop asked why Japanese always have bigger left feet than right. Ryūhoku pondered this, then decided, "Samurai in our country from the time they are boys wear two swords. This means that they put more strength into their left foot, and it naturally becomes bigger than the right foot. I asked my friends about this, and they all agreed with me."[21]

Even the rare unpleasant experience gave Ryūhoku food for thought. When he saw a drunken man smash a window in the hotel restaurant, he reflected, "For the first time since coming to Europe several months ago I saw someone who was so drunk he resorted to violence. This [the fact that one seldom sees such behavior] is a glory of life in the West."[22] He seems to have been thinking of the many violent drunks he had seen in Edo.

Ryūhoku's life of pleasure in France, Italy, and England was perhaps occasioned by the need to relieve his depression over the fall of the shogunate. He showed his loyalty toward the deposed régime in an unusual manner: he became an unqualified admirer of Napoleon III, whose own régime had fallen just two years after the Meiji Restoration. While in Paris he learned of the death in England of Napoleon III, and composed a *kanshi* of mourning in which he declared that now the German kaiser would be able to sleep soundly, sure there was no one capable of overturning his reign.[23]

Much of Ryūhoku's diary is devoted to his travels in Italy. He went as a tourist, perhaps the first Japanese to spend time anywhere in Europe without even the semblance of official duties. He visited Turin, Milan, Venice, Florence, Rome, and Naples. He was interested in Roman history, and even composed a *kanshi* in honor of Brutus:

> No need to ask: is it loyal or disloyal to kill one's lord?
> In the flash of a sword point a hundred plans turn to nought.
> Who can avenge the rancor of a thousand years?
> In the broken tile, the remaining stones, I mourn the ancient palace.[24]

It is surprising that the conservative Ryūhoku should have expressed admiration for the man who killed Julius Caesar, but the poem's emphasis is on the dreams of the great men of the past, now turned to broken tiles and scattered stones. Ryūhoku's sympathies were always with deposed rulers. While in Florence he was informed that the people of the city remained loyal to the deposed grand duke of Tuscany and did not offer their allegiance to the king of Italy. He wrote in his diary, "When the king of Italy visits this city, extremely few people take off their hats as a mark of respect." But when in Rome, inspecting the ruins, Ryūhoku accidentally encountered the king of Italy, he joined other people in removing his hat, to which the king responded by removing his own. "He is not in the least arrogant," commented Ryūhoku.[25]

Ryūhoku returned to Paris after completing his tour of Italy. He felt as if he had "returned to his old home."[26] It was just at this time that he received his first letter from home. He was happy to have a letter, though it reported that his youngest daughter had died. He asked rhetorically, "How could I not shed tears?"[27] But the next words in the diary report that he went drinking with a friend. It is possible to interpret Ryūhoku's casual attitude on learning of his daughter's death as a stoicism that concealed deeply felt emotion, but, more likely, this man of pleasure was not overly concerned about what happened to his family.

During his last weeks in Paris he visited the Louvre again to admire the paintings. He went to the theater. He bought a watch. He visited the grave of the Empress Josephine. He dined here and there. On April 25 he said goodbye to the abbot Gennyo, who was leaving for Germany. Ryūhoku wrote that he felt the pangs of parting, but he had hardly seen the abbot during his stay in Paris.

When Ryūhoku left Paris for the last time, he went to say farewell to the couple who ran the small, inexpensive hotel where he had lived the longest. He wrote, "I had stayed a long time at the Corneille, so I said goodbye to the master and his wife. It was almost like saying goodbye to blood relations."[28]

On April 27 Ryūhoku sailed from Calais to Dover. The English Channel, as usual, was rough and Ryūhoku estimated that only two of the more than fifty passengers failed to vomit. When he went through customs he bribed an official with two shillings, in return for which his baggage was hardly examined. This man-of-the-world was already adept at getting along in Europe.

In England he visited Madame Tussaud's waxworks museum, Windsor Castle, and various other sights. At Windsor he wrote a *kanshi* expressing his admiration for England:

> *In all four directions no one complains of cold or hunger;*
> *Her Majesty sits, arms folded, deep in her palace.*
> *I ask you to observe how people enjoy strolling in her garden;*
> *As in the garden of the sage kings, deer cluster, swans fly.*[29]

The poem suggests how impressed Ryūhoku was to see quite ordinary people wandering freely through the grounds of the castle, a sight unimaginable in the shogun's palace. He surmised that the grounds were open because the queen of England had no reason to fear anyone, as nobody was cold or hungry.

Ryūhoku's enthusiasm for England did not prevent him from making harsh remarks about the pall of smoke that hung over London and the other English cities, a side effect of the industrial revolution that had made the country prosperous. Kume Kunitake, who visited England before he went to France, wrote of his relief when he breathed fresh air again. Ryūhoku, who traveled in the opposite direction, was unhappy over the change, but managed all the same to enjoy his stay in England, as a *kanshi* written by the Thames suggests:

> *Smoke from the train mingles with smoke from the steamers;*
> *It is dark in all directions, one can't see the sky.*
> *Suddenly a gust of wind blows, sweeping away the smoke;*
> *And a lovely sunset can be seen beyond London Bridge.*[30]

Ryūhoku boarded ship at Liverpool for New York. The ship called at Queenstown (Cobh) in Ireland, and many passengers, all in the steerage class, came aboard. Two days later, when Ryūhoku took a stroll on deck for a breath of fresh air, he saw the immigrants bound for America from Germany and Ireland. He commented, "The lower classes look much alike, whether in East or West." The unpleasant haughtiness reflects for a moment Ryūhoku the *bunjin*, who kept himself aloof from the vulgar masses. The diary as a whole has little of the humor that characterizes Ryūhoku's other writings, but it has a conspicuously literary gloss. Earlier Japanese diarists who visited Europe seem to have written their diaries with an awareness that history was looking over their shoulders, but Ryūhoku wrote for his and our enjoyment.

Notes

1. *Bunjin* were "men of letters"—men who were devoted to the ideal of the gentleman and amateur. Their writings, both poetry and prose, were usually in classical Chinese, in emulation of the Chinese *wen-jen* whom they admired.
2. The Sino-Japanese pronunciation of Yanagibashi (Willow Bridge) is *ryūkō*; hence the title.
3. Kawaguchi Hisao, *Bakumatsu Meiji Kaigai Taiken Shishū*, p. 475; also p. xxviii. The text of the diary (in *yomikudashi* style—rearrangement of Chinese text in Japanese word order, etc.) is given in photographic reproduction at the end of this book. References to poems are in Arabic; to the diary in Roman. See also *Narushima Ryūhoku*, p. 117.
4. *Bakumatsu*, p. 480; p. xxix. *Narushima*, p. 118.
5. *Bakumatsu*, p. xxix. *Narushima*, p. 118.
6. *Bakumatsu*, p. 481; p. xxix. These are the final two lines of the quatrain.
7. *Bakumatsu*, p. lix. *Narushima*, p. 135.
8. *Bakumatsu*, p. xxix. *Narushima*, p. 118.
9. Ryūhoku gives temperatures throughout in Fahrenheit, as did Kume Kunitake in his diary.
10. Kawaguchi, *Bakumatsu*, p. 483; p. xxx. *Narushima*, p. 119.
11. *Bakumatsu*, p. 484; p. xxxi. *Narushima*, p. 119.
12. *Bakumatsu*, p. xxxiii. *Narushima*, p. 120.
13. *Bakumatsu*, p. xxxiii.
14. *Bakumatsu*, p. xxxviii. *Narushima*, p. 123.
15. *Bakumatsu*, p. 499; p. xxxix. *Narushima*, p. 123.
16. *Bakumatsu*, p. xxxix. *Narushima*, p. 124.
17. This is my guess at the name of the restaurant, designated by Ryūhoku as

Zangurei-rō. Maeda Ai in *Narushima Ryūhoku,* p. 181, suggested Taverne Anglaise, a restaurant near the Boulevard des Italiens; but in that case there would have been no *z* in *Zangurei*.

18. Kawaguchi, *Bakumatsu*, p. xxxix. *Narushima*, p. 124.
19. *Bakumatsu*, p. xl. *Narushima*, p. 124.
20. *Bakumatsu*, pp. xlv, xlviii. *Narushima*, p. 127.
21. *Bakumatsu*, p. xlix. Both swords were worn on the left side of the body; Ryūhoku was probably thinking of the weight of the swords on that side of the body.
22. *Bakumatsu*, p. liv. *Narushima*, p. 132.
23. *Bakumatsu*, p. 504.
24. *Bakumatsu*, p. 514.
25. *Bakumatsu*, p. lxiii. *Narushima*, p. 137.
26. *Bakumatsu*, p. lxv. *Narushima*, p. 139.
27. *Bakumatsu*, p. lxvi.
28. *Bakumatsu*, p. lxvii. *Narushima*, p. 140.
29. *Bakumatsu*, p. 518.
30. *Bakumatsu*, p. 519.

Bibliography

Kawaguchi Hisao. *Bakumatsu Meiji Kaigai Taiken Shishū*. Tokyo: Daitō Bunka Daigaku Tōyō Kenkyūjo, 1984.
Maeda Ai. *Narushima Ryūhoku*. Tokyo: Asahi Shimbun Sha, 1976.
Narushima Ryūhoku, Hattori Bushō, Kurimoto Jōun in Meiji Bungaku Zenshū series. Chikuma Shōbo, 1969.

Travelers in Asia

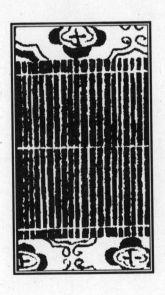

Bridges in the Clouds,
Rain in the Gorges

J apanese travelers of the early Meiji era were not restricted to those who journeyed to Europe and America. For the first time in centuries the Japanese were able to visit China. The ships bearing missions from Japan to Europe often stopped in Shanghai, and the diaries kept by the members of the missions recorded impressions of a country that was far more familiar to the Japanese than anywhere in the West; but China also sometimes seemed shockingly unlike the idealized picture that had been created in their minds by the works they had read of Chinese literature, history, and philosophy.

The appeal of China was particularly strong among samurai who had received extensive training in the Chinese classics. The experience of visiting sites associated with the martial and literary heroes known from childhood was categorically different for them from the interest of visiting George Washington's house or the tomb of Napoleon; these sites were not simply curiosities but confirmed special ties with the sources of samurai culture.

Among the Japanese who kept diaries describing their travels in China, Takezoe Shin'ichirō (1842–1917) is often credited with having created a masterpiece of the travel diary. His diary, written in *kam-*

bun (prose in Chinese), San'un Kyōu Nikki (Diary of Bridges in the Clouds, Rain in the Gorges), describes a journey made in 1876 from Peking to Chungking, then down the Yangtze River to Shanghai. The journey took 110 days. Takezoe was accompanied by a Japanese, Tsuda Seiichi, and a Chinese whom he refers to as Chih-hsin.[1]

Takezoe was born into a learned samurai family in Kumamoto and received an orthodox education under Confucian scholars. He served the Kumamoto clan, and in 1868 made a trip to Shanghai to arrange for repairs to a steamship bought by the clan. After the Meiji Restoration he entered the diplomatic service and was assigned in 1875 as the secretary of the Japanese Legation in Peking, where he served under the celebrated diplomat and advocate of Western thought Mori Arinori (1847–1889). In his diary Takezoe recalled how reports he heard there of the wonders of the scenery in Szechuan had filled him with the desire to see the sights with his own eyes.[2] He undoubtedly knew two accounts of travel in Szechuan by Chinese of the Sung dynasty, Lu Yu and Fan Ch'eng-ta. His post in Peking gave Takezoe the opportunity to make the journey. He was the first Japanese to visit Szechuan since the monk and poet Sesson Yūbai early in the fourteenth century.

When, some 550 years after Sesson, Takezoe left Peking to set out on his journey, he recalled these lines by the poet Chia Tao (779–843):

> Now, when unexpectedly I cross the Sang-kan again,
> And look off at Ping-chou, I think, "That is my home."

Chia-Tao while living in Ping-chou had yearned to be back in his hometown of Hsien-yang, but after ten years in Ping-chou he realized, as he crossed the Sang-kan River to go to still another post, that Ping-chou was now his home. These were the same lines that had inspired Bashō to write at the opening of his Nozarashi Kikō (Exposed in the Fields),

aki totose	Autumn makes ten years;
kaette Edo wo	Now I really mean Edo
sasu kokyō	When I talk of "home."[3]

Takezoe had resided in Peking for less than a year, but the thought of leaving behind Japanese friends who would help him if he fell ill or console him if he was depressed, and of setting forth with only one Japanese companion into an unknown land, made him feel the same emotions that Chia Tao and Bashō had felt long before.

On May 7, 1876, Takezoe and his companions crossed the Pao River and entered An-hsien district. From here on westward, he wrote, rice was not grown and people ate wheat. It was upsetting for Japanese not to be able to get rice when they traveled in America and Europe, but it was probably even more unsettling to be in the same Orient and still not get rice. But this was only the first of the problems that beset Takezoe on his way to Szechuan.

The next day, between T'ang-hsien and Pao-t'ing, they were surrounded by a mob of beggars along the road. Takezoe likened their voices, begging for alms, to autumn cicadas singing in the trees, a more poetic description than the one other Japanese travelers to the West gave to the jabbering of the beggars they encountered. An even more vexing problem was the blinding dust from the road, whipped by the hot winds. The two Japanese, riding in a cart, wrapped themselves in blankets to protect themselves. When they reached their destination, they looked at the driver of the cart: his dark face had turned white and only his eyes glared darkly. "He looked so much like a demon that we had to laugh."[4]

On the ninth they reached Hsin-lo district, a place so desolate that the land could not be cultivated. Takezoe wrote that the people sustained themselves on a kind of gruel they made from grain mixed with leaves from the elm, camellia, and date trees they grew. Others, he says, ate nothing but leaves. It is hard to take this as literal truth, though he was describing what he had actually seen, but there is no reason to doubt his statement that, because the region lacked firewood or charcoal, people dug roots for fuel and used dried horse dung in place of charcoal. Takezoe recalled that when he spent a winter in Shantung, the smell on the *kang* where he slept was so terrible that he asked what caused it. They were burning horse dung.[5]

Whenever possible, the Japanese left their inn before daybreak in order to avoid the dust stirred up along the roads by other people. On the thirteenth they crossed what Takezoe called a "sand river."[6] The river bottom was absolutely dry, and when they attempted to cross it by cart, the sand swallowed up the wheels, and they could not extricate the cart even with the help of three horses. Only after they had hired a fourth horse could the cart at last be pulled up on the opposite bank of the dried-up river. That night they spent in Han-tan (Kantan). There was a carefully tended shrine to Lu-sheng (Rosei), but nothing to remind them of the story (familiar to every educated Japanese of the time) in which Rosei slept on a magic pillow at the inn in Han-tan and lived in his dream a whole lifetime during the few minutes while his meal was being prepared.

The inns where the Japanese spent the nights were extremely primitive. For about a month after they left Peking there were no facilities for bathing and, as Takezoe reported when at last he was able to bathe again, his face and body were caked with grease and dirt, and the odor made him nauseous.[7] One night, when he got up and lit the lamp, the sound of flies buzzing in his room was like that of water boiling. He recalled that a Chinese poet had once mistaken the sound for the crowing of cocks, and he commented, "It was not without reason."[8]

Despite the many hardships of travel in China, there is no suggestion in Takezoe's diary that he wished he had not been so foolhardy as to make the overland journey from Peking to Chungking. Wherever he went there were mementoes of the Chinese past he knew so well. Sometimes, as when the travelers passed the native place of Han Wei-kung (1008–1075), there was only a small shrine in the fields to commemorate the man, but Takezoe was thoroughly familiar with the achievements of this scholar and statesman, and the knowledge made even an insignificant place seem memorable.

At other places the monuments were more impressive. When the Japanese reached T'ang-yin-hsien they admired the splendid mausoleum where Yüeh Fei (1103–1141), the brilliant general, was worshiped. Yüeh Fei, born the son of a tenant farmer of Han Wei-kung, had risen from the ranks to lead the Southern Sung army that in 1141 defeated the invading Chin army. Han Wei-kung was remembered now only by an inconspicuous shrine, but Yüeh Fei was idolized as a savior of the country. Takezoe described the rooftop tiles, beautifully carved in various shapes, soaring above the green trees of a grove. Stone monuments with carved inscriptions stood in rows in all four cardinal directions. Takezoe, admiring the calligraphy of the inscriptions, declared that he could tell the characters of the writers from their handwriting.

Outside the gate of the mausoleum Takezoe saw the statues of Ch'in Kuei (1090–1155) and his wife and another of Chang Chun (1086–1154) with his hands tied behind his back. Ch'in Kuei and Chang Chun had opposed Yüeh Fei's policy of resisting the Chin invaders and entered into negotiations with them. Yüeh Fei was thrown into prison and later killed there. For this reason, people passing the statues outside the gate invariably spat on them. But, Takezoe reasoned, if Kao Tsung (the first emperor of the Southern Sung dynasty) had not intended to kill Yüeh Fei, not even a hundred Ch'in Kueis could have vented their poison in this way; therefore, the murderer of Yüeh Fei was not Ch'in Kuei but Emperor Kao Tsung.[9]

None of the Japanese who visited the West possessed this kind of knowledge about the countries they saw. Even a modicum of knowledge of European history would have given to Cairo or Lisbon an allure that no Japanese felt. Takezoe, traveling under conditions that were infinitely worse than any experienced by Japanese who visited the West, probably derived more pleasure from his travels than they. Sometimes he was fascinated by an old inscription, sometimes intrigued by different possible interpretations of well-known historical facts. Nothing he saw from the past was without interest.

However, historical associations could not completely blot out the extreme discomfort to which Takezoe was subjected. One night he woke from dreams to hear a noise like that of a waterfall. He investigated, and discovered it was made by donkeys chewing hay. He commented, "I understood for the first time the aptness of the line, 'From my bed I hear the scrawny horses chewing the remains of the hay.'"[10] At inns in northern China the rooms for guests were separated from the stable by only a thin partition, and the neighing of horses or the braying of donkeys sounded as if they came from the traveler's pillow.

On May 19 Takezoe and his companions saw bamboo for the first time since leaving Peking seventeen days earlier. The sight of fresh green leaves after the dusty desolation through which they had been traveling made Takezoe wonder if the miserable conditions were not the fault of the people themselves. If they had devoted their energies to planting and cultivating trees, there would soon be forests, and wood would be plentiful. The wood could be used to build more substantial houses than the mud dwellings characteristic of the region, eliminating the nuisance of weeds sprouting from the walls or of the houses crumbling in a rainstorm. The branches could also be used for firewood in place of horse manure or roots.[11]

Takezoe's unquestionable admiration for Chinese culture did not blind him to the sorry state of Chinese society at the time. The worst feature was the widespread consumption of opium, which seemed to grow more conspicuous at each successive stage of the journey. In the areas north and south of the Yellow River everyone planted opium, and the farther west one went, the more opium one saw. Takezoe declared that in the region where he was traveling, all the local people smoked it. In Shan-hsi province seven out of ten, men and women alike, smoked opium. The annual cost of the opium consumed by each person, he calculated, was not less than twenty gold pieces. The population of China was said to be four hundred million; so even if only one-tenth of the population smoked and only one-fortieth smoked the more expensive imported opium, the annual expenditure would come to ten million pieces of gold. Takezoe reasoned,

> If smoking were good for the body, the expense would be worth it. Or, if it did neither good nor bad, perhaps it might not be worth worrying over. But it is in the nature of opium to consume the energies of the smoker and shorten his life. This poison is worse than venom. I fear that in another one hundred years' time the four hundred millions of China will be utterly enervated and the race will approach extinction. The father and mother of the people [i.e., the emperor] should take measures as soon as possible.[12]

Chinese food eaten along the way also depressed Takezoe. After leaving the ancient capital of Lo-yang, the Japanese stopped at Tzu-hsien. They asked for rice, only to be told there wasn't any. The people of this part of the country ate wheat, which they made into dumplings or buns. Even if they had rice, all they did was to remove the husks, then store it until it rotted, smelled, and produced insects. "Soup is made by boiling pieces of pork in oil. They also boil in oil pepper, onions, and garlic. None of it is fit to be eaten."[13] And, of course, it was not unusual to suffer from stomach pains or diarrhea.[14] It is a tribute to Takezoe that he did not allow these personal discomforts to alter his basic love of China and its culture.

The worst misery Takezoe experienced in China was caused by the total lack of even elementary comforts in the inns. In general, he informs us, Chinese inns provided nothing more than a place to sleep. Travelers had to bring their own bedding. Worse, "in the north there are no toilets. People all do their business in pigpens. The pigs always make this their meals. If somebody goes there, the pigs joyfully assemble around his behind, and no matter how hard he tries to drive them away, they won't leave. It is really unbearable."[15] The first place the Japanese encountered toilets was Hsi-an-fu. The toilets were dirty, but they were better than nothing.

The first place where they could bathe after leaving Peking were the Li-shan Hot Springs, the site of the Ch'ing-hua Palace of a thousand years before. Takezoe wrote that he felt marvelous after bathing. Even quite ordinary comforts assume great importance when one travels under such conditions. And, of course (though Takezoe did not bother to mention the fact until he had completed the journey), he was tormented every night by bedbugs, which the Chinese called "stink bugs" (chou-chung), an evocative name. At first, until he got used to their presence at every inn where he spent the night, he could not sleep.[16]

It is interesting to compare Takezoe's impressions of China with the roughly contemporaneous account of Japan by the intrepid Englishwoman Isabella Bird (1831–1904), who traveled in the summer of 1878 (just two years after Takezoe's journey to Szechuan) from "Yedo to Yezo," shunning most of the principal cities along the way in favor of "unbeaten tracks." Here is her description of an inn at Kuruma-tōge, near Nojiri in the mountains of central Japan: "I found nothing that I could eat except black beans and boiled cucumbers. The room was dark, dirty, vile, noisy, and poisoned by sewage odours, as rooms unfortunately are very apt to be."[17]

And here is her description of Japanese of the region: "These people wear no linen, and their clothes, which are seldom washed, are constantly worn, night and day, as long as they will hold together[18] . . . The persons of the people, especially of the children, are infested with vermin, and one fruitful source of skin sores is the irritation arising from this cause . . . The married women look as if they have never known youth, and their skin is apt to be like tanned leather. At Kayashima I asked the house-master's wife, who looked about fifty, how old she was (a polite question in Japan), and she replied twenty-two—one of many similar surprises."[19]

Isabella Bird was far from being excessively critical of conditions in the places she visited. Later in her journey she declared, "Considering that I have often put up in small hamlets off the great routes even of Japanese travel, the accommodation, minus the fleas and the odours, has been surprisingly excellent, not to be equalled, I should think, in equally remote regions in any country in the world."[20]

She was also ready to praise the Japanese landscapes, as in this description: "It was a lovely summer day, though hot, and the snowy peaks of Aidzu scarcely looked cool as they glittered in the sunlight. The plain of Yonezawa, with the prosperous town of Yonezawa in the south, and the frequented watering-place of Akayu in the north, is a perfect garden of Eden."[21]

Takezoe, after enduring the hardships of inns along the way, would also be rewarded by magnificent scenery when he at last reached Szechuan.

On June 9 Takezoe and his companions reached the first goal of their journey, the *sandō* at I-men-chen. A *sandō* (like a *kakehashi* in Japan) was a narrow path, resembling a ledge, built of wood planks along the side of a precipitous cliff. (As far as I know, there is nothing like a *sandō* in the West, and for that reason I have translated it as "bridge" in the title of Takezoe's diary.) By extension, it came to mean any dangerous path through spectacularly steep mountains. Bashō wrote of the *kakehashi* in Kiso:

kakehashi ya	Bridge along the cliff—
inochi wo karamu	Clinging for their very lives
tsuta momiji	Ivy and maple leaves.

The *sandō* in China were even more frightening, judging by Takezoe's description:

Mountain torrents issue from the numberless mountains, and strangely shaped rocks stand in ranks. We crossed a mountain torrent to tread the perilous opposite shore. The narrow path twists around the side of the mountain, and when one looks up at the sky it is as from the bottom of a well. Two *li* farther on we crossed through a barrier, the ancient Ta-san Barrier. The mountains grew ever steeper and the path ever more dangerous. A thousand fathoms below was a gulch with a fiercely raging torrent that made a noise like thunder and was shaped like a cloud. We had descended some ten *li* from the barrier when suddenly a downpour rained on us like cannon balls. We got down from our sedan chairs and rested for a while.[22]

The mountains, for all their dangers, were more congenial to the Japanese than the dusty plains. Takezoe noted nostalgically that the mountain people made things of wood that looked like the souvenirs sold at Hakone. The green of the mountains and the bright color of the rhododendrons and other flowers made the place seem (to use Isabella Bird's word) like another Eden. A Taoist priest invited them into a temple building where the Japanese were treated to tea and food. Behind the building, a flight of stone steps with a carved stone balustrade led up to the top of the mountain. Takezoe wrote, "There are pines and bamboo, the green mingling among the blue, absolutely pure, without a particle of dust. We wandered here and there for a long time, the feeling of dustiness suddenly evaporated. This is truly a wondrous place of purity."[23]

The next day the Japanese reached the point of confluence of the Hsia and Pao Rivers, and saw the ruins of San-chiao-cheng. Before long, they crossed another river in a small boat, and reached Wu-ch'u-p'u. Takezoe wrote, "Cascades in the mountains pour down with a never-ending roar, and the blowing wind raises spray like scattered jewels. The water of the Pao, collecting in pools, is an indigo blue, and where it surges over rocks seems to be throwing off snow. In its course are weird boulders and strange rocks, some like coiled dragons, others like wild horses, lie beside the waves. And the *sandō* threads its way through all this. This part of the journey was like traveling through a painting."[24]

Still farther on was the Thousand Buddha Cliff. Here the *sandō* had been constructed in the T'ang dynasty by a man who had also carved images of Buddha along the sides of the cliff. Later, many other men added sculptures of Buddha, in every posture and with every expression. In the Ch'ien-lung era (1739–1795) a farmer who was cultivating the mountainside found over twenty stones that seemed to have supernatural origins. He reported this to the authorities, and an official subsequently raised funds to build a temple in which the stones were worshiped. Takezoe, a good Confucianist, was enraged by this act of what he considered to be deluded piety: "It is forgivable for ignorant people to be superstitious, but what does it mean when an official promotes such nonsense?"[25]

Beyond Thousand Buddha Cliff the dangerous part of the *sandō* came to an end. While traveling in the dusty flatlands Takezoe had feared that when they reached the *sandō* in Szechuan they would have to make their way through dense forests where tigers and panthers roamed, and that it would be impossible to get any decent food to eat; but they discovered that the lands between the mountains were cultivated, and there were even rice paddies. Beans and wheat had been planted in every cranny of the cliffs, and wherever they went they could hear the sounds of chickens and dogs, the traditional sounds of a peaceful Chinese village. Oxen and sheep were so numerous they blocked the roads. At dangerous places along the way steps had been cut into the cliffs and there was even a railing to help the traveler. The cities they passed were thriving, and the inns excellent. An uninterrupted stream of palanquins went by day and night. Even in the small towns along the road the food was delicious, and the inns were prepared to accommodate guests with comfort. Takezoe commented, "Ah, there is always something one couldn't have guessed in the things of this world."[26]

On July 2 Takezoe and his companions arrived in Ch'eng-tu. The following day Takezoe visited an antique shop. He declared that there was nothing worth looking at, whether calligraphy, paintings, or antiques. But there were bookshops everywhere, and the shelves were full of books. Takezoe remarked, "One can tell this is a place where literature has flourished."[27]

The last part of Takezoe's journey, from Ch'eng-tu to Chungking, then down the Yangtze to Shanghai, was made in relative comfort. For the first time Takezoe mentions having met a Chinese with a background similar to his own, the scholar Ch'en Hsi-ch'ang, whom he met in Ch'eng-tu and who accompanied the Japanese as far as Chungking. Ch'en told Takezoe about the anti-Christian riots in Chungking. Churches and hospitals associated with them had been burned, and the rioters had not been satisfied until they had destroyed every last church.[28] In the regions of China through which Takezoe had passed, life was so hard that people could think of little else but obtaining food and firewood, but here they had the leisure to be stirred by ideology.

Takezoe's diary is a polished example of literary *kambun*. He also published a companion volume of *kanshi* composed on the journey. Both in prose and poetry he so vividly captured the experiences of his journey that his work has been admired in China as well as in Japan.

Notes

1. This seems to be his personal name only and not his full name.
2. Yonaiyama Tsuneo, *Nyūshokki*, p. 263.
3. See my *Travelers of a Hundred Ages*, p. 292.
4. Yonaiyama, *Nyūshokki*, p. 267.
5. *Ibid.*, p. 268. A *kang* is a kind of earthen platform under which a low fire is kept burning to warm the person sleeping above.
6. *Ibid.*, p. 273.
7. *Ibid.*, p. 294.
8. *Ibid.*, p. 275.
9. *Ibid.*, p. 276. There is another, even more impressive shrine to Yüeh Fei in Hangchou.

10. *Ibid.* I have not been able to identify the quotation.
11. *Ibid.*, pp. 279–80.
12. *Ibid.*, p. 284.
13. *Ibid.*, pp. 285–86.
14. *Ibid.*, p. 296.
15. *Ibid.*
16. *Ibid.*, p. 353.
17. Isabella L. Bird, *Unbeaten Tracks in Old Japan,* p. 93.
18. *Ibid.*, p. 94.
19. *Ibid.*
20. *Ibid.*, p. 185.
21. *Ibid.*, p. 133.
22. Yonaiyama, *Nyūshokki*, p. 301.
23. *Ibid.*, p. 304.
24. *Ibid.*, p. 305.
25. *Ibid.*, p. 318.
26. *Ibid.*, p. 323.
27. *Ibid.*, p. 329.
28. *Ibid.*, p. 350.

Bibliography

Bird, Isabella L. *Unbeaten Tracks in Old Japan.* Tokyo: Tuttle, 1973.
Keene, Donald. *Travelers of a Hundred Ages.* New York: Henry Holt, 1989.
Yonaiyama Tsuneo. *Nyūshokki.* Osaka: Yagō Shoten, 1944.

Travels in the North

Not all the Japanese explorers of the 1860s and 1870s went abroad. Both the islands of Hokkaidō and the Chishima (Kuril) archipelago to the north, and the Ryūkyū Islands far to the south, though considered to be Japanese territory, awaited exploration by Japanese from the three main islands. It is true that there had been Japanese settlers at Matsumae and a few nearby places in Hokkaidō, and the remoter regions to the north had been explored by such men as Mamiya Rinzō (1775–1844), but the first person to leave writings of literary interest about the area was Matsuura Takeshirō (1818–1888), who emerges from his diaries as an appealing figure and a strong and persuasive advocate of justice for the Ainu.

During the course of his lifetime Matsuura visited every one of the sixty-eight provinces of Japan, and left diaries describing most. He was born in Ise in 1818 and from an early age was stirred by the urge to travel and by an almost equally strong urge to become a Buddhist priest. At the age of twelve he entered the private school of a Confucian scholar in Tsu where he acquired the knowledge of the Chinese classics displayed in his diaries, both in his allusions to Chinese literature and in the *kanshi* he composed during the journeys.

Matsuura's travels began in 1833 when he went to Edo for further study, taking advantage on the way home of the opportunity to travel in the mountains of central Japan. From then on, most of his time was spent on his journeys. In 1838, while in Nagasaki, he fell seriously ill, and recovered owing to the care of a Zen priest. In gratitude (but also because he had long aspired to become a priest), Matsuura was ordained as a Zen priest at the age of twenty-one. The first temple he was assigned was on the island of Hirado, and this inspired him to travel to other islands in the Japan Sea including Iki and Tsushima. He wanted to go on to Korea, but an acquaintance, an elderly scholar, urged him to go instead to the north where, because of Japanese indifference, the Russians were gradually making encroachments.

About this time Matsuura learned that during his long absence from home (apparently he never wrote or received letters) both his parents had died. He returned to Ise and in 1844 held services for them. He also visited the Great Shrine of Ise. Buddhist priests were forbidden to worship at the shrine, so Matsuura wore a wig to conceal his shaven head. While there he announced—for reasons he did not reveal—that he had renounced his profession of Buddhist priest. Henceforth he would be an explorer.

In 1845 Matsuura made his first journey to Ezo (Hokkaidō). The local Japanese authorities were strict about allowing casual visitors into the domain. In order to allay their suspicions, he obtained credentials as a merchant. He visited the north three times between 1845 and 1850, not only the parts of Hokkaidō already familiar to the Japanese but the southern part of Sakhalin (Karafuto) and the islands of Kunashiri, Etorofu, and Shikotan in the Kuril chain. He became fluent in Ainu, which helped him enormously in his explorations.

In 1853, when a Russian fleet arrived at Nagasaki with the declared purpose of establishing the boundary between Russian and Japanese territory on Sakhalin, Matsuura's opinions, as an expert on the north, were eagerly sought by patriots, and he went to Kyoto to discuss with members of the nobility the best ways to protect Japan from the menace of foreign intrusion. By this time he was a convinced believer in *jōi* (expel the barbarians!), an attitude he seems never to have renounced.

Matsuura returned to Sakhalin in 1856 and single-handedly explored the interior. At the end of the year he was stricken with so serious an illness that for a time he expected to die, but he fortunately recovered, and soon resumed his explorations with undiminished energy. His diaries, which narrate his travels from 1856 to 1858 (though they were not published for another five or more years), are of exceptional interest, not only for his descriptions of the places he visited but for what they revealed about him. He does not state why he made these dangerous journeys, but he probably hoped to reaffirm Japanese possession of the northern islands.

Kita Ezo Yoshi (Additional Account of Northern Ezo) opens with a brief statement of the proposed itinerary. The party of eight men, including both Japanese and Ainu, would cross over to Sakhalin from Sōya, and after exploring the west coast, make their way to the east coast. Matsuura anticipated that the journey would present extreme hazards, and for this reason restricted the size of the party. It was essential to travel light, and he prescribed exactly what each man would be allowed to carry in the way of clothing and other equipment. The list began:

> Item. Clothes to be carried are a short jacket (*hanten*), breeches (*momohiki*), underwear, and a cotton garment (*mempuku*). No cloak. A rain hat, a sash three feet long, an oiled rain cape. Straw sandals to be carried at the waist. However, night clothes are not allowed. For this purpose, each person is to carry one padded garment.
>
> Item. Each person should carry a teacup and a pair of chopsticks. A walking stick is optional.
>
> Item. A candle, a bamboo match-cord, birch chips and spills should be carried.[1]

Other permitted items included a hand towel, flintstones, a fan, and medicine. After the last of the seven articles Matsuura wrote, "Absolutely nothing that is not specified above is to be carried."[2] This would not be a journey of the kind described by the famous diarists of the past, nor a state-sponsored mission of the kind that would soon be sent to distant countries, but a painful and possibly dangerous encounter with the harshest aspects of nature found in Japanese territory.

Japanese who traveled to Europe or America at the end of the shogunate period generally provided themselves with Japanese food to eat on the journey, but when Matsuura and his companions were about to set off for Sakhalin he warned them, "Nothing will be easy on this trip. You will have to eat what the natives eat—fish, grass roots, and whatever else the country provides. But in order to comfort yourselves a little psychologically, you are allowed to take along one bag of rice and a cup of salt."[3]

At various places in his diaries Matsuura described in detail what he ate. In *Shiribeshi Nisshi* (Daily Record of Shiribeshi), the account of a journey in the first month of 1858, there occurs an unforgettable description of a meal of bear meat. Matsuura and his Ainu guides were tired and hungry. They came to a cave that looked like a bear's den, but there was no sign of a bear. They decided to spend the night. Then, perhaps by way of diversion from the grimness of the journey, Matsuura wrote on the wall a *kanshi* in which he described his weariness and his eagerness to eat a bear's paw, a dish often praised by the Chinese as the ultimate delicacy.

The Ainu could not read what he had written and asked what it said. Matsuura answered, no doubt in jest, that he wanted to eat a bear. They replied with the utmost seriousness, "If you are so eager to eat a bear, sir, we'll catch one for you." The four Ainu thereupon set off for the mountains, bows and arrows in hands. That evening they returned not with a bear but with four badgers. The next day, while Matsuura rested in the cave during a fierce snowstorm, the Ainu again went off into the mountains and returned this time with two badgers and four weasels. But that day they had seen bear tracks, and they knew that a bear was nearby. Here follows Matsuura's description of how they killed and ate the bear:

> I climbed up to a high place about forty or fifty yards away and watched. The men thrust pointed sticks into the cave, but the bear remained inside, roaring in anger. The dogs wagged their tails joyfully, two of them dancing around as if they meant to enter the cave; but the Ainu, restraining them, fired three or four poison arrows inside. This made the bear roar all the more furiously, until I thought that the cave would collapse under the reverberations. Then the men, clearing a path in the snow, drove the dogs into the cave. The bear grew all the more crazed as the poison began to take effect, and came roaring out of the cave, heading directly at Tonenbaku. But he, not in the slightest perturbed, cried out, "Damn you, *heureho*!" (The natives call a bear cub a *heureho*, and always use this word when confronting a bear.) He got his arm firmly around the neck of the bear which, though its strength was visibly failing, continued to shake and roar. Tonenbaku drew his knife and thrust the point in from under the bear's legs all the way to the ribs. His skill was really astonishing.[4]

When the other Ainu saw that Tonenbaku had killed the bear, they at once set about cutting up the meat. First, they offered some to the gods of the mountains and sea. Next, they dragged the carcass into the cave where they had spent the previous night, and proceeded to devour the meat, raw or grilled. Matsuura wrote, "The fresh blood froze to their beards, and their hands were stained with blood. They looked exactly like devils in paintings. It was a terrifying sight."[5]

Matsuura did not say whether or not he ate any of the bear meat he had so lightheartedly requested. The sight he describes was horrifying enough to take away the appetite of even a very hungry man.

But on other occasions he ate Ainu food, though he did not necessarily enjoy it. For example, here is his description of some millet dumplings he ate: "The way they make it is to pound millet into a powder, mix it with flour made of lily root, add salmon roe, roll it into balls, and then boil them. They gave them to me just as they were, but the natives fry them in deep fish oil. The taste is extremely unusual."[6]

He also related how he was invited to a meal by an *otona* (headman), and used this experience to poke fun at Japanese who refused to eat Ainu food: "They went out and brought back some viper grass and mountain arum root which they cooked for me. They said as they served it that this was the potato of the natives. It tasted delicious. They said the Japanese refuse to eat it, because they think it is poisonous, but they informed me that if you remove the hard part at the core it is not in the least poisonous. I ate seven or eight for lunch without the slightest ill effect."[7]

On still another occasion he was invited to dinner by an elderly *otona* whom he described in these terms: "The *otona* Arayuku (seventy-four years old) wore a wide-sleeved kimono of Ōsugi pale green damask, and a jacket of Santan[8] brocade. Two boys stood by his side, one holding his sword and the other his tobacco pouch ... His white hair fell over his shoulders. He stroked his reddish beard, which all but covered his knees. He came out to meet me, leaning on a stick. His appearance was imposing, and he seemed every inch the chief of a fiefdom."[9]

When all the guests were seated, the second son of the chief greeted Matsuura with Ainu words that meant, "It's been a long time, hasn't it?" Everyone was surprised that the man should have known Matsuura, but the chief's son explained to the others that in 1856 they had traveled together to remote parts of the country. Then, "he came before me and politely expressed his thanks for my kindness at that time. I, too, thought it was truly extraordinary to meet here someone I had known deep in the mountains, and I was feeling happy about this when the second son, addressing the others in the gathering, said, 'This gentleman has been all the way to Orokko,[10] Santan, and Taraika,'[11] at which everybody showed me greater respect than ever."[12]

Dinner consisted of choice cuts of bear meat, deer intestines, and slices of frozen salmon. Naturally, there was also plenty to drink. Matsuura was clearly a member of the gathering, not an observer. The Ainu were his friends and he was happy to share their food, as he would share his food with them. There is no suggestion of condescension in his attitude: he never appears to be congratulating himself on his willingness to eat at the table of inferiors. Unlike those Japanese whose fear of being poisoned made them refuse to eat certain Ainu dishes, it was obvious to Matsuura that if food was actually poisonous it would kill the Ainu as well as the Japanese. No doubt Matsuura had to overcome many prejudices before he could enjoy an Ainu meal, but he made the effort, and in the end he unaffectedly joined in the pleasure of a feast with them.

Matsuura was able to a remarkable degree to enter the lives of the Ainu and frequently expressed his admiration for them. His travels would have been impossible without their help, and his life was in their hands when they traveled through dangerous places. Again and again he found refuge in their homes. He was impressed by their bravery and fortitude, but (contrary to the general belief of Japanese at the time), he also found them intelligent, and he devoted many pages of his diaries to describing their generous actions. When something puzzled or disturbed Matsuura during his travels, he would always turn to the Ainu for guidance. On his journey to Shiribetsu, for example, he was overjoyed to find water after five days of thirst, but when he drank the water, it was bitter. He asked an Ainu why this was so, and was told, " 'The water is bitter because it comes from a mountain where *todo*[13] and Ezo pines grow. Water from mountains with birches, walnut trees, and ginger plants tastes sweet.' Now that I heard the reason, it certainly seemed so. Water from mountains with *todo* and pines even looks a little different—rather sooty. The natives have investigated even such things. This was not the only thing I have learned from them. I have again and again benefited by their knowledge."[14]

No one has ever described his countrymen more harshly than Matsuura in his work *Kinsei Ezo Jimbutsu Shi* (Account of Ezo People in Recent Times). He gave example after example of Ainu who, because of their simple goodness, had been exploited by the Japanese, who possessed the power to make the Ainu obey. For example, once, when Matsuura and his companions were traveling in Sakhalin and needed a place to spend the night, they asked for shelter at the house of an old man who gladly took them in. After a time, when it had become dark, the old man took down from a shelf a five-stringed koto, which he played as he sang. Matsuura was struck by the man's devotion to music and asked another Ainu about him. He was told, "Many melodies were preserved from ancient times on this island, but because we were forced by the *unjōya*[15] to work in the fishery, and had to do this so often, the number of people who could still play the music rapidly decreased until finally there was nobody left at all. The only one who still plays it in the bay region is this old man."[16]

Before he left, Matsuura was presented with an old koto and told, "The Ezo people who lived around this bay long ago used to play this instrument to soothe their feelings, but now there is no time to enjoy it. Ever since they established the *unjōya*, we have done forced labor all year round. You can tell from the fact that nobody can play this instrument anymore just how bitter our lives have been. When next some gentleman comes here from the country they call Edo, please tell him of this."[17]

In Matsuura's stories of the Ainu of recent times, the agents of the Japanese presence in the north figure as destroyers of Ainu culture, merciless exploiters of the Ainu men, and brutal seducers of the

Ainu women. He related the stories of three Ainu women who had been the victims of the Japanese. The first, an old woman with two daughters, had been left to live alone in the mountains. Her elder daughter, Peratoruka, had attracted the attention of a Japanese guard named Toramatsu, who tried in every way to get her to yield to him. He arranged to have Peratoruka's husband sent to a distant fishing ground, and took Peratoruka with him to his own fishing ground. In the end, Peratoruka had no choice but to do what Toramatsu demanded. Her sister was also separated from their mother, and her sons were forced to work for the Japanese. When one of the sons asked an official for permission to visit his grandmother, the Japanese cursed him and declared, "What need have you to visit an old woman who's been left in the mountains because she can't work any longer? She's in the mountains—let her live as she pleases in the mountains, and then let her croak."[18] The brutality of the man might seem unbelievable if Matsuura had not furnished many instances of similar behavior. The various officials did not treat the Ainu like human beings.

Matsuura's attitude toward the Ainu was quite unlike that of most Japanese of the time. In every instance he sympathized with them. He saw how the houses in their villages were dwindling in numbers, and records with unflinching honesty the poverty that was too terrible to behold. He seems to have thought of the Ainu rather as Europeans of the eighteenth century thought of the "noble savage." Voltaire, in his play *Alzire*, set in Peru at the time of the Spanish conquest, expressed his belief in the moral superiority of the civilization of the defeated people to the brute force of the conquerors' civilization. Later, in the nineteenth century, James Fenimore Cooper portrayed American Indians who, though they lacked the benefits of a European education, were not only brave but heroic, and fully possessed of moral integrity. Matsuura's Ainu knew nothing of Confucian teachings, but they displayed filial piety naturally. They were friendly and generous toward the Japanese, though the latter treated them like animals, and the special warmth they showed Matsuura was a sign of the gratitude they felt toward a Japanese who had taken the trouble to learn their language and customs.

Matsuura never forgot, however, that he was Japanese, and constantly worried over the possibility that the Russians might deprive Japan of its northern possessions. He remembered with respect his predecessors as explorers of Ezo, especially Kondō Morishige, Mogami Tokunai, and Mamiya Rinzō, and he listened eagerly when some aged Ainu recalled having seen these men. Like them, he desired nothing more than to strengthen Japanese control over the region, but unlike them, he did not think of the Ainu as a people unrelated to the Japanese. Again and again he pointed out instances of the cultural kinship between the two peoples. The Ainu, he declared in a diary, preserved the ancient Japanese language and customs even better than the Japanese themselves. He found that the Ainu place-names sometimes included words relating to Shinto religious rites;[19] and wrote about some Ainu dances he had witnessed, "I was moved with gratitude, indeed so overcome that words cannot describe it, to think that the manner of dancing of the capital has survived here, in a corner of Chishima."[20]

The old Ainu culture, exemplified by the legends related in the *yukari*, the epic poems that were recited for hours at a time, also appealed to Matsuura, as we know from the mentions of recitations scattered throughout his diary, such as the following: "I spent the night in the shade of a mountain. I gave the natives sake, and they enjoyed it all night long, sitting around a bonfire. A man named Samemon sang *yukari*, and everybody happily joined in the refrain. Their pleasure was extreme and lasted until dawn, without anyone feeling in the least the severe cold emanating from the eternal snow."[21] Matsuura was probably the first Japanese to take pleasure in these songs. But much of the old Ainu culture was being rapidly destroyed. Matsuura, after describing the traditional Ainu dyeing, wrote, "I thought there wasn't anyone any longer who knew the method of dyeing, but I was deeply impressed to hear that it still survives in these mountains."[22]

The lament for disappearing arts is a familiar strain in the accounts of people who seem doomed to extinction. The Japanese had hastened the end of the Ainu by sending the able-bodied men to the coastal settlements or distant fishing grounds, taking the women for their wives; and in many once-prosperous villages only the old and infirm were left. Matsuura heard that the population of one village had been halved during the fifty years since the Japanese first exercised control of the region. His informant commented, "If things go on in this way, I worry about what will happen to the native race in another twenty years."[23]

Matsuura did not, on the other hand, shrink from describing the unpleasant aspects of his life among the Ainu. During his travels in the Tokachi region, for example, he had what he described as the worst experience of any journey:

> One thing that bothered us was that for some time we had all been suffering from diarrhea and had to relieve ourselves often. The toilets of the natives consist of nothing more than two thick pieces of wood laid parallel in the middle of the fields. One squats on these to do one's business. There is no roof, no walls around it, nothing at all. Tonight it was raining, so [without going into the fields], I stepped outside and somewhere or other exposed my behind. At once some dogs, soaking wet and intending to eat my excrement, thrust their muzzles under my behind and fought, biting one another, to see who would get first choice. The wet hair of their muzzles brushed against my behind, splashing mud over it and also over my crotch and my clothes. There was nothing I could do about this nuisance.[24]

One is reminded of Takezoe Shin'ichirō's account of a toilet at a Chinese inn.

Travel in the north was extremely unpleasant most of the time. During much of the year (and not only in the winter months) it was bitterly cold. Matsuura's description of a journey made in the snow at the beginning of the second month (early in March in the solar calendar) is memorable:

> The ground is so muddy underfoot that sometimes one sinks all the way down to one's hips. The pain is indescribable. The wind is not a wind from this or that direction but something that swoops like a whirlwind, blowing up the snow. One feels as if one's face has been slashed open; one's hands and feet feel no sensation; and one's mouth won't move. The sky, which has been perfectly clear, turns dark in a moment, then bright again the next moment. There is no accounting for the transformations. When I looked off to the right, the place I was to go looked like a head with an *ebōshi* on top, and below it was a sheer drop of several hundred *jō*.[25] I thought that if I were blown over by the wind I would fall to the bottom of the valley. I still shudder in body and spirit at the thought of that precipitous cliff. But even if I get past the dangerous places today, what kind of places await me farther on?[26]

Even in summer it was chilly in the mountains, and Matsuura and his companions were otherwise tormented by insects—mosquitoes, horseflies, flies, gnats—that often kept them from sleeping. Wild animals made the journey dangerous. In *Shiretoko Nikki* (Shiretoko Diary) he wrote, "When it got dark, bears came from their hiding places and ate with a crunching sound the fish bones we had thrown away. It was a desolate sound."[27] Elsewhere, wolves passed close by them:

"Two or three wolves began to howl furiously at a place that I estimated was four or five hundred yards away. Their howling was somehow even more unearthly, more desolate than the roaring of a bear. As the wind blew through the rushes, it occurred to me that perhaps the wolves were hungry in the snow and would come to eat our food. I could not sleep."[28]

Matsuura was deeply attached to Ezo, despite the hardships of the life. He mentions several times his excitement, upon looking at a landscape, to realize that it was as big as a whole province in other parts of Japan. Most unusually for a Japanese of that time, when he heard of some mountain that had never been climbed, he was eager to be the first to conquer it, however difficult the ascent.[29] Ezo was a land of adventure for Matsuura, but more than the wonderful, un-spoiled scenery, it was the Ainu who drew him back.

He was not the only visitor to Ezo who was charmed by the Ainu. Isabella Bird, who claimed to have been the first European woman to have made a foray into the country of the aborigines, re-ferred to the Ainu as savages, but was obviously entranced by them. She wrote of one of the first Ainu men she saw, "I think I never saw a face more completely beautiful in features and expression, with a lofty, sad, far-off, gentle, intellectual look ... His manner was most grateful, and he spoke both Ainu and Japanese in the low musical tone which I find is a characteristic of Ainu speech."[30]

Later, when she crossed a river, two Ainu men helped her. She wrote, "They were superb-looking men, gentle, and extremely cour-teous, handing me in and out of the boat, and holding the stirrups while I mounted, with much natural grace. On leaving, they ex-tended their arms and waved their hands inwards twice, stroking their grand beards afterwards, which is their usual salutation."[31]

Miss Bird spent three days and two nights in an Ainu hut, not (as in Matsuura's case) because she needed shelter from the elements, but because she was boundlessly curious about people. Her mixed feel-ings about the Ainu were summed up in one long sentence:

> They have no history, their traditions are scarcely worthy the
> name, they claim descent from a dog, their houses and persons
> swarm with vermin, they have no letters or numbers above a
> thousand, they are clothed in the bark of trees and the un-

tanned skins of beasts, they worship the bear, the sun, moon, fire, water, and I know not what, they are uncivilisable and altogether irreclaimable savages, yet they are attractive, and in some ways fascinating, and I hope I shall never forget the music of their low, sweet voices, the soft light of their mild, brown eyes, and the wonderful sweetness of their smile.[32]

Miss Bird was mistaken when she pronounced the Ainu to be "uncivilisable," but she was sincere when she described what in the Ainu so attracted her. Matsuura does not mention the voices, the eyes, or the smiles of the Ainu, but the attraction these people exerted over him is no less evident. The most remarkable sentence in his diaries occurs after mention of his arrival at the Japanese settlement in Ishikari. "For the first time in forty-two days I had my hair dressed, took a bath, and lay down under a quilt, but I felt as if I had lost my humanity."[33] One would have imagined that for a Japanese, indeed, for any civilized man, a bath and clean clothes after forty-two days of dirt would be heaven itself, but Matsuura believed that he had lost something precious. He had once more become Japanese, involved in a Japanese world, and could no longer experience the "real life" of the Ainu, with whom he had traveled as a brother.

Matsuura's writings earned him many enemies among the Japanese officials in Ezo. This was hardly surprising, in view of his attacks on the ruthless actions of the various oppressors of the Ainu, some of whom he named. One official with whom he remained on good terms was Muragaki, the governor of Awaji, who was stationed in Hakodate, the main Japanese settlement in Hokkaidō, before going to America, and later returned to this post.

Matsuura did not go back to Ezo after the Meiji Restoration, but he had the distinction of giving the main island its name, Hokkaidō—North Sea Island. Perhaps his enemies were too strong, but perhaps also be feared that the Ainu way of life he had loved no longer existed.

Notes

1. Yoshida Takezō, *Matsuura Takeshirō Kikō Shū,* III, p. 537.
2. *Ibid.*, p. 538.
3. *Ibid.*
4. *Ibid.*, pp. 248–49.
5. *Ibid.*, p. 249.
6. *Ibid.*, p. 371.
7. *Ibid.*, p. 328.
8. Santan designated what are today the maritime provinces of Siberia.
9. Yoshida, *Matsuura*, III, p. 358.
10. The Orokko were a Tungusic people who lived mainly in Sakhalin and the maritime provinces of Siberia.
11. Possibly Taraku Island, near Shikotan.
12. Yoshida, *Matsuura*, III, p. 358.
13. A kind of evergreen common in northern Japan. *Todo* is derived from an Ainu word; the usual Japanese name is *ōshirabiso*.
14. Yoshida, *Matsuura*, III, p. 253.
15. Offices of the Japanese on Hokkaidō where during the Tokugawa period taxes were collected from the Ainu in kind or in forced labor.
16. Yoshida, *Matsuura*, III, p. 23.
17. *Ibid.*
18. *Ibid.*, p. 18.
19. *Ibid.*, p. 423.
20. Chishima was used for the Kuril Islands, but sometimes also for Hokkaidō. Matsuura saw the dances at Nosappu on the east coast of the island.
21. Yoshida, *Matsuura*, III, p. 232.
22. *Ibid.*, p. 514.
23. *Ibid.*, p. 488.
24. *Ibid.*, p. 362.
25. An *ebōshi* was a ceremonial hat worn by nobles when formally costumed. A *jō* was about ten feet, or three meters.
26. Yoshida, *Matsuura*, III, p. 249.
27. *Ibid.*, p. 467.
28. *Ibid.*, p. 344.

29. *Ibid.*, p. 401.
30. Isabella L. Bird, *Unbeaten Tracks in Old Japan*, p. 225.
31. *Ibid.*, p. 232.
32. *Ibid.*, p. 255.
33. Yoshida, *Matsuura*, III, p. 299.

Bibliography

Bird, Isabella L. *Unbeaten Tracks in Old Japan*. Tokyo: Tuttle, 1973.
Yoshida Takezō. *Matsuura Takeshirō Kikō Shū*, 3 vols. Tokyo: Fuzambō, 1975–77.

Exploration of the Southern Islands

On April 18, 1893, Sasamori Gisuke (1845–1915), a samurai who had lately returned from the Kuril Islands, where he had spent three painful months "roving over hill and dale, miserably fed and clothed, and suffering many privations,"[1] was summoned by the minister of home affairs, Inoue Kaoru (1835–1915), who wished to discuss Sasamori's report on conditions in the north. During the course of their conversation the subject turned to the Ryūkyū Islands, at the very opposite end of Japan. Worry over Japan's defenses to the north had prompted Sasamori, a fervent patriot, to see for himself the actual state of affairs. His concern over the Ryūkyūs was aroused for similar reasons. Inoue, however, was more interested in discovering what might be done to increase sugar production in Okinawa, and thereby reduce Japan's dependence on imported sugar. He asked Sasamori if he would be willing to go there and make an investigation.

Sasamori was certainly an unlikely person to send to Okinawa in the summer. He came from Hirosaki in the north of Japan, was unaccustomed to heat, and knew nothing about sugar. (At the opening of his diary Sasamori confesses that he did not know whether sugar grew on trees or was a kind of plant.)[2] However, a rich industrialist named Kimbara Meizen (1832–1923), who had been impressed by Sasamori's report on Chishima, urged him to study conditions in Okinawa in the same spirit, sure that it would be of benefit to the nation, at least indirectly. Kimbara was the backer of Sasamori's travels in the Ryūkyū Islands.

Sasamori was pleased to be entrusted with this mission. He had long been convinced that the indifference to the Ryūkyūs displayed by the Japanese government had resulted in a threat to Japanese security. However, when he said goodbye to his family and friends before leaving Hirosaki he was anything but cheerful. He could not help worrying about the two dangers lying ahead of him on the journey—poisonous snakes and disease, especially malaria and filariasis. He tells us (with surprising frankness for a samurai) in the first entry of the diary,

> At the time of my departure I had already prepared myself to die, and even though I forced a look of manly cheerfulness on the outside, in fact tears of blood welled up in my breast at the thought that this was at once a separation for life and a separation by death. When I think back on my feelings at the time, I see that the dejection in my heart was a kind of hallucination, grief and joy sweeping over me by turns in the same room with my family and friends. Reader, I ask you to forgive the above state of mind.[3]

The last sentence tells us that Sasamori expected that the diary would be published and read. This undoubtedly inhibited his expression at times; conversely, the rare occasions when he openly voiced his emotions were given special intensity because of his normal reluctance to indulge in personal comment. Before publishing the diary, Sasamori went through the manuscript, cutting passages that seemed excessively critical of the political situation in the Ryūkyūs and suppressing the names of some officials whom he had described with harshness, but his observations are presented honestly, and there is no mistaking his shock over the misery in which many of the people of Okinawa lived.

From the beginning of his stay in Okinawa he was confronted with a contradiction between what he wanted to believe and his actual experiences. It was absolutely essential for him to believe that the people of the southern islands were Japanese; otherwise, he would have to recognize the claim of China to the islands or else the legitimacy of the kings of the Ryūkyūs. For this reason he refused ever to use the words *naichijin*—people from the Inner Country, a commonly used term for the three main islands of Japan. He explained, "People call all the other prefectures except for Okinawa *naichi*. But Okinawa is not a foreign country. I consider it inappropriate for this reason to make a distinction between 'inner' and 'outer' in the case of the Ryūkyū Islands, and I shall use the term 'the other prefectures' for what other people call *naichi*."[4] But having made this resolution, which he never broke, he was compelled again and again to admit that the people of the southern islands were unlike the rest of the Japanese in crucial respects.

The first major difference was that of language. Sasamori, as a native of Hirosaki, undoubtedly knew from personal experience how difficult it was for outsiders to understand the dialect spoken in that part of Japan. When it came to the language of Okinawa, he insisted that it too was just a dialect of Japanese, but he was obliged to admit that he could understand almost nothing. From the day of his arrival in Naha, the capital of Okinawa, he was faced with this problem: "When I landed there was a crowd of several hundred women gathered on the dock. Old and young alike were struggling to get to the front, pushing and shoving back and forth. Some held a bottle in one hand, others carried on their head a small parcel wrapped in cloth. The strangeness of their appearance and the noise they made defies description. Nothing they said was intelligible. I could barely make out that they wanted so many *kan* or so many hundred *mon* for something."[5]

The next day Sasamori felt even more exasperated over not understanding the language. He wrote in his diary, "Today I lost
my way again and again. I kept asking people I met, but I couldn't
understand a word they said. There was nothing I could do about
it."[6] Even a month later, he still could not understand anything, and
he had to rely on an interpreter. He worried that his ignorance of the
Ryūkyū language might offend (or amuse) people.[7] When Sasamori
later visited the outer islands he made the dismaying discovery that
each one had a different, mutually unintelligible dialect.[8]

The languages spoken in the Ryūkyū Islands are as different
from standard Japanese as French is from Italian, but Sasamori was
indignant when he heard Japanese say that "the physique and language of the inhabitants of the islands show the influence of the western lands;[9] it makes me more and more suspicious of such people."[10]
He pointed out that the language spoken in Okinawa contains various words that had become archaic in Japanese, such as *kozo* for "last
year," or *miki* for sake, and gave other examples of place-names and
personal names that retained old Japanese forms. His most earnest
wish was to prove that, despite the apparent differences, the Okinawan language is actually pure Japanese.[11]

Sasamori was determined from the beginning of his stay in Okinawa to accommodate himself to the local way of life. Despite his
resolution, however, he could not help being affected by the heat. He
recalled:

> Last year I spent the summer in Hokkaidō and Chishima.
> That is how it happened that I wore all summer the clothes I
> would wear in winter in *naichi*.[12] I didn't wear summer
> clothes—whether lined or unlined—even once. But when
> someone who has never been exposed to the blazing, year-
> long heat of summer in the tropics suddenly arrives there, it
> needs hardly be said what a physical shock he receives. That
> explains why, ever since I arrived in Naha, my head has been
> heavy all day long, and feels the way it did in old days in the

fief when I used to wear a helmet. I developed a fever, and my ⸱⸱ body ached so much I could not stand.[13]

There was nothing Sasamori could do about the heat, and he does not mention it again, though it remained blazing hot during his entire five months in Okinawa. When he traveled, he wore Okinawan dress, to the surprise of people he met.

"When I was given a formal welcome by the officials, I did not wear either a *haori* or a *hakama*.[14] I seem to have astonished everybody by wearing underwear of unlined banana-hemp cloth,[15] a white obi, drawers and leggings, and straw sandals."[16]

When he and some local people set out on a tour of inspection of Kunigami, at the northern end of the island of Okinawa, the others all carried Japanese-style lunch boxes, but Sasamori followed local customs: "I was the only one to have rice balls wrapped in banana leaves. When the others saw me open the leaves they couldn't help but laugh. I suppose this was because they thought that, since I had come on a special mission from Tokyo, I would carry a lunch box in the style of an official stationed in Okinawa, but instead (to their astonishment) I carried exactly the same kind of lunch as a woodcutter or country bumpkin."[17]

For all his desire to prove that Okinawan customs were basically the same as Japanese, Sasamori did not pretend that this was true of Okinawan food. The most elaborate Okinawan meal he describes was at a restaurant to which he was invited by the governor. His account does not make the place seem very attractive:

"The eaves were three or four feet lower than the fence. This made the room dark even at midday, and the heat was extreme. One room served both as a banquet hall and a place to sleep. There was nothing special about the interior decorations, but the place was indescribably cramped. There is not much difference between this place and a prison cell. The natives consider this to be a high-class place to buy pleasure."[18]

Sasamori admired the young geishas and liked their songs, even though he could not understand the words. Unfortunately, an ailment kept him from doing justice to the dinner, but he describes it with respect: "After tea and cakes they spread out delicacies from the mountains and the sea. The main dish is pork . . . I am told that they can make dozens of wonderful dishes, all from pork . . . I imagine that even Western people, for whom meat is the principal item of the diet, would have to yield to them in their skill of preparing pork."[19]

Sasamori visted an abbatoir in which pigs were slaughtered with such efficiency that "meat-eating foreigners who had a look at the plant were astonished by the skill."[20] He heard a rumor that in the Kōka era (1844–48) a Frenchman had visited Okinawa and taught the people the art of slaughtering pigs.

However much Sasamori admired the dexterity of the Okinawan butchers, he still seems to have missed Japanese cuisine. He described a meal he prepared for himself while on the island of Iriomote: "I took out some of the rice I had brought with me and boiled it. I bought an egg and put it in the rice bowl, and poured onto it a little of the soy sauce I had brought along. This was my evening meal. There were no pickles and no miso. And, of course, no soup. There is really a poor man's journey."[21]

Despite Sasamori's insistence that the Okinawans and the Japanese were of the same race and culture, he kept being made aware of dissimilarities. The extent of Chinese influence in Okinawa seems to have surprised him. When he visited Shuri Castle he could not help but recognize that the buildings were modeled on Chinese rather than Japanese examples.[22] There were Confucian temples with statues of Confucius, and the Confucian classics were the basis of what education existed in Okinawa. It may seem strange that a samurai whose own education had consisted largely of learning to read and write *kambun* should have been surprised by similar traditions in Okinawa, but he could not detect the kind of process of naturalization of the Chinese classics that had occurred in Japan. Confucian culture in Okinawa seemed to involve a worship of China itself, and the old documents of the Ryūkyū kingdom were dated with Chinese rather than Japanese reign-names.

Some Japanese, worried over this situation, advocated destroying the Confucian statues and temples, in the belief that as long as they were tolerated, it would be impossible to rid the Okinawan people of their worship of China. Sasamori was shocked by this proposal:

"Ah, they said the Confucian temples should be destroyed and the statues broken, but that the people should not be deprived of their Japanese spirit. I never would have expected there to be such heedless advocates of enlightenment. Their stupidity was really to be pitied, but how could so deplorable a development be permitted? Fortunately, there were intelligent people at the time and they did not allow the temples to be destroyed. This is truly a matter of rejoicing for the nation."[23]

He urged instead that the Confucian temples in Okinawa be cleaned and restored. His respect for Confucius was too great to permit vandalism. Chinese influence in Okinawa was not restricted to the Confucian temples. Sasamori noticed that at the crossroads in every village there were stone monuments inscribed with the names of a Chinese hero who was believed to ward off harm, and that people pasted on their doors slips of red paper with the names of gods who protected the house.[24] They also followed the Chinese practice of burning paper in a special stone structure. He wrote, "If the villagers have old paper they bring it here and burn it inside. They never use old paper for toilet paper, like people from the other prefectures. This may be because they venerate written words as gods and feel they must repay the gods' favors. The veneration of writing must be accounted a good custom."[25]

Some prominent Okinawans who found China more congenial than Japan had traveled to China to ask for help in restoring the old order.[26] The Chinese, for their part, refused to admit that the Ryūkyū Islands were Japanese territory until they were defeated in the Sino-

Japanese War of 1894–95; but there was little they could do to end the Japanese occupation. Members of the old aristocracy in particular made appeals to the Chinese for their protection, but Sasamori was sure that such appeals could have not the slightest effect.[27]

Shō Tai, the last king of the Ryūkyū Islands, after reigning thirty-one years was compelled by the Japanese authorities in 1879 to move to Tokyo and to give up his throne in return for being made a marquis. The king himself was naturally resentful over being deposed, and the people of Okinawa—not only the nobility but also many common-ers—opposed the Japanese action. Sasamori, though certainly no par-tisan of the king, felt obliged to record instances of the worshipful respect still accorded to Shō Tai and his family. For example, on June 19 Prince Kitashirakawa (1847–1895), a representative of the Jap-anese government, paid a state visit to Okinawa. He called on Shō Tai (who had been allowed by the Japanese to return to Okinawa in 1884) to present his compliments. He also offered his respects at the royal tombs. Despite these conciliatory gestures, not one member of the six or seven major noble families accepted Prince Kitashirakawa's invitation to a banquet held a few days later. When the prince was to tour the island, the officials at the prefectural office asked permission to use Shō Tai's palanquin, only to be informed that there was no such thing; but when the prince was about to leave the island, word came that the palanquin existed after all, and it was brought to him. Sasamori, who refused to call the ex-king anything but Mr. Shō, com-mented, "A complete contradiction! What discourtesy!"[28]

He then described the reception given by the people of Okinawa to Prince Kitashirakawa:

When the prince toured the various sites, the streets of Naha were full of spectators. The police inspector and the entire con-stabulary turned out, and they informed the people on the

proper way to show their respect, but some obstinate Okinawans resisted the police. However, if anyone of Mr. Shō's
family should go by, they bow down to the ground to express
their respect. That is why nobody from the other prefectures
who happens to be here can control his anger over their disrespect. Ah, these two or three incidents tell us more than enough
about how the people of Shuri and Naha feel about us.[29]

Sasamori noted with indignation, "One thing that attracted attention on this occasion was that even though Mr. Shō and his family
had rickshaws at their disposal, they went in palanquins, differing in
no particle from the coming and going of a daimyo's retinue in the
old days. Moreover, the Okinawans showed this procession the pro-
foundest marks of respect, far more than toward the prince."[30]

Later, when he went to Shuri, he noticed, "In front of every
house along the road from Naha they had spread mats, and men and
women sat formally in rows. I asked the reason, and I was told,
'Today, at the invitation of the governor, Shō Ten [Shō Tai's son] and
his family are to pass. Everybody has turned out to pay their respects.'"[31] Their attitude recalls Narushima Ryūhoku's description
of how the people of Florence displayed greater respect for the deposed grand duke than for the new king of Italy.

The Japanese considered various solutions to the problem of what
to do about this potential source of disorder and perhaps even rebellion. Some favored "showing the virtue of conciliation in order to in-
duce them to support the main tenets."[32] Others insisted that the only
safe course was to move Shō Tai and his whole family to Tokyo. The
problem was not restricted to the disposition of the Shō family, but involved the attitude of many Okinawans that the Japanese were in-
truders. Sasamori reported that there was not a single instance of an
Okinawan marrying a person from "the other prefectures," nor was
there a single person from "the other prefectures" who had taken up
permanent residence in Okinawa.[33] In contrast, "Even though people

from Europe and America belong to a different race, they often become naturalized in our country and marry Japanese."[34] He came to the sad conclusion: "The natives' feeling is one of strong attachment to the restoration of the old régime, and for this reason their attitude has not been satisfactory to this day."[35]

Sasamori was absolutely certain it was better for the Okinawans to be under the enlightened rule of the Meiji government than under the former system, when they had their own king but paid tribute to both the lords of Satsuma and the emperor of China. However, he had the integrity to listen to contrary opinions and to quote them in his diary. For example, he met on Amami Ōshima a man of some importance who told him, "The old régime resembled despotism, but because it looked after the islanders with kindness, as if they all really belonged to one family, conditions were not as confused as they are now. When backward islanders acquire a superficial modernism or, in extreme cases, hope for the implementation of a system of towns and villages, the results are actually far less satisfactory than under the old régime."[36]

Sasamori refused to assent to the paternalism implicit in this attitude. He desperately wanted to believe that the people of the southern islands were Japanese and, as subjects of the emperor, should enjoy the same privileges as any other Japanese. His survey of life in the islands came as a shock to someone with these convictions. Even before he left Hirosaki he had known of the health problems, but he was not prepared for the dreadful reality. The first and most terrible shock came on June 19, 1893, when he was making a survey of the Kunigami region of Okinawa. He noticed a few small huts that had been built in an otherwise deserted area and, wondering who lived there, asked the policeman who accompanied him. The latter replied, "Lepers." Sasamori said he would like to have a look, but the others with him tried to dissuade him, saying, "The smell is something terrible. Don't try to get any closer."

Sasamori relates in his diary,

I answered them, "They may be lepers, but they are still children of His Majesty, the emperor. Even if nobody else wants
to join me, I definitely want to see them." I scrambled up a
rocky height and reached the huts. They were hovels, not four
feet high, and about twelve feet on all sides. Hay was spread
on the earthen floor. I saw a woman about twenty and a girl
about seven. Their entire bodies were rotting, and I could
smell them from some distance, even before I reached their
hut. One look was enough to make my hair stand on end.[37]

Nothing Sasamori saw later on was quite as horrifying as this experience, but when he left the main island of Okinawa in order to inspect the outer islands, people warned him, "It's the time of year
when sickness is prevalent on the outer islands. Do take care of yourself."[38] But even before he encountered sickness, he was confronted
by poverty of a degree he had never known before. He wrote about
one hamlet on the island of Ishigaki,

I arrived at the Nagura guardhouse. No sign of anyone. The
guardhouse was in a state of extreme dilapidation, in miserable
condition as one could tell at a glance; it was like an abandoned
old shrine in some remote village in the other prefectures.
There were six houses in the whole village, with a population
of ten men and six women . . . The state of dilapidation of the
six houses was far worse than that of the guardhouse, in a condition one could never see in the other prefectures . . . Ah, if
the Ryūkyūs were a possession of China I could look on such
conditions with indifference, but when I thought that these
were subjects of the Japanese Empire, His Majesty's children,
as a sentient being the sight made me want to cry out in lamen-
tation, and even that would not be enough.[39]

Even in the most wretched village, where the inhabitants seemed
to possess absolutely nothing, the tax collectors were merciless, and

the officials, members of the old samurai class, were lazy and corrupt, utterly indifferent to the misery around them.

Wherever Sasamori traveled in the outer islands, he encountered disease. Malaria seems to have been the most prevalent, but he generally lumped together all tropical diseases as *fūdobyō* (endemic diseases), and it is hard to be sure exactly which disease he meant. No medicine was available to cope with the symptoms of malaria. Sasamori wrote in indignation,

> Quinine is the principal medicine used in treating this disease, and it is the accepted opinion among doctors that the patient must not neglect to take it every day. I hope that in the future trial plantings of the trees will be made, and the results examined. However, as is the way in backward regions, it is difficult to get anything accomplished. The village officials say such things as, "What does the trial planting of trees have to do with me, an official?" and show even less interest in considering this than the ordinary citizen. Is this not the height of the deplorable?[40]

Sasamori carried with him a supply of quinine that he gave to malaria patients he encountered. In every instance the quinine proved to be effective, but there was no other medical assistance available. When he went to the island of Iriomote, he asked if there were any doctors, and was told that until two years before there had been a hospital in one village, but that it had been closed. He wrote in his diary, "Ever since then, there has been an itinerant doctor, but he made a tour here only once, last August, and this year he has not come even once. This is an area of disease without a hospital, without a doctor. I have visited the fourteen villages on the island of Iriomote, a disease area where there are 1,214 people, and on behalf of the people of this contagion ward, I protest to the world."[41]

In Sasamori's original manuscript the last phrase was, "I protest to the empire of Japan."[42]

Sasamori had come close to admitting that even under enlightened Japanese rule (as opposed to the feudalistic rule of the Ryūkyū kings), some Japanese subjects were treated far worse than others. Disease, uncontrolled by medicine, had drastically reduced the population of many of the southern islands. He discovered on consulting old records of Komi village on Iriomote that in 1753 the population had been 767 persons, and the village itself had been considered to be "a prosperous place that typifies the entire island of Iriomote."[43] Now the population was 142 persons, and "when I walked through the village and examined the remains of the houses that used to be here, there were more than eighty. What man, regardless of whether he is wise or foolish, as long as he has blood in his veins, could fail to feel compassion for this heartrending situation?"[44]

In the village Sasamori met the mayor. Here is his description of the man: "A corpulent man who appeared in formal costume. He wore a wide Chinese brocade sash over a banana-hemp kimono, and a *haori* over it. His appearance at first glance seemed no inferior to that of a high-ranked official, and I was told that he was a leading official on the island."[45]

The man spoke Japanese. (Sasamori, unwilling to suggest that the language of *all* Okinawans was not Japanese, adopted the local usage and said the man spoke "Yamato language."[46]) Sasamori asked if there were any people suffering from endemic diseases. He continued,

> As usual, the answer was no. When I had strolled through the village a little while before I had seen several sick people, and I pursued the matter, at which he merely bowed his head. I couldn't stand the mystery, and I suggested we start talking with our brushes.[47] [I wrote,] "Year after year the population decreases and the tax burden gets heavier and heavier. You should really feel compassion for the people's suffering. What

do the senior people of this place plan to do in the future to relieve the distress?" Answer: "I am someone who uses his
salary to support his family. I don't know what would be good
to do in order to prevent the population from decreasing and I
don't know any way to relieve poverty. It was simply because
of seniority that I was assigned to this place."

At this point Sasamori exploded with wrath: "If I were to try to
read what is in his mind, it would be that it is quite sufficient as long
as the samurai class can keep the commoners under control and
support their own families. It is all too evident that they judge that
the life-and-death sufferings of the commoners are no concern of
theirs."[48]

The situation with respect to education in the southern islands
was almost as bad as the health problem. There was supposed to be a
Confucian school in Komi village, but "the fact is that there are now
no teachers and no pupils and the school has ceased to exist."[49] No
schooling was available for the children of the more than seven hundred people who lived in the area. Sasamori saw before the village office on the island of Ishigaki a sign openly stating that there were no
schools.[50] Even in districts of Okinawa where schools existed, only a
small proportion of the children of school age attended. For example,
in one village in the Nakagami district of Okinawa there were 75
boys and 6 girls attending school out of over 1,600 children of school
age.[51] In the Kunigami district there were two schools with four
teachers, but only 61 pupils (52 boys and 9 girls) out of 1,178 children.[52] On the island of Miyako he was told by a teacher that the
school had been temporarily closed because of some local disturbance. Sasamori was enraged:

"To prevent pupils from attending school because the parents are
dissatisfied with the government is to treat their own children with
contempt. Their stupidity is pitiable."[53]

Although education was by no means widespread in the Ryūkyū
Islands, some Japanese were reluctant to admit that educating the

children in the region was of any value unless it inculcated the principle of devotion to the Japanese state. They said, " 'What is the meaning of education anyway if it does not preach loyalty and patriotism? What is the purpose of education? If one doesn't teach the way of loyalty and patriotism, and one still wishes to lead children on the path to the good, how is this to be achieved?' "[54]

Sasamori did not agree. He feared that if an unquestioning adherence to the principle of loyalty and patriotism became the central feature of education in the Ryūkyū Islands, it might easily lead to a revival of allegiance to the Ryūkyū royal family and to China. This was what he feared most of all; his interest in the southern islands stemmed originally from his concern over the defenses of Japan, and if the people of the islands were alienated by inept propaganda, this would be a disaster for Japan. He therefore insisted, in good Confucian terms, that children at school be taught the philosophic meaning of loyalty and patriotism so that there would be no danger of misunderstanding the terms or using them with reference to the wrong ruler and the wrong country. "Moreover, if one does not teach this because one fears the consequences, how does it differ from prohibiting the use of fire because one fears a conflagration? Who would not laugh at such stupidity?"[55]

The situation in the Ryūkyū Islands, as Sasamori clearly revealed, was desperate. Disease was rampant. Taxes were ruthlessly collected even from those least able to pay. Most children were denied an education. In many villages the population was dwindling and in some there were no children. The local officials were corrupt and indifferent to the suffering of the people. Japanese rule of the islands had obviously not brought about prosperity.

Sasamori stubbornly refused to admit that, apart from a few dissimilarities, the Japanese and the Okinawans might be different peoples. He frequently alluded to the legend that Minamoto Tametomo (1139–1177) had escaped from Izu and made his way to Okinawa, where he founded a dynasty of kings. He was also inclined to believe that after the Battle of Dannoura, at which the Taira forces were decisively defeated, some Taira warriors had fled to Ishigaki. He related, "I went to the hamlet of Karahama. I saw signposts marked 'Yamato graves' and 'Yashima graves.'[56] I got down off my horse and went into the woods. Some ten paces into the woods there was a cave containing human bones. I lit the incense I had brought with me and offered a prayer for their souls."[57] Sasamori was assured that these were the bones of Taira warriors, but (as a Confucianist who believed in "investigating things and refining one's knowledge"), he announced his intention of taking one skull back to Tokyo and having it examined by experts there. "If they should decide that these are actually Taira remains, I intend to build a shrine and to worship them." Sasamori referred to the skull several times later in the diary and, true to his word, after carrying the skull with him throughout his second circuit of the islands, he took it to Tokyo where he turned it over to an expert.[58]

Regardless of whether or not some inhabitants of the Ryūkyū Islands were descendants of Minamoto Tametomo or of the Taira warriors, there was undoubtedly a mutual feeling of alienation between the local people and "the people of other prefectures." The Japanese frequently accused the Okinawans of being ungrateful. For example, in a village where there were no doctors, the local policeman often doubled as a physician, but if the sick person recovered, he never thanked the policeman. One such policeman asked Sasamori, "Is it because they think it is only natural for a policeman to cure people? Or is it because they are cold-hearted? I have treated I don't know how many people, but it hasn't done the least bit of good."[59]

Sasamori quoted someone who had told him, "The history books always say that their ways are simple and honest and so on, but they don't deny that these people have a tendency to be cold-hearted."[60] Sasamori's informant further related that every year no fewer than one hundred people traveled from the main islands to the Ryūkyūs. During the ten years between 1879 and 1889 well over a thousand people had come to the islands, but not one had remained. The man went on, "It is not only that the customs and the language are different, but [those from elsewhere] cannot help disliking their unfeeling-ness. Unless by chance there are feelings of mutual affection, it is like living temporarily in a foreign country. They consider us to be for-eigners, and because most natives share this feeling, there is a ten-dency for us, too, to think of them as foreigners."[61]

Even if men from the other prefectures took native women as their wives or mistresses, they never took them back to the "other prefectures" when they returned. Perhaps this was because the women insisted on remaining behind. "I have the impression that the wives are determined not to leave the island and go to Japan, a for-eign country, even if it means separating from their husbands and children."[62] Or perhaps, as the case of Minamoto Tametomo (who tried unsuccessfully to take his Okinawan bride with him back to Japan only to be prevented by the turbulent seas) suggests, "Ever since that day, going to Honshū has been for women something for-bidden by the gods of the sea."[63] More likely, the men were embar-rassed to show their "foreign" brides to their families at home. But, regardless of the cause, it was evident to Sasamori's informant that lasting marriages between Japanese and Okinawans were impossible. One can imagine how disappointed Sasamori was by this disagree-able conclusion.

It is noteworthy that virtually every person with whom Sasamori talked while he was in the southern islands was (to judge from the names) from "the other prefectures." The village officials were Oki-nawans, but every official of consequence was from *naichi*, as were all the policemen and almost every prosperous merchant. Sasamori took this as a matter of course and never commented on it. Instead, he vented his indignation on the only natives of the region with whom he had dealings, the local officials. When he called at some village of-fice, there was usually nobody there.[64] Even when he did succeed in meeting an official, the man's irresponsibility generally infuriated Sasamori, as in the following instance:

"When I asked the village official if there was any endemic disease [malaria], as usual he answered that there wasn't any. When I made an actual inspection, I discovered that one man, two women, and one child were actually suffering from this sickness. When I gave them some quinine pills I had brought with me, they joined their hands in prayer and thanks for my kindness. I was so enraged that when I left the village I swore at the official. He bowed to the ground before me and did not say one word."[65]

Perhaps the situation was not really the fault of the officials, who were badly paid and had to fend for themselves and their families, as Sasamori recognized.[66] The same held true of the doctors, whose failure to visit the outer islands had so incensed Sasamori. When Sasamori asked a doctor why he let months go by without visiting some islands, the doctor cited the miserable fees that were paid for visits to the epidemic areas. "How many people do you suppose there are who, in order to earn ten yen a month, will brave ten thousand miles of angry waves and go into a disease-ridden desert?"[67] Doctors were not immune to malaria, and they often ran out of quinine. They had to pay for the quinine they administered to the patients, but often the patients could not reimburse them. The villagers, afraid that the doctor would demand payment, often hid sick persons when he visited and they actually hated it when he came.[68]

Clearly, the responsibility rested with the government in Tokyo, but Sasamori was too loyal a samurai to consider the political implications of the disastrous situation in the Ryūkyū Islands. Undoubtedly he was much relieved to depart.

Sasamori several times compared the Okinawans with the Ainu. He believed that the agricultural techniques of the Ainu were superior,[69] but on the whole he thought that the Okinawans were more advanced, even though the fertility of their soil had made them lazy:

"Although one may attribute it to the inveterate habits of the people, it is the natural fertility of the land that makes them easy-going and lazy, reluctant to exert themselves even if this means con-tenting themselves with coarse food and badly made clothes. As a place of corrupt public morals, they are beyond comparison with anywhere in the other prefectures."[70]

This view, recorded in his diary shortly before he left the south-ern islands, suggests disenchantment with a place he wanted des-perately to like, and his comparison of the Okinawans to the Ainu suggests, despite his denials, that some doubt lingered in Sasamori as to whether or not the Okinawans should really be considered Japanese.

Before Sasamori left Hirosaki to go south, he had worried about the poisonous snakes in Okinawa. He mentions only casually in his diary that he killed four deadly snakes on his travels.[71] On another occasion, while in a dark toilet, "Something cold licked my behind. For a moment I was panic-stricken, imagining that I was being at-tacked by a poisonous snake. Ah, I thought, what a shame to die be-fore I can accomplish my plans! I really felt bitter toward heaven. I threw away my umbrella and let the rain fall over my whole body. Then I thought about it calmly, and tried rubbing the place, and I re-alized that I hadn't been bitten by a poisonous snake! I had been as-saulted by a pig! My joy can be imagined."[72] Sasamori (like Takezoe and Matsuura before him) had been licked by a hungry but not frightening animal. It must have made him painfully aware just how far from "the other prefectures" he was.

Notes

1. Azuma Yoshimochi, *Nantō Tanken*, I, p. 7.
2. *Ibid.*, p. 10.
3. *Ibid.*, p. 8. The entry is dated May 10, 1893. That evening Sasamori left for Aomori, the first stage of his journey.
4. *Ibid.*, p. 14.
5. *Ibid.*, p. 17. One *kan* was 960 *mon*, a copper coin (with a square hole). This

currency was superseded in 1872 by the sen and yen, but the old manner of referring to money apparently persisted in Okinawa.

6. *Ibid.*, p. 18.

7. *Ibid.*, p. 70.

8. *Ibid.*, p. 176. He gave the breakdown of the languages spoken on Miyako Island as: 45 percent Miyako dialect; 20 percent Japanese; 25 percent Okinawan; 8 percent Yaeyama dialect; and 2 percent Chinese.

9. The word *seido* designates any country to the west of Japan. It probably refers to China here.

10. Azuma, *Nantō Tanken*, II, p. 80.

11. *Ibid.*, p. 81.

12. Although Sasamori objected to the use of *naichi* when making a distinction between Okinawa and the rest of Japan, he used it to distinguish Hokkaidō and the northern territories from the islands of Honshū, Shikoku, and Kyūshū.

13. Azuma, *Nantō Tanken*, I, p. 45.

14. Parts of traditional formal wear. The *haori* is a cloak, and the *hakama* is a kind of divided skirt. This would have been the costume expected of Sasamori as a visitor sent by the government.

15. Cloth woven of fiber from the banana plant (*bashōfu*); also known as abaca cloth. The typical textile of Okinawa.

16. Azuma, *Nantō Tanken*, I, p. 70. The frontispiece of Azuma's book is a picture of Sasamori, apparently showing him as he looked in Okinawa. In addition to some of the items of clothing mentioned, a fan (*uchiwa*) is suspended around his neck. He carries in his left hand a large black umbrella, and in his right what seems to be a towel, probably to wipe off sweat.

17. *Ibid.*, p. 69.

18. *Ibid.*, II, pp. 120–21.

19. *Ibid.*, p. 121.

20. *Ibid.*, I, p. 137.

21. *Ibid.*, p. 200.

22. *Ibid.*, p. 20.

23. *Ibid.*, p. 35.

24. *Ibid.*, p. 107.

25. *Ibid.*, pp. 108–9.

26. *Ibid.*, p. 42.

27. *Ibid.*, II, p. 200.

28. *Ibid.*, I, p. 131.
29. *Ibid.*, pp. 131–32.
30. *Ibid.*, p. 133.
31. *Ibid.*, II, p. 123.
32. *Ibid.*, p. 204.
33. *Ibid.*
34. *Ibid.*
35. *Ibid.*
36. *Ibid.*, pp. 243–44.
37. *Ibid.*, I, p. 86.
38. *Ibid.*, p. 171.
39. *Ibid.*, p. 189.
40. *Ibid.*, p. 202.
41. *Ibid.*, p. 214.
42. *Ibid.*, p. 269.
43. *Ibid.*, p. 211.
44. *Ibid.*
45. *Ibid.*
46. Yamato was the usual Okinawan appellation for *naichi*, the three main is-
    lands of Japan in premodern times.
47. This suggests that although the mayor is said to speak Japanese well,
    Sasamori thought that when it came to complicated matters it was prefer-
    able to write out questions and answers, in a manner similar to that which
    Japanese and Chinese, who did not speak each other's language, employed.
    Or perhaps he simply wanted the mayor's answers in writing.
48. Azuma, *Nantō Tanken*, I, p. 211.
49. *Ibid.*, p. 262.
50. *Ibid.*, II, p. 39.
51. *Ibid.*, p. 149.
52. *Ibid.*, I, p. 73.
53. *Ibid.*, p. 175.
54. *Ibid.*, II, p. 4.
55. *Ibid.*
56. Yashima may be a reference to the battle of Yashima (in Shikoku) where
    the Taira suffered the second of three major defeats in the warfare at the
    end of the twelfth century.
57. Azuma, *Nantō Tanken*, II, p. 26.
58. *Ibid.*, p. 298.

59. *Ibid.*, p. 36.
60. *Ibid.*, p. 122.
61. *Ibid.*
62. *Ibid.*
63. *Ibid.*
64. *Ibid.*, p. 98.
65. *Ibid.*, pp. 18–19.
66. *Ibid.*, p. 19.
67. *Ibid.*, p. 59.
68. *Ibid.*, p. 60.
69. *Ibid.*, I, p. 80.
70. *Ibid.*, II, pp. 215–16.
71. *Ibid.*, p. 216.
72. *Ibid.*, I, p. 240.

Bibliography

Azuma Yoshimochi. *Nantō Tanken*, 2 vols., in Tōyō Bunko series. Tokyo: Heibonsha, 1982–83.

Writers
Abroad

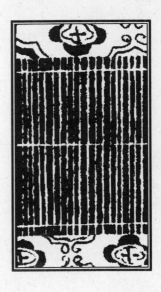

The Diaries of Mori Ōgai

During the late Tokugawa period a small number of Japanese traveled abroad for study, sometimes with official permission but more often illegally. These young men had decided that the only way to save Japan, at a time when its existence seemed threatened by the intrusion of foreign powers, was to go to those countries and master their sciences, especially the science of war. Yoshida Shōin (1830–1859), though a passionate advocate of *sonnō jōi* (revere the emperor and drive out the barbarians!), attempted to make his way to America by stowing aboard Commodore Perry's flagship *Powhattan* when it was anchored off Shimoda. He failed in this attempt, but other Japanese, often with the connivance of foreigners who were resident in Japan, managed to travel to America or Europe.

Their troubles were by no means over once they reached foreign soil. First they had to learn a foreign language and to become accustomed to unfamiliar ways. They sometimes encountered great kindness, but often they were looked upon as curiosities, and, to their dismay, well-intentioned persons exerted pressure on them to become Christians. Quite apart from the mental stress, they often were confronted with weather more severe than any they had known in Japan, and they contracted tuberculosis and other illnesses, as we know from the graves of young Japanese in foreign cemeteries. While living abroad, they were most often completely on their own; there were no diplomatic or consular officials to aid them in emergencies.

The situation for the Japanese abroad improved markedly after the opening of the country, and by 1882 there were Japanese, often with government grants, studying at the principal universities of Europe and America. Of all the Japanese sent abroad at this time Mori Ōgai (1862–1922) was probably the most successful in his relations, not only with his teachers but also with the people among whom he lived. He kept two diaries that chronicled his experiences at this time. The first, *Kōsai Nikki* (Diary of a Voyage to the West), opens on August 23, 1884, when he left Tokyo for Yokohama where he was to board a ship bound for Europe, and ends with his arrival in Germany on October 11 of that year. The second diary, *Doitsu Nikki* (German Diary), opens on the following day and continues almost to the end of Ōgai's stay in Europe three and a half years later.

Ōgai, an army officer by profession, had received on June 17 the order, "You will proceed to Germany and study public hygiene, and in addition you will investigate military medical practices." He would be traveling on orders and not of his own volition, but there is no mistaking his joy over being sent abroad: "When once I had completed my studies at the university I was eager to go, as soon as possible, to the West. It was clear to me that present-day medicine had come to us from the West. Even supposing one can read their writing and pronounce their words, unless one has personally set foot on their soil, it is no more than an ingenious exercise in translation."[1]

Ōgai was by no means sentimental at the prospect of leaving Japan for a period of four years. While his ship was still in Japanese waters he composed a *kanshi* in which he insisted on the closeness of Japan to the rest of the world, though it was far more common to remark on its isolation. He mentions in the poem Hayashi Shihei (1738–1793) who, some ninety years earlier (in 1786), in his *Kaikoku*

Heidan (Military Talks for a Naval Country) had pointed out that an unbroken stretch of water links Japan to the West:

> *Why shed such tears on saying goodbye?*
> *East or West, surely people are people.*[2]
> *Do you remember what old Hayashi wrote:*
> *Shinagawa's waters touch the Atlantic.*[3]

Ōgai had nine other Japanese as his companions on the voyage to Europe. He celebrated his new friendships by composing a *kanshi* in which he epitomized each of the Japanese. The tone is humorous, especially in the description of himself:

> *Mori alone seems tranquil and unconcerned;*
> *His snores are like thunder, but who dares rebuke him?*

The poem concludes:

> *One year, when they complete their stay in Europe,*
> *And return home, what reputations will they enjoy?*[4]

Although the conclusion suggests some uncertainty about how the Japanese students will fare once they return to Japan, the prevailing note of not only this poem but also the whole diary is youthfully optimistic.

Each of the places glimpsed from the ship inspired Ōgai to compose a *kanshi*. Some are in an elegiac mood that probably owes more to convention than to his actual feelings. Shipboard life was a good deal pleasanter than at home, as he related in this poem:

> *Life aboard ship is not busy the way it is at home;*
> *I get my fill of sleep and wake as dawn comes through the porthole.*
> *A boy rings a bell a couple of times to rouse me from bed,*
> *And offers me coffee, a cupful of fragrance.*[5]

Undoubtedly it was more agreeable to be awakened by the tinkle of a bell than by a bugle, and also pleasant to have coffee brought by a steward. Another *kanshi* relates how, when it was hot, a steward came to turn on an overhead fan. Aboard ship the young Ōgai led the life of a gentleman.

The first port of call was Hong Kong. There was a Japanese consulate and Ōgai went there before going anywhere else. He was treated to a Japanese meal, and wrote of the raw fish and vegetables, rice and pickles, "The meal sufficed to wash from my mouth the taste of the Western food I had been eating for ten days."[6] That night, however, Ōgai returned to the ship to sleep. He explained, "That was because of the fear of robbers." These are almost exactly the same words that Narushima Ryūhoku used in his diary for 1872 to explain why he did not spend the night ashore. Hong Kong may indeed have been dangerous at night, but this was only the first of many resemblances between Ōgai's diary and Ryūhoku's. Perhaps Ōgai, like the poets of the past who sought out places mentioned in poetry by their predecessors, was consciously following in the footsteps of Ryūhoku. Unquestionably, he was familiar with Ryūhoku's diary.

In Hong Kong Ōgai visited a public garden, the zoo, and a hospital, but was unable to secure permission to visit the British military barracks. Like earlier Japanese visitors to Hong Kong, he was impressed by what the British had done to turn an unimportant little island into a thriving center of commerce. One of his *kanshi* concludes:

> *Who could have predicted this overgrown, uninhabited spot*
> *Ceded to the British would one day harbor countless ships?*[7]

The visits to Saigon and Singapore elicited further expressions of admiration for the colonial powers, including a *kanshi* on Singapore in which Ōgai pictured the British as alchemists who had transformed the base metal of the island into gold.[8]

Ōgai visited a Buddhist temple while he was in Ceylon. The description of his visit is typical of the telegraphic style he used in this diary, no doubt in imitation of the classical Chinese writers of the past: "I went into a Buddhist temple. There is a statue of Shakyamuni in Nirvana, and flowers are offered in ceramic vessels. A smell of incense pervades the building. The faces of the priests are like images of arhats.[9] They wear yellow surplices and leather shoes.[10] Sutras inscribed on palm leaves are kept in the temple. The writing resembles Braille."[11]

The most important statement in *Diary of a Voyage to the West* occurs near the end, after Ōgai has reached Germany. He writes, "I have arrived in Cologne in Germany. I understand German! I've come here and I've been able to escape the malady of being deaf and dumb. This is really a delight."[12] Ōgai was delighted that the German he had learned in Japan was intelligible to German people; his proficiency would be a critical factor in his successful residence abroad.

It did not take Ōgai long to fit into German society, but initially at least he must have experienced some difficulty with the fine points of German etiquette. We can infer as much from his account in *German Diary* describing his courtesy call on the army surgeon Hashimoto Tsunazune after his arrival in Berlin in October 1884. He recorded,

> When I entered his room I made a profound bow only to be admonished by Mr. Hashimoto. "Bowing so low you all but touch your head to the ground is simply not done," he said with a wave of his hand. Later, when I asked people about this, I was told that in Europe before a child can be said to be educated he must study with a dancing master who carefully teaches him how to stand, how to sit, how to show respect, how to kneel. For this reason, after one has lived here a long time and spent time exclusively with the local people, when one suddenly sees the crude behavior of a Japanese it is unbearably funny.[13]

Ōgai seemed to have learned this lesson quickly. At any rate, there is no suggestion in his diary that he was ever subjected to mockery because of his "crude behavior." About two years later, however, he met a Japanese at the Café Royal about whom he wrote, "He was short and thin and had a dark complexion. He startled the people at nearby tables by executing a Japanese-style bow in his Western clothes."[14] When Ōgai met the same man on New Year's Day 1887 he reported, "He is still Japanese-style."[15] By this time Ōgai was so accustomed to German ways that "Japanese-style" had come to seem comic to him, too.

Ōgai was wearing a Japanese military uniform when he arrived in Berlin, but the army attaché ordered him to wear civilian clothes because the uniform made him too conspicuous. Ōgai had no choice but to follow orders though he had difficulty squeezing the money for a suit of clothes from his meager allowance.[16] But the attaché was right: it was easier for Ōgai to mix with other students in civilian clothes than in a uniform. A few days later he recorded that when he went to call on the professor under whom he was to study he wore a black coat and white gloves for the occasion. The gloves were purchased, but he borrowed the coat from another Japanese.

Ōgai seems to have had no trouble in making friends with his fellow students. He was invited to join a singing society, and soon afterward an article appeared in the newspaper stating that distinguished guests of the society included the grand duke of Mecklenburg and "the Japanese army doctor Mori."[17] A few months later he was asked by an acquaintance if he would become a member of the Kreuzbrüder. He recorded, "I had no idea what this might be, but I accepted for the fun of it." He accordingly went through the rites of initiation. One of the rules of the organization was that every newly inducted member had to relate three mistakes he had made in his life. (However, affianced or married members were obliged to relate only two mistakes.) Ōgai commented, "There were many other pranks of a similar nature. Probably they use the money that accumulates in fines to help the poor."[18] It can hardly be doubted that Ōgai was popular with his fellow students, and he enjoyed his life at the universities of Leipzig and Munich as few Japanese students had done before.

Hardly had Ōgai arrived in Germany than his superiors gave him quite contrary recommendations as to how he should spend his four years abroad. The army surgeon Hashimoto advised him to devote his full energies to the study of public hygiene: "Other people have been sent from Japan to investigate all aspects of Germany in detail. You should devote yourself exclusively to the study of hygiene, and only hygiene."[19] The next day (October 13, 1884) Ōgai met Aoki Shūzō, the Japanese minister, an imposing man with a flowing beard, who told him, "Yes, it's a good thing for you to study hygiene. But when you get back home you will probably find it difficult to put directly into practice what you have learned. Theories of hygiene are of no use to people who go around with the thongs of geta inserted between their toes. Learning does not consist merely of reading books. If you examine carefully the ways of thinking of Europeans, their lives, their manners, that alone will be quite sufficient an accomplishment for your study abroad."[20]

Ōgai does not say which advice he preferred, but when he went the next day to consult Hashimoto about his course of study in hygiene, he was given a schedule that he was expected to follow. First, he was to go to Leipzig for study with Professor Franz Hoffmann, then to Munich for Professor Max von Pettenkofer, and finally a period in Berlin studying under the great Robert Koch. Ōgai essentially followed this program, but he also managed to heed Minister Aoki's advice and observe life in Europe.

Ōgai attended the theater frequently while he was in Germany. He never indicates that he had trouble understanding the dialogue even of classical plays, a tribute to his proficiency in German. Occasionally in his diary he praises an actor, but his chief interest in the theater may have been the sharing of the pleasure of the German people around him. Unlike many Japanese who traveled in Europe, Ōgai seems to have been uninterested in scenery or natural beauty, though he occasionally devoted a few lines to the description of a public garden or to mention the flowering of cherry trees. Here is one such passage:

"I went into the garden. The plants and flowers were in full bloom. There were many marble statues. Behind them was a grove of chestnut trees. They had red and white flowers. There are many pigeons. They have a white ring around their necks. They are rather larger than the Japanese variety."[21]

The laconic expression is evidence that this diary, though now in Japanese, was originally composed in classical Chinese; the flatness of the tone suggests Ōgai's lack of interest in such sights. When he rented a room in Munich, for example, it was only afterward that he discovered the kind of view it commanded: "I happened to glance outside and saw the sunlight shining on the green of Teresia Meadow, and the statue of the goddess Bavaria rose high in the sky. To the south of the meadow, mountains could be seen in the distance. When I first rented this room I paid no attention to this extraordinary view. I had to laugh at my own inattentiveness."[22]

In contrast to his indifference to scenery, Ōgai evinced unusual interest in faces, and almost always gave a brief description of the appearance of people he met before he related the subject matter of their conversation. This was true not only of Europeans but also of the Japanese he met in Germany. His description of army minister Ōyama Iwao (1842–1916): "He is a tall man with a dark complexion and a face pitted with pockmarks. His voice is very gentle, almost like a woman's."[23] This, needless to say, is only a brief sketch of first impressions, but such sketches do not appear often in other diaries of the time. They indicate that Ōgai's chief interest while in Germany was in the people he met.

Probably no earlier visitor to Europe participated as fully as Ōgai in the life of the country in which he resided. His first New Year's Day in Germany was spent not in doleful thoughts about how far he was from Japan but in merrymaking with the Germans. He wrote,

"It is the custom here to celebrate the New Year at midnight of the first day. I welcomed in the New Year at the dance hall of the Crystal Palace. At the stroke of midnight everyone gathered there, and acquaintances and strangers alike called out, *'Prosit Neu Jaar!'* and shook hands."[24] There is no suggestion in the diary of the kind of awkwardness one sees today when Japanese soccer players, after scoring a goal, imitate the Europeans in embracing one another. Ōgai seems to have been able without difficulty to fit into a convivial, distinctly un-Japanese milieu.

A week later Ōgai again visited the Crystal Palace, this time for a masked ball. One might have expected of Ōgai, especially if one knew him only as the austere figure of later years, that he would have stood apart from the crowd, an aloof bystander and observer of other people, but he wrote in his diary, "Iijima and I went in, both wearing Turkish hats and covering our faces with black masks."[25] A year later, shortly after his arrival in Munich, he attended another masked ball, this one held as part of the carnival festivities. The dances reminded Ōgai of "our old-style Bon dances." He did not hesitate long before joining the celebration. He related,

"I went to the place again, this time wearing a mask with a big nose. There was a girl wearing a white costume marked with green crests and a black mask who came up to me and invited me to dance. I said, 'I am a foreigner. I don't know how to dance.' She said, 'In that case, please come with me and have a drink.' I invited the girl to a table and ordered liquor. I enjoyed myself thoroughly. On the way back I showed the woman to her door."[26]

She asked him to visit her again, but he never did, and he was unable to determine whether or not she had been sincere in her invitation. It is intriguing that Ōgai first identified himself to the girl as a foreigner (*gaikokujin*) rather than as a Japanese. Perhaps he preferred not to let it be known that a Japanese had attended so undignified a gathering.

Ōgai had no trouble mastering German etiquette. When his friend Wuerstler, an army surgeon, invited him to a party in honor of his wife's birthday, he stopped at a florist's, bought a potted plant, and had it delivered to the Wuerstlers' home.[27] Later, when introduced to the queen at a reception held at the palace of the king of Saxony, he kissed her hand.[28] He was also capable of handling less agreeable situations. When the aunt of his professor in Leipzig died, he saw the coffin to the grave.[29] As a foreigner, regardless of the country, one of the most difficult things is knowing what to do at a funeral. Everyone else knows the etiquette, having attended other funerals, but the foreigner is likely to be paralyzed with the fear of committing some terrible gaffe. Ōgai had the requisite dignity and self-confidence to perform even this unfamiliar task.

While in Germany Ōgai associated not only with Germans and fellow Japanese but also with people of many other nationalities. At Frau Vogel's restaurant in Leipzig where he ate his midday meals he met a Greek, an American, and an Englishman, and when he returned to the restaurant after an absence he discovered that now four Englishwomen and a Frenchman regularly ate there. Presumably he spoke German with all of them, and was pleased to discover that his German was better than most. He specifically mentioned a Swedish officer he met at the royal palace who was not proficient in German.[30]

On another occasion, when Ōgai delivered a talk in German at a reception held in honor of Gustav von Lauer, the "army surgeon-general and surgeon to the king," he followed a Russian and an American who had expressed their respects. Ōgai noted in his diary,

I stated that I, too, had for a long time been a great admirer of the literature and the military system of Germany and that this evening's gathering had amply repaid my long-cherished hopes. Although my talk was by no means worse than that of the American doctor, whose German nobody could understand, I felt chagrined that I had not astonished the listeners by my eloquence. In short, I still lack sufficient self-assurance. All the same, the army surgeon Mueller stood up and came over to me and praised me lavishly. Then, facing the crowd, he

shouted in a loud voice, "This is the student I have trained."
He looked very pleased with his achievement.[31]

Ōgai had obviously created a favorable impression on the Germans. The various foreigners Ōgai met seem to have felt comfortable in his company. He related how an American named Thomas had confided his unhappiness over not being able to marry. He said that tuberculosis ran in his family and he was unwilling to transmit it to his children; but there was a girl back home whom he loved, and he could not keep from writing her, though he knew that he should not. He showed Ōgai her photograph. Ōgai consoled Thomas: "'Koch has just discovered the tuberculosis bacillus. We can now dispel the old superstitions about this fatal disease. At present you are in sound condition. You should marry a strong and healthy wife and have strong and healthy children.'"[32]

This was precisely the advice Thomas craved. Two nights later, much restored in spirits, he and Ōgai went to a dance hall about which Ōgai wrote, "This dance hall was not built for upper-class guests. The women who come here are for the most part hostesses and the like."[33] Neither Ōgai nor Thomas seems to have been averse to such surroundings.

When Ōgai left Leipzig for Munich he was seen off at the railway station by two Japanese, a Scot, and an American. Naturally, however, his closest relations were with Germans—his teachers, fellow students, landladies, and at least one woman friend. On January 20, 1886, a party was held to celebrate Ōgai's twenty-fourth birthday, a day after his actual birthday because his host, the distinguished army surgeon Wilhelm Roth, was busy on the nineteenth. Over twenty people attended. As birthday presents Ōgai received a figurine of a village girl and a bull, a calendar, and Robert Koenig's history of German literature. These were not elaborate gifts, but quite possibly Ōgai had never received a birthday present while in Japan. On the first page of the book the army surgeon had inscribed a poem meaning roughly: "It is much too difficult to learn Japanese, but we thank from our hearts our dear pupil. May this book recall to him even after he returns home his years in Germany!" The poem is terrible, but the sentiments were unquestionably sincere. Ōgai's diary entry for the day concludes, "After that, what with the fine wine and the rare delicacies, it was about 12:30 when we parted, having had a thoroughly delightful time."[34]

Ōgai was by no means unmoved by the affection shown him by his European friends. Just before he left Leipzig for Munich a farewell party was held for him, attended by many guests, from the head of the army hospital down. Ōgai recorded in his diary, "During the toasts Roth read a poem of his own composition. Halfway through he broke into sobs and could not stop. I also was shedding tears without realizing it. When we were about to part he said to me, 'My feelings about you are not the same as those of the other Saxon doctors who have come today. I think of you really as my good friend. Please let me hear from you from time to time, and let me know how you are. It will comfort me.'"[35]

It is easy to imagine what effect these words had on the young Mori Ōgai. He boarded a train for Munich later the same day, sharing a compartment with the Russian army surgeon Walberg (actually, a Finn serving in the Russian military). Ōgai wrote in his diary, "On the way we discussed the degrees of intimacy in friendship. We had already sworn to be like brothers and never forget each other, and we finally began to call each other *du*. Walberg is a physician and a poet. He enjoys writing adventure stories. Many of his works have been performed at theaters in Finland and have been much applauded."[36] Ōgai could not have foreseen it, but in the future he, too, would be known as a "physician and poet."

Of course, not every European he met was so agreeable, but Ōgai did not easily take offense. For example, he was twice mistaken for another Japanese studying in Germany, a Captain Ijichi. Some Japanese might have been irritated to the point of demanding, "Do all Japanese look alike to you?" But Ōgai merely smiled. Again, he related how when he was about to board a train a man came up to him.

"He was imposingly built and his red face was framed by a white beard. He bowed to me and said, " 'You're Japanese, aren't you? Excuse me for saying so, but I could tell from one glance at your face that you were Japanese, though you also have features resembling those of people from west of the Pamirs. My name is Johannes Ranke. I am by profession an anthropologist. It would give me great pleasure if I might have your photograph.' "

Ōgai might well have been annoyed at being treated as an interesting anthropological specimen, but he gave Professor Ranke the perfect answer: "I had heard your name even before I left Japan . . . I have enjoyed reading your works on physiology and have greatly benefited from them. I am perfectly glad to give you my picture, but I would like one of you in exchange."[37]

Ōgai did not always remain unruffled by consciously or unconsciously hostile attitudes. One evening he attended a lecture given by a doctor who had traveled in East Asia. "When he mentioned the unsanitary condition of the streets in Korea and China, people all turned toward me with sneers on their faces. Then, when his lecture came to the point where his ship anchored in Nagasaki, he had not a single word of comment on the city. If I had not been present, who knows what abuse he might have leveled at Japan?"[38] In a sense it was courteous of the German doctor to refrain from mentioning unsanitary conditions he may have seen in Japan, for fear of hurting the feelings of the Japanese in the audience, but the implications were obvious, and Ōgai noticed the cold smiles on the faces of the other people present. But he refused to allow such moments (and surely there were others that he did not mention in his diary) to sour his happy stay in Germany.

Ōgai frequently mentioned the beauty of the German women he saw, whether waitresses in the cafés or ladies of the upper classes. Here is his description of a woman he happened to meet at the

Ladies' Association (wives and fiancées of army surgeons) at the military hospital in Dresden: "The most beautiful of the women was Frau Ewers. She has lacquer-black hair, snowy white skin, large eyes, and a prominent nose—all in all, a beauty. Her chin rather projects, but not so much as to be considered a fault."[39]

Needless to say, it was easier for Ōgai to approach women of the lower classes than the members of the Ladies' Association. In the cafés he saw many prostitutes, heavily made up and obviously waiting for customers. He commented, "Among them a few have the charm to stir a man's heart. But there is something unpleasant about their faces. It is hard to explain exactly what this is, but one can tell at a glance that they are prostitutes."[40] Ōgai considered prostitution a disease of society, but thought it was useless to prohibit it. In Berlin there were no houses of prostitution. "That is why the coffee shops have become the haunts of prostitutes. In extreme cases they stand on street corners, beckoning to customers and selling their love. It is hard to say which corrupts social customs more, such women or the brothels."[41] Ōgai nowhere indicates that he ever had relations with a prostitute, perhaps because he intended to publish his diary, but possibly also because such relations—if they occurred—did not seem important enough to be mentioned.

Although Ōgai was reticent about his own involvements with German women, he did not hesitate to describe those of other Japanese men living in Germany. One night when he returned to his lodgings in Leipzig, the maid told him that her lover was waiting to meet Ōgai. No sooner did she pronounce these words than a man wearing a Japanese *yukata* (bathrobe) showed himself. He had come to Germany to study psychopathy.[42]

Ōgai never suggested disapproval of such relations on moral grounds, but he sometimes disapproved for aesthetic reasons, as when he described the former waitress at the Café Minerva who had become the mistress of the painter Harada Naojirō (1863–1899): "Her appearance is most unattractive. She is thin and her face is pale. She is also devoid of intelligence. Their love has all but glued the two of them together."[43] While Harada was still attending art school in Germany a beautiful girl had fallen in love with him. She was the daughter of a professor, a woman with raven-black hair, snowy white skin, and eyes that sparkled with intelligence. She spoke English and French, and was such a good writer that it was said more than half of her father's books were actually written by her. She seemed to desire nothing more than to keep house for Harada, but he told her that he already had someone with whom he lived. Ōgai commented, "I could not help feeling baffled . . . Harada was by nature a man as clear as water.[44] That was what I always loved in him. That is why I feel deep regret when I see him behaving as at present."[45] Four months later Ōgai saw Harada off at the railway station. He was returning to Japan, but his mistress, the former waitress, was to be left behind though she was now with child.[46]

Ōgai's diary mentions another Japanese, Ogata Korenao, who died in Italy leaving an Italian wife and their child. Ōgai wrote, "Korenao is not the only one to have had a child while in Europe . . . It is not to be wondered at, from the standpoint of human feelings if a man makes the decision to leave abroad the child who was the result of his dissipating the loneliness of lodgings in a foreign country. However, it is most deplorable if he fails to send money for the child's education and leaves the mother and child to die of starvation."[47] Ōgai understood that loneliness understandably causes men to seek comfort from available women, but he believed a man whose relationship has resulted in the birth of a child must not be irresponsible.

What, then, of Ōgai himself? Not only is there no overt mention in his diary of physical involvement with a German woman, but he gave as the principal reason for changing his lodgings in Berlin the undesired friendliness of Trudel, the seventeen-year-old niece of the landlord. He wrote, "At night she would visit my room and ensconce herself on my bed chatting, and do other such irritating things."[48] Trudel always declared that she would rather die than live the placid life of a housewife, and she manifested contempt for scholars, calling Ōgai the principal offender. "I hated and avoided her," Ōgai writes. It seems clear, even from Ōgai's account, that this fun-loving girl was interested in him and was trying to divert his attention from his books to her. But Ōgai not only refused to yield to temptation, he also moved to another part of the city.

We might imagine, if we had only Ōgai's diary as our source of information, that he was an unusually straitlaced young man, but (as everyone even slightly interested in Ōgai knows) a German woman followed him to Japan when he returned, arriving only a few days later. Ōgai refused to meet her, so his brothers persuaded the woman to go back to Germany. There are enough blank spaces in Ōgai's diary, especially the part that covers his stay in Berlin before he left for Japan, to accommodate a love affair. Naturally, we have no information on how deeply Ōgai was emotionally involved with the woman, but his refusal to see her in Japan, rather out of character for a man of his moral convictions, suggests that he thought of their liaison as merely a diversion.

It was long assumed that the woman who followed Ōgai to Japan was the model for Elise in his story "The Dancing Girl," and that Ōgai himself (who called the work an *Ich Roman*) was the Japanese student who abandons his mistress; but various Ōgai specialists have recently advanced the theory that "The Dancing Girl" was based not on Ōgai's own experiences but on those of another Japanese army surgeon. The arrival of the German woman in Tokyo, combined with the subsequent appearance of "The Dancing Girl," may have prevented Ōgai from publishing this diary. He may have feared that people might connect the woman and the story, and that the diary would confirm their suspicions. The original diary may even have contained open references to Elise, a compelling reason not to publish it. The original manuscript has been lost, and the one we now possess, in the hand of a professional copyist, presumably embodied Ōgai's later thoughts on his stay abroad. It was not published until 1937, fifteen years after Ōgai's death.

❖ ❖ ❖

While in Germany Ōgai spent considerable time with fellow Japanese. He was by no means the kind of student who, while living abroad, refuses to associate with his countrymen because he fears this will keep him from learning a foreign language or understanding the way of life of the foreign people. However, he was not a student of the opposite variety either, the kind who clings to his countrymen as a protection against the alien society in which he finds himself. Five days after his arrival in Berlin there was a farewell party for three Japanese who were about to return to Japan. "Seventeen people of the sacred land (*mikunibito*) gathered,"[49] Ōgai wrote without irony.

Although Ōgai had virtually nothing to say in his diary about food, he undoubtedly yearned at times for Japanese food, as we can surmise from several entries. Shortly after discovering that the lover of the maid in his boarding house in Leipzig was a Japanese named Sakaki, he wrote, "This evening we—Sakaki, myself, and the others—cooked rice and ate it."[50] On New Year's Day of 1886 Ōgai joined with some German friends in drinking punch at midnight. The next morning he got up at nine and had a cup of coffee. Then, he relates, "I thought of people at home far away lifting their chopsticks over New Year's food."[51] But such moments of homesickness were rare.

Ōgai seems to have missed most of all Japanese with whom he could discuss literature. The other students probably did not share his interests. Of course, it was not difficult to find Germans with whom he could discuss European literature, but for all his love of European writing, Ōgai undoubtedly also felt a need to keep abreast of developments in Japanese literature. He mentions, for example, that a friend lent him several volumes of the political novel *Kajin no Kigū* (Chance Meetings with Beautiful Women, 1885), by Tōkai Sanshi, and says that it "greatly assuaged the loneliness of the traveler."[52] This was a peculiar book from which to derive comfort while in a foreign country—it takes place mainly in America and Europe—but probably it gave him pleasure just to read literary Japanese.

Various Japanese visited Ōgai during his stay in Germany, of whom the most welcome was Inoue Tetsujirō (1855–1944), a philosopher who was also a pioneer of the new poetry. Ōgai described the occasion in these terms:

"His appearance is peculiar and he has a few pockmarks on his face. He has the gift of eloquence, and when he gets carried away by his conversation it is as if nobody else was there. He showed me his collection of poems and the draft of his history of Oriental philosophy. Tonight was the first time since coming to Germany that I have conversed about Oriental writing. My joy was indescribable."[53]

The last part of Ōgai's stay in Germany was spent in Berlin. Ōgai became far more involved in Berlin with Japanese society than he had been in Leipzig or Munich, where he was free not to meet any Japanese if he so chose. In Berlin there was the Yamato Club which Ōgai was expected to attend. This association of Japanese residents of Berlin had contradictory purposes, as Ōgai himself noted in his diary. The first purpose was social, the second serious. The convivial aspects kept people from enjoying the serious lectures, and the serious aspect caused some members to reprove others for their idle chatter.[54] It was not the kind of association to which Ōgai would have devoted much of his time.

Ōgai wrote little about his studies with Robert Koch, one of the founders of the science of bacteriology. It appears that while in Berlin much of his time was taken up with guiding Japanese visitors, and he became involved in the intrigues of the local Japanese society. This may be why the end of the diary is conspicuously less interesting than the earlier parts.

The most dramatic event during Ōgai's stay in Germany was the death of Ludwig II, the king of Bavaria, along with his physician who tried to restrain the king when he drowned himself in Lake Starnberg. The king's celebrated extravagance was a sign of madness, but it is ironic that this extravagance proved so beneficial to later generations. The operas of Wagner he patronized are among the treasures of mankind, and his castles, absurd though they are, rank among the tourist attractions of Germany. Ōgai, in his story "Utakata no Ki" (A Record of Foam on the Water) attempted to explain (in highly romantic terms) the mystery of why the king had been fatefully drawn to the lake.[55]

An event of even greater importance to Ōgai personally was the address given in March 1886 by Edmund Naumann, a professor of geology who had taught at Tokyo University from 1875 to 1885, when his contract was terminated. He was awarded the Order of the Rising Sun shortly before his return to Germany. Ōgai expressed surprise in his diary that Naumann should, despite the decoration, have harbored unfriendly feelings toward Japan. Perhaps Naumann resented being dismissed after having performed conscientiously as a teacher, but it probably did not occur to Ōgai (or to the officials who dismissed Naumann) that he might have supposed that he had tenure.

Naumann was unquestionably well versed in the geology of Japan, though not all Japanese geologists agreed with his findings, but he chose to talk in Munich about quite different matters. According to Ōgai's diary, "He discussed the geography, customs, politics, and scientific technology of Japan. A fair number of his remarks were hostile. For example, he said, 'Gentlemen, if you but consider the state of Japan's advance into the realm of civilization, you will realize that the degree of civilization the Japanese have attained is inferior to that of Europe. Do not suppose that they have been incensed into displaying a spirit of enterprise. This situation has been forced on them by foreigners, and could not be prevented."[56]

Naumann concluded his talk with a humorous anecdote about some Japanese who bought a paddle steamer and sailed it abroad. When at last the ship returned to Japan the engineer did not know how to stop the ship, so it wandered about nearby waters until the engine gave out. Naumann concluded, "Japanese scientific technology is for the most part on this level. I hope that some day it will escape from this unfortunate situation."

Ōgai was enraged by the talk. Professor Roth, noticing his agitation, approached and asked Ōgai what had upset him so. Roth had thought that Naumann's lecture was meant to express his hopes for the progress of Japan. This opinion, from a man Ōgai respected, made him feel all the worse, but he said nothing. When they were seated at table afterward Naumann explained why he had not become a Buddhist during his years in Japan: "It was because Buddha said women have no souls."[57] Ōgai, who realized how difficult it would be to disprove Naumann's theories about the future of Japan, was delighted to hear this particular bit of stupidity, which he disproved by citing passages from the Buddhist sacred texts that mentioned women who had gained enlightenment.

Ōgai, with the encouragement of German friends, eventually published a rebuttal of Naumann's views. It did not silence the man, but it undoubtedly helped Ōgai to clarify his own ideas on the nature of Japanese culture.

Ōgai's diary provides a clearer picture of life in Europe than any of the official diaries that describe Japanese missions abroad. He lived as a student among students of different nationalities, and observed their life at close hand. His position as an army surgeon entitled him to invitations to functions at the palaces of Saxony and Bavaria, but he is most interesting when he writes about the people he knew best—the students, their girlfriends, the strangers he encountered daily on the streets. He noticed the old woman who stood on a corner selling cherries wrapped in pieces of newspaper, and he observed elegantly dressed ladies buying the cherries and eating them as they walked, an unimaginable scene in Japan. Ōgai also bought some cherries from the woman, and commented, "The size is about that of the first joint of the thumb. The taste is extremely good."[58] It is hard to imagine earlier Japanese visitors to Europe compromising their dignity to the extent of eating cherries—or anything else—as they walked down the street, but the young Ōgai cheerfully entered the ways of life of the people around him.

The students, far from treating Ōgai as an incomprehensible stranger from the opposite end of the earth, accepted him as one of their own. He was invited to be present at a duel between two students and did in fact attend, though he did not approve of dueling: "It has very little to recommend it, and the evils are enormous." Dueling was strictly prohibited by law, and only persons in the confidence of the duelists were invited to be present, an indication of the trust Ōgai inspired among the other students.[59]

Ōgai characterized himself in his *German Diary* as a man who liked a spartan life.[60] This may have been by way of disassociating himself from the pleasure-loving Japanese students whom he knew. But Ōgai's actions, as described in the diary, do not necessarily seem spartan. He seems to have consumed a very large amount of beer in the company of students, perhaps because he believed that the best way to know other men is to drink with them. He also behaved at times in a conspicuously unmilitary manner. On one occasion, when he went for a hike by a lake near Munich, he tells us, "There was an old man who sold balls on rubber strings. I bought two or three and gave them to some children."[61] He was intrigued by Gypsies, and on a sudden impulse he once invited two Gypsy children to accompany him and a Japanese friend to Nymphenburg.[62]

Specialists in the writings of Mori Ōgai have succeeded in identifying almost every person and building he mentions in *German Diary*. It is invaluable as a source of biographical information about an important period in the life of a major writer. Events and impressions recorded in the diary would be utilized by Ōgai when writing works of fiction, and this aspect of the diary has also been thoroughly examined. But it is not often enough stressed that the diary is of great interest in itself, quite apart from what it tells us about the life of the author. The tone is almost always cheerful, although Ōgai must have experienced periods of frustration and even dejection while studying abroad. This is not an aspect of his life that he chose to describe in his diary, which, he seems to have believed, should not be a confession. It is instead the account of a young man's discovery of another civilization and of himself in the process.

Notes

1. Text in Kawaguchi Hisao, *Bakumatsu Meiji Kaigai Taiken Shishū*, p. 801. The original text is in *kambun*, but I have used Kawaguchi's *yomikudashi* version.

   Ōgai alludes here to the Chinese story of the man from Ying who sent a letter that contained some incorrectly written material to a minister of Yen. The minister exercised great ingenuity in making a plausible translation of the letter, though the contents were obscure.

2. Ōgai actually refers to two stars, *shin* in the west and *shō* in the east, which were believed to be so far apart they never met; but he denies the famous statement of Tu Fu (712–770) that human beings, like these stars, were fated never to meet.

3. Kawaguchi, *Bakumatsu*, p. 805.

4. *Ibid.*, p. 809.

5. *Ibid.*, p. 812.

6. *Ibid.*, p. 814.

7. *Ibid.*, p. 820.

8. *Ibid.*, p. 828.

9. In Theravada Buddhism (the kind practiced in Ceylon and elsewhere in Southeast Asia) an arhat was a holy man who had reached the highest degree of enlightenment. Halls filled with five hundred images of *arakan* (usually known as *rakan*), each with distinctive features, are found in China, and there were smaller-scaled examples in Japan as well.

10. *Kesa* (*kassya* in Sanskrit), the word translated as "surplice," in Southeast Asia is a length of material worn as a garment, hanging over the body diagonally from the left shoulder to the right armpit. In China and Japan it survives only vestigially. Ōgai was surprised by the bright color. He was also surprised that the priests wore shoes of leather; Japanese priests would have avoided using the hides of animals for this purpose.

11. This seems improbable, but Ōgai's text gives (in kanji) *buraiyu*. Passage quoted from Kawaguchi, *Bakumatsu*, pp. 833–34.

12. *Ibid.*, p. 852.

13. *Ōgai Zenshū*, XXXV, p. 20. All references to *German Diary* are from this volume of the *Complete Works*.

14. *Ibid.*, p. 94.

15. *Ibid.*, p. 105.

16. *Ibid.*, p. 23.

17. *Ibid.*, p. 26.

18. *Ibid.*, pp. 42–43.

19. *Ibid.*, p. 20.

20. *Ibid.*, p. 21.

21. *Ibid.*, p. 30.

22. *Ibid.*, p. 80.

23. *Ibid.*, p. 21.

24. *Ibid.*, pp. 24–25.

25. *Ibid.*, p. 25.

26. *Ibid.*, p. 77.

27. *Ibid.*, p. 48.

28. *Ibid.*, p. 68.

29. *Ibid.*, p. 26.

30. *Ibid.*, p. 46.

31. *Ibid.*, p. 71.

32. *Ibid.*, p. 36.

33. *Ibid.*, pp. 36–37.

34. *Ibid.*, p. 67.

35. *Ibid.*, p. 76.

36. *Ibid.*

37. *Ibid.*, pp. 83–84.

38. *Ibid.*, p. 57.

39. *Ibid.*, p. 60.

40. *Ibid.*, p. 71.

41. *Ibid.*, pp. 71–72.

42. *Ibid.*, p. 39.

43. *Ibid.*, p. 91.

44. This is an allusion to the *Analects* of Confucius, who defined the quality of friendship as being "colorless as water," meaning that it was free of excessive or cloying emotions.

45. *Ōgai Zenshū*, XXXV, pp. 91–92.
46. *Ibid.*, p. 101.
47. *Ibid.*, p. 88.
48. *Ibid.*, p. 114.
49. *Ibid.*, p. 21.
50. *Ibid.*, p. 40.
51. *Ibid.*, p. 63. Ōgai specifies *zōnisen*, a tray with *zōni*, a kind of soup with rice cakes served at New Year.
52. *Ibid.*, p. 108.
53. *Ibid.*, p. 51.
54. *Ibid.*, p. 134.
55. There is a translation of this story by Richard Bowring under the title "Utakata no Ki," *Monumenta Nipponica* 29:3, 1974.
56. *Ōgai Zenshū*, XXXV, p. 74.
57. *Ibid.*, p. 75.
58. *Ibid.*, p. 34.
59. *Ibid.*, pp. 83–84.
60. *Ibid.*, p. 83.
61. *Ibid.*, p. 95.
62. *Ibid.*, p. 88.

Bibliography

Bowring, Richard John. *Mori Ōgai and the Modernization of Japanese Culture.* Cambridge: Cambridge University Press, 1979.

Brazell, Karen. "Mori Ōgai in Germany," *Monumenta Nipponica* 26:1–2, 1971.

Kawaguchi Hisao. *Bakumatsu Meiji Kaigai Taiken Shishū*. Tokyo: Daitō Bunka Daigaku Tōyō Kenkyūjo, 1984.

Mori Ōgai. "Utakata no Ki," trans. Richard Bowring, *Monumenta Nipponica* 29:3, 1974.

Ōgai Zenshū, 38 vols. Tokyo: Iwanami Shoten, 1971–75.

Rimer, J. Thomas. *Mori Ōgai*. Boston: Twayne Publishers, 1975.

The European Diary
of Natsume Sōseki

The visits to Europe of the two best known writers of the Meiji era, Mori Ōgai and Natsume Sōseki (1867–1916) were both described in diaries. No two diaries are less alike. Ōgai's diary is almost unvaryingly cheerful; Sōseki's is bilious in tone and he hardly mentions a single thing that pleased him. In part the difference can be explained in terms of the ages of the diarists when they arrived in Europe. Ōgai was twenty-two when he went to Germany, but Sōseki was already thirty-three by the time he reached England. Quite apart from the personalities of the two men, it was easier for a young man like Ōgai to accommodate himself to unfamiliar surroundings than for a married man with responsibilities such as Sōseki. Ōgai was able to associate with German and other students on terms of equality, but Sōseki, both because of his age and his feelings of dignity, never associated with British students or, indeed, any intellectuals apart from the tutor he hired.

Again, the times were different. When Ōgai went abroad in 1884, it was the height of the era of the Rokumeikan, the ballroom where Japanese of the upper classes, all in European dress, dined and danced in the European manner, in order to demonstrate that Japan

had emerged from feudal darkness. There was a strong predisposi-
tion at this time to accept almost uncritically any form of knowledge
and even any form of etiquette from the West. But by the time that
Sōseki went abroad in 1900 a wave of *Nippon shugi* (Japanism) had
struck the Japanese intellectual world, and even a man as critical of
contemporary Japan as Sōseki did not wholly escape the influence
of this change of attitude. Finally, Ōgai went abroad in the best of
health and never had occasion to complain in his diary even of a cold,
but Sōseki's diary contains ominous mentions of the medicines he
took for the stomach ailment that would eventually prove fatal. Part
of Sōseki's ill humor may have stemmed from physical as much as intellectual causes.

Sōseki kept a diary only during infrequent periods of his life, unlike Ōgai, whose diaries span almost his entire career. Sōseki probably thought of his diaries not as compositions that might be published
some day in their original form but as source materials to be used in
the future when writing works of literature. The entries are generally brief reminders to himself of what he did or thought on a certain
day. For example, the entry for November 12, 1900, states merely,
"Traveled on the *underground railway*. Heard Ker's *lecture*."[1] (Itali-
cized words are in English in the diary.) It would have been interesting if Sōseki had described his sensations on traveling for the first
time on the subway, but he seems to have been resolved never to utter
a word of surprise over anything he encountered abroad. It would
have been equally interesting to have his comments on the lecture by
Professor William P. Ker, a celebrated scholar of medieval literature
who was known as an inspiring teacher. Did Sōseki have trouble in
understanding the lecture despite his remarkable knowledge of English? Or was the lecture so vividly engraved in his mind that he
thought it unnecessary to mention its contents in his diary? He does
mention eight days later hearing a lecture by Ker that was interesting
(*omoshirokarishi*), but that was the limit of his praise.

Sōseki sailed from Yokohama on September 8, 1900. After a brief
account of the bout of seasickness that almost every Japanese traveler

experienced, he consciously or unconsciously expressed attitudes that would typify his reactions not only to the voyage but also to his entire stay abroad:

"I had packed the works of Kitō and Shōha in my suitcase, and I thought I would read a bit, but I found it quite impossible. The surroundings stink so much of Westerners that it was beyond me to take pleasure in anything like haiku."[2]

Sōseki was passionately fond of haiku and composed some during the voyage to Europe. It was not surprising that he brought with him collections by two minor haiku poets, both disciples of the great Buson; but for him to have been reading these haiku as he headed for England, the country whose language and literature were his special field of competence, suggests that he was attempting to defend himself from the alien culture that threatened him. He wrote in his diary that he was unable to read the haiku of Takai Kitō and Kuroyanagi Shōha because of the Western people around him. Presumably, this does not refer to people who were actually in his cabin but to the alien atmosphere that was somehow generated, and which pervaded the whole ship.

A younger scholar of English literature would probably have felt excited at the thought that he was surrounded by people who spoke only English, and he might have attempted to get some conversational practice before arriving in England, but it is clear that Sōseki felt something close to physical revulsion in the presence of so many foreigners. He wrote in his diary,

Ever since leaving Yokohama, except for the people traveling with me, there have been nothing but foreigners to left and right. Among them there was one Japanese, and, thinking it might be amusing, I spoke to him, only to discover to my astonishment that he was a Portuguese born in Hong Kong. I was delighted when another Japanese came aboard in Kobe, but—who would have guessed it?—he turned out to be a half-breed, begotten by an Englishman on a Chinese woman. I'll have to be careful from now on lest I make some terrible mistake. Watch your step![3]

There is something so nasty about these remarks that it is difficult to excuse them, even coming from a great writer. The use of the verb *tsugau*, normally used only of animals coupling, here indicates a contempt for another human being that was unworthy of Sōseki but, unfortunately, typical of his attitude at the time. Sōseki did not hesitate to use such words as *ketō* or *ketōjin*[4] for foreigners of any kind, and he was equally uncomplimentary about the Chinese in Shanghai and Hong Kong who bothered him by their noisiness. As soon as he went ashore in Hong Kong he headed for a Japanese inn, though it proved to be too filthy for him to stay there.

By this time Japanese travelers were by no means rare, and when he arrived in Singapore a native who spoke some Japanese took him on a guided tour of the botanical garden and museum (which Sōseki pronounced as being "not especially impressive"), and then to the Matsushima-ya where he had lunch. Sōseki recorded in his diary, "This seems to be the Japan town. I wandered along the streets where prostitutes ply their trade. It gave me a funny feeling."

In Colombo, Ceylon, he hired a horse carriage and visited a Buddhist temple in which there was a sacred relic, but the place was so badly run down that, he wrote, "there is absolutely nothing worth seeing."[5] When people along the roads threw flowers into his carriage and in return begged for money, calling at him, "Japan! Japan!" Sōseki opined, "The people of a ruined country are contemptible."[6]

Sōseki's arrival in Naples seems to have cheered him somewhat. At any rate, he praised the cathedral and noted with interest the countless sculptures and excavated artifacts from Pompeii in the magnificent archaeological museum. He wrote not a word about the scenery of the Bay of Naples or about Vesuvius, though travelers were normally overwhelmed by its scenic beauty. On the whole, Sōseki was indifferent to scenery, and in his descriptions of architecture or works of art he rarely wrote more, even about works he admired, than single words such as "splendid" (*rippa*) or "impressive" (*sōgon*). He seems to have been embarrassed to have liked Naples. He explained, "I suppose I was impressed because it was the first place I had gone ashore since coming to the West."[7]

Sōseki traveled from Naples to Genoa by ship, and from there by train to Paris. When he arrived at the station in Genoa he was surrounded by the confusion typical of any large Italian station, and was desperately anxious until he found a travel agent who spoke English and put him aboard a train for Turin, where he was to change for the Paris train. The Turin train was crowded, and whichever compartment he put his head into he was informed that it was fully occupied. "I spent a good deal of time wandering around in a daze, led by the porter. In the end I squeezed in among some *ketōjin*. They all stared at my face."[8]

When Sōseki arrived in Paris he was bewildered by the unfamiliar city, not knowing which way to turn. Aboard ship some fellow Japanese had taught him a few words of French, which were sufficient to reach the lodgings of a fellow Japanese. While in Paris he visited the Exposition, climbed to the top of the Eiffel Tower, and (guided by a Japanese acquaintance) strolled along the boulevards. All he recorded of his impressions was, "It looks about fifty times as splendid as the Ginza on a summer night."[9]

The next day Sōseki ate a Japanese dinner and went to a music hall. He commented, "The prosperity and degeneracy of Paris are something astonishing."[10] He returned several times to the Exposition, but his only recorded impression was, "The Japanese ceramics and Nishijin silks stood out most prominently."[11] After a week in Paris he headed for London.

Sōseki dutifully went sightseeing in London. He visited the Tower, London Bridge, and the Monument, and attended the theater with a Japanese acquaintance. He wrote not a word about his impressions, though surely he was familiar with these places from the books he had read even before he left Japan. As a specialist in eighteenth-century English literature, he presumably knew the play he saw at the Haymarket Theatre, Sheridan's *School for Scandal*, the best-known English comedy of the century. One wonders why he felt no excitement.

Sōseki's descriptions of the sights of London are laconic. "Saw the British Museum. Saw Westminster Abbey."[12] That was all he had to write about those famous places. But the very fact that he systematically went from museum to museum suggests that, perhaps despite himself, he was responding to the culture of the people whose language and literature he had long studied.

It did not take Sōseki long after his arrival in London to start characterizing the English and contrasting them with the Japanese, as in the following examples, written on January 3, 1901:

"They make way for other people. They are not self-centered like the Japanese.

"They insist on their rights. They do not find this a botheration as the Japanese do.

"They are proud of England. Just the way the Japanese are proud of Japan."

He concluded by urging himself, "Try thinking of which country one has better reason to be proud."[13]

These observations have a little of the humor we associate with Sōseki's early writings, and they also suggest he was aware of some of the good qualities of the English, but a darker side of his experiences emerges in his diary entry for the next day: "Try spitting while you are taking a stroll through the London streets. You will be astonished at what a pitch-black clot comes out. Millions of people in this city are every day breathing in the smoke and dust and dyeing their lungs with the color. Whenever I blow my nose or spit it gives me such a bad feeling I feel ashamed of myself."[14]

The dirty atmosphere in England had been commented on by earlier Japanese visitors, who generally expressed relief when they arrived in France, where industrialization had not advanced to the same degree, but Sōseki, though he obviously disliked the air pollution, had another thought, more complicated than any expressed by previous visitors. He wondered why people who lived in so polluted an atmosphere had such fair skins, and concluded that it was probably because the pollutants weakened the light of the sun. This leads to the most famous passage in his diary:

"I thought I saw a short and peculiarly ugly man coming toward me along the street, only to realize that it was myself, reflected in a mirror. It has only been since coming to this place that I have realized we really are yellow."[15]

One would search in vain for a similar passage in the diary of Mori Ōgai. Sōseki's feelings of racial differences induced him to write harshly about the *ketōjin*, but sometimes he also described himself with self-contempt. The contradiction implied in such attitudes would recur in his writings. Even in *Kusamakura*,[16] the most poetic of his works, every time the hero, a painter, compares something European to its Eastern equivalent, it is in terms of the superiority of the latter. He expresses distaste for elaborate European pastry, contrasting it with the shimmering beauty of Japanese *yōkan* (bean jelly). He declares his preference for Chinese poetry to *Hamlet* or *Faust*, and asserts that European poetry never manages to free itself from the world of commercial transactions.

If Sōseki (or the hero of *Kusamakura*) worked entirely within Japanese traditions, there would be no conflict. But Sōseki wrote novels that owed little to the Japanese *monogatari* (tales or stories) and much to the novels of Britain and the United States, and at the time he wrote this diary entry he was a scholar of English literature by profession. Similarly, the painter in *Kusamakura* worked in oils, and did not follow Japanese painting traditions. The spiritual conflict between East and West revealed in these contradictions has been experienced by many Japanese since Sōseki's day, and this may be one reason his popularity has never diminished.

Sōseki discovered while living in London that most of the English people with whom he associated—his landlady, the shopkeepers, the tailors, and so on—knew less about English literature than he did. This was not surprising: he was a scholar of English literature and most of them were poorly educated. Probably, despite their British nationality, they were unable to understand the books he studied. This discovery must have cheered him. Though he does not say so in his diary, Sōseki undoubtedly felt at a disadvantage when compared to British scholars of English literature, and it probably comforted him to realize that he knew more about the subject than the majority of the inhabitants of the British Isles.

He wrote in his diary,

> You mustn't think that just because they are English their knowledge of literature is necessarily superior to yours. Most of them are so busy with their family businesses that they haven't the time to open a book of literature or anything resembling one. They haven't even the time to read a *respectable* newspaper. It doesn't take long when talking with someone to realize this. Of course, it's their own country's literature, so people don't want to admit their ignorance. Either they save appearances by saying that they are so busy they have no time to read, or else they go on pretending that they know literature. This no doubt is because in their hearts they feel ashamed to know less than a Japanese. There's no point as far as I am concerned in pursuing a topic that leads nowhere and is annoying to the other party, so I make it my practice to shift the subject at an appropriate moment.[17]

Sōseki related how at the University of London students would go up to the professor after a lecture to ask how the names of Keats or Landor were spelled, and how the old man who lived in the same lodging house asked after they had gone together to a performance of *Robinson Crusoe* whether it was really true or just a story. The old man's wife, though she had never read more than a couple of novels in her whole life, gave herself airs of being well educated, and after she had used some quite ordinary word in her conversation she would ask Sōseki if he understood what it meant. Sōseki continued,

"The conversation was in the language of her native country, so obviously I could stand on my head and still not be as fluent. But what they call *cockney* is not very elegant language and I don't understand it."[18]

Sōseki's unshakable mood of depression, more than any particularly unpleasant experience, made his stay in England an almost unbroken series of gloomy days, relieved only when he was able to spend time with some congenial Japanese acquaintance. His irritation with the English pervades the pages of his diary. He took weekly lessons from William J. Craig at five shillings a time. In later years Sōseki would write more appreciatively of this Shakespearean scholar, but the most vivid mention of Craig in the diary is: "I went to Craig's. I requested him to correct my composition. He wants an *extra charge*. He is despicable."[19]

His remarks on the various people in whose houses he lodged were never flattering, as the following will suggest: "The people in the house went to see a dog show. The weather's bad and it's snowing. The people here are just like animals—they pay no attention to the weather."[20]

He was sometimes invited to tea by English ladies who were sorry for the Japanese man so far from home or perhaps hoped to convert him to Christianity. On one such occasion he wrote, "Invitation from Mrs. Edghill to tea. I must go. I hate the thought."[21] On another occasion he wrote of being invited to a house in Dulwich. It was snowing fiercely, but he felt obliged to go. When he arrived he was ushered into a small drawing room where a group of ladies were already assembled, waiting for him:

> There was nothing for me to do but to sit down. I looked to my right and then to my left, but I didn't recognize one of the women around me. I did not even know the lady of the house. I thought what an uncouth woman she must be to invite a foreigner, a Japanese at that, to an *at home*. I suppose she invited me out of a sense of duty. And I also went out of a sense of

duty. Tea was served. We exchanged a few absolutely banal remarks . . . It was a complete waste of time. What a stupid thing
Western society is! I wonder who could have invented such
a straitlaced society. What pleasure can one derive from it?[22]

The longer Sōseki remained in England, the greater the gap he
felt between himself and the English. In terms that anticipated the
opinions he expressed in *Kusamakura*, he wrote, "Western people like
cloying things. They also like gaudy things. One can tell this from
their theater. One can tell this from their food. One can tell it also
from their architecture and their decorations. One can tell it even
from the way husbands and wives embrace and kiss. This is all reflected in their language, and accounts for the scarcity of wit or tran-
scendental observation in their literature."[23]

He constantly contrasted European with Japanese tastes, always
indicating preference for the Japanese. Yet this cannot have been his
entire conviction. If it had been, he would surely have abandoned his
study of European literature and immersed himself in the composition of haiku and *kanshi*. For all his opposition to the uncritical adoption by the Japanese of everything Western, he realized that the
process had not gone far enough. He wrote,

> They say that Japan woke up thirty years ago, and that, more-
> over, it suddenly leaped to its feet as if at the sound of a fire
> alarm. But this awakening was not a real awakening. It was
> performed in a state of confusion. The absorption of things
> from the West was so rapid that there wasn't time to digest
> them. This is true not only of literature but of politics and
> business as well. It's all over with Japan unless it really opens
> its eyes.[24]

It is not clear whether Sōseki believed he himself had opened his
eyes, but we may be sure from what he wrote in the rest of the diary
that nothing was likely to remedy the terrible depression from which

Sōseki was suffering. On July 1, 1901, still in London, he wrote in his diary, "Of late I have been feeling extremely out of sorts. The most trivial things upset me. It makes me wonder if I am not suffering from some nervous ailment."[25] Sōseki's depression prevented him from enjoying his life in England, but without the experience of this depression he might not have created the masterpieces of his later years.

Mori Ōgai and Natsume Sōseki led totally dissimilar lives in Europe. Their reactions to their experiences typify the Japanese travelers of the past century, with an important difference: their diaries, unlike those kept by most travelers, are of considerable literary importance. From this time on, the diary, whether a real one composed each night before the writer went to bed or a false diary like those kept by the ladies of the Heian court, written long after the events described, emerges as an important genre of modern Japanese literature. It became a commonplace of criticism to say that a diary was the finest work produced by an author. I doubt that this claim could be made for Natsume Sōseki's diary, but it possesses unique importance as a document describing the great phenomenon of our century, the meeting of East and West.

Notes

1. *Sōseki Zenshū*, XIII, p. 20. References to Sōseki's diary are all taken from this volume.
2. *Ibid.*, p. 8.
3. *Ibid.*
4. The word *ketō* meant literally "hairy Chinese," and *ketōjin* was "hairy Chinese person." This term of abuse, found in Japanese literature as far back as Chikamatsu Monzaemon's play *Kokusen'ya Kassen* (The Battles of Coxinga, 1715), originally was used with the meaning of "dirty Chinese," but in Sōseki's time it was used for Europeans, who were hairier than the Chinese. The term was sometimes used jocularly, but it was generally (as here) a term of abuse.

5. *Sōseki Zenshū*, XIII, p. 12.
6. *Ibid*.
7. *Ibid*., p. 16.
8. *Ibid*.
9. *Ibid*., p. 17.
10. *Ibid*.
11. *Ibid*., p. 18.
12. *Ibid*., p. 19.
13. *Ibid*., pp. 29–30.
14. *Ibid*., p. 30.
15. *Ibid*.
16. The title means literally "pillow of grass," but the English translation by Alan Turney is called *The Three-Cornered World*.
17. *Sōseki Zenshū*, XIII, p. 32.
18. *Ibid*.
19. *Ibid*., p. 39.
20. *Ibid*.
21. *Ibid*., p. 41.
22. *Ibid*., pp. 42–43.
23. *Ibid*., p. 48.
24. *Ibid*., p. 49.
25. *Ibid*., p. 70.

Bibliography

Natsume Sōseki. *The Three-Cornered World*, trans. Alan Turney. London: Peter Owen, 1965.

Sōseki Zenshū, XIII. Tokyo: Iwanami Shoten, 1975.

The Diaries of Niijima Jō

The Japanese of the nineteenth century who had the least trouble in getting along with Europeans and Americans were undoubtedly those who became Christians. In the nineteenth century being a Christian involved a great deal more than being baptized and attending church. Both the missionaries and their Japanese converts were certain that believing in Jesus was the only way to be saved. There was no question of ecumenical understanding between Christianity and other religions; the missionaries who covertly began to preach Christianity to the Japanese at the end of the shogunate era were convinced that Buddhists, however admirable they might be in the conduct of their lives, were doomed to perdition because they refused to acknowledge the one true religion. The missionaries believed therefore that, however arduous and unrewarded their labors might be in a country unfriendly to their religion, it was their inescapable duty to preach the gospel. Some of these men were undoubtedly intolerant and misguided, but their joy when they succeeded in saving Japanese souls was genuine.

Niijima Jō (1843–1890) was one of the first Japanese Christian converts of the modern period (as opposed to the many of the sixteenth and early seventeenth centuries). In a memoir of his life, written in English in 1885, he described his early years for the benefit of his American foster parents. He dedicated the narrative to them with these introductory words: "To Mr. and Mrs. Alpheus Hardy, To whom I owe more than to my own parents for their boundless love and untiring interest manifested in my welfare, both temporal and spiritual."[1]

Niijima's personal name was originally Shimeta. He described the origin of this unusual name as a product of his grandfather's joy on learning that, after four granddaughters, he at last had a grandson. The grandfather exclaimed, "*Shimeta!*" (I've got him!) and this became the boy's name.[2] He was given a strict education in the Confucian classics and in martial sports, in keeping with his status as the eldest son of a high-ranking samurai of the Annaka fief; but at the age of fourteen he was chosen to study Dutch, and eventually became proficient enough in that language to read texts of physics and astronomy.

He recalled,

> One day I happened to walk on the shore of Yedo Bay and caught a sight of the Dutch warships lying at anchor. They looked so stately and formidable! When I compared these dignified sea-queens side by side with our clumsy and disproportioned junks, nothing further was needed to convince me that the foreigners who built such warships must be more intelligent and a superior people to the Japanese. It seemed a mighty object lesson to rouse up my ambition to cry out for the general improvement and renovation of my country.[3]

As yet Niijima knew nothing about Christianity. His chief concern was to save Japan from the menace represented by the Dutch warships. To this end he determined to master the sciences, especially the art of navigation. The year he saw the Dutch ships was 1860, the same year that the first Japanese embassy traveled to America, but

Niijima, who was then seventeen, naturally was not given the opportunity to accompany the mission. Two years later, however, he was permitted by the daimyo of the Matsuyama fief, a close relative of the daimyo of the Annaka fief, to make a round-trip journey between Edo and Bitchū Tamashima on the Inland Sea aboard the *Kaifū Maru*, a schooner built in America.

Niijima at this time was far from being the moral paragon he became in later years, as we can guess from a passage in his diary describing his visit to Tamashima: "When I asked a native of the town where the liveliest place was, he said Yanahara and added, 'You'll find brothels there. That's where you should go.' He gave me detailed directions on how to get there . . . I walked two or three blocks north, turned to the left and then went another two blocks, and finally turned to the right and went another three blocks or so. There was a whole row of brothels, very splendid looking, and I could only suppose that it would be extremely enjoyable to have a drinking party there, and get the women to sing and dance."[4] In later years, when Niijima wrote the account of his life that he offered to his foster parents, he described his shock on observing the "base and licentious life" led by the crew of the *Kaifū Maru*.[5]

He was torn at this time between his allegiance to the daimyo of Annaka, who was loyal to the shogunate, and his own preference for *sonnō*—reverence for the emperor. Just about this time a friend lent him the Japanese translation of *Robinson Crusoe*,[6] and this aroused a strong desire to visit foreign countries. Some time afterward, the same friend lent Niijima some works of Western geography and history that had been published in Chinese translation by missionaries. He was especially intrigued by some Christian books published in Shanghai and Hong Kong.

At first Niijima read with skepticism, but references to God as the "Heavenly Father" moved him deeply, probably because there was no similar concept in either Buddhism or Confucianism. He wrote in the book he dedicated to his foster parents,

Having recognized God as my Heavenly Father, I felt I was no longer inseparably bound to my parents. I discovered for the first time that the doctrines of Confucius on the filial relation were too narrow and fallacious. I said then: "I am no more my parents', but my God's." A strong cord which had held me strongly to my father's home was broken asunder at that moment. I felt then that I must take my own course. I must serve my Heavenly Father more than my earthly parents.[7]

There had been countless instances of Japanese who had "left their houses" (*shukke*) to become Buddhist priests, believing that worldly attachments must be severed before a man can obtain salvation, but for Niijima, who had been raised on Confucian principles, leaving to become a Christian was a tremendous decision, made especially difficult because of his deep devotion to his parents. Once he had made the decision, the next step seemed clear: he must go abroad and study with foreign teachers of the gospel. At the time it was strictly prohibited for Japanese to go abroad unless as a member of an official mission. A few had succeeded in making their way to foreign countries anyway, with the aid of Europeans resident in Japan, but Niijima did not know a single European or American. It was at this point that he learned that the same schooner on which he had sailed to Tamashima would be going to Hakodate in Hokkaidō, and he managed to get permission to make the voyage.

Niijima thought that it would be relatively easy to obtain passage aboard one of the foreign ships that had been calling at Hakodate since it was opened to international traffic in 1859. He did not tell his family what he had in mind, but they seem to have guessed. At the farewell dinner he drank a cupful of water (*mizu sakazuki*), a traditional way to signify a long parting, and his grandfather (who had been upset when he learned that Niijima had been reading *Robinson Crusoe*) composed the haiku:

ikeru nara	If you can manage it,
itte mite ko yo	Go, have a look and come back:
hana no yama	The mountain of flowers.

Cheered by this unexpected support, Niijima felt "full courage to start from home like a man."[8]

Niijima's diary *Hakodate Kikō* (Journey to Hakodate) records his experiences aboard the *Kaifū Maru* during its voyage from Edo to Hakodate in the third month of 1864. The record of the journey opens as Niijima was hoping somehow to meet the former castaway Nakahama Manjirō (1827–1898), who had spent ten years abroad before returning to Japan.[9] Two acquaintances he met by chance in the streets of Edo asked him if he would like to go on a sailing ship to Hakodate. This was a quite unexpected stroke of good fortune. He forgot about meeting Manjirō, and at once set about making preparations for his departure. However, unless he obtained permission of the daimyo of his fief and of the Matsuyama fief (which owned the *Kaifū Maru*) he would not be able to go anywhere. He went to see the inspector (*metsuke*) of his clan stationed in Edo, and secured the man's promise to help him. Permission was granted four days later. Niijima was deliriously happy, it goes without saying. He wrote, "I was unable to restrain my joy, and without realizing what I did, I let out a great shout. I cried, 'Ah, Heaven has not abandoned me! The success or failure of my plans hinges on this one stroke of fortune.'"[10]

When he was on the point of departing, however, disquieting thoughts passed through his mind. He wrote, "My mother's expression at this time was one of unbearable grief. I felt exceedingly sorry for her. However, if some future day, after I have accomplished my project, I return home and requite the boundless debt of gratitude I owe her, I shall prove that I definitely was not an unfilial son."[11] Obviously, he was tormented not by the thought of a couple of weeks at sea but by his realization that this would be only the beginning of a long separation from his family.

The *Kaifū Maru* set sail from Shinagawa on the twelfth day of the third month. As the ship headed slowly north, Niijima was in extremely high spirits. He wrote in his diary, "I am so happy that I have composed a poem." This was the poem:

mononofu no	A warrior has
omoi Tatsuta no	Resolved that unless he wears
yama momiji	Brocade like the leaves
nishiki kizareba	Of Mount Tatsuta in autumn,
nado kaeru beki[12]	Why should he ever come back?

This is not a good poem. The reader is likely to cringe at the hackneyed poetic devices such as the pun on *omoitatsu* (to resolve) and Tatsuta, a place traditionally associated in the old poems with red leaves floating on the water. But Niijima's resolve not to come back unless in glory—wearing brocade, in the old phrase—testifies to the earnestness of his purpose.

On the twenty-third the *Kaifū Maru* anchored at Katsuura. Niijima went ashore with the other members of the crew and celebrated (at a party held in a restaurant) their good fortune in not having gone aground the previous day on a shoal at the mouth of Okitsu Harbor. He wrote in his diary, "We were lucky some geishas had arrived the day before from Edo. So we ordered sake, food, and geishas too. Soon afterward, food and drinks arrived, as did two geishas. They sang in sensuous voices and made us all drunk."[13]

It sounds as if it was a very lively party, but Niijima added to this description, probably some years later, the statement, "This is an extremely immoral place, quite frighteningly so."[14] He repeatedly commented with distaste, at whatever ports the ship called on, the large number of prostitutes he noticed: "In each house there are a couple of them, or even four or five. I was told that the total number was more than a hundred. This is because many merchant ships call here."[15]

The *Kaifū Maru* with Niijima aboard arrived in Hakodate on the twenty-first day of the fourth month. As soon as he got ashore he headed for the school (*juku*) taught by Takeda Ayasaburō (1828–1880). Takeda had originally devoted himself to the martial arts, but in 1845 he went to Osaka, where he studied Dutch at the school run by Ogata Kōan, the same school where Fukuzawa Yukichi was to study. Takeda subsequently also learned English and French. His experience in dealing with the Russian fleet that visited Japan in 1853 aroused his interest in the regions to the north; he feared the Russians planned to seize Japanese territory. He entered the service of Muragaki Norimasa, the magistrate of Ezo, and planned defenses in the area.[16]

No doubt Niijima had heard from two friends who were studying at Takeda's school of the latter's reputation both as a scholar of foreign languages and as an advocate of national defense. When he visited the school, however, he was told the friends were both away. One had left for Edo on a shogunate ship; the other had disappeared, but rumor had it that he had contrived to leave the country with the aid of the Englishman with whom he had been studying English. This report seems to have suggested to Niijima a course of action to follow.

Niijima, frustrated in the hope of seeing his friends, made inquiries in Hakodate about Takeda's school, and was unimpressed by what he learned. "I was told that at present there are four or five students and there was no one especially good at reading; and that Takeda himself had gone off to Edo. Furthermore, because there were so few students, it was pointless to hire a man to do the cooking, involving an expense, so each person ate either at home or at an inn. This was extremely inconvenient for me, and I thought I would go to the house of some Western person."[17]

The next day, as he reported in his diary, he went to see someone he knew at the Takeda school and said he would like to discuss his plans. The man invited Niijima and two other men to a restaurant, and treated them to food and liquor. Niijima related,

After the wine cups had flown back and forth for a while[18] and we were all in extremely good spirits, I told my friend of my wish to live at the house of a Western person. He replied, "I know a Russian priest named Nikolai. He is intelligent and a man of wide knowledge. That is probably why he was ordered by the czar of Russia to come here and learn Japanese. He recently lost his Japanese teacher and he's been frantically looking for a new one. Why don't you go to the house of this Russian priest? The man also knows English, and he might be able to help you a little with your study of English." I made up my mind I would go to the Russian's house, and asked my friend to introduce me.[19]

Niijima's friend came to his lodgings a week or so later and conducted him to the house of the Russian priest. The friend explained to the priest Niijima's desire to study English and his disappointment with Takeda's school. Nikolai at once agreed to take on Niijima as his Japanese tutor. Two days later Niijima moved into the Russian's house. In his room there was a bed (which Niijima, unfamiliar with beds, described as a "sleeping place high enough to discourage fleas") and a big desk.[20] Nikolai was impressed by the determination of the young man, which had carried him all the way to Hakodate, and treated Niijima with the greatest kindness.

It took a little time for Niijima to grow accustomed to the Russian's ways. "This priest does not eat breakfast. All he takes is some Chinese tea with sugar and a few biscuits. He poured tea for me, too, and urged me to eat as many biscuits as I liked."[21] Nikolai arranged for a Russian officer to visit the house daily to give Niijima his English lesson. Although Nikolai was reputedly competent in English (as well as in German, French, Greek, and Latin), he seems not to have felt confident enough to tutor the young Japanese.

Niijima had suffered for years from poor eyesight, apparently the result of a severe case of measles, and he asked if he might be treated at the Russian hospital. The next day he visited the hospital and was astonished both by the superior facilities and by the doctors themselves who, unlike Japanese doctors, charged no fees. "They give expensive medicines even to people who are so poor they are like beggars, whatever is needed for their sickness. The only thing they hope for is that when the patient has completely recovered from illness *he will feel fond of the Russians*."[22] He contrasted this kindness with the hospitals established by the Japanese government, where the food was terrible (because hospital officials made money from the food allowance), the medicines inadequate, and the premises dirty.

However, the superiority of the Russian hospital in Hakodate and the kindness with which the Japanese patients were treated induced fears on Niijima's part as to the ultimate effect on the local population:

> It upsets me greatly to think that if the people of Hakodate continue to receive help from Russia for years at a time, they may in the end desert our government and eagerly turn to the Russians instead. Ah, why does our government not realize what the long-term policy of the Russians is? Here we have a dike through which just a little water leaks. But even though it is just a little, unless repairs are made at once, the water will finally destroy the dike, ravage the farmland, carry off the houses, and harm the people. Ah, unless our government quickly repairs the slightly damaged dike that is Hakodate, in the end the water of Russia will destroy the whole dike; the people will be carried off by the water; and no measures will be able to prevent this.[23]

On the eighth day of the fifth month Niijima began work as Japanese tutor to the learned Russian priest: "I began today to read the *Kojiki* with Nikolai," he wrote.[24] Nikolai apparently wished to read the most ancient religious text of the Japanese, and Niijima, though he probably had never before read the *Kojiki* (Record of Ancient Matters), a considerable task even for a scholar of Japanese literature, consented, no doubt because he benefited from the information about the West that Nikolai from time to time during the lessons imparted to the young Japanese:

"According to what the priest says, about the time of our Emperor Richū (in the fifth century A.D.), Russia was *barubarī* (meaning, without decorum and without knowledge?), and the entire people did nothing but fight wars and pillage wherever they went. Moreover, it was the custom that a man could not get a wife unless he had killed someone, nor could a woman get a husband unless she had killed someone."[25]

Niijima continued to give Nikolai lessons in the *Kojiki* almost every day. In return, he not only acquired some English but picked up news of the foreign community in Hakodate. For example, on the twenty-first day of the fifth month the Portuguese consul died. On the following day all the foreign ships in the harbor had their flags at half-mast in mourning, but the Japanese ships did not do the same. Niijima was indignant: "It seems as if they do not know the courtesy appropriate to an allied country. This is really most to be deplored."[26]

Niijima's diary continues without any more remarkable event being noted than a shift in textbook from the *Kojiki* to a popular book on loyalty and filial piety. Then, in the entry for the fourteenth day of the sixth month of 1864 there occurs the electrifying statement: "Tonight, after nine o'clock, with the help of Fujiya Unokichi I secretly went with him by small boat to an American merchant ship which I was able to board."[27] Niijima had been smuggled aboard a foreign ship, violating the prohibition on Japanese subjects leaving the country. Although he does not mention the details in his diary, in a short memorandum he wrote two years later while in America, he explained how on the twelfth day of that month he had been taken to see the captain of the American ship:

> When I told him of my desire to study the learning of his country, and to sail around the world, he was deeply moved by my aspirations, and finally said that he would help me to carry

them out. He told me that his ship was sailing at dawn on the fifteenth, and I promised to get aboard the ship by nine on the night of the fourteenth. I returned to the Russian's house, and sold all of my possessions—everything except my books, my swords, and my clothes—and prepared to sail.[28]

On the thirteenth he had his photograph taken, and sent it to his home as a memento of himself. On the fourteenth, after it got dark, he left Nikolai's house with his scant possessions, hiding his swords under his clothes. He went to the shore and found the small boat that a friend had readied for him and rowed out to the American ship. He recorded in the memorandum, "Because this was something no one had ever tried before, I rowed with desperate strength, and at last was able to board the ship. I felt elated at my success, but I could imagine how my parents would grieve for me, and before I knew it I had composed a poem:

ika ni sen	What am I to do?
aa ika ni sen	Ah, what am I to do?
ika ni sen	What am I to do?
fubo no nageki wo	Thinking of my parents' grief,
ika ni to ya sen[29]	What indeed am I to do?

Unfortunately, this pedestrian verse is a typical example of Niijima's poetry. But all the same, it is notable that, like the diarists of the past, at times he felt compelled to encapsulate his thoughts in poetry.

Although neither the diary nor the memorandum mention it, the ship was searched by Japanese officials before it sailed, but Niijima, with the connivance of the Americans, had been hidden in a locked room and escaped detection. As long as the ship remained in Japanese waters he was still in danger. Even once the ship had safely left Japan, he was alone among strangers whose language he could hardly speak.

The first experience of Niijima's new life that he chose to record in his diary occurred about a week after he had been smuggled aboard the American ship. On the twenty-first day of the sixth month he wrote, "I have just washed three sets of underwear. While I was at home I never washed my own clothes, but I have resigned myself to it now, saying that it is for the sake of my studies, and that to know hardship personally is part of learning."[30] For a young man of the samurai class, washing his clothes was humiliating, but his willingness to perform this menial task was a proof of the earnestness of his endeavor. But even as he washed his clothes, a disquieting thought struck him: if his parents were somehow to learn of the hardships he was undergoing, they would surely weep profusely for him. In true samurai fashion, Niijima forgot neither his dignity nor his parents.

Another, more immediate problem beset him. The smattering of English he had acquired in Hakodate was totally inadequate for him to express himself aboard the American ship. He wrote on the same day, "Because I am still unable to communicate with people, I have to take orders from Chinese. But one day I will tame them like dogs or pigs."[31] Presumably he was able by writing characters to carry on a rudimentary "conversation" with the Chinese, but it must have been galling for a proud samurai youth to have to take orders from men who were probably no more than cooks or cabin boys. In an account of his life he wrote in later years, he described how "when I emptied into the ocean a tub of water after washing the dishes, I inadvertently tossed a spoon overboard. The Chinese steward frightened me by saying that the captain would beat me. I took out all the Japanese money I had, went to the captain's cabin, and confessed to him by making gestures with my hands and shoulders, begging him to take the money for the lost spoon. To my great surprise, he smiled and refused to take the money."[32]

The captain, at least in Niijima's recollections of later years, was a kindly man. Taking a Japanese aboard his ship was risky: if the Japanese authorities had discovered what he had done, he would have been forbidden to visit Japan again. However, Niijima could not pay for passage, and he had to work aboard the ship. Initially, this went against the grain for him as a samurai. In a *kanshi* he composed the day after his unpleasant experience with the Chinese, he spoke of being "made use of by the foreigners."[33]

The captain was not interested in teaching English to the young Japanese. Niijima accordingly asked another American to teach him, but the lessons did not go well. He recorded in his diary, "Because he was just as greedy and mean as the captain, it happened that, after he had taught me seven or eight words, and pronounced each word three or four times, and I still couldn't imitate him, he let out an angry cry, put his hands on my nose and jaw and forced open my mouth. 'Now say *do*!' he said."[34]

Niijima's description of the captain as "greedy and mean" does not accord with the favorable account of the man found in his recollection written twenty years later. The diary is no doubt more trustworthy, but in the recollections there is an interesting passage that is not in the diary. After having been mauled by his short-tempered teacher, Niijima rushed down to his cabin for his sword to avenge himself. He wrote in English, "When I caught my sword and was about to dash out of the room, a thought came to me at once that I must take a serious consideration before I should take such an action."[35] In the end, he persuaded himself that he would have to bear such a trifling humiliation in view of the likelihood that he would endure much worse in the future, and he resolved that he would never resort to his sword for any reason. This was the first step away from his training as a samurai.

On the twenty-fourth Niijima looked off to the east for a last glimpse of Japan, but all he could see of the Land of the Gods was clouds. A more momentous event in Niijima's new life occurred later the same day, as he recorded in his diary. "Last night I had my hair cut to a little more than five inches. This morning this is the way my hair looks."[36] He included at this point a sketch of himself with his new, shortened hair, a compromise between the topknot of a samurai and a Western-style haircut. On the following day still another, vastly more important development occurred in his life: "Today I read a little of the Bible that I had borrowed from Captain Savory. I felt just as if I had returned home and seen my parents again. The joy in my heart was extraordinary."[37] This was Niijima's first meaningful encounter with the Bible, which would become the mainstay of his life in later years.

Soon afterward, as the ship was approaching Shanghai, Niijima took another bold step: "Today, at the mouth of the Yangtze, I cut my hair."[38] He underlined the importance of this second cut by giving the date in full: "Last day of the sixth month of the first year of Genji, the Year of the Rat." He kept a little of his shorn hair, but threw the rest into the sea, composing a *kanshi* in which he asked the sea, if it had a soul, to carry the hair to his family in Japan. He promised that when he had accomplished his great mission, he would once again grow his hair long in the samurai manner.[39] No doubt he felt forlorn at abandoning his identity, but later that day the navigation officer of the ship gave him a hat, and when Niijima put it on, the officer said he looked like a Frenchman. Niijima wrote in his diary, "My joy was higher than Mount Fuji."

The ship that had taken Niijima from Hakodate to Shanghai was to return to Japan, and he therefore had to find another ship that would take him to America. A British sailor who visited the ship promised to return that evening and guide Niijima to a British ship that was about to sail, but he failed to appear as promised. Niijima commented sadly, "I learned for the first time how untrustworthy other people are."[40] In the meantime, the captain of the ship decided to put Niijima to work in the hold. "The stink of the bottom of the ship assaulted my nose, and I thought that I was going to get sick at any moment. It was really a terrible hardship." This seems to have been one of the worst experiences of Niijima's whole life.

Fortunately, he was able to find passage on another vessel, an American ship called *The Wild Rover* that would be sailing to Boston by way of Southeast Asia and the Cape of Good Hope. Niijima wrote, "I felt as if I had escaped the tiger's mouth and had at last entered a realm of delight."[41]

On the eleventh day of the seventh month of 1864 Captain Taylor of *The Wild Rover* summoned Niijima and informed him that he was about to fire his Chinese cabin attendant and that he wished Niijima henceforth to keep his cabin clean and in order. This was the work Niijima was to perform in lieu of paying for his passage.

The captain further told Niijima, "I shall call you by the name Joe."[42] Evidently, the captain could not pronounce the name Niijima, and had decided on Joe as it had the virtue of being short and easy to pronounce. If Niijima resented being called by a foreign name, he does not say so. Indeed, in later years he officially took the name Jō, and when he wrote in English he signed his name Joseph Neesima.

Captain Taylor also warned Niijima to be careful because there was a Japanese "embassy" in Shanghai.[43] Niijima replied in English, "I know three men of Embassy, and a man of three is my good friend. Therefore I must shelter myself in this ship."[44] Niijima feared that if he were seen by another Japanese, even a close friend, he would be arrested and sent back to Japan.

Niijima saw in the harbor a steamship displaying both Japanese and British flags, and was told that the ship was carrying the Japanese embassy back to Japan from Europe. That day, for reasons not stated in the diary, he presented the captain with his sword. He wrote, "I gave my long sword to the captain of the ship. He was extremely pleased."[45] He had surrendered one more vestige of his life as a samurai. In his memoirs, written in English, Niijima explained, "I presented my long sword to the captain, requesting him to take me to the United States, and I agreed to work out my passage without pay." But when the Chinese cabin attendant was fired and Niijima replaced him, he discovered that his duties were far more taxing than he had supposed. He wrote, "All the work I must do makes me feel as if I had entered another tiger's mouth. But the captain is very pleasant, and he is extremely polite when using me."[46]

Niijima noticed in the harbor a ship with an unfamiliar flag and asked Captain Taylor its nationality. He was told it was Siamese, and this made him say with a sigh, "The ship had braved a thousand miles of waves to come here to trade. Ah, why do ships from the Land of the Gods never come?"[47] This may have been the first time that Niijima realized how unusual a phenomenon it was for a country to be closed to the outside world.

However, Niijima's patriotism was undiminished. On the twentieth the captain informed him of the report that Britain was sending troops to attack Japan because the Japanese had opened fire on British ships and an Englishman had been cut down and killed. Niijima was once again moved to sad thoughts, this time expressed in a *kanshi*, perhaps because of his heightened emotions. He was well aware how poorly equipped the Japanese troops were in weapons and supplies, and how they lacked capable leaders; but he was sure that the Japanese would fight the British to the death, and even if the British army defeated the Japanese army, the people would never surrender. The British would never be able to take Japan unless they slaughtered every last Japanese soldier, and in the meantime the Japanese, having experienced many battles, would once more be a strong nation.[48] Needless to say, none of these warlike sentiments would be repeated in the account of his life Niijima wrote in 1885. By this time it was clear that Captain Taylor's report had been incorrect. More important, Niijima was no longer the samurai he was in 1864.

The months Niijima spent aboard *The Wild Rover* were largely uneventful, as we can infer from the absence of diary entries for most days. Occasionally, nostalgic recollections of his parents induced him to compose a haiku or a *kanshi*, and he always identified Sundays, perhaps because of his increasing interest in Christianity, but more likely because it was a welcome day of rest. On the twentieth day of the ninth month the captain told him about an attack by British, French, and Dutch warships on the forts along the straits at Shimonoseki, but Niijima made no comment in his diary. The ship slowly made its way along the Chinese coast to Hong Kong, arriving on the fifth day of the eleventh month.

Three days later Niijima made this entry in his diary: "I sold my short sword to the captain for eight dollars."[49] He gave no explanation of why he had parted with the last remnant of his samurai status, but in the memoir written twenty years later he was more explicit:

> While I was in Hong Kong I wanted to buy a copy of the Chinese New Testament, but found that my Japanese money would not pass there. So I requested the captain to buy my small sword for eight dollars. Some time after I obtained that money, the captain gave me permission to go on shore with the Chinese steward to get a sight of the city. Then I had a fine chance to purchase a copy of the New Testament in a Chinese bookstore.[50]

It is not clear why Niijima failed to mention in the diary his purchase of the Chinese translation of the New Testament. Perhaps he felt apprehensive about showing interest in a religion that was still officially prohibited for Japanese, but his diary is so fragmentary by this time one is led to conjecture that he had lost the habit of describing in full his daily experiences.

The ship meandered on its course, visiting Saigon, Manila, and Sumatra. On the fifteenth Niijima gazed at the full moon alone, with nobody to share his feelings. His thoughts turned toward home, and he composed some poems. The most moving in meaning, though hardly distinguished as a poem, was:

meigetsu ni	When I ventured to ask
fubo wo ikan to	The full moon in its glory,
tazunureba	"How are my parents?"
iwazu kotaezu	It said nothing, replied nothing,
tada akaaka[51]	But only shone the brighter.

Another poem written at this time suggested his exasperation. It bears the prefatory note, "Written out of an excess of suffering over having to perform painful labors day after day":

kaku made to	I had in advance
kanete kakugo wa	Vowed to endure whatever
seshi naredo	Hardship came my way,
kaku kaku kaku to	But I never imagined
joshi to omowaji[52]	It would be like this, this, this.

The Wild Rover made its way around the Cape of Good Hope on May 30. (By this time Niijima had ceased to use the lunar calendar in his diary.) After the long, boring voyage, the sight of distant mountains gave him pleasure and brought back memories of home. On June 18, 1865, *The Wild Rover* passed close to St. Helena. Unfortunately for Niijima, who wanted to have a look at Napoleon's grave, the ship had adequate supplies and there was no need to put in.

On July 24 the ship at last reached Boston. Niijima wrote in his diary, "Today I landed at Boston. I bought the biography of Robinson Crusoe. Cost, one and a half dollars."[53] *Robinson Crusoe* was an appropriate book for a Japanese about to begin life, all alone, in a continent far from home.

Soon after his arrival in Boston, Niijima said goodbye to *The Wild Rover*, aboard which he had lived almost a year. He met the owner of the ship, Alpheus Hardy, who immediately showed unusual kindness to the young man, even buying him warm clothes to stave off the rigors of the New England winter, though it was still some time away. Hardy was to be Niijima's great benefactor in America, as he acknowledged implicitly when he assumed his "official" name, Joseph Hardy Neesima. Hardy's interest in Niijima may have been aroused originally merely because the young man had lived so long aboard one of his ships, but surely some other factor was also involved. Niijima's determination and perhaps his exceptional nobility of character were communicated to Hardy especially by the brief essay that Niijima wrote in English, at Hardy's request, explaining why he had left Japan. For his part, Niijima seems to have sensed, now that he had met Hardy, he was in safe hands. The diary called *Kōkai Nikki* (Diary of a Voyage) concludes with a *kanshi* in which

Niijima declared that, having traveled a thousand *ri* in order to accomplish his resolve, he would not be affected by homesickness.

The first problem ahead of Niijima was to learn English properly. Hardy asked acquaintances if Joseph (as he was known) might live with them. They hesitated, wondering how they could share their house with someone who scarcely knew English and who was unfamiliar with their ways. They may also have felt uneasy about having a heathen under their roof. But, after reading the account that Niijima had written of himself in his crude English, they opened their hearts. On January 2, 1866, after Niijima had lived at the house of Miss Hidden about three months, she wrote Hardy in these terms:

"I have no fancy or desire to take boarders, and should not in this instance except for the peculiar circumstances. We have made him a regular member of the family; he sits with us all the time and shares the privileges of the family."[54]

On the previous day Niijima had written Hardy a letter in his artless but charming English describing his happiness: "O, dear Sir, I feel your kindness and goodness from the top of my head to the extreme of my feet, and I wish you to know that since I came here how happy I am, and how successful as follows." He described his studies—arithmetic, English, geography and, above all, the Bible, which he read with fascination, memorizing the parts he deemed most important.

Six months later Miss Hidden wrote Mrs. Hardy, "From the first I have felt that it was a privilege to have his influence thrown in my way . . . My dear Mrs. Hardy, I feel that as God in his providence has given you the means and the heart to take this heaven-directed wanderer into your charge, you have found a diamond of which the world is not worthy, of which you may well be proud."[55]

Niijima entered Amherst College in September 1867. He was admitted by exception because he had not studied Greek and Latin, then required, but he performed so brilliantly in his studies that he was chosen at graduation to represent his class. He naturally did not forget his parents or Japan. A letter sent to his father, in which he described his life in America and his resolve never to abandon his parents, is especially affecting.

Niijima kept several diaries in English while he was in America and others in Japanese in which he described travels in Japan after his return. They are all of interest, but cannot approach the testament of the early diaries that tell us so unforgettably of his great physical and spiritual adventure.

Notes

1. Translation from *Meiji Bungaku Zenshū*, XLVI, p. 27. This autobiographical essay, "Watakushi no Wakaki Hibi," was written in August 1885.
2. Niijima also gave an alternate explanation: he was born in the fourteenth year of the Tempō era [1843] shortly after New Year, when the decorations called *shime* were still on display.
3. English text in *Meiji Bungaku Zenshū*, XLVI, pp. 34–35.
4. *Niijima Jō Zenshū*, V, p. 6. All quotations from Niijima's diaries come from this volume.
5. *Meiji Bungaku Zenshū*, XLVI, p. 35.
6. Two translations of *Robinson Crusoe* were made during the last years of the shogunate. The first, made in 1850 from a Dutch translation of the English, did not appear until after the Meiji Restoration; the second was published in 1857. See my *Dawn to the West*, I, pp. 60, 63, 78.
7. *Meiji Bungaku Zenshū*, XLVI, p. 36.
8. *Ibid.*, p. 37.
9. Manjirō was stranded on a desert island in 1841 when his fishing boat sank in a storm. He was rescued by an American whaling ship, taken to America, and given training as a cooper. He later became a gold prospector in California. He returned to Japan (via Okinawa) in 1851. Although he had (unwittingly) broken the law that prohibited Japanese from going abroad, he was forgiven because his knowledge was needed. He served as the interpreter for Commodore Perry in 1853, and from 1860 was the chief interpreter of the shogun. He later taught not only English but also navigation and whaling.
10. *Niijima*, V, p. 9.
11. *Ibid.*, pp. 9–10.

12. *Ibid.*, p. 11.

13. *Ibid.*, p. 12.

14. *Ibid.*

15. *Ibid.*, p. 15.

16. For a good, short account of Takeda Ayasaburō, see Numata Jirō et al., *Yōgakushi Jiten*, p. 434. The Muragaki mentioned here is the author of the diary that described the first Japanese mission to the United States.

17. *Niijima*, V, p. 19.

18. Probably meaning that, in the Japanese way, each man, after drinking some sake, gave his cup to another man and filled it. The exchange of cups (*ken-shū*), though no longer as common as in the past, persists as a mark of conviviality.

19. *Niijima*, V, p. 20.

20. *Ibid.*

21. *Ibid.*

22. *Ibid.*, p. 22. The last words are underlined in the text.

23. *Ibid.*

24. *Ibid.*

25. *Ibid.*, pp. 22–23.

26. *Ibid.*, p. 35.

27. *Ibid.*, p. 37.

28. This passage is taken from the diary "Hakodate Yori no Ryakki," in *ibid.*, p. 72.

29. *Ibid.*

30. *Ibid.*, p. 38.

31. *Ibid.*

32. From "Watakushi no Wakaki Hibi," in *Meiji Bungaku Zenshū*, XLVI, p. 40. A similar text is given by Arthur Sherburne Hardy in *Life and Letters of Joseph Hardy Neesima*, pp. 39–40.

33. *Niijima*, V, p. 39.

34. *Ibid.* Perhaps the problem was that Niijima was rendering it as "zu." The syllable *du* does not occur in Japanese words.

35. Hardy, *Life*, p. 39.

36. *Niijima*, V, p. 40.

37. *Ibid.*

38. *Ibid.*, p. 41.

39. *Ibid.*

40. *Ibid.*, p. 42.

41. *Ibid.*
42. *Ibid.*, p. 43.
43. This no doubt refers to the mission, headed by Takenouchi Yasunori. See above, p. 53.
44. *Niijima*, V, p. 43.
45. *Ibid.*
46. *Ibid.*
47. *Ibid.*, p. 44.
48. *Ibid.*
49. *Ibid.*, p. 54.
50. Hardy, *Life*, p. 40.
51. *Niijima*, V, p. 61.
52. *Ibid.*, p. 62.
53. *Ibid.*, p. 67.
54. Letter from Mary E. Hidden to Mr. Hardy, dated January 2, 1866; in Hardy, *Life*, p. 51.
55. *Ibid.*, p. 67.

Bibliography

Hardy, Arthur Sherburne. *Life and Letters of Joseph Hardy Neesima*. Boston: Houghton, Mifflin, 1893.

Keene, Donald. *Dawn to the West*, 2 vols. New York: Holt, Rinehart and Winston, 1984.

Meiji Bungaku Zenshū, XLVI. Tokyo: Chikuma Shobō, 1977.

Niijima Jō Zenshū, V. Kyoto: Dōhōsha Shuppan, 1984.

Numata Jirō et al. (eds.). *Yōgakushi Jiten*. Tokyo: Yūshōdō, 1984.

Diaries
by
Politicians

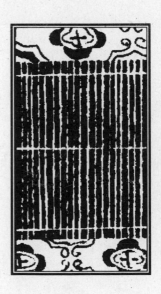

The Diary of Kido Takayoshi

Niijima Jō met Mori Arinori in Boston on March 15, 1871. At the time Mori's official position was Lesser Minister Resident in the United States of America (*gasshūkoku chūsatsu shō-bemmushi*). Mori promised to help Niijima obtain a passport if he should wish to return to Japan; Niijima's crime in having left Japan illegally had been forgiven. Mori and Niijima met several times during the next few months and became friendly enough for Niijima to ask Mori's assistance in establishing an American-style university in Japan. He seems already to have been planning the future Dōshisha University in Kyoto.

Early in the following year, Niijima had word from Mori of the forthcoming visit of a mission headed by an envoy extraordinary and ambassador plenipotentiary, and he was asked to come to Washington to explain the American educational system to the members of the mission. On March 20, 1872, Niijima met Tanaka Fujimaro (1845–1909), councillor for education. Two days later, Kido Takayoshi (1833–1877), the associate ambassador of the mission, wrote in his diary, "I met Nishijima for the first time today. In order to pursue his studies, he sneaked out of Japan seven or eight years ago and came to this country. He has already graduated from a university, and at present he is devoting himself faithfully to education. He is a friend I can rely on."[1] (Kido seems to have misheard Niijima as Nishijima.)

The next day Niijima wrote his foster parents, Mr. and Mrs. Hardy, that he had been invited to accompany Councillor Tanaka to Europe and requested their permission, which they gladly gave. Niijima had evidently impressed not only Kido but also other members of the mission. On April 1 Kido wrote in his diary, "Prince Nabeshima, Tanaka Fuji[maro], Nishijima Shimeta, and others have left this place. It is only since coming here that I have first conversed with Nishijima. His kindness and sincerity sharply contrast with the frivolity and superficiality of those who recklessly call for 'enlightenment' these days. When I am with him I feel as if I have found an old friend, and I derive no small benefit from our conversations. He is someone to depend on in the future."[2]

Kido mentions Niijima once again in his diary. Niijima traveled through Europe with Tanaka, inspecting educational institutions. His itinerary was not the same as for other members of the mission, but Kido and Niijima met again at the hot springs in Wiesbaden, Germany, where Niijima had gone for nervous exhaustion and rheumatism. On May 26, 1873, he noted that Niijima (this time he gave the name correctly) had called on him.[3]

That is all that Kido had to say about Niijima. Even these few crumbs of impression provide an interesting sidelight on Niijima, who evidently had greatly pleased Kido. This is worthy of note, not only because Kido was generally unfavorably disposed toward Christians but because he so seldom in his diary described anyone with warmth. The diary, though invaluable for its account of political conflicts at the beginning of the Meiji era, is notably lacking in the human interest that normally gives Japanese diaries their special appeal. Kido knew most of the important political figures in Japan, and during his travels abroad met various monarchs and statesmen who must have produced some kind of impression on him, but in the diary he maintained a resolutely stoic attitude. Although a passionate man, he preferred to think of himself as a Confucian recluse, untouched by the commotion of the external world. Even if we admire this stance, it is hard not to regret that he did not give more of himself to the diary.

Kido's short life (he died at the age of forty-four) was full of excitement. He was born into an influential family in Chōshū and as a youth became a disciple of Yoshida Shōin, the spiritual leader of the *sonnō jōi* movement. He was not only learned in the Confucian classics but also an expert swordsman, and studied Western military tactics with the pioneer expert Egawa Tarōzaemon (1801–1855). He urged military preparedness on the daimyo of the Chōshū clan, and personally participated in many of the martial events preceding and accompanying the Meiji Restoration. He narrowly escaped death in 1861 when the Satsuma clan was suppressing extremist elements in Kyoto. His perils at this time were shared by a beautiful courtesan who protected him and enabled him to escape. In 1866 he secretly drew up the formal alliance with Saigō Takamori (1827–1877) of the Satsuma clan that led directly to the overthrow of the shogun's government and the restoration to power of the emperor. One of the most powerful men of the new régime, he was responsible for the move of the capital from Kyoto to Edo (Tokyo). Even Japanese who know nothing of his biography have heard about the exploits of his youth, when he was known as Katsura Kogorō. There is hardly a more romantic figure in modern Japanese history.

When we turn to his diary, kept between the years 1868 and 1877, our expectations are high. The diary is indeed far more detailed and varied than those kept by other statesmen of the period, but all the same, it is likely to prove a disappointment for anyone who is not especially interested in political history. The early years covered by the diary are remarkable chiefly for the number of times Kido's day ended in a drinking party and sometimes in a state of total inebriation. On a higher plane, the interest he displayed in calligraphy is striking; he was again and again asked for samples of his writing. His diary is otherwise given over to repeated expressions of frustration because his policies had not been adopted, but it is seldom clear exactly how his wishes were being foiled. One has the exasperating feeling after reading the diary that one does not know him much better than before.

The fault is partly one of style. Compared to Kume Kunitake's splendid description of the travels of the Iwakura mission to America and Europe, Kido's writing is dull and virtually without incident or personal comment. He mentions that he climbed to the top of the Arc de Triomphe and then visited Nôtre-Dame, but he has not a word to say of his impressions.[4] Is it possible they made no impact on him? When at Brighton in England he accidentally saw the exiled Napoleon III, the Empress Eugénie and the prince imperial riding in a carriage, he wrote not a word of even the most conventional commiseration.[5] If Kido had been a colorless politician, it would be easy to understand this silence, but we expect more from the dashing Katsura Kogorō.

No doubt Kido intended his to be a public diary, and for that reason omitted personal feelings (though he was not ashamed to reveal his drunkenness). The failure of this diary to convey the personality of the man is typical of others by statesmen, and contrasts with the individuality found in the literary diaries of the time.

Notes

1. *Kido Takayoshi Nikki*, II, p. 147. See also the translation by Sydney DeVere Brown, *The Diary of Kido Takayoshi*, II, pp. 140–41.
2. *Kido Takayoshi Nikki*, II, p. 152. See also Brown, *The Diary*, II, pp. 144–45.
3. *Kido Takayoshi Nikki*, II, p. 383.
4. *Ibid.*, p. 296.
5. *Ibid.*, p. 216.

Bibliography

Brown, Sydney DeVere. *The Diary of Kido Takayoshi*, 3 vols. Tokyo: University of Tokyo Press, 1983–86.

Kido Takayoshi Nikki, 3 vols., in Nihon Shiseki Kyōkai Sōsho series. Tokyo: Tōkyō Daigaku Shuppankai, 1967.

The Diary of Ueki Emori

The most personal of the diaries kept by statesmen of the Meiji era was undoubtedly that of Ueki Emori (1857–1892). The diary opens on February 15, 1873, when he was sixteen. The young man had performed brilliantly at the clan school in his native Kōchi (on the island of Shikoku), and he was chosen to study at a newly founded private school in Tokyo called Kainan Shigaku, which was primarily devoted to Western learning. Ueki sailed for Kōbe three days later and, after several days of sightseeing in Osaka, he boarded another ship that reached Tokyo on February 23. On March 2 he visited the graves of the forty-seven loyal retainers of the lord of Akō at the Sengaku Temple. So far, he was behaving like a model young samurai on his first visit to the capital, and his diary contains little to attract our interest.

By 1875, however, the diary (which hitherto has consisted almost exclusively of brief entries mentioning where Ueki went that day or to whom he sent a letter) becomes more interesting as new, untraditional elements entered his life. On June 9, for example, he ate bread for the first time. On November 22 he had his first drink of milk, and on December 14 his first taste of sherry, which made him drunk.[1] On

January 20, 1896, he celebrated his birthday by drinking wine and eating beef soup.[2]

His intellectual life also picked up at about the same time. He noted (on the same day that he ate his first piece of bread) that he had returned a borrowed copy of the *Meiroku Zasshi*, a journal published by leading advocates of "civilization and enlightenment," and before long he was associating with the members of their society.[3] He attended lectures on educational and political matters and read John Stuart Mill's *On Liberty* in the translation published in 1871 by Nakamura Keiu (1832–1891). He visited the Irifune-chō church on a number of occasions, and plied the minister, an American, with questions about religious doctrine.[4] He regularly attended lectures held at Keiō University, the bastion of Fukuzawa Yukichi's advocacy of enlightenment. He visited the licensed quarter in Yoshiwara, though it is unclear whether he went merely to see dances or if he indulged in other pleasures (which form so memorable a part of later sections of his diary).

So far little distinguished Ueki's first years in the capital from the similar experiences of any young samurai intellectual, but almost without any warning the following entry appears for March 15, 1876: "I went to the Tokyo court with a town flunky, and at one o'clock sentence was passed in the courtroom on Oka Takayoshi and myself. We were condemned to two months of imprisonment. About four in the afternoon I went into prison."[5] Ueki does not reveal why he was sent to prison, but it was apparently because of an article he had contributed to the newspaper *Yūbin Hōchi* a month earlier. The article, entitled "Hito wo Saru ni suru Seifu" (Governments that Make Men into Monkeys), when read today appears harmless: Ueki seems to be saying merely that ideas are what distinguish men from monkeys, and if a ruler deprives people of the right to have ideas of their own, he is in effect turning them into monkeys. Ueki had wondered about the advisability of publishing such an article at a time when censorship of the press was becoming increasingly severe. On February 28 he had consulted with Oka Takayoshi, a former editor at the Hōchi

Company, about the regulations on punishment for contributions to newspapers;[6] now both were in prison together.

Ueki remained in prison until May 13. He noted in his diary that he had shared Cell 22 with various intellectuals, including Narushima Ryūhoku. He had also profited by the enforced leisure to read the Confucian classics, including *Tso Chuan*. His two months in prison in such good company and with such books to read no doubt contributed to Ueki's education.

After Ueki left prison he naturally felt obliged to write about his experiences, and later in 1876 he published an article with the arresting title of "Jiyū wa Senketsu wo mote Kawazaru Bekarazaru Ron" (Why Liberty Must Be Bought with Fresh Blood). His ideas on freedom were much influenced by those of the liberal politician Itagaki Taisuke (1837–1919). He first heard Itagaki lecture in Kōchi, and his participation in the *jiyū minken undō* (movement for freedom and people's rights) for which he is best known was inspired by admiration for Itagaki. After his release from prison, Ueki lived for a time in Itagaki's house in Tokyo, and served as tutor to one of his daughters. When Itagaki returned to Kōchi in February, 1877, Ueki followed him.

Ueki was also much affected by Christian thought. His diary again and again mentions attending church and hearing sermons. For example, on January 7, 1877, he wrote: "Sunday. Read *The Family Library*.[7] In the afternoon went to hear the sermon at Nikolai.[8] It had already ended when I arrived. So I went to Verbeck's[9] to hear a lecture on the Bible. At night I stopped by a lecture given at Yagenbori on the Bible."[10] Ueki also read many Christian writings, as we know from another diary he kept of his readings. We also know, thanks to the researches of Ienaga Saburō, that Ueki published under a pseudonym various articles written from a Christian point of view. One finds in these writings such statements as "At present, the religion of our party is a pure Protestantism that follows our party's revered Bible—in other words, the faction of freedom."[11] It was probably the Christian insistence on the existence of duties that are higher than one's obligations to the state that attracted Ueki more than theological matters. He attended Protestant, Catholic, and Russian Orthodox churches indiscriminately.

Even after his release from prison, Ueki remained a dangerous man in the eyes of the police. His diary mentions various occasions when he was summoned for questioning. On May 13, 1878, he recorded in his diary, "At night a policeman came and asked me repeatedly about what I did before and after my trip. Later, I was summoned to the East Substation where I was interrogated by a police inspector and asked about my travels."[12]

In September of that year he visited Kyoto as a tourist. He wandered from temple to temple, crisscrossed the main bridges near the Gion area, and finally found a place to stay near the Sanjō Bridge. He wrote, "Tonight a detective has come to stay in the room next to mine."[13] Detective or no detective, Ueki was much too excited to remain in his room, and he rushed back and forth across the Kamo River taking in the sights, from time to time drinking lemonade or eating shaved ice. Wherever he went he was followed by detectives. He noted, "Today the two detectives ran out of wooden clogs and are barefoot. They also showed how greatly distressed they were when, after twelve, I still hadn't eaten lunch."[14] Following Ueki around Kyoto must have been an exhausting task for the poor detectives.

It seems clear from the diary that Ueki's only purpose in staying in Kyoto was to enjoy the sights and the other pleasures of the old capital, but the police were suspicious. On October 24, after he had been in Kyoto for more than a month, he complained, "Every day when I go out, two detectives invariably follow me. They are always following me, close or far away, regardless of the time of day or night, and they never leave me for a minute, even when I go to the public bath or the hairdresser."[15] He supposed that this attention from the police was owing to his having, on a previous visit to Kyoto, met some persons who were suspected of being subversive.

Soon, however, he developed a quite different interest in Kyoto from the temples and bridges—the various women whose favors he bought. He had slept with geishas in other cities, but his favorites were those in Kyoto, and that may be why he kept returning to this city. For example, on April 24, 1880, he left Osaka for Kyoto: "I went to the theater in Gion and saw the dances of the *maiko* [apprentice geishas] from the Yasaka quarter. I stopped by Ueda Take's place in Gion and sent for the geishas Kosato and Tsuruyo. I ended by spending the night."[16] The next day, after visiting the Exposition and seeing the Imperial Palace, "I bathed at the Maruyama Baths and sent for the Kyoto geisha Tamatsuru."[17] Three days later, on April 27, he went to the Society of Patriots,[18] and followed this by buying a geisha named Yukimatsu.

Brief entries concerning his active political life alternate in the diary with equally brief mentions of his exceptionally active sexual life. On May 3 he states simply, "Sent for Wakamatsu." The diary entry for the next day is: "Sent a request for the copyright of a book on freedom of speech." On May 22 he gave a lecture attended by about five hundred people. The next day, back in Osaka, he sent for the geisha Wakamatsu. The entry for May 24 is: "I have caught a bit of gonorrhea." Not discouraged by this development, he sent for Wakamatsu once again on the twenty-fifth.

Ueki seems to have felt no conflict between the high ideals he expressed publicly and his private sessions with the women he bought. On October 8, 1880, he reported in his diary, "At night I gave a speech at the Minami Theater on Shijō. There were more than three thousand in the audience, and it was an extremely festive occasion. At eleven I went to the Yōkarō in Shimabara, and sent for Hatsuyuki-dayū."[19] Surely few diaries record such contrasts between public and private behavior!

On February 1, 1881, Ueki had a most peculiar dream: "I dreamed that I slept in the same bed with the emperor. I also slept under the same covers with the empress and had sexual intercourse with her."[20] From this point on, Ueki frequently referred to himself in the diary as the emperor (*tennō*) and he used appropriate honorifics to describe his own actions. For example, on July 30 a party was held to celebrate daily publication of the newspaper *Kōchi Shimbun*. Ueki noted, "The emperor deigned to be present."[21] On August 3 Ueki (referring to himself) wrote, "The emperor is staying at the Jiyūtei in Motomachi." On September 24 of the following year (1882), while in Sendai, he wrote in his diary, "At night Chiyoura of the Shinchikurō visited His Majesty, bringing along a maid. His Majesty also went to the Shinchikurō. He sent for a hundred *maiko* and watched them perform."[22]

Beginning in 1883 Ueki used a different system of dating each year. This year he identified first as "the year 2543 since the founding of Japan," but later as "the year 1883 since the birth of the Holy Master of the West," and finally as "the twentieth anniversary of the birth of the Great Emperor of the World."[23] The words *great emperor* (*daikōtei*) refer to Ueki Emori himself, but for some reason he said that he was twenty years old, rather than his actual age of twenty-six. (On New Year's Day two years later he rectified the error by giving the number of years since his descent into the world as twenty-eight.)

On February 13, 1883, however, he struck a disquieting note: "The emperor has had a venereal disease since the middle of last month."[24] Ueki seems to have been paying the price of his nightly revels, but he was by no means reformed. On March 13, 1884, he wrote, "The emperor at night made a stately progress to Yoshiwara. At the Kōzenrō he sent for the courtesan Nagao."[25] The date January 1, 1887, was expressed in terms of the years since the descent to Japan of the legendary Emperor Jimmu, since the birth of Jesus, and since the commencement of the reign of the Kuang-hsü emperor in China. It was also "the thirtieth year of the descent of the Great Emperor of the World."[26] Similar entries are given for New Year's Day of 1890 and 1891. One of Ueki's last references to himself as the emperor is in the entry for December 10, 1887, where he wrote simply, "The emperor has venereal disease."[27]

Ueki nowhere explained why he kept referring to himself as the emperor. Perhaps it was because of antimonarchical sentiments. On

August 2, 1879, he had a dream that he remembered in these terms: "At night I had a dream. I was in Tokyo, and somebody got furious with me because, he said, I had failed in my argument to express reverence for the emperor, or perhaps it was that I said something close to advocating a republican form of government. Anyway, he sent two youths to stab me. I was slightly wounded, but did not die."[28]

Perhaps this dream conveys political views that existed in Ueki's subconscious, though he seldom felt bold enough to express them openly. In January 1880 he wrote an article in which he declared that although some people feared a republican form of government, if truly understood and put into practice it would prove a blessing to the nation.[29] But, however convinced Ueki may have been of the superiority of a republic to a monarchy, it was prudent not to express these views openly, as he knew from the months he spent in prison for having published much less controversial opinions.

The strange dreams that appear in Ueki Emori's diary help to give it an interest not found in the diaries of other politicians of the era. He is remembered today as one of the most progressive thinkers of the Meiji era, but in reading his diary the frequent mentions of the women with whom he slept are apt to make one forget that he was a leading advocate of equal rights for women. One forgets, too, the lectures he gave on subjects that demonstrated his enlightened opinions, and the books of modern European thought that he read. His dreams, the most memorable parts of the diary, were not always erotic. For example, in October 1882 he dreamed he went to France and met Herbert Spencer and discussed his philosophy.

Ueki felt no shame over hiring women's bodies; it was perfectly acceptable in the society in which he lived for a man to have one or more mistresses, and visits to prostitutes, though not often mentioned by other diarists, were taken as a matter of course. Ueki is remembered instead for such articles as "Danjo Dōken ni tsukite no koto" (Concerning Equal Rights for Men and Women), written in June 1879, perhaps the first instance of a Japanese openly advocating equal

rights. Earlier Japanese who had visited America and Europe sometimes urged improved treatment of women, but not equality. Ono
Azusa, who had studied abroad and had later helped to found Tōkyō
Semmon Gakkō, the antecedent of Waseda University, was unusually liberal in that he believed unmarried women had equal rights
with men, but he feared that if husbands and wives enjoyed equality
it would destroy the necessary harmony within families.[30]

Ueki, perhaps in the attempt to understand and justify his strong
sexual urges, published in September 1878 an article entitled "Ningen
Isshō Hana no Gotoshi" (A Person's Life Is Like a Flower) in which
he insisted that the period of life when sexual intercourse is most desired is the glory of all forms of existence. The essay begins,

> I am asked, "What do you mean by flower?" and I reply, "I
> mean by flower the sexual union of flowers. The time when
> the stamens and the pistils unite sexually is the full blossoming
> of the flower, its glory" . . . Ahh, the flower is the sexual union
> of flowers. How alike, how alike this is for human beings . . .
> What is called in the world "civilization and enlightenment"
> [bummei kaika] is none other than something created with
> ardor at a time when human beings, male and female, give
> free play to their sexual desire and join in achieving the truest
> pleasure.[31]

Ueki may have been influenced by an article by Tsuda Mamichi
(1829–1903) on sexual desire, which appeared in an 1875 issue of
Meiroku Zasshi. Tsuda had argued that sexual desire was the greatest
gift of the Creator to human beings, and had rejected the arguments
of Buddhists who held that desire was sinful and Confucianists who
held that it was injurious. Ueki may even have been influenced by
similar views expressed many years earlier by Hirata Atsutane
(1776–1843).[32] But his diary entry for August 29, 1880, suggests still
another possible influence: "At night I left the Tsurutei and went to

Shimabara.[33] I went to the Yōkarō and diverted myself with Hana-mado. It was just the same as Socrates amusing himself with a cour-tesan."[34]

It has sometimes been suggested that Ueki wrote his famous editorial against prostitution, published in February 1882, while enjoying himself in a brothel, but there is no evidence to support this. It is clear, all the same, that his advocacy of equal rights for women began while he was still indulging himself with prostitutes. He recognized the difficulty of abolishing prostitution in the near future, and urged that efforts should be made in the meantime to educate prostitutes in the principles of liberalism (*jiyū shugi*). This, he held, would benefit not only the prostitutes but also their customers.

Perhaps it was to this end that he decided to teach some prosti-tutes popular-rights songs (*minken kayō*) and dances (*minken odori*). Diary entries for August 1881 touch on his efforts:

> **2nd**. At night I went for a stroll along the riverbed by the quarter. I took in the evening cool with Saka Yoshizō and others. At eleven o'clock more than thirty geishas from the Yōkirō appeared and danced. The emperor climbed to an eminence and observed them.
>
> **3rd**. The emperor from today is staying at the Jiyūtei in Hom-machi ... Later, he summoned some geishas and drank sake.
>
> **4th**. Went to the Risshisha.[35] Discussed the Constitution.
>
> **5th**. ... Went to the Risshisha, heard a lecture on Christianity, then went to the riverside.
>
> **6th**. At night joined Kurohara Heisaku, and then went to the Shikuntei with both dancing masters. We assembled all the geishas and trained them in these dances.[36]

We find in the diary (entry for August 29), not long after these events, the laconic statement, "Spent the day quietly by myself. Drew up a draft of the Japanese Constitution."[37] It is hard to believe that the man who a week earlier had helped to teach geishas the latest dances was now engaged in anything as serious as the framing of the first constitution, but the combination of pleasure and politics occurs again and again in Ueki's diary. For example, on December 8, 1881: "There was a general meeting of the members of the Jiyūsha [Liberal Society] and they held a party in my honor. Over seventy people attended, and I gave a talk on my belief that freedom must be the central axis of our movement. Many geishas also came to listen."[38]

Ueki's dreams and daily life sometimes present the same combination. On April 26, 1882, he wrote in his diary,

"Tonight I dreamed that I had raised an army to bring about a revolution in Japan. I went to amuse myself at the Kameya. In the afternoon I hired a rickshaw and headed toward Kōbe on the way back home. The two men who pulled the rickshaw went so fast it was like flying. After a while we arrived in Kōbe. I wandered around to various places amusing myself. At night I went to Fukuhara and sent for the geisha Kotama."[39]

Ueki had extremely little to say in his diary about his marriage. The entry for July 20, 1881, states merely, "This evening a marriage ceremony with Yamawaki Kamejo was performed."[40] The entry for July 24 says, "Tonight I went to the Yamawakis. This is my first visit as their son-in-law."[41] He says nothing more about his wife nor about why his marriage was soon afterward annulled. He did not remarry.

Mentions of brothels sharply diminish and eventually cease to appear altogether in the diary after he began to give lectures on the necessity of abolishing prostitution. As a member of the Kōchi Prefectural Assembly, he sponsored a bill prohibiting prostitution that was passed with only one opposing vote. He was much in demand as a speaker before gatherings of associations of high-minded ladies. On May 23, 1889, he noted in his diary, "At the request of the Tokyo Women's Christian Temperance Union I gave a lecture at the Sukiyabashi Hall on monogamy."[42] His dreams (as recorded in the diary) still turned at times to beautiful women. He wrote about his first dream of 1884: "Last night I dreamed I went to England and met a beautiful woman."[43] Ueki in fact never went abroad. His development as a human being, recorded with startling frankness in his diary, suggests that it was no longer necessary for Japanese to travel abroad in order to become modern men.

Notes

1. *Ueki Emori Shū*, VII, p. 81.
2. *Ibid.*, p. 84.
3. The society was called the Meirokusha—*mei* for Meiji, *roku* for sixth, and *sha* for society. Mori Arinori proposed the founding of a society for the promotion of "civilization and enlightenment" in the sixth year of Meiji; hence the name. For a good short account of the society, see the article by Jerry K. Fisher in *Kodansha Encyclopedia of Japan*, V, p. 161. The magazine, which appeared in 1874 and 1875, has been translated by William R. Braisted in *Meiroku Zasshi: Journal of the Japanese Enlightenment*.
4. *Ueki Emori Shū*, VII, pp. 65–67, 75–76, 79.
5. *Ibid.*, p. 88.
6. *Ibid.*, p. 87.
7. *Katei Sōdan*. I have not traced this collection.
8. Presumably, the Nikorai-dō, the popular name for the Cathedral of the Resurrection, a Russian Orthodox church, founded by Archbishop Nikolai (1836–1912), that is still a prominent landmark in Tokyo.
9. Guido Verbeck. See p. 91.
10. *Ueki Emori Shū*, VII, p. 111.
11. Ienaga Saburō, *Ueki Emori Kenkyū*, p. 90.
12. *Ueki Emori Shū*, VII, p. 153.
13. *Ibid.*, p. 165.
14. *Ibid.*, p. 171.
15. *Ibid.*, p. 172.
16. *Ibid.*, p. 234.
17. *Ibid.*
18. Aikokusha, formed by Itagaki Taisuke in 1875, developed by 1880 into a major political organization with close to a hundred thousand members. Its aims were highly serious.
19. *Ueka Emori Shū*, VII, p. 247.

20. *Ibid.*, p. 258.
21. *Ibid.*, p. 270.
22. *Ibid.*, p. 303.
23. *Ibid.*, p. 309.
24. *Ibid.*, p. 313.
25. *Ibid.*, p. 338.
26. *Ueki Emori Shū*, VIII, p. 26.
27. *Ibid.*, p. 39.
28. *Ueki Emori Shū*, VII, p. 205.
29. See Sotozaki Mitsuhiro, *Ueki Emori to Onnatachi*, p. 53.
30. *Ibid.*, p. 49.
31. Ienaga, *Ueki*, p. 196.
32. See my *Japanese Discovery of Europe*, p. 168.
33. A licensed quarter in Kyoto.
34. *Ueki Emori Shū*, VII, p. 244.
35. Self-Help Society, founded in 1874 by Itagaki Taisuke and others in the Freedom and People's Rights Movement. The name was taken from the translation of Samuel Smiles's *Self-Help*, which had appeared in 1870.
36. *Ueki Emori Shū*, VII, p. 271.
37. *Ibid.*, p. 273.
38. *Ibid.*, p. 282.
39. *Ibid.*, p. 292.
40. *Ibid.*, p. 270.
41. *Ibid.*
42. *Ueki Emori Shū*, VIII, p. 80.
43. *Ueki Emori Shū*, VII, p. 333.

Bibliography

Braisted, William R. *Meiroku Zasshi; Journal of the Japanese Enlightenment.* Cambridge, Mass.: Harvard University Press, 1976.

Ienaga Saburō. *Ueki Emori Kenkyū.* Tokyo: Iwanami Shoten, 1960.

Keene, Donald. *The Japanese Discovery of Europe.* Stanford, Calif.: Stanford University Press, 1969.

Kodansha Encyclopedia of Japan, 9 vols. Tokyo: Kodansha, 1983.

Sotozaki Mitsuhiro. *Ueki Emori to Onnatachi.* Tokyo: Domesu Shuppan, 1976.

Ueki Emori Shū, 10 vols. Tokyo: Iwanami Shoten, 1990.

Diaries
by
Women

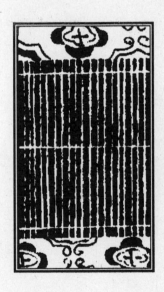

Koume's Diary

It is easy to form the impression that the Meiji Restoration caused the entire country to be inundated with influences from abroad. Even Japanese whose lives were not directly affected by the political changes must have been influenced at least indirectly by the new learning and the new inventions imported from the West. This impression is confirmed by old photographs such as the one showing Iwakura Tomomi, the nobleman who headed the mission sent to America and Europe in 1871, dressed in formal Japanese attire but wearing Western shoes. Woodblock prints from the same period depict fashionable young women with their hair done in exotic styles that clearly originated abroad. Prints of the 1880s persuade us with their depictions of the Rokumeikan (Hall of the Belling Deer) that similar ballrooms must have existed in all parts of the country, as part of a national effort to absorb the new European culture. Indeed, picturesque examples of houses with gables and bow windows, built in the age of "culture and enlightenment," are still to be found in all parts of Japan, from Hokkaidō to Kyūshū.

The diaries kept by men of the time, especially the kind of men I have been considering, contain repeated references to the new culture. Even men who never went abroad read books that stirred their interest in new social or political ideals. The enormous success of translations or adaptations of foreign works of literature that preached such ideals as parliamentary democracy or self-help proves how ready many Japanese men were for change. By way of contrast, very few diaries by women of the period have been published, and their contents contrast strikingly with those kept by men. It may be only an accident that this disparity exists. Hundreds or perhaps thousands of diaries by women of the early Meiji era may lie in storehouses somewhere, food for bookworms; or, in the worst cases, the descendants of these women, having decided that no one would ever be interested in some rambling account of unimportant events found in an old lady's diary, may have destroyed the diaries or used them for scrap paper.

The diary of Kawai Koume (1804–1889) is perhaps the most extensive to have been printed. It has entries for the years between 1849 and 1885, though for some years there are only brief jottings, and other years, including the first eight years of the Meiji era, are a blank, presumably because the manuscript has been lost. Most of the entries are uninteresting. The weather is invariably described in detail, and much space is devoted to visits to and from people who are now totally forgotten. Even if Koume had been lucky enough to know people who are still remembered today, her diary would probably not have provided any fresh glimpses into their characters because she so seldom wrote anything personal about her acquaintances. The preparation of meals, heating the bath, and similar tasks of Japanese women of the time are described, but are unlikely to retain the attention of a modern reader for very long. The chief attraction of the diary is its evocation of the life of an educated, artistically talented woman, who lived in Wakayama, so far from the center of "civilization and enlightenment" that it barely intruded on her consciousness.

Koume's diary provides an interesting contrast with those kept by men of her time, who give the impression that the encounter with foreign ideas, things, and people had immeasurably altered the lives of all Japanese. Her diary is evidence of the strength and persistence of Japanese tradition, especially among women.

Koume was educated in *kangaku*, the Confucian classics, by her grandfather and in waka poetry by her mother. Her diary reveals her abiding interest in *kangaku* by its mentions of attending lectures given by her husband, the Confucian scholar Kawai Baisho, on various Chinese classics. She gives no examples of the poetry she composed in Chinese, but a number of her waka, none very skillful, are included. Her chief artistic interest was painting. She studied at first with a local teacher, but later with Noro Kaiseki (1747–1828), a pupil of the celebrated Ike no Taiga (1723–1776), who had established himself as the leading painter of watercolors in the province. Koume was an extremely swift and versatile painter, and she received a steady stream of requests for paintings, *fusuma* (sliding-screen) pictures, and so on, especially after the death of her husband in 1871.

Koume rarely referred to the prices she charged for her pictures, but it appears that they were by no means high, as we can gather from an entry in her diary for 1871:

> Yesterday a man came from Mr. Sakai Kiyoshi with a letter saying, "This is not to press you for the paintings I requested the other day, but if they are finished, would you please turn them over to my man? Also, I do not intend to secrete these paintings, so would you please tell me what I owe you?" I had no choice but to answer, but without telling the man what I had previously charged people, I said plainly that my fee was twelve sen for each painting. He at once put down the money and left. There is something really sordid about this, and it certainly gave me an unpleasant feeling, but it can't be helped, given the times. There were six ink paintings with light coloring, for a total of seventy-two sen.[1]

Even in the early Meiji era seventy-two sen for six paintings must have been a minimal charge. Koume probably gave away most of her paintings, and that probably made her feel that accepting money was demeaning. But, since this was the enlightened new Meiji era, she could not protest this violation of the old, uncommercial ways.

Koume nowhere provided information on when she first began to keep a diary or why she kept one, but in an entry for 1877 she wrote,

"For the past few days I have been reading over my old diaries. Last year I had the idea of copying out a list of events going back to 1804, the year I was born . . . but I simply hadn't the time. Recently I have been able to find a little more time. I am already of such an age that I don't know how much longer I can last. Once I am gone, nobody will know about the past. I myself regret that I never asked my mother directly about her life."[2]

It is evident from this passage that Koume kept her diary in order to preserve from oblivion the events of her life, no matter how trivial. Did she sense that she was living in an age of rapid changes and that people of the future would want to know what it was like to have been a samurai's wife? Or was she, like many other diarists, writing mainly so that her son would know the life his parents had led before he was born? It is hard to be sure, but it can scarcely be doubted that Koume took seriously her self-appointed task of serving as the historian of the household, and she provides information that is difficult to find elsewhere about the lives of other women of the time.

One of the surprising features of the household of the Confucian scholar Kawai Baisho was the amount of sake consumed each day. Again and again Koume noted that she had served drinks to guests, even early in the morning, and there are frequent mentions of her husband, or sometimes both her husband and herself, getting extremely drunk. An entry for 1851 opens, "My husband has a hangover. He can't get up out of bed. Everybody is still resting." Later the same day she added (after going to visit someone):

"I got terribly drunk. I went back home and lay down, oblivious to everything . . . About two in the morning my husband got up, lit a fire, and made tea for me. Eventually I sobered up a little. This sort of thing is really a mistake."[3]

The experience seems not to have chastened Koume. Two years further on we find such passages as, "In the evening Yasubei came. I served him sake, and my husband and I got drunk with him, horribly drunk."[4]

These are by no means the only mentions of drunkenness in the diary. Sake was very much a part of the daily lives of Koume and her husband. She seems always to have taken a little drink before she began a painting. More appealing to contemporary readers than Koume's accounts of drunken parties are the quiet scenes she depicted in the lives of samurai intellectuals (*bunjin*) of the old régime, such as her description of a picnic under the cherry blossoms in 1859. Of course, there was sake, but on this occasion nobody got drunk: "We amused ourselves by painting pictures and composing Chinese poetry and *haikai* together."[5]

This delightful event took place at a time when Japan's long peace and, it might be said, its very existence were being threatened. The year 1859 was a terrible one in Wakayama. There was an epidemic of cholera about which Koume wrote, "So many people died we couldn't count them all."[6] And there was not only cholera. Unripe fruit fell from the trees, and the cotton crop was a poor one. There was consolation in the rice harvest, which promised to be unusually abundant, but the crop was ravaged by an invasion of insects. There was so little to eat that even birds became scarce. Never before, Koume wrote in her diary, had so many disasters afflicted people all at once.[7] But they somehow survived even without obtaining assistance from elsewhere.

Judging by her diary, Koume's life had been scarcely touched by the West before Commodore Perry's fleet appeared off Uraga. It is true that she often mentions tobacco, but by now this was no longer an exotic, foreign plant; and she even served beef to her guests as early as 1849;[8] but on the whole the life that she and her family led hardly differed from that of Japanese of a century or two earlier. The situation changed dramatically in 1853. Koume wrote in her diary on the seventeenth day of the sixth month that a foreign fleet had been sighted, and that the foreigners had demanded the right to lease the island of Ōshima off the Izu coast. According to the same, unfounded rumor, this demand had been refused by the Japanese, and preparations to resist the foreigners were being rushed to completion. The next rumor recorded by Koume was that a fleet of British and French ships had demanded possession of Ōshima, threatening otherwise to attack.[9] Even in Wakayama, far from Izu, guns were being distributed to samurai, and frantic attempts were initiated to improve their gunnery.

Rumors continued to fly. On the eighth day of the seventh month Koume reported that the shogun, Ieyoshi, had died. Rumor had it that he had fallen from a tower from which he was peering through a telescope at the British fleet. Koume commented, "I still don't know if this is true or not. In any case, there's a rumor that the world is coming to its end."[10] Still other rumors reported that the British ships were now demanding an annual tribute of fifty thousand *koku* of rice. Strange prophecies, some in the form of riddles or rebuses, also circulated. For example, Koume mentions a riddle she had heard about two daikon radishes (*nihon no daikon*) to which moxa treatment (*kyū*) had been given. The riddle was interpreted as a pun meaning that Japan (*nihon*) was in grave peril (*daikonkyū*).

On the twentieth Koume wrote in her diary that an order had been issued by the shogun's government that Confucian scholars should be ready to help prepare an answer to be given to the letter delivered by the Americans. On the same day an acquaintance came to display armor to be used in the event of war—tunics of chain mail, gauntlets, and broadswords."[11] Koume's son Yūsuke was ordered to report for rifle training, and her husband was appointed officer in charge of sea defenses.[12] Koume composed an anti-American waka:

kage ni nomi	If they stop hiding
kakuroi mo sede	In shadows and come into
hi no moto ni	The light of the land

kitaraba tokuru   Of the rising sun, they will melt,
Amerika no fune[13]   Those ships from America.

The point of this waka is found in the puns: the name America contains the word *ame*, meaning sweets that will melt (*tokuru*) in the fire (*hi*) of *hi no moto*, the Land of the Rising Sun.

Despite the disquieting news of Perry's fleet, however, the lives of Koume and her family in Wakayama continued much as before. Her husband taught the Confucian classics at the clan school, and there were frequent parties from which he usually returned home drunk. Koume regularly visited the castle, and no doubt that was where she learned of political developments elsewhere in the country. She also heard of the outrageous behavior of foreign sailors on shore, and described one such incident in these terms:

> Recently the foreigners have been rampaging through Edo. I heard that children have been throwing stones at them, and that they have been scolded for this by the authorities. There has also been the case of three foreigners who fell to slashing at one another. One was slashed from the forehead down to the mouth, a second slashed aslant from the shoulder, and the third ran off after wounding the other two. The whereabouts of the assailant are unknown.[14]

A European or American woman of this time would probably have felt squeamish about mentioning such matters, but Koume was a samurai's wife and she found it natural to report in detail the actions of the battlefield. She was also aware, even though her own life was unchanged, that she was living in a time of violence and danger to Japan:

> These are not easy times to be living. Long ago, Kamo no Chōmei in his *Account of My Hut*[15] described how, at about the time of the Yōwa era [1181–1182], before the outbreak of the

war between the Minamoto and the Taira, there were various
portents such as an earthquake, a cyclone, deaths from starvation, a great fire, and then the fighting started. I too in the past
witnessed unpleasant, even dreadful things, but now, in addition to everything else we have this terrible epidemic and,
worst of all, invaders have come from abroad, and internal
warfare is about to break out. These are most disheartening
and frightening times. I don't pray for long life; I pray only we
will escape unharmed.[16]

Koume apparently never actually saw a foreigner, but she heard
stories of their unspeakable ferocity. She heard, for example, of a foreigner who bought a trained monkey from a Japanese, then proceeded to boil it alive and eat it on the spot.[17] A little later (in 1861), a
British ship appeared off the Wakayama coast, and a crowd gathered
to have a look at it. A girl of fourteen or fifteen disappeared, and was
not sent back from the ship for two days. An order was issued that
persons were not to go sightseeing even if foreign ships came back
again.

The general anxiety was heightened by the sharp rise in food
prices and the noticeable increase in crime. Koume heard that
sworded samurai (or at least *rōnin*, lordless samurai) were stealing
food intended for beggars, and she wondered what was happening to
the world.[18] Armed robbers roamed the countryside, and Koume reported their activities in detail in her diary. But she seems to have
been naturally cheerful, and her gloomy comments on the state of the
world are always relieved by her accounts of more pleasant events.
The traditional pleasures remained, and brought comfort amid the
painful uncertainties of daily life, as we can infer from this waka by
Koume:

> haru no hi ni   While gazing at
> Shiogamazakura   Shiogama cherries
> nagamureba   On a day in spring,

karaki yo nari to   Who could possibly suppose
tare ka omowan[19]   This is a sorrowful world?

Koume continued to report in detail on the roving bands of armed men who terrorized the countryside. Unlike the women diarists of the Japanese past, she clearly did not believe that such matters did not concern her. Sometimes her information came from official sources, but more often she reported mere rumors, as she was aware. One rumor she treated seriously was of a disturbance in 1864 at Tennōzan in Yamazaki. "There is one unit composed of women, and another of priests, and they are both strong and daring. The priests are meat-eating, have wives, and either let their hair grow long or have it cut short in the foreign style. Their faces are sunburned the color of red lacquer. They wear body armor and carry pikes."[20] She followed this entry (written in the middle of the seventh month, normally the hottest time of the year) with, "In Edo people are wearing lined kimonos, and snow has fallen in Nikkō, I hear, but this is not definite." Her final comment in her entry of that day was, "Dear me, every single thing I hear is unpleasant."[21]

Koume's life, despite all the rumors, continued much as usual. When visitors came, she offered them sake; when a baby was born, she prepared *sekihan*.[22] Perhaps the most striking feature of Koume's diary is its picture of the continuity of a woman's occupation, even in the midst of turbulent changes. The opening of Japan to the West exercised virtually no influence on Koume's life. She never ate Western food, never wore any item of Western clothing, never had any contact with Europeans or Americans, never expressed in her diary the least interest in what was happening in foreign countries. This might be more easily understood if she had been a badly educated woman, but Koume was very well educated, and from 1867 there are mentions in her diary of reading newspapers from Kyoto or Osaka. Occasionally she even copied into her diary long passages from the newspapers, but only of items relating to Japan.

The first mention of a foreign thing in the diary is of a gift she received in 1867: "I received a present of a little glass bead that comes from some foreign country. If one looks inside, one can see a woman. She really looks as if she is alive. There's something frightening about it, and the face is coarse. It is fitted onto the outer rib of a fan, and it costs seventeen *momme*. It would be nice if the face was attractive, but there is something sinister about it."[23] Even after the Meiji era began, there is scarcely a mention of anything foreign, though she lists a blanket (*furankettō*) among the possessions taken by her son when he moved.[24]

The diary entries for the last months of 1867 are filled not so much with apprehension over the menace of the West as with rumors of prodigies that had occurred in Japan. Koume was told by someone with a relative in the capital about a remarkable happening. She described what she heard with the cautionary note, "It is just too strange. I'll set down only the outlines." Here is her summary:

"It has been reported that a few days ago an Edo woman descended quite naked from the sky over Nagoya in Owari. Later, various gods descended from the sky in Mino, Kai, Yamato, Nara, and other places and danced there. And, even more recently, a great crowd of gods descended south of Kyoto and elsewhere. The weather was clear and they could quite plainly be seen coming down."[25]

Then follows a list of divinities (beginning with the great goddess Amaterasu) who descended from the skies, together with the presents they brought, including charms, amulets, and wooden images. People in the places where these prodigies had taken place responded by dressing fancily for the occasion and making offerings of food and drink. The account continues,

Women dressed as men and men as women. There were all sorts of startling effects in their costumes, and they made music with songs, samisen, drums, flutes, gongs, and bells. And they danced around shouting, "*Yoi ja nai ka, yoi ja nai ka, yoi ja nai ka*."[26] They danced their way through the streets, taking the hands of anyone they happened to meet—even strangers and even samurai—and cried, "Won't you dance? Won't you dance?" The music and the shouting lasted from dawn until late at night. The festival lanterns and small lanterns were indescribably splendid. Day after day the dancing has been at its height, and there is no sign that it is likely to end today or tomorrow.[27]

These events were known to Koume only from secondhand reports, but there can be little doubt that she believed them. Moreover, the marvels that had occurred in Kyoto were soon manifested in Wakayama. In her diary entry for the sixth day of the twelfth month of 1867 Koume reported that *oharai* (paper offerings) had fallen from the sky at various places, including the house of an old woman who lived near the harbor. Overcome with awe, the woman felt she must offer sake to the gods in return, but had no money to buy it. She pawned a kimono and with the money obtained she bought the sake. The next morning when she got up she discovered that the kimono she had pawned was in her house once more, together with fifty *ryō* in gold. Koume concluded her account with the remark, "I don't know if it is true or not."[28] She showed commendable skepticism, but elsewhere in the diary she gave so many accounts of miracles that one can only suppose she believed in them.

Five days later, she described the latest prodigy: *gohei* (pendant strips of paper) had fallen from the sky. She wrote, "A great crowd of people swarmed in. I heard that in the end, they had to bolt the door. The crowd seized the packloads of persimmons and tangerines. They were told that they didn't belong to the owner of the house, but had been left there by someone. They paid no attention, but tore the packs apart shouting, '*Yoi ja nai ka, yoi ja nai ka.*'"[29]

Also at this time, an image of Kannon had fallen from the sky into the house of another old woman. This precipitated fresh festivities and great rejoicing to the familiar cries of "*yoi ja nai ka.*" Koume, looking back over recent events, wrote,

Ever since the last part of the tenth month all kinds of strange things have fallen from the sky—talismans of the gods, images of the buddhas, gold, silver, copper coins, rice, and other things. This is something extraordinary, never heard of before, and quite impossible for me to describe adequately in my ugly handwriting. The townsmen, farmers, and even people of the highest station were awestricken, and there were many different observances. People attended wearing splendid, costly costumes, and there was dancing and singing that lasted I don't know how many hours, all day and night. This was a most amazing sight."[30]

Amidst the echoes of *"yoi ja nai ka"* it was announced that the shogun had tendered his resignation to the emperor. Koume, imagining the moment when Tokugawa Yoshinobu bade farewell to his retainers, was overcome with compassion. She expressed her anxiety over the future of Japan, now that it was deprived of the shogun's wisdom.[31]

Following the gap of eight years from 1868 to 1876, the diary resumes with Koume living with her son and his family, her husband having died in 1869 in his seventy-eighth year. In the same year, the clan academy in which he had taught was abolished and a new school established that was open to children of all classes.[32] In January 1876 her son, Yūsuke, was appointed a teacher of the seventh grade at the new school. His income, together with the money that Koume received for her paintings and calligraphy, which were now much in demand, enabled the family to live comfortably. Koume had acquired a new interest, the theater. She lists in her diary most of the plays she saw, names the principal actors, and states the admission fees paid. She went not only to Kabuki but also to Nō and to the puppet theater. She does not mention her husband except in connection with memorial services held on the anniversaries of his death.

The most memorable event of her last years was the Satsuma Rebellion of 1877. The first mention in the diary set the tone for later ones: "They came around selling newspapers, so I bought one. Cost, two sen. Description of the fighting at Kumamoto in Higo [province]. Government troops are gradually being reinforced. Still not clear who will win. [The government troops are] entrenched in the castle. Provisions are short, but anyone who ventures outside the castle gets killed at once. What a sad thing it is!"[33] There is no note of excitement in Koume's account, only sadness that government soldiers are being killed. She had absolutely no sympathy for the rebels: "The Satsuma rebels are all extremely wicked people. They are so bad that even if they had ten heads to cut off, that would still not be enough."[34]

A few days later she wrote, "The outcome of the fighting in Kagoshima has still not been decided. Many people have died—they say more than four hundred from this province alone . . . The other day some heads came back, I am told. So far only the heads of troop commanders have been sent back. The others will come back after they have been pickled in salt and name tags have been attached to their ears."[35] One can imagine how horrified a European lady of the time would have been by severed heads pickled in brine, but Koume remained to the end a samurai's wife.

Koume's information on the Satsuma Rebellion was mainly hearsay, but we can believe her when she writes about the effects of the war on people in Wakayama. She wrote on April 14:

> Fine weather today. The flowers are opening. But somehow news of the war makes me uneasy. They are now mustering troops. They had been paying thirty yen to volunteers, and some men—very, very few—were glad to go, but that wasn't enough, so after considering one thing and another, the government finally ordered men directly . . . Next, I gather, they started mustering all men over seventeen and under forty. And they don't pay them even one yen. I hear they have mustered eight thousand men in Kii [province] alone."[36]

Koume's criticism of the war became more pointed as the result of reading the newspapers and observing its effects on the people around her. She wrote,

"His lordship has come back here. He has been asked to raise a large number of troops, but nobody, absolutely nobody wants to go, and there seems to be no chance he'll raise the needed number. It is unreasonable, after always having treated the samurai as useless creatures, to expect them to serve when there is an emergency.[37]

This unexpected glimpse of what the Satsuma Rebellion meant to people of the time, unlike anything I had previously read, repaid the effort of reading the many pages of Koume's diary, written throughout in an unengaging style. Koume's thoughts are inartistically expressed, but they have the ring of truth, and for that reason are often more affecting than what one finds in diaries of greater literary appeal. The telling of the truth, however unflattering to the writer, has been characteristic of diaries by Japanese women ever since the time of *Kagerō Nikki* (The Gossamer Years).

Notes

1. Shiga Hiroharu and Murata Shizuko, *Koume Nikki*, III, p. 47.
2. *Ibid.*, II, p. 302.
3. *Ibid.*, I, p. 45.
4. *Ibid.*, p. 76.
5. *Ibid.*, p. 148. *Haikai* was another name for haiku.
6. *Ibid.*, p. 202.
7. *Ibid.*, p. 206.
8. *Ibid.*, p. 24.
9. *Ibid.*, p. 107.
10. *Ibid.*, p. 108.
11. *Ibid.*, p. 110.
12. *Ibid.*, p. 129. His title was *kaibōgakari*.
13. *Ibid.*, p. 135.
14. *Ibid.*, p. 197.

15. A reference to *Hōjōki*, the celebrated essay written in 1212 by Kamo no Chōmei (1155–1216).
16. Shiga and Murata, *Koume Nikki*, I, p. 119.
17. *Ibid.*, p. 275.
18. *Ibid.*, p. 241.
19. *Ibid.*, p. 249. The "cherries" are, of course, the blossoms, not the fruit.
20. *Ibid.*, II, p. 36.
21. *Ibid.*, p. 37.
22. "Red rice"—glutinous rice (*mochigome*) boiled with red beans—considered even today to be festive, and consumed on felicitous occasions.
23. Shiga and Murata, *Koume Nikki*, II, p. 182.
24. *Ibid.*, p. 228.
25. *Ibid.*, p. 202.
26. *Yoi ja nai ka* means literally, "It's good, isn't it?" This was the cry of people during the wave of dances and similar activities that swept the country during the last days of the shogunate. Imamura Shōhei's film *Ee ja nai ka* (1980) is a good illustration of these events.
27. Shiga and Murata, *Koume Nikki*, II, p. 204.
28. *Ibid.*, p. 209.
29. *Ibid.*, p. 211.
30. *Ibid.*, p. 214.
31. *Ibid.*, p. 215.
32. *Ibid.*, III, p. 282.
33. *Ibid.*, II, pp. 291–92.
34. *Ibid.*, p. 294.
35. *Ibid.*, p. 296.
36. *Ibid.*, p. 298.
37. *Ibid.*, p. 300.

Bibliography

Shiga Hiroharu and Murata Shizuko. *Koume Nikki*, 3 vols., in Tōyō Bunko series. Tokyo: Heibonsha, 1974–76.

The Diary of Higuchi Ichiyō

From the time the diary of Higuchi Ichiyō (1872–1896) was first published in 1912, it was acclaimed as a masterpiece, her finest work. Baba Kochō (1869–1940), who was largely responsible for publishing the diary intact, without yielding to requests that sections be deleted which might be injurious to the reputation of Ichiyō and the people mentioned therein, wrote at the time, "We consider the diary to be among the most important of Ichiyō's writings. Convinced as we are that the diary reveals in the clearest possible manner the character of an outstanding woman, we could not bear for it to be consigned to oblivion."[1]

The diary has since been widely read by persons attracted to Ichiyō by her stories, by the films based on the stories, or by the woman herself. However, a suspicion that Ichiyō did not always tell the truth has clung to the diary; that she may have invented some incidents and suppressed others that showed her in an unfavorable light. Some scholars also insist, despite Baba's claim that the diary was published unexpurgated, that he and the other editors must have made various deletions. Even supposing they are wrong, and that the editors in no way tampered with the original text, the diary is so conspicuously literary that we can only assume that Ichiyō, despite her claim in the diary that she did not write for other people's eyes, at least subconsciously wished to publish the diary, following in the traditions of the great Japanese women of the past, manipulating her account of events in order to heighten their literary quality.

Ichiyō's sister Kuniko stated that Ichiyō on her deathbed asked her to burn the diary. There is no way to confirm whether or not this was true. Perhaps, as Ichiyō specialists have suggested, Kuniko, fearful lest the diary harm her sister's reputation, herself invented the deathbed request.[2] Fortunately, Kuniko (like most other people who have been asked to burn diaries) disregarded her sister's instructions. But, we may wonder, what precisely made Kuniko (or anyone else) fear that publication might harm Ichiyō's reputation? We know, with the advantage of hindsight, that the diary has instead contributed to the creation of the legend of Higuchi Ichiyō—the genius who struggled throughout her life against oppressive poverty, whose only love never reached fruition, and who died of tuberculosis at the age of twenty-four after having written several stories that rank among the masterpieces of modern Japanese literature. If the diary had been burned, we would have been left only with the writings—the stories and a vast number of uninteresting short poems—and the gossip and reminiscences of people who knew her. She would certainly not be idolized as she is today. Reading the diary, it is hard to find a single passage, let alone a single day's entry, that one would wish to delete. Whoever was responsible for the diary in its present form—whether Ichiyō herself or the editors—deserves our gratitude. It is a remarkably affecting work.

Of course, the diary, by its very nature, is not as flawlessly constructed as "Takekurabe" (Growing Up) and the two or three other stories for which Ichiyō is especially remembered, but it is absorbing from beginning to end as the account of the life of the first important woman writer of Japanese prose in five hundred years. However, some scholars who have studied the diary with great care have reached the conclusion that Ichiyō's character was not above reproof.

It is not that they have been shocked to read of her frequent visits (despite her mother's disapproval) to the house of the novelist Nakarai Tōsui (1860–1926), nor even by her strange relationship with the fortune-teller Kusaka, but by what they consider to be her disingenuousness. Others have opined that her determination to succeed was backed by a ruthless streak. Wada Yoshie, a leading authority on Ichiyō's writings, believed that the diary should be read as an autobiographical novel that contains a generous admixture of fiction. With respect to Ichiyō's decision to break with Tōsui, the most dramatic incident in the diary, Wada wrote:

> Viewed objectively, all that happened was that she rejected Tōsui's help after she realized it was useless depending on him to sell her stories and provide the necessary income for living expenses. She decided to rely instead on Tanabe Kaho. It was as simple as that. And so it came about that Ichiyō utilized the scandal of her supposed relations with Tōsui to establish ties with *Miyako no Hana*.[3] If Tōsui had possessed sufficient influence to help her make her debut successfully, or if Ichiyō could have counted on his providing a steady allowance for living expenses, she would certainly not have made a formal break with him, no matter how much of a commotion people at the Haginoya [school] might have raised. Tōsui, it might be argued, was a writer down on his luck who was betrayed by Ichiyō.[4]

Regardless of whether or not one accepts Wada's harsh interpretation of Ichiyō's motives, it is noteworthy that a scholar who had devoted many years to the study of Ichiyō should have reached such a conclusion. Normally, biographers fall in love with their subjects, even when they write about people who are far less attractive than Ichiyō. But even scholars who are more sympathetic to Ichiyō than Wada have expressed doubts about the credibility of the diary. One of them, discussing Ichiyō's first meeting with Tōsui, noted that six days later Nonomiya Kikuko, who had introduced Ichiyō to Tōsui, visited her, but the account of Kikuko's visit in Ichiyō's diary does not mention Tōsui. He wrote,

"If they actually talked about Tōsui, why should she have failed to mention this in her diary? The least Ichiyō could have done would have been to express her gratitude to Kikuko for having introduced her to Tōsui, who gave her such a kind reception . . . This leads us to the conclusion that her account of her meeting with Tōsui was not factual but a part of the world that Ichiyō had created."[5]

Such comments suggest that Ichiyō has remained an enigma even to the scholars who know her best. Perhaps that is true of all literary geniuses, who may not be able to help but alchemize unimportant or even sordid experiences into the stuff of movingly beautiful writing. Ichiyō could no more record her daily experiences with literal accuracy than Mozart was capable of creating a tune and not developing it. Her diary belongs to the oldest traditions of the genre in Japan, going back to *The Gossamer Years*, whose author wondered, even as she insisted that she wrote only the truth, whether some falsehoods had not crept into her account of the facts.

Ichiyō began to keep a diary in 1887, when she was fifteen years old. It is not clear what prompted her to do so. Of course, it is by no means unusual for a girl of fifteen to wish to confide her emotions to a diary, but Ichiyō's was distinguished from most others kept by writers of the Meiji era by its archaic diction, a pseudo-Heian style that she maintained throughout, regardless of the subject discussed.

The opening sentence of the first volume of her diary is typical: "It was, I think, about the fifteenth day of January that I went to my teacher's house for the first writing practice of the new year."[6] The words she used to express this quite ordinary event were conspicuously archaic. For example, the first word, *midorigo*, was an old word for infant. Here, it was not used in that sense—Ichiyō was obviously not writing about infants— but to lead into the old name for January, *mutsuki*, a word that begins with *mutsu*, meaning diapers, a term intimately connected with infants. It is hard to imagine a young woman in England or France writing in 1887 a diary that was phrased in the language of *Beowulf* or *La Chanson de Roland*.

We may well wonder why a girl of fifteen should have chosen to record her experiences and thoughts in a language so remote from her daily speech. It was not exceptional at this time for a woman to keep a diary in classical Japanese, but to use Heian language and wordplay was not typical. It has been suggested that Ichiyō hoped that using this language would improve her literary style. If that was the case, she was sadly mistaken. Any reading she did in contemporary Japanese literature should have made it clear to her that only a new literary style, closely based on the spoken language, could capture the essence of the new Japan.

Perhaps Ichiyō kept the diary mainly for the practice it gave her in calligraphy.[7] We know how important calligraphy was, not only to Ichiyō but to all young ladies of the time. A diary entry written in May 1893 contains an extended passage on calligraphy beginning, "Handwriting, more than anything else, expresses a person's character."[8] At the Haginoya, the school Ichiyō attended as a girl, students were taught mainly calligraphy and the composition of waka poetry, both deemed indispensable accomplishments for a young lady of the upper class. Ichiyō fully shared the attitudes on women's education embodied in the school curriculum, though she was far from being a member of the upper class. (She was able to stay at the Haginoya by working as the principal's assistant.) Ichiyō's diary frequently mentions the hours she spent improving her handwriting, and the diary may have served the function of reminding her to practice daily. But even if she had kept the diary in a literary style closer to that of writers of her own day, she could still have practiced calligraphy, if that was her chief consideration.

I wonder if Ichiyō's decision to write in a pseudo-Heian style did not originate in the subconscious identification she made between herself and such ladies of the Heian court as Sei Shōnagon and Murasaki Shikibu. She professed the intention of describing in her diary not the remote, elevated subjects that the poets of waka had treated but humble matters that were closer at hand: "I know nothing about Fuji in the days when smoke rose from the peak, but I have written instead about the dust at the foot of the mountain."[9] However, she immediately followed this declaration with an elegantly phrased reflection that seems to have stemmed directly from *The Pillow Book of Sei Shōnagon*: "They say that in spring it is the dawn that is most beautiful, but are not the evenings even more to be cherished? As it gradually grows dark, after we have spent the whole day dallying in the shade of flowering trees, the sound of a temple bell echoes faintly, and even the voices of the crows returning to their nests have a tranquil sound."[10] Mention of "crows returning to their nests" was unpoetic in terms of the conventional poetic diction; perhaps Ichiyō considered this to be a sample of "dust at the foot of the mountain." Other passages in the early diary are less like entries than lists in the manner of *The Pillow Book*.

Ichiyō's interest in literature, initially at any rate, was almost exclusively confined to the Japanese classics and a few works written in Chinese. We know from the diary which books she read and where she read them. She often visited the public library in Ueno Park. Her description of the library in summer is of a modern scene, though the language is reminiscent of Murasaki Shikibu:

> At the library I was squeezed as usual into a cramped little space, and I feared it would be unbearably hot, but perhaps because the ceilings are high and the windows are big, I was delighted to discover that the wind blowing in made it actually rather cool. Whenever I go to the library it puzzles me that there are always many male readers, but generally not a single woman. In any case, I take my place among the men, write down the name of the book, look up its number, and take it to the desk, where I am told that I have made a mistake and will have to rewrite the call slip all over again. My face grows hot and my body feels as if I were shivering all over.[11]

Ichiyō does not mention what books she read in the library on this particular occasion, but on September 25, 1891, she borrowed the *Nihongi, Kagetsu Sōshi*, and *Tsukinami Shōsoku*.[12] This was a forbidding selection even for a bluestocking such as Ichiyō. She confessed that she found it difficult to understand the section of the *Nihongi* (Chronicles of Japan) devoted to the Age of the Gods, but she was stirred from her drowsiness by reading *Kagetsu Sōshi* (A Tale of Flowers and the Moon), and she felt helplessly envious of the smoothly flowing style of the author of *Tsukinami Shōsoku* (Letters on Commonplace Matters). On later visits to the library she borrowed various classics of Japanese literature of the tenth to thirteenth centuries. She also read books and magazines that she borrowed from acquaintances.

Ichiyō's readings testify to her determination to obtain a thorough grounding in traditional Japanese literature, but we cannot help being struck by the inappropriateness of the books she chose as preparation for becoming a professional writer in the 1890s. She did not read any translations of European literature, though by this time many were available. (She mentions in her diary only having read an article on *Macbeth* and an account of the life of Schiller.[13]) She obviously knew *The Tale of Genji* extremely well, was familiar with the standard collections of waka, and with Heian literature in general. Among modern Japanese writers she knew only a few short stories by Kōda Rohan (1867–1947) and Ozaki Kōyō (1867–1903). In the last year of her life she read a translation of *Crime and Punishment*. It is strange that, as a budding writer, she was not more interested in the work of her contemporaries, in Japan or abroad. Most puzzling of all is the total absence of references to Ihara Saikaku (1642–1693), the Japanese novelist who influenced her work most conspicuously.

Ichiyō was eager to appear in print once she began to write stories. She desperately needed the money, and writing fiction was a more agreeable way of earning money than washing other people's laundry, a principal source of income before she started to publish stories. But she also wanted the fame. It seems not to have occurred to her to publish her diary, either as she wrote it down or in a modified form. Indeed, she repeatedly insisted in the diary that she had no intention of ever letting anyone else see it. She declared in an entry for April 1891,

"Since this diary was not intended from the start to be shown to other people, my brush has no flowers, my writing has no shine. These are merely notations jotted down from time to time, and some passages contain such gross self-praise as to be quite shaming. Many others are so crude in their expression as to make a laughing-stock of me."[14]

A year later she wrote at the beginning of another section of her diary,

"This is not something I have prepared in order to show to others, but if in the future I look back on this account of my past, I am sure that many things will seem most peculiar and even demented, and if by some mischance other people should see it they will surely say, 'This is the work of a madwoman.'"[15]

It is hard to imagine, however, that the diary was written solely for Ichiyō's amusement. The act of writing it must have taken up several hours each day, and undoubtedly cut down on the amount of time available for composing works of fiction that she might have sold to magazines or newspapers. At times the only source of income for Ichiyō, her mother, and her sister Kuniko was what she received in payment for her stories, and if writing the diary had not seemed of great importance to Ichiyō she would hardly have devoted so much time to it. I wonder if she was not somehow aware that the diary would prove to be the major work of her short life.

It is customary to write about Ichiyō's diaries as if she wrote only one, but they were composed as a series, each given a separate title, probably another indication of literary intent. The earliest diary, describing events of 1887, is called *Mi no Furugoromo*. This title contains a pun on *mi no furu* (to have an experience) and *furugoromo* (an old kimono), the latter referring to the old kimono her parents gave her in lieu of something more festive to wear at a party at the Haginoya. The other girls were dressed in new and beautiful clothes, but Ichiyō had to be content with a secondhand kimono, all that her father could afford.

Ichiyō wrote about the title of her next diary, *Wakaba Kage* (In the Shade of Spring Leaves), "Although I call the diary 'In the Shade of Spring Leaves,' its pretentions are confined to the title; it was not inspired by felicitous hopes for a prosperous future."[16] She appended to these remarks a poem in which she likened herself to the *hototogisu*, a bird that is said to sing in the shade of verbena blossoms and to transmit sad messages from the world of the dead. The title she gave the diary implies that, despite the promise of young leaves, she was living in a world without much hope. All the same, the young leaves also suggested the first sprouting of the two most important aspects of her life, her writing and her love for the minor novelist Nakarai Tōsui.

The early death of her father was a serious blow to Ichiyō. He was still alive while she attended the Haginoya, and though she felt ashamed of her clothes when she compared them to the costumes worn by the other young ladies, she had not suffered real privation. Her poems were generally awarded the highest marks, and she had reason to believe that she was the most esteemed of the thousand "disciples" of the head of the school, Nakajima Utako. As long as Ichiyō's life was not shadowed by the dread of acute poverty, she seems not to have differed much from the other girls at the Haginoya. The waka she composed were conventional, and when she went to see the cherry blossoms at Ueno her reactions differed little from those of poets of a thousand years earlier. She thought that she was fortunate indeed because she had so many wonderful friends at the Haginoya: "I have many school friends. I also have many intimate friends and the number of friends keeps growing. I must not say which is which, but these young ladies are my elder sisters, and serving them makes them all the dearer to me."[17] It seemed likely that she would be chosen as Nakajima Utako's successor.

The situation changed markedly after the death of Ichiyō's father (and her elder brother), when the household finances deteriorated. The tone of her remarks about her friends at the Haginoya changed. She wrote in her diary,

"These ladies of the upper class are my friends, but there is a barrier between us, and I always find it humiliating to wait on them, to laugh at their jokes even when they are not funny, and to be obliged to pretend to rejoice over things that do not please me."[18]

There are also increasing references in the diary to Ichiyō's mother borrowing money. Ichiyō and her sister did needlework, but the income was pitifully small. At this stage she decided to emulate her classmate, Tanabe Kaho, who had made money by publishing a story. The need for money gave her the courage to meet Tōsui. Some accounts have it that she knew him because she was doing his laundry, but she does not mention this. Indeed, her diary reveals instead the pride she retained as a samurai daughter.[19] She even questioned the propriety of making a living as a writer. She said of her first visit to Tōsui, "When I first met him, I still thought it was deplorable for a woman to engage in such an occupation, but since I was doing it for my family, I had no choice."[20]

The description Ichiyō gave in her diary of this meeting with Tōsui was surely written with other readers in mind. It is wonderfully well composed, and her account of her timid greeting to Tōsui is even funny:

"I was still such a novice in such matters that I felt my ears grow hot and my lips become dry, and, unable to remember what I had intended to say, all I could do was to bow profusely, without saying a word. It embarrasses me when I think what an idiot I would have seemed to anyone else!"[21]

The self-portrait is even more interesting than Ichiyō's description of Tōsui. She wrote of him,

"Mr. Nakarai must be about thirty. I realize that it is unladylike of me to comment in detail about his figure and appearance, but I will set down my impressions exactly as they came to me. When he gave a little smile he really looked just like the kind of man with whom even an innocent child of three might feel at home. All the same, he is most impressive, no doubt because he is considerably taller than average and well built."[22]

Nakarai explained to her why he was obliged to write potboilers, instead of the books he really wanted to write:

> The various novels he has recently been publishing were not written with any sense of pride. It was difficult for him to look scholars or men of distinction in the face when they criticized or even attacked his stories. But what was he to do? He wrote not in the hope of fame but in order to feed and clothe his parents, brothers, and sisters. Of course, he was prepared to be criticized, since what he wrote was dictated by the needs of his family, but if some day he ever had the chance to publish a novel after his own tastes, he would probably not accept criticism so readily. He concluded with a great laugh, and I thought he really had meant what he said.[23]

The account is affecting, even if we doubt that Tōsui was in fact capable of writing works of superior literary quality. In any case, not many scenes of first meeting linger as long in the reader's memory. At this early stage in her career Ichiyō's talents were more evident in her diary than in her stories.

The best-known part of the diary is undoubtedly her account of her love for Tōsui. If she had not met him and described him so evocatively, he would certainly be completely forgotten today. He was never more than a hack writer to whom Ichiyō by chance had access when she decided to embark on a literary career. He does not seem to have been able to give her much guidance, judging by her first stories, but his willingness (and even eagerness) to spend time with this rather plain, timid young woman suggests that he, too, felt something akin to love from their first meeting. Tōsui had made a vow after the death of his wife never to remarry, but it was rumored that he was a frequent visitor to the licensed quarters. It would not have been surprising if such a man had taken advantage of an inexperienced girl, but (on the contrary) he warned her of the danger of gossip if she visited him too often: "I am not exactly decrepit, and you, after all, are of marriageable age. These are extremely unfavorable circumstances for future meetings."[24]

However, it did not take long for gossip to start at the Haginoya concerning the relations between Ichiyō and Tōsui. When she informed him of this gossip, he protested the innocence of his interest in her, but Ichiyō decided under pressure that she would have to break with him, and even refused his offer of an introduction to Ozaki Kōyō, the most prominent figure in the literary world of the day.

Despite the resoluteness of her step, she found that she could not control her longing to be with him, and after some months began to visit him again. Even when her mother expressly forbade her to visit Tōsui when he was ill (the mother was sure he had a venereal disease), Ichiyō, after an initial show of obedience, secretly went to his sickroom. Her account of this visit is masterly. Tōsui's charm is nowhere more apparent than when he asks her to inscribe one of her poems for him.

"He took out some paper, a smile on his face, and grinding the ink himself on the inkstone said, 'I know what a great imposition it is, but please write for me a couple of your poems—old poems or anything else. I had thought of sending someone to ask this of you, but I knew how unlikely you would be to write anything without a struggle, so I have kept it to myself."[25]

The diary contains various disquisitions by Ichiyō on the subject of love, including such passages as,

"People do not know that I love in this way. They may suppose in their shallow and foolish way that mine is a love like most others, and look upon me with mockery. So be it. It will not bother me to be laughed at. It will not bother me to be slandered. That is because the god of my love is unwilling to be so lacking in affability as to concern himself with such petty trifles."

At other times, however, Ichiyō wondered about the propriety of her visits to Tōsui, especially when she went to the hideout where he did his writing.

"He and I sat facing each other, separated only by a *nagahioke*.[26] He said in his usual smiling way, 'Come closer!' but I felt cold sweat pour at the thought of how it would weigh on my conscience if I did what he asked, in a place where there was nobody else, in defiance of the adage 'boys and girls should not share the same mat once they reach the age of seven years.'"[27]

Nowhere does Ichiyō suggest that she became physically intimate with Tōsui, but she seems to have been much tempted. In November 1892 she went to see Tōsui and afterward wrote in her diary, "Since no one else was around, I edged up closer to him and murmured, 'It upsets me that it has been such a long time since I saw you last. I feel unbearably lonely not to have anyone with whom I can discuss my problems."[28]

Tōsui replied, "Is there anything I can do to help you?" He whispered the suggestion that they go to the street behind the house, a lonely place where no one would see them, and they could talk undisturbed. Ichiyō refused. It was precisely because she disliked furtive behavior that she had taken the bold step of visiting him. She wrote, "I left feeling as if everything was still in the air."

Ichiyō's attraction to Tōsui seems to have been mainly physical. Two years after their first meeting, in her diary entry for May 27, 1893, she described her feelings for Tōsui with the greatest intensity:

"When sorrow overtakes me, I yearn for him. When I feel weak, I yearn for him. But I must not talk of him or his clear eyes or his fragrant breath. Anything, no matter what it is, if it is his, strikes to my heart and makes me sad."[29]

Tōsui's attractiveness as a man did not, however, blind Ichiyō's awareness of his failings as a writer. He brought her a copy of his two-volume novel *Kosa Fuku Kaze* (A Wind Blows the Northern Desert) as soon as it was published. She praised the appearance of the book, but after she read it noted in her diary, "Tōsui's style is inherently crude, lacking in brilliance or charm. Moreover, he makes no effort to improve his writing, but seems to be concerned only with adding twists and turns to the plot."[30] She was moved by the novel all the same, not because of its literary value but because it reminded her of him. When a friend from the Haginoya spoke harshly about the novel, Ichiyō disagreed, protecting Tōsui, but she noted privately in her diary, "It is certainly not a work of perfect beauty." Tōsui gave her some useful advice on how to make her stories more salable (mainly by reducing the number of archaic words), but there seems to have been no spiritual or intellectual bond between them.

On March 21, 1893, a young man in the uniform of the First Higher School paid Ichiyō a visit. He identified himself as Hirata Ki-ichi, an editor of the literary periodical *Bungakkai*. He came to inform her that her story "Yuki no Hi" (A Snowy Day), which had been scheduled to appear in the second issue of the magazine, would appear in the third issue instead because of the large number of articles that simply had to be published immediately. The conversation shifted to the subject of contemporary writers and the general situation of literature in Japan. She wrote in her diary,

"He seems to crave something in between profundity and subtlety in literature. He said that Saigyō, Kenkō, and Bashō were exemplars of 'the same hearts in different people.' . . . I was infected by his enthusiasm and became quite loquacious. I couldn't think of him as someone I was meeting for the first time."[31]

Probably Ichiyō had never before talked with anyone on such literary matters. Her conversations with Tōsui seem to have been confined mainly to the commercial aspects of being a writer. Hirata had read Ichiyō's story, "Umoregi" (A Buried Life), and thought he could detect the influence of Kōda Rohan. Ichiyō, not the least offended, smiled, surprised and pleased that a man should have read her story. Hirata for his part was delighted to have found a kindred spirit and opened his heart to Ichiyō concerning his dissatisfaction with the Japanese educational system. Although the students at his school were the cream of the young Japanese intelligentsia, he had not succeeded in making a single friend. "They're all like objects produced from an identical mold. You'd have great trouble finding individual excellence, no matter how far you searched."[32]

He traced his inability to get along with other students to his grief over the death of his father. This struck a responsive chord in Ichiyō, whose father and elder brother had both died. Hirata told her that he was still only a third-year student because he had failed mathematics one year. He continued, "The teachers are not interesting, and I am not happy with my classmates. I feel a general sense of the transience of all things, and I turn for companionship day and night to *Essays in Idleness*."[33]

As Ichiyō chatted with Hirata, she discovered that Hirata Kiichi and Hirata Tokuboku, whose essay on Kenkō she and her sister had admired, were one and the same. She was impressed that anyone so young was capable of such deep feelings. When the school term began in April she waited for another visit from Hirata, but he failed to appear. However, not even this soulmate had displaced Tōsui in her affections.

A crisis occurred in July 1893 when Ichiyō and her family, putting aside the contempt for trade that stemmed from their samurai background, decided that they had no choice but to open a little shop somewhere. After much searching for a suitable place (and seeing sordid poverty at close hand), Ichiyō finally settled on a house near the gate of the Yoshiwara pleasure quarter. In order to open their little shop, Ichiyō and her mother raised capital by selling the last of their paintings and examples of calligraphy that had been acquired by Ichiyō's father. They borrowed money too, but they never managed to assemble enough to buy the stock needed for the shop. They sold sundries and cheap confectionery to children and others of the neighborhood. Here is how Ichiyō described the place:

> The house is on the one road that goes from Shitaya to Yoshiwara. Words cannot describe what it is like after dark, what with the noise of rickshaws thundering by and the glare from

their headlights as they fly back and forth. Rickshaws on their way to Yoshiwara keep going until one in the morning, and the noise of returning rickshaws begins echoing from three in the afternoon. Never in all my life can I remember anything like the feelings of the first night I slept here after the move from the profound silence of our house in Hongō. The house is one in a row, and rickshaw men live on the other side of the thin wall. I wonder what it will be like after we begin our business. Even such people are potential customers, and we must do our best not to offend them. People have told us that the neighborhood of the licensed quarter is a bad place as far as human relations are concerned. I can imagine how we will be scorned for not having a man in the house, and how many painful experiences we are likely to have.[34]

At this point in the diary she gives an autobiographical account of her childhood, rather contradicting the claim that she did not intend anyone to read the diary. Perhaps she felt it necessary to explain to herself why a girl of good family, educated in a school for young ladies, should have had to run a shop outside the licensed quarter. Although she does not say so, Ichiyō probably resented her mother's old-fashioned ideas on the appropriate education for women: the mother was convinced that too much learning did a girl no good, and that her time was better spent in learning to sew and to take care of a house.[35] Years earlier, her father had thought Ichiyō should attend school a while longer, and had asked her what she herself preferred. She recalled, "I was born timid, and I couldn't pronounce anything definite about either alternative, and though it made me so unhappy I all but died, I stopped going to school."[36]

At school the teacher had praised her as the brightest pupil in the class, and she grew so accustomed to praise that she felt sure she could accomplish anything she set her heart on, but in fact she left school at the age of twelve, and from then on went to the Haginoya, a kind of finishing school for young ladies, instead of pursuing a real education. If she had received the education for which she was qualified by her intelligence, the family might never have been reduced to such miserable circumstances.

Ichiyō wanted to write, but the shop left her little opportunity. Most of her time was consumed in trips to wholesalers to obtain stock, and sometimes she had to carry heavy burdens that strained her delicate physique. At first business was fairly good. Another shop in the neighborhood that sold similar wares had to close. But profits were minimal, and soon it was Ichiyō's shop that could no longer operate. She wrote in her diary on June 16, 1895, "There is not a penny of savings in the house, and we haven't paid the rent we have owed the agent since last month."[37]

The future seemed bleak, but although Ichiyō thought that she had broken her ties with the literary world when she opened the shop, the editors had not forgotten her. Hirata visited her at the shop in October 1893. He asked her for another story for *Bungakkai*. A few weeks later another editor of the magazine sent her a reminder that the story was due. She wrote in her diary, "It's still not ready, and I've been up all night for two nights running." When the story appeared in the December issue of *Bungakkai* she received payment of one yen fifty sen. Even if one yen was worth ten thousand times what it is today, this was scarcely adequate compensation, but Ichiyō was the only paid contributor to the magazine, a mark of the esteem in which she was held and also of the sympathy of the editors.

Ichiyō's reputation continued to grow. Perhaps the most unusual feature of her career is that from the outset, even when her stories were distinctly immature, she was frequently asked to contribute to the leading magazines. Hirata, an early enthusiast for her writings, brought other literary people to her house. Soon people were saying that she had created the Japanese women's literature of the future.[38] The praise was welcome, though it brought in no money.

In January 1895 Ichiyō published in *Bungakkai* the first installment of "Growing Up." Her life outside the Yoshiwara gate had provided her with the materials for the work, but her diary does not give clues as to which persons or incidents served as the models. Unlike the earlier, more romantic stories, "Growing Up" was written with a realism born of actual observation. It is easy to imagine that Ichiyō actually knew the prototypes of Midori, Nobu, Shōta, and the other children growing up in the licensed quarter. Her poverty and the humiliation of having to fawn on customers to sell the cheap wares in her shop had provided her with material that she could never have gleaned at the Haginoya. Her readings in Saikaku and other writers of the Tokugawa period had also helped her to create a literary style that was no longer (like the diary) a pastiche of Murasaki Shikibu.

By the end of her short life she was widely recognized as perhaps the most outstanding writer of her day. The last entry of her diary, written on July 20, 1896, mentions that Kōda Rohan, the novelist she had worshiped from afar, had visited her earlier that day to ask for a manuscript. Toward the end of her life she neglected the diary, probably because she was fully occupied with her stories. Many people came to visit her during her last days. The novelist Izumi Kyōka was so impressed that he styled himself Ichiyō's disciple. Unlike some geniuses, Ichiyō was recognized during her lifetime, but she did not live long enough to enjoy her fame.

Notes

1. Quoted in Odagiri Susumu, *Kindai Nihon no Nikki*, p. 225.
2. *Ibid.*, p. 218.
3. *Miyako no Hana* (Flower of the Capital) was an important literary magazine.
4. Wada Yoshie, *Higuchi Ichiyō Den—Ichiyō no Nikki*, p. 140.
5. Nishio Yoshihito, *Zenshaku Ichiyō Nikki*, I, p. 69.
6. The text is: *Midorigo no mutsuki shitate tōka amari itsuka to ieru hodo ni nan keiko hajime tote shi no moto ni makadekeri.* I have slightly changed the text by indicating voiced consonants, though Ichiyō did not distinguish between voiced and unvoiced. See Nishio, *Zenshaku*, I, p. 17.
7. See *ibid.*, p. 5.
8. *Ibid.*, II, p. 419.

9. *Ibid.*, I, p. 105.

10. *Ibid.* Ichiyō is referring here to the celebrated opening words of *Makura Sōshi*.

11. *Ibid.*, I, p. 84. Here is the beginning of the passage in the original: "*Toshokan wa rei no ito semaki tokoro e oshiireraruru nareba, sa koso atsusa mo, tae-gatakarame to, omoishi ni . . .*"

12. The *Nihongi* (or *Nihon Shoki*), compiled in 720, is the first of the six imperial histories; it is written in classical Chinese. *Kagetsu Sōshi* is a *zuihitsu* (brief essays on random topics; literally, "following the brush") by Matsudaira Sadanobu, written in 1818. *Tsukinami Shōsoku* consisted of letters written by Udono Yonoko (d. 1788), a pupil of the scholar of National Learning, Kamo no Mabuchi. The collection was published posthumously in 1807.

13. See Nishio, *Zenshaku,* II, p. 67. One other foreign work she knew was the Korean novel *Kyūunmu* (Cloud Dream of the Nine), part of which she copied out. See *ibid.*, p. 134.

14. *Ibid.*, I, p. 46.

15. *Ibid.*, II, p. 128.

16. *Ibid.*, I, p. 46.

17. *Ibid.*, p. 118.

18. *Ibid.*, II, pp. 74–75.

19. Her father, an ambitious farmer, had gone to Edo and purchased samurai status shortly before the Meiji Restoration, but Ichiyō always referred to herself as a samurai's daughter.

20. Nishio, *Zenshaku*, II, p. 138.

21. *Ibid.*, I, p. 51.

22. *Ibid.*

23. *Ibid.*

24. *Ibid.*, p. 54.

25. *Ibid.*, II, p. 409.

26. An oblong brazier, bigger than the usual hibachi.

27. Nishio, *Zenshaku*, I, p. 177. The quotation is from the Chinese classic *Li Chi*.

28. *Ibid.*, II, p. 280.

29. *Ibid.*, p. 444.

30. *Ibid.*, p. 346.

31. *Ibid.*, p. 369.

32. *Ibid.*, p. 370.

33. *Ibid. Tsureguregusa* (Essays in Idleness) is a *zuihitsu* collection written by the priest Kenkō, probably around 1330.
34. *Ibid.*, III, p. 59.
35. *Ibid.*, p. 75.
36. *Ibid.*
37. *Ibid.*, p. 371.
38. This particular comment was made by the novelist Kawakami Bizan (1869–1908).

Bibliography

Danly, Robert Lyons. *In the Shade of Spring Leaves*. New Haven: Yale University Press, 1981.

Higuchi Ichiyō. "Growing Up," trans. Edward G. Seidensticker, in Donald Keene, *Modern Japanese Literature*. New York: Grove Press, 1956.

Nishio Yoshihito. *Zenshaku Ichiyō Nikki*, 3 vols. Tokyo: Ōfūsha, 1976.

Odagiri Susumu. *Kindai Nihon no Nikki*. Tokyo: Kōdansha, 1984.

Wada Yoshie. *Higuchi Ichiyō Den—Ichiyō no Nikki*, in Shinchō Bunko series. Tokyo: Shinchōsha, 1960.

The Diary of Tsuda Umeko

In the eleventh month of 1871 Tsuda Umeko[1] (1864–1929) set sail for America as one of the first five girls to study abroad. She was chosen at the request of her father, Tsuda Sen, a retainer of the Sakura clan, who possessed considerable knowledge of the West. In 1867 he had traveled to San Francisco as a member of a mission, and had remained in America for about six months. (He sent his topknot back to his wife in Japan.) Later, he served as a translator and interpreter, and during the final days of the shogunate he was sent to Nagasaki. While on this journey he wrote his wife, urging her to have Umeko begin her studies, though she was only four years old at the time. Tsuda Sen's interest in education for women had been stimulated by his stay in America.[2] It was expected that Umeko and the four other girls would spend ten years abroad, a most ambitious project.

Umeko did not record her first impressions of America until many years later. Beginning in 1891 she wrote in English a series of essays describing her experiences and reflections on notable world events. She attributed to Count Kuroda Kiyotaka (1840–1900), the deputy director of the Hokkaidō Colonization Office, the bold plan of sending female Japanese students to America, and expressed her

amazement that "even five girls were found in the length of the kingdom whose parents would permit them to start on this perilous and
dangerous undertaking."[3] She speculated that perhaps no more than
five girls had "applied or desired to go . . . At any rate, there was no
special reason for our selection, as there was no particular influence,
rank, or power possessed by our relatives. It had merely happened
that we came from families who had come in contact with the new
foreign element, and who were far-sighted enough to understand
what this opportunity might mean to us in the future."[4]

Before their departure for America the girls were summoned to
the imperial court to be received by the empress. Umeko recalled,
"This was the first time the empress ever had received in audience the
daughters of Samurai, and the reception of these little girls was indeed
a wonderful sign of the times and marked a new era for Japan."[5]

No articles of foreign clothing could be obtained for the girls in
Japan, so they set out in Japanese clothes. Once they arrived in San
Francisco, their clothes attracted gaping crowds, but Mrs. De Long,
the wife of the American minister to Japan, who accompanied them,
refused to buy them any American dresses because (according to
Umeko) "that lady enjoyed the sensation we created, and the fame of
our arrival."[6] Only after they reached Chicago were they finally permitted to buy American costumes "but not until we had asked many
times, and had at last appealed to Prince Iwakura, the head ambassador, to command that some clothing be got for us."[7] Then, as now,
foreigners craved to see Japanese women in their "pretty native
robes."

There is an enchanting photograph of little Tsuda Umeko taken
soon after she obtained her first American clothes. She stands, her
legs crossed and her right arm leaning on some object, in a rather
melancholy pose. White stockings and highly polished shoes are vis-
ible below her skirt, but it is the hat, decked with feathers and rib-
bons (and larger than her head), that dominates. Umeko's expression
is grave, suggesting that at this time the deportment expected of a little samurai girl was the same as for an American girl.

In a letter written in March 1872 to his benefactors, Mr. and Mrs. Hardy, Niijima Jō mentioned meeting two of the five Japanese girls in Washington. He wrote, "One of them is about fifteen years of age, and another is only eight years old, the second daughter of my old schoolmate, who is now a prominent officer in the country. She is a little cunning and acute thing I ever saw. I had very pleasant conversation with them and dined with them too. They don't understand what the ladies in the families speak to them; so when I go there to see them they are delighted to see me and ask me ever so many questions."[8]

Umeko later recalled that at first the five girls lived together in a house in Washington. "We talked Japanese to our heart's content, and did almost what we liked in the large, roomy house. Our governess could not manage us, as she might have done had we understood English . . . After our daily English lesson in the morning, we would go out frequently to the Japanese legation and spend the time there amusing ourselves, or we would be taken out to walk by some of the attaches or secretaries, who would often go with us to the shops and buy for us all the toys and pretty things which pleased our fancies."[9] This life lasted only about six months, when some Japanese officials discovered that the girls were not learning English and separated them, sending them to live with different families.

Umeko's writings in English demonstrate that before long she acquired a mastery of the language. In May 1895 a magazine published in New York declared, "From reading the article on Japanese women in the war [the Sino-Japanese War of 1894–95] by Miss Ume Tsuda, no one would suspect that she was not born to the use of the English language."[10] Her proficiency in English was such that it is puzzling how she remembered her Japanese during the eleven years spent in America. It is true that after she returned to Japan in 1882 she studied the Japanese classics and calligraphy, but it would not have been surprising if she had completely forgotten her native language. I have met some Japanese who after a much shorter time abroad have had difficulty in speaking their own language. No doubt

Umeko had exceptional ability not only to learn foreign languages but also to retain her own.

In reading the diary she kept in 1898 and 1899, as well as the fragment of a diary written in 1917, I was struck by the perfection of Umeko's English, but as I read, it also occurred to me that the diary might be more memorable if she had made a few mistakes suggesting her efforts to acquire a language so unlike the one she had first known.

It would be wonderful if the diaries kept by Umeko when she first visited America were some day discovered. If they exist, we should surely find in them many fresh reactions to the unfamiliar world into which she was suddenly plunged. What was it like for a small child to be surrounded by people who were obviously friendly but whose words and gestures were unintelligible? Seventeen years later she wrote reminiscences that are interesting in themselves but probably not as faithful to the experiences as a diary written on the same day would have been. For example, when the train carrying the Japanese from San Francisco to the East Coast stopped in Omaha, she recalled that American schoolgirls went to see the Japanese. "They all smiled at us Japanese children and clapped and kissed their hands, which we thought was very polite and kind," she wrote.[11] But had the Japanese girls actually understood that the American girls were being polite when they blew kisses? It is hard not to suppress the feeling that only later, perhaps much later, did little Umeko appreciate the gesture of the Omaha schoolgirls.

Again, she wrote about American food: "We ate the food given us, not having anything else, but we did not know beforehand what any dish was, nor how it would taste. Our first experience with butter was at Sacramento, when we each took a spoon, and helped ourselves to a mouthful of it, and found to our great disgust, that it was not palatable, to say the least."[12] But it is hard to believe that she never saw butter aboard the American ship when crossing the Pacific or at her hotel in San Francisco. A diary would surely be more reliable.

A few letters survive from her first years in America. The very first letter in English, written was she was nine years old, was sent to her father in Japan. It is appealingly childish and has a few mistakes.[13] Another, of much greater interest, was sent in 1875 to Mr. Lanman, in whose house she lived in Washington, responding to his request for her thoughts on what improvements ought to be made in Japan. Umeko gave these opinions:

> I think it is wrong to make everything different to what it at present is in Japan; we ought to keep a great many things as they are. For instance, I should like Japan to keep its native language, native dress and native style of writing; but I should like to see in my country, American as well as Japanese schools . . . I wish all the people would become Christians; and all the temples converted into churches. It would be too much trouble and expense to build new churches, but we might take out all the idols and symbols of idolatry.[14]

These are extraordinary sentiments for an eleven-year-old girl, and if we had no other evidence we might suppose she wrote the letter afterward and pretended it was an early composition. She clearly was most precocious, and even though she left Japan when she was only eight, she retained a clear impression of her life there, and was able to compare Japan and America with objectivity: "I am sure I should like to sleep in a Japanese bed again, but I would not care for the pillow."

Umeko's diary of 1898 opens with a description of sightseeing in London. She went to the Tower of London, St. Paul's Cathedral, the Guildhall, and Westminster Abbey. Hardly a word in the diary (written entirely in English) indicates that the writer is Japanese, though she says of Westminster Abbey, "it is so large and the ceilings are so high, it gives one a feeling of awe—something like the feeling that the temples of Nikko do in Japan."[15] The comparison is surprising. The gloomy interior of Westminster Abbey hardly resembles the elaborately decorated shrines at Nikkō, and the scale is totally dissimilar. Did Umeko really feel something akin in the atmospheres of the two, or was this perhaps a reminder to herself that Japan also had imposing monuments?

Umeko's journey to America and England in 1898 was her third trip abroad, and she had already spent about fourteen years outside Japan. She seems to have been entirely assimilated into Western society, and her references to Japan (such as her putting on a kimono to please her hosts) seem contrived rather than heartfelt. Her life abroad, far from representing a privation, as it did for some Japanese, was more interesting and enjoyable than life in Japan. She wrote while in Cambridge, "I can hardly believe myself here. I go out so little in Japan. It is indeed a great change for me."[16] Later, in London again, she wrote, "I am having plenty of invitations to tea and to lunch so many I can not accept them all . . . I feel so much the relaxing of the responsibility I had while in Japan, and to have these months of freedom is a very great thing indeed for me."[17]

Some aspects of life in England undoubtedly reminded her of Japan. Both countries had stable societies, contrasting with the American insistence on equality and upward mobility. Umeko wrote while in London,

"Noticed the school children all going home with maids and attendants. This is more like Japan than America. The children are taught to be very polite. They got up & stood when I came in, and when I went out . . . I was much pleased at their manners. In America, there is entirely too little of that. I don't see why the children should not stand when a superior in the school comes in."[18]

Umeko was able to fit easily into American or English society first of all because she spoke English so well, and second because she was a devout Christian, at a time when people in the West were less tolerant of other religions. Some early Japanese visitors to Europe had felt repugnance when they entered the great churches; others had admired the architecture and perhaps the music, but had not felt even as much of a spiritual experience as they might have felt at

Nikkō—but Umeko was at home. Undoubtedly the fact that she was an Episcopalian also helped to make England congenial, and she talked with the highest rank of the Anglican clergy.

When she met the archbishop of York, she relates, "I told him that I really wished to do something, and to grow in grace and that I had had many advantages, but I must do something to pass them on to others, and how the weight of responsibility hung on me, although I was so unworthy of the blessings that God had given me in comparison with so many of my fellow country-women, that often I felt I would be glad of not having seen and known and heard so much."[19] This long sentence is not Umeko's English at its best, but the sentiments expressed were unquestionably sincere.

When reading Umeko's diary, one feels close to her, but never as close as one feels to the women who wrote diaries during the Heian and Kamakura periods. Perhaps this is because she was not as susceptible to worldly passions as those women who recorded the anguish of parting, the death of lovers, and the terrors of warfare. Nothing in the diaries indicates that she fell in love, and her references to war (the Sino-Japanese War) are patriotic rather than despairing.

On occasion Umeko seemed depressed, but never for long. On December 29, 1898, she wrote, "I am so feeble in faith. But I do long for more faith and a better life and especially that my heart may be so full of love and sympathy that it may outflow to those around me who need it. More love, more sympathy, to others I need, I know it. I know my past has been far from worthy of me. May God grant that the future may be better. My faith is so weak and dim."[20]

This entry, which, in another woman's diary, might have indicated disillusion or loss of faith, in Umeko's case seems to suggest that she had imposed on herself impossibly lofty ideals, and would never be content with what she achieved. Such thoughts gave way by the end of the entry for the same day to: "1899 is upon us—what will the new year be like? 1898 has been such a great and wonderful surprise for me. Such a wonderful, wonderful year it has been, altogether!"[21]

Apart from occasional references to Japanese she met in England and to letters that arrived from home, there is nothing to suggest she was ever homesick. She wrote about one of her former pupils that she looked "thin and pale. She is very lonely too, poor child."[22] But if Umeko meant by "too" that she was also lonely, she conceals this. She seems to have been far too busy ever to feel lonely. The people she met in England were extremely hospitable, not because she was Japanese but because she fitted easily into their society. There is no reference to anyone staring at her or asking her stupid questions about Japan, even though Japan was for most Europeans almost as remote as the moon. Umeko's natural dignity, combined with her effortless command of English, made her the first truly cosmopolitan Japanese.

She was teased while in England about her American accent,[23] and the English did not hesitate to criticize the Americans to her. She nevertheless retained her affection for Americans: "I can't say I share their opinion of American men. I like them better than I do the Englishman, who is not so genial on the whole it seems to me. They are very polite etc. but they are certainly colder. On the other hand, I do not like the fiery Frenchman."[24]

The few pages of a diary written in 1917 have quite a different tone. Umeko, lying in a hospital bed in Tokyo, seems genuinely depressed, mainly at the thought that she might die before her work was completed. For the first time—however briefly—her diary acquires literary interest.

"One might easily have expected and asked for ten or fifteen years more of life, but when one thinks of the young men going to war, noble, brilliant young men, the flower of their country, and of the awful suffering and death to which they go, and it seems so cruel and useless, then why, because to me, my own life has not seemed to be for selfish or useless purposes, should I expect, ask or pray for long life?"[25]

For a moment this woman, normally so serene and purposeful, seems to join the Japanese women of the past for whom the diary was not merely a record of events but an outlet for the deepest emotions.

Notes

1. At the time she was known as Mume. She did not change her name to Umeko until 1902, but I shall call her by one name throughout.
2. And, years later, by a conference he attended in 1871 in Tokyo at which Japanese officials discussed with Americans the question of education for women. See *Tsuda Umeko Monjo*, p. 558.
3. *Ibid.*, p. 77.
4. *Ibid.*
5. *Ibid.*
6. *Ibid.*, p. 81.
7. *Ibid.*
8. Arthur Sherburne Hardy, *Life and Letters of Joseph Hardy Neesima*, p. 122.
9. *Tsuda*, pp. 83–84.
10. *Ibid.*, p. 57.
11. *Ibid.*, p. 83.
12. *Ibid.*, p. 82.
13. *Ibid.*, p. 473.
14. *Ibid.*, p. 17.
15. *Ibid.*, p. 264.
16. *Ibid.*, p. 273.
17. *Ibid.*, p. 290.
18. *Ibid.*, pp. 267–68.
19. *Ibid.*, pp. 295–96.
20. *Ibid.*, p. 296.
21. *Ibid.*, p. 297.
22. *Ibid.*, p. 288.
23. *Ibid.*, p. 274.
24. *Ibid.*, p. 320.
25. *Ibid.*, pp. 366–67.

Bibliography

Hardy, Arthur Sherburne. *Life and Letters of Joseph Hardy Neesima*. Boston: Houghton, Mifflin, 1893.
Tsuda Umeko Monjo. Kodaira-shi: Tsuda-juku Daigaku, 1989.

Mineko's Diary

It is not likely that anyone would take the trouble to read the diary of Mori Mineko (1848–1916) if she had not been the mother of the great Mori Ōgai. The specialist in Ōgai's writings will be grateful even for the occasional crumbs of information found in the pages of this laconic diary, but other readers are likely to regret that Mineko's sense of decorum did not permit her to unbend and tell us what her life was really like.

We know, for example, from Ōgai's story "Hannichi" (Half a Day)[1] that the relations between his mother and his second wife were extremely strained. The wife so disliked the portrait of herself in the story that she prevented publishers from including it in the various collections of Ōgai's works that appeared before her death. The relations between the two women were undoubtedly tense, but the diary does not clarify them. We wish that Mineko, even if she could not be objective, had at least presented her side of the story, but that was not her purpose in keeping the diary. Unlike the Heian court ladies, and even unlike her younger contemporary Higuchi Ichiyō, she did not consider the diary to be a confidant to whom she could entrust her secrets. She had quite the opposite intent: she expected Ōgai to read the diary when he returned from service in the Russo-Japanese War. A brief explanation of her reasons for keeping a diary is found in an entry dated April 17, 1904:

"Of late many letters I have sent to Rintarō,[2] who is with the Second Army in Hiroshima, have not been received. I imagine he knows about the things I have told him, but just to be safe, I have decided also to keep a diary."[3]

Mineko clearly intended to show Ōgai her diary, but nothing in it indicates whether or not she did so after his triumphal return from the battlefield. She continued to keep a diary afterward: it seemed to have become a habit. She normally wrote the diary a day at a time, but the remote tone of some entries may have been occasioned by her having neglected the diary for a week at a time, only later setting down recollections of what had happened.[4]

After Ōgai's return from the war, he showed his family the diary he had kept while overseas, as we know from an entry in Mineko's diary: "At night Kimiko read the Manchurian part of the diary."[5] The impersonality of Ōgai's wartime diaries, certainly when compared with those he kept while in Germany, may have been caused by his expectation that people at home would read them.

Quite apart from the diaries, Ōgai was an exceptionally faithful correspondent while in China. Mineko's diary mentions receipt of letters from the front several times a week. She almost never refers to the contents of the letters, and does not mention that most of them were addressed not to herself but to Ōgai's wife, Shigeko, who was living not in the Mori household but in her parents' house. Ōgai's letters are lively and sometimes embellished with poems of his own composition, but Mineko (though she answered every letter immediately and frequently sent him food and other needed items) was determined to live up to the role of a samurai's mother. She had no use for sentimentality, and her letters were firm rather than affectionate.

Mineko's diary was written only ten years after the last of Higuchi Ichiyō's, but a far greater period of time seems to separate the two women. Unlike Ichiyō, whose style was an approximation of

Heian-period Japanese, Mineko wrote in modern language that differed little from the colloquial. One notices also the large number of mistakes in spelling and in the use of characters in Mineko's diary, though her social class was far above Ichiyō's. She seems not to have been as well educated, or, it might be more accurate to say, the content of her education had been different. Mineko never mentions the Heian classics in her diary, and the only kind of premodern Japanese literature with which she was familiar was Kabuki drama. On the other hand, she read considerably more of European literature (in translation) than did Ichiyō, and she even saw European plays performed. Her diary entry for November 22, 1907 (when she was sixty-two years old), was, "I went to the Hongō Theater. *Hamlet* was really interesting."[6]

It was not only in literary tastes that Mineko was more modern. Ichiyō never mentions eating European or even Chinese food, but Mineko's diary is dotted with references to such exotic items as Western pastry, sandwiches, and ice cream, as well as meals of European and Chinese food.[7] When she sent food to Ōgai at the front, it was generally foreign: "I sent in a strong wooden box five [boxes of?] chocolates, three [cans of?] milk, two sausages, two [bottles of?] ink, and four pounds of cube sugar."[8] She was also familiar with such inventions as the phonograph and motion pictures.[9] She even seems to have been interested in Western-style painting, as this entry suggests: "At two o'clock I went to the museum. I looked only at the oil paintings. I ate dinner in Ueno. I walked home from Nezu."[10] All in all, for a woman of that time and background, she was well abreast of foreign tastes, presumably as the result of her son's influence. Her comfortable income (certainly when compared to Ichiyō's penury) permitted these luxuries; but the times had also changed, and if Ichiyō had lived ten years longer it is likely that she too would have participated to some extent in the imported culture.

A few entries suggest that Mineko could have written a more literary diary. After the death of her mother in July 1906, she decided to inter the mother's ashes at Tsuchiyama in Shiga Prefecture, where her father's remains were buried. She did not actually leave Tokyo for this purpose until October. She related in the diary,

> I left Shimbashi at ten. This was my first time ever beyond Hakone. I had heard about the scenery around Fuji, and about Fuji itself visible above the white clouds, but actually seeing it was quite another matter. We went along with Fuji on our right only for it to appear on our left, and then on the right again before we lost it from sight. The sea appeared occasionally, then hid itself again. Seeing from a distance masses of sorghum hanging to dry under the eaves of houses I wondered what it was. But everything I saw was unfamiliar.[11]

After spending the night in Nagoya, she went on by train to Mikumo, and from there by horse carriage to Tsuchiyama. She wrote in her diary, "That day I suddenly felt unwell. The noise of the carriage reverberated painfully in my head. At twelve-thirty I reached Tsuchiyama. I brought my mother's ashes to the grave of my father, whom I have remembered every morning and night for fifty-four years, and buried them there. What a strange thing fate is! I wondered who would bury my ashes and where. At the thought tears came in spite of myself."[12]

For a moment we hear the voice not of a general's mother but of an ordinary woman, and we know that Mineko concealed beneath her severe exterior thoughts and emotions that she chose not to express. If one tries while reading Mineko's diary to form an impression of what she was like as a person, the diary does not supply many clues. Even when she wrote about the illness of her grandchildren, she maintained impassivity: "Furitsu [Fritz] has been ill since about the tenth. Lately it has been worse. Mariko seems to have whooping cough. No fever, just coughing. Furitsu's sickness has turned into pneumonia, and sometimes his breath stops."[13] This is the entire entry; not a word suggests she was worried, though undoubtedly she was.

The next entry, written after the diary had been neglected for over two months, opens with this puzzling notation: "April 3. My diary for this year began." This is followed by a description of sightseeing in Kyoto. Mineko does not mention it, but Furitsu died on February 5. The shock of his death may explain the empty pages in the diary. Perhaps she thought it unseemly to mention private grief in a diary that others might see.

Mineko hardly expressed a single like or dislike in the three hundred pages of her diary. Her most outspoken opinions relate to the theater. She attended Kabuki regularly, and went to modern plays, especially those written by her son. The theater was virtually her only recreation. From time to time she passed judgment on something she saw. Generally she was severe. For example, she wrote in 1905: "Went to the Kabuki Theater. The 'Eighteen Famous Plays of Danjūrō'[14] were performed by actors well matched in their ineptitude. There must have been many people who, remembering [actors of] the past, wept."[15]

A mother's natural partiality toward the work of her son did not temper the severity of Mineko's judgments. On December 1, 1906, she attended a performance of Ōgai's *Nichiren Shōnin Tsuji Seppō* (The Holy Man Nichiren's Sermons at the Crossroads) and commented, "It wasn't good, but it was somewhat interesting."[16] In Kyoto she attended a performance of Shimpa plays given by Kawakami Otojirō and his troupe, and vouchsafed a few words of praise:

> I went at six to the Kabuki Theater.[17] They were performing
> *The Crown*,[18] which they are still doing in Tokyo. I didn't think
> it was all that interesting, but Kawakami is really an enthusi-
> ast, and doesn't stint in anything he does. As for the audience,
> it is what one would expect in Kamigata.[19] They go to the the-
> ater, and without thinking they might be interfering with other
> people's pleasure, they chat, they eat, and while they eat they
> don't listen to the dialogue. I paid no attention to them, but sat
> quietly in my place. I really could not help but admire a man
> who can rise above the limitations of "patriot actors."[20]

Mineko's account of the disturbance in September 1905, when mobs of people dissatisfied with the results of the peace conference following the Russo-Japanese War burned the police boxes and churches,[21] is a highlight of a diary that is generally lacking in excitement, but ultimately the greatest interest of Mineko's diary is what she tells us, even indirectly, about her son.

As long as the war continued Mineko was anxious about Ōgai's safety, but once the fighting ended her chief concern was his triumphal return. After many delays, Ōgai finally reached Tokyo on January 12, 1908. Mineko wrote in her diary, "Soon afterward the train arrived. I could hear the sounds of a band, and then Rintarō's face could be seen at a train window. Everybody was pushing for a better look. He said a few words. Then he got off the train and boarded a horse carriage that had come from the Ministry of the Imperial Household and headed for the palace."[22]

Later that day, Ōgai arrived at Mineko's house, where he met innumerable acquaintances who had come to welcome him back. Mineko wrote, "At eleven at night, I urged him to go to his wife's place in Shiba. Mariko, after not having seen him in two years, had just a glimpse of him at the station today." If we can accept this statement at face value, Mineko, despite her bad relations with Ōgai's wife, urged him to go visit his wife and daughter.

The tension between the two women grew steadily more acute, as we can infer from several ambiguous diary entries. The relations between Ōgai and his wife, Shigeko, were exacerbated especially by the publication of "Half A Day." Mineko wrote on March 10, 1909, "Shigeko is away again. On the fourth a story called 'Half A Day' appeared in the magazine *Subaru*. He described Shigeko in the story, and it has caused a lot of trouble. She may have left on account of it."[23] But on May 31 Mineko wrote, "Today Shigeko was quite submissive. Rintarō and I are both happy. I wonder if it isn't because of the story."[24]

If Mineko's diary contained a few more entries describing what actually went on in Ōgai's house, it would be an invaluable source of information about the private life of an exceedingly reticent man, but Ōgai no doubt inherited his reticence from his mother, a samurai mother of the old school.

Notes

1. There is a translation of this story by Darcy Murray in *Monumenta Nipponica* 26:1–2, 1973.
2. Rintarō was the personal name of Ōgai. (Ōgai was his *gagō*, or artistic name.)
3. Yamazaki Kunihiro (ed.), *Mori Ōgai: Haha no Nikki*, p. 60.
4. This is suggested by such entries as "This morning I wrote my diary for the first time in a long time." (Yamazaki, *Ōgai*, p. 69.)
5. *Ibid.*, p. 201. Kimiko was Ōgai's younger sister, Koganei Kimiko.
6. *Ibid.*, p. 314.
7. *Ibid.*, pp. 111, 142, 148, 149, 180, 191, 204, 282, 291.
8. *Ibid.*, p. 100. The ink was presumably not for drinking.
9. *Ibid.*, pp. 221, 311.
10. *Ibid.*, p. 281.
11. *Ibid.*, p. 255.
12. *Ibid.*
13. *Ibid.*, p. 328.
14. *Kabuki jūhachiban*. These eighteen plays (or parts of plays) were often considered to constitute the basic repertory of Kabuki. They were chosen about 1830 by the seventh Ichikawa Danjūrō as the representative plays performed by his "family."
15. Yamazaki, *Ōgai*, p. 171.
16. *Ibid.*, p. 260.
17. She refers to the present Minami-za in Kyoto.
18. *Ōkan*. This is probably the play by Osada Shūtō (1871–1915), published in 1909.
19. Another name for the Kansai, in general the region around Kyoto and Osaka.
20. Yamazaki, *Ōgai*, p. 256. "Patriot actors" is a rough translation for *sōshi yakusha*. Kawakami Otojirō (1864–1911), the central figure of the Shimpa theatrical tradition, first achieved prominence during the Sino-Japanese War with his productions of patriotic plays.

21. *Ibid.*, p. 166.
22. *Ibid.*, p. 198.
23. *Ibid.*, p. 353.
24. *Ibid.*, p. 354.

Bibliography

Yamazaki Kunihiro (ed.). *Mori Ōgai: Haha no Nikki.* Tokyo: San'ichi Shobō, 1985.

The Diary of
Shimomura Toku

One will not find the name Shimomura Toku in a Japanese biographical dictionary, no matter how detailed. Only a few fragments of the extensive diary she kept from 1912, the year she sailed from Yokohama to Seattle, until her death in 1963 have ever been printed. But she serves as a fine exemplar of the many Japanese who emigrated to the United States and elsewhere during the Meiji era.

Toku was born in 1888 in Saitama Prefecture. She graduated from the Japanese Red Cross Tokyo Nursing School, where she studied nursing and midwifery. During the Russo-Japanese War she served aboard a hospital ship that stood by during the Battle of Tsushima. After her return to Japan she was awarded the Order of the Sacred Crown, Eighth Class, for her meritorious actions. She subsequently was put in charge of the clinic at a spinning mill in Kawagoe. One day a factory supervisor suggested to her an arranged marriage with his younger brother, who was working in Seattle. The brother had gone to America intending to study dentistry, but at the time was washing dishes in a restaurant.

Toku does not seem to have hesitated long about becoming a

"picture bride." In preparation for the journey she had her hair bobbed, and changed from Japanese to Western clothes. She also paid a visit to her future husband's family in Shiga Prefecture.[1]

Toku described her first meeting with her future in-laws. She had been expected in the afternoon but arrived in the morning. "Everybody was taken aback by my sudden appearance, and there was a great commotion. Having become a member of the family of my dear husband, I went to the parlor and felt my heart pound as I sat before my husband's photograph."[2] She remained with her new family about ten days. When she left for Saitama to see her own family, she wondered when she would again visit Shiga Prefecture, and hoped that it would be with her husband. Probably the thought did not cross her mind that she might never again set foot on Japanese soil.

Toku's ship, the *Awa Maru*, sailed a month later, on February 28, 1912, from Yokohama. She was accompanied by the supervisor, her future brother-in-law, who had business in America. Hardly had the ship left the harbor than it began to rock violently. Toku noted in her diary, "I was the only one who ate dinner tonight."[3] On the following day, "I went out on deck, but the rain and waves were fierce. Grateful that I had not become seasick, I lay in my bunk reading a book."[4] Perhaps Toku's experiences as a nurse on a hospital ship had given her sea legs.

The bad weather continued. As usual in such cases, the crew members incorrectly predicted again and again that the weather would improve the following day, or else declared that in all their years at sea they had never encountered such terrible storms. Toku noted on March 3, "The ship is listing more than forty-five degrees. At night it is even worse. I feel so utterly helpless, worrying about whether we'll ever reach our destination. I prayed to our Heavenly Father, our only strength. I had been unable to sleep, but I at last shut my eyes." This was a first expression in the diary of Toku's abiding faith in Christianity that would carry her through crises even more painful than storms at sea.

Toku was married soon after she arrived in America. The life of the newlywed couple was by no means easy. Page after page of Toku's diary describes the hardships they suffered. Opening at random one of the volumes of this extremely long diary, I found this entry for April 4, 1915:

"My husband says he doesn't feel well. But in America, however painful it may be, one works just the same as usual, and one is not allowed to rest. He went to work in spite of his illness. He finally came back home about ten o'clock. He said he had asked for day work. Living by his side, I can't help worrying when I see how he suffers all day long from exhaustion."

On May 12 of that year Toku herself was taken ill and wrote, "I spent the whole night in pain. The baby is crying because it's hungry, and my husband is worn out. I felt so forlorn that I cried out without realizing it, my voice choked, 'Ah, what a place to have emigrated!'"

Of course, even if Toku and her family had been in Japan, on occasion they would have fallen ill, and perhaps their financial situation would have been even worse; but in Seattle, far from their families, in a country whose ways they really did not understand, the sense of isolation was acute. But they survived. Toku's skill as a midwife was in demand, and she delivered over a thousand babies during the twenty-eight years from her arrival in 1912 until 1940, when she made her last delivery, her grandson, now a professor. Her husband was never able to study dentistry, but eventually managed to earn a decent living. Everything changed abruptly in December 1941.

On the sixth Toku wrote only a brief note in her diary: "Spent the whole day on household chores. Christmas is coming so I spent the day making plans for presents and cards." She still wrote classical Japanese, but English words were conspicuous.[5] The next day's entry was in a totally dissimilar mood:

When I got back home from church I heard the news, like a bad dream, that Japanese airplanes had bombed Hawaii. It was so unexpected that I was stunned. It was just the time for the cooking lesson of the Ladies' Society, but I left halfway through and returned home. I sat before the radio again and listened to the news. They said that this morning at six o'clock Japan had declared war. Our future looks darker and darker. All I could do was pray, "God, be with us!"

The entry for December 8 is similar in tone:

It finally got light after a night of uneasiness. All I can do is pray. I spent the whole day sitting in front of the radio and listening to the news. Tonight from eleven o'clock there is a blackout. It lasts until ten minutes to eight tomorrow morning. With the outbreak of war, the leaders of the Japanese community in this city have been rounded up and are being held in the immigration office . . . God be with us in the darker and darker days ahead! From today all assets of Japanese have been frozen. Money deposited in banks cannot be withdrawn.

On December 9 Toku wrote in her diary, "Today was also spent in anxiety. All I could do was pray, 'God protect our America!'" In these words one has a foretaste of the tragedy that would afflict Toku and many other Japanese during the next three years. Toku had probably never consciously thought of herself as being an American. Her life in America was spent almost entirely among Japanese and Japanese-Americans, and to the end she probably remained unable to speak English well. But she called her grandson by his American name, and "home" for her no longer meant the village where she was born in Saitama (or anywhere else in Japan) but Seattle. When she called on God, she asked Him to protect not Japan but America.

During the days immediately following the outbreak of war between Japan and the United States, Toku spent much of her time anxiously listening to the radio. She seems at first to have been reluctant to leave the house, fearful that she might encounter some manifestation of anti-Japanese feeling. On December 12 she wrote, "I spent the whole day in the house. I hear that permission has been given from today to withdraw one hundred dollars from the bank. This is in order to preserve the lives and safety of us enemy aliens. I felt more than ever the generosity with which America treats us."

Two days later, she wrote, "The weather was good. A long, long week has ended. I went to church feeling that it was because we are Christians that we have the special privilege of gathering on this Sunday. In the choir we sang together Hymn 307 from our hearts. With heartfelt feelings of prayer and with tears we sang and wept."

Toku's deep religious convictions never wavered even under the most trying circumstances, and she expressed her gratitude for every human gesture. On December 17 there was a further relaxation of restrictions, and Japanese were permitted to engage in business again. Toku's reaction was: "I felt grateful, thinking, 'It's because we're in a democracy.' " On Christmas Day she wrote, "Christmas in wartime. We celebrated it quietly at home. I am truly thankful that the whole family can get together happily and eat roast chicken."

On February 19, 1942, President Franklin D. Roosevelt, bowing to pressure from the military, signed an executive order that authorized the secretary of war to exclude potentially dangerous persons from military zones. Two days later General John De Witt, the military commander of the Western Defense Command, issued a proclamation establishing military zones along the Pacific Coast, and in the middle of March an order was issued stating that all persons of Japanese ancestry were required to leave the West Coast. Naturally, this came as a terrible blow to Shimomura Toku and the many others in the Japanese community of Seattle, but there was no protest. Toku's family was eventually evacuated to Minidoka, in the desolate wastes of southern Idaho.

Toku's diary for 1942 describes her tragic experiences without a suggestion of self-pity. On the day that she and her family were sent to an internment camp, not the same one to which many of her friends had gone, she wrote, "There are no words—not lonely, nor anything else—adequate to express my feelings. Ah, how sad I am there is a war!" But when a dance party was held in the mess hall at

Minidoka at the end of the year, she wrote, "The solicitude of the government has made it possible for us Japanese to welcome in the New Year this way, with everything we need." She expressed gratitude for the ample food, and even pleasure that she did not have to plan meals, let alone cook them. She always found consolation in religion, though many persons interned with her undoubtedly wondered why they and 150,000 other people were being punished for crimes they had not committed and had never dreamed of committing.

Toku's diary makes us aware of the tragedy that sometimes befalls people who love two countries. Similar tragedies have occurred many times in the past, but the events were close enough to me to feel personal shame, as an American who was not interned, that such events could have happened. Toku and her family returned to Seattle after the war ended and were able to resume the life that had been so brutally interrupted. Her diary insists that she was happier in her last years than ever before. One hopes this is true.

Notes

1. This section of the diary was printed by Itō Kazuo in his *Zoku Hokubei Hyakunen-zakura*.
2. Itō, *Zoku*, p. 16.
3. *Ibid.*, p. 19.
4. *Ibid.*
5. The sentence just translated is, in the original, "*Kurisumasu* mo chikazuki-tareba *puresento* ya hagaki no *puran* ichinichi sugoseri." In the following sentence such English words as *kukingu resun* (cooking lesson), *redeo* (radio), and *dekureya waa* (declare war) occur.

Bibliography

Itō Kazuo. *Zoku Hokubei Hyakunen-zakura*. Seattle: Hokubei Hyakunen-zakura Jikkō Iinkai, 1968.

Poets
and
Novelists

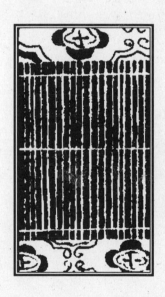

An Undeceitful Record

Kunikida Doppo (1871–1908) kept a diary between 1893 and 1897. The diary, *Azamukazaru no Ki* (An Undeceitful Record), is especially detailed for the first two years, the entry for each day often running to several pages. The first noticeable feature of the diary is its internal nature. Doppo rarely mentions the weather, unlike almost every other diarist of his time. He is also so vague about his daily activities that it is often difficult to guess how his days were spent. For example, in October 1893 he was appointed as a teacher at the Tsuruya Gakkan, a school in Saiki, Ōita Prefecture, but there is hardly a mention of what he taught, and not one pupil or colleague is named. He never indicated even whether he liked or disliked teaching. Practically the only allusion to his teaching is the following, extremely typical utterance:

"Yesterday I went to the school for the first time and, facing the twenty-odd pupils, I voiced my greetings on the occasion of my first lecture and our first meeting. After setting the daily lesson, I left. Make me love these children and, ah, let me not mislead them!"[1] Unfortunately, he never gave any indication in his diary as to whether or not this prayer was answered.

Instead of the description of the events of each day that we expect in a diary, Doppo gives us instead a good deal of self-analysis, declarations of religious and literary convictions, and condemnations of the evil in the world. Surely there are not many diaries as consistently serious as Doppo's. The word *majime* (serious) is one of the key words of the diary, as in this passage:

> A serious life, serious study, serious efforts—are these not the true characteristics of a man who senses his duty, thinks of human life, believes in the sacred? But, when one looks carefully about one, how few serious people there are in the world! Most things that people do, say, work at, or plan stem from inertia or else from habit, and there is almost nothing that does not stem from physical desire. I, too, am well aware this is so. Why is it people cannot easily become serious? It goes without saying it is because they lack sincerity.[2]

The Japanese are often said to be a serious people, and Doppo's insistence on this virtue, here and elsewhere in the diary, seems to be in keeping with Japanese traditions. I wonder, however, if the source of his insistence on seriousness was not Longfellow's "Life is real! Life is earnest!" Earlier in the diary Doppo wrote *Jinsei wa majime nari*, a close translation of "Life is earnest!"[3] Similarly, Doppo's frequent mentions of the importance of *shinshiritei* (sincerity), though in keeping with the traditional Japanese virtue of *makoto*, probably came directly from Carlyle. Doppo wrote, "I have come to realize that when Carlyle wrote in *On Heroes* that the basic quality of the hero was sincerity, and when Emerson wrote that the genius is religious, their meaning was exactly the same."[4]

Doppo borrowed such concepts from abroad. The existence of foreign sources was less important than the fact that his beliefs were not merely fancy importations but were part of his flesh and blood. Perhaps he was the first Japanese writer who did not distinguish his tastes and beliefs from those of the European and American writers he admired, but accepted theirs as universal truths.

Doppo's earnestness, displayed on every page of his diary, is appealing, but sometimes seems immature or even childish. His favorite word was *aa* (ah!), which he used repeatedly, especially when expressing his wonderment over nature, humanity, and other objects of contemplation, as in this passage:

"Ah, nature! Beautiful, boundless, unpredictable nature!

"Ah, humanity! Continuously being born, and continuously dying on this earth—humanity!

"Ah, human beings! Human beings that go on breathing, controlled by the great kingdom of time!"[5]

Sometimes, not satisfied with a single *aa*, Doppo doubled the effect as in *Aa aa shizen, ware nanji wo yobu toki ni oite, mune ni kaen no uzumaki okoru wo kanzu*. (Ah, ah Nature. When I call upon you, I feel flames whirl in my breast.)[6] Or he even triples his sighs in this fashion: *Aa aa aa ware kotoba wo shirazu*. (Ah, ah, ah, I do not know the words.)[7]

Along with his cries of *aa* there are many mentions of tears, which come in different varieties: "I try to stanch the silent tears, the hot tears, the tears of indignation, but they cannot be stanched."[8] In one of his rare accounts of eating and drinking, Doppo described how he invited a friend to dinner:

"In the afternoon I invited Mr. Imai Tadaharu and boiled some beef for him. We drank beer and chatted. At one point I resolutely and at length admonished him, showing him what I had written, and asking him to examine himself at once. He swallowed silent tears and I also wept. We swore that we would improve our characters, consider human feelings, reflect on life, and become closer and closer friends."[9]

The mention of "what I had written" presumably refers to the criticism of Imai that Doppo had recorded in his diary entry of two days earlier. It begins,

"Thinking of close friends and acquaintances, it came to me that my relations with Mr. Imai Tadaharu have greatly changed in recent days, and I wept. When I think back on it myself, I realize that I have maintained almost the same simple, ingenuous feelings in my relations with him as when we first became friends, at the age of fifteen or sixteen, but he has already sullied the pure springs of affection with the muddy waters of age, ambition, and envy."[10]

Doppo was sure that it was essential to maintain the purity of the "springs of affection" (*jōsen*) of boyhood, and not allow them to be defiled by the "muddy waters" (*dakusui*) of adulthood. We may admire Doppo's idealism, but these words of self-reflection and criticism hardly seem those of an adult. He himself wrote, "I am not suited to discussions with others. I have not yet become sufficiently mature to discuss anything on the highest level of seriousness."[11] This judgment was too severe, but it indicates that Doppo was aware that his high-flown ideals enjoyed little currency in the world of adults.

Entry after entry in Doppo's diary begins with a statement of his true nature: "I am a child of nature. I have ideals and faith. I have enterprise. I am a human being."[12] Doppo followed this declaration with a poem Emerson had quoted at the beginning of "Self-Reliance." Doppo, however, was far from possessing self-reliance. His analyses of his weaknesses occupy many pages in the diary. Here is what he wrote immediately after quoting Emerson:

> This is precisely what my self-confidence must be. Therefore, if in the future I act out of laziness, reveal little of the virtue of magnanimity, have only a faint sense of self-abnegation, show no calmness of purpose, and lack the energy to pursue rigorously and diligently to their accomplishment the enterprises I undertake, my goals and my affairs, this will mean that I have set at naught my ideals and faith, that I have become a sycophant of society, that I have killed the human spirit within me. In a word, it will mean that I have committed suicide.[13]

Doppo was so unremittingly severe with respect to even his most trivial faults that at times we may be tempted to smile at so much self-conscious insistence on incorruptibility, but at other times we may wish some incident had reminded Doppo that laughter is also a part of human life.

As we read it is easy to form the impression that Doppo spent most of each day either in painful self-examination or else in writing his diary. He is constantly berating himself for his vices, as in the following entry:

> Just as maggots hatch in rotten meat, just as larvae spawn in stagnant water, poisonous insects and evil-smelling snakes swarm in my corrupt carnal desires and devour my heaven-bestowed divine spirit; and all of heaven and earth—beauty, good, love, fire, loftiness, peace, depth, mystery, darkness—disappears before me. May the cold sword of death, the icy pond of extinction, slash my rotten flesh! May the blazing fires and furious flames of the great universe consume this rotten flesh of mine![14]

It is not clear what occasioned this outburst, though it undoubtedly referred to Doppo's sex life. What had he done? Had he yielded to temptation and consorted with a prostitute? Or perhaps committed masturbation? If he did not always tend to describe his sins in highly colored terms, we might imagine (at the least) that he had raped a nun. In a letter he wrote his friend Mizutani Makuma he declared,

> Neither great thunder nor divine lightning can save me; neither frozen lakes nor frozen seas can halt the corruption of my flesh. The sensual world that fills my eyes attacks me like a

snake; the poisonous fog that fills my whole heart, my whole body, has already destroyed me completely. I have become so corrupted that I am almost too insensible to listen to your words . . . I have become something as ugly as a dung fly that hovers in dull and torpid sunlight. No, probably I have been like that from the start. Deceived by the foul odors rising from a cesspool of fleshly desires, I was unaware of this myself . . . I am exhausted from walking the tightrope between death from madness and degeneration. I am sure that I must have deceived you to this very day. I have all along been corrupt flesh, and how I have made you corrupt too, to this day. Forgive me! Forgive me! I have corrupted many people. After all that has happened, I absolutely must do something.[15]

Doppo, characterizing this letter as "a peculiar missive," decided not to send it. Fortunately, it did not take much time for Wordsworth to elevate and purify his spirit, and, he says, "Writers like Emerson deepened my wisdom."[16] He attended church regularly and read the Bible often. He never gets more specific about the nature of his terrible sins nor, for that matter, does he devote much attention to the diversions in his life. Occasionally he took a walk with a friend, and once in a great while he visited places of entertainment such as *yose*[17] or *jōruri*.[18] On one occasion he even got drunk, as he recorded in a confessional entry. He accidentally met Mizutani (with whom he had a reconciliation), who invited him to lunch. Doppo related in his diary,

"Mizutani said, 'I'll treat you to beef.' While the beef was cooking, I had to order sake. The sake arrived. I had one cup and then another. Finally I got very drunk, for the first time since, when I was a boy of twelve or thirteen, I swilled down a great deal of sake and got drunk."[19]

Doppo decided that it must be because drunkenness is the source of immorality that the sages of all times have forbidden people to drink. "I had made a vow never to drink sake, but I had now drunk it all the same. In other words, I had lied."[20] He declared that he would try never to drink again, but he would not make the same vow as before because, "Vowing and then lying is a thousand times more immoral than sake." I wonder if I am the only one who feels uncomfortable when reading the diary of such a moralistic young man?

Doppo's ideas were derived largely from his readings in European literature, but he also read the Confucian works that were closely associated with the traditional education of the samurai class. He mentioned some of his books in a diary entry for February 1893: "Emerson, Carlyle, Hugo, Wordsworth, Burns, Goethe, the *Analects*, Wang Yang-ming, Chuang Tzu, and a history of England, all in a row, stare down at me from the shelf."[21]

If the works of Shakespeare, Milton, Tolstoy, and a few Japanese authors were added to this list it would more or less constitute the books Doppo read during the years covered by his diary. Most of these works appealed to him not because of their literary beauty but because of the intellectual or spiritual stimulation they provided. He more often commented on the effect that a particular book had on him than on its contents.

For example, he borrowed from the popular historian Tokutomi Sohō (1863–1957) a biography of Jean-Jacques Rousseau by John Morley. Two days later he wrote in his diary that he had read the preface several times, suggesting not only that it had impressed him but also that he did not read English easily. One phrase in the preface struck him particularly—"steadfast faith in human nature." He commented,

> The phrase "steadfast faith in human nature" captures exactly my recent emotions, and I felt as if I had obtained a kind of light. When I consider the role of the poet, it is to hear the faint sounds and plaintive notes that this life of ours produces in the innermost depths of the human heart, to explain it and to

teach it. In other words, it is more important for him to listen to these faint sounds and plaintive notes than to listen to Christ, Confucius, Wordsworth, or, for that matter, Shakespeare or Wang Yang-ming. It is more important to listen to them than to the murmuring of one's own spirit. The reason for listening and then expressing them is that this is the way the poet has to teach humanity.[22]

There can be little doubt that Doppo was profoundly affected by Morley's phrase, but it is unlikely any reader today would be equally affected. Doppo, constantly seeking inspiration from his readings, was capable of finding enlightenment even in a quite ordinary sentiment. He stated how he benefited from his readings: "There are works in which lofty and profound thoughts and emotions are set down. If I read these books, I shall obtain their lofty and profound thoughts and emotions."[23] Doppo esteemed Wordsworth and Burns less as poets than as teachers whose poems revealed to him some vital truth or expressed thoughts and feelings within his own heart that he had never formed into words. After reading Wordsworth's "Resolution and Independence," he wrote in his diary, "Ah, Wordsworth has sung what was in my heart."[24]

Doppo insisted again and again in his diary that he must become a poet,[25] but the poems he wrote at this stage of his life consisted mainly of exhortations along the lines of, "Ah, nature, I beg you, tell me your meaning," or "Liberty! come and save me!"[26] The most important influences Doppo received from his readings in Wordsworth and Burns were probably unconscious—their concern with ordinary people, ordinary landscapes, ordinary goodness.

Early in his diary Doppo, in one of his frequent bouts of self-analysis (but more cheerfully than usual), predicted a glorious career for himself:

I am cosmic. I am ideal. And because I am cosmic and ideal, I plan to enter politics. My life's work is revolution. It consists of making our national government a free government, our people a people that stands on truth and ideals, our national destiny that of a pioneer in the progress of the peoples of the whole world. That is why I shall stand in the world of politics. It is absolutely not because of any political—that is to say, ambitious, worldly, carnal—desire . . . I must go forward with the conviction that I am a gentleman whose style is prophetic, a politician who will be the great realizer of a great revolution.[27]

Doppo's first employment was with *Jiyū Shimbun* (The Liberal Newspaper).[28] The experience seems to have disillusioned him with practical politics, but (as a devout Christian) he maintained the hope that he might become the Niijima Jō of the political world. He was not really suited to be a journalist, as he soon discovered:

"Human life, the cosmos, work, duty, life and death, nature, beauty, eternal life—these have all disappeared from my emotions. Newspapers, magazines, receptions, money—these things have bit by bit come to be on my tongue and to control in large part my intelligence and feelings."[29]

Doppo castigated himself for the desire for fame that he detected behind his political ambitions. He declared that this was the cause of his spiritual anguish. He realized now that he must return to the ideal of "love, faith, and labor." "If not," he told himself, "I am sure to die of madness."[30] But he was still not sure what to do with his life. "I am in a fog as to whether I should become a man of letters or a man of politics." But the next day he reached an unexpected conclusion: "I hope to become a teacher." The day after that he changed his mind once again:

"Last night was for me an extremely important night. Last night I resolved decisively to make literature my career in this world. That is to say, I believe that serving as a 'teacher of mankind' to the fullest extent of my abilities and to end thus my stay in this world is most suited to my destiny, and that this will give value to my life."[31]

His repeated changes of opinion regarding his future reflected not only his own uncertainty but the different advice given to him by two men he especially respected, Tokutomi Sohō and the Christian minister Uemura Masahisa (1858–1925). Tokutomi urged Doppo, if he really wished to become a newspaper reporter, to go to the provinces. He said, "After you have polished your skill for a year in the provinces, you can make your debut in Tokyo."[32] Uemura, entirely agreeing with Doppo's own preference for remaining in Tokyo, promised to do what he could to help find Doppo a suitable job. But when Uemura asked Doppo what he would like to become, he was unable to state his real hope, that he might become a poet.[33]

In October 1893 Doppo finally made a decision. He accepted the teaching post at Saiki on the island of Kyūshū. There he would indeed become a teacher as he had hoped, though the reality of teaching school would not, in the event, bring any pleasure. More important, by going to a small town far from Tokyo he was to come close to the world of nature described by Wordsworth and Burns, and in this sense to become a poet. Doppo's life did not change markedly after he arrived in Saiki. As usual, the diary is full of self-criticism in a familiar vein:

> Tetsuo[34] is very sensitive. Whether he faces right or turns left, he cannot stop feeling things. He is now sitting here. The last ten days have gone by. Ten extremely busy days of his life have gone by. However, he has remained throughout in an almost passive position. He sees this, he hears that. But he has been incapable of making even one important invention. To put it in a word, he has confusedly spent these days which should have been of the greatest importance in nothing more than a passive *passion*. His ten days' activity have not made him into a *wild soul* standing proudly in the shrines of the gods, in the midst of nature, between heaven and earth, but instead have caused him to discover for himself that he is among the human shadows of the world of social receptions.[35]

He mentioned only briefly his teaching program: from 3:30 in the afternoon he taught lower-form pupils from the second volume of the national readers; from 4:30 he taught "reading"; from 8:30 in the evening he taught algebra; and from 9:30 he lectured advanced pupils on Swinton's *World History*. But he was attracted far more to the ordinary people he saw in Saiki than he was to the school:

"Some are aged fathers, some unsophisticated men, some happy-looking couples for a lifetime. Then there are sensitive, melancholy youths, innocent boys—ah, are these not also poems?"[36]

The people he had seen in Tokyo never inspired him to write poetry, possibly because they in no way resembled the people who appear in the poems of Wordsworth and Burns, but here Doppo saw such people. He called for his muse to inspire him: "Ah, where are you, my god of poetry? Where does the muse live?"[37]

The simple life surrounding Doppo inspired him as it had inspired the English Romantic poets: "Ah, *simple life*! And amidst the greatness of nature, the life of man like foam on the water! And the great cosmos!"[38] When he strolled outside the town, he saw the blue water of mountain streams and, here and there, thatch-covered cottages. He attended church in Saiki. There were only four people in the congregation besides Doppo and his younger brother, but "this small band lifted their voices in song, swallowing the tears as they prayed. They were few in number, but they did not lose their dignity."[39]

Gradually Doppo became aware that each of the people he met had a story. When he took a ferry, he noticed with the eyes of a poet (or a novelist) the boatman: "I am sure it would be interesting if I went into this ferryman's shack and listened to his story. Is he not also someone I should include in my 'tale'?"[40] The boatman was not the only one to interest him. "For me this is a lovable village, and I am sure that it can furnish me with the seeds of many stories. What kind of people and what kind of stories shall I discover in this village?"[41] When he took the ferry he listened to the conversations of the other passengers. "Their talk is all new to me . . . This riverboat, too, is definitely material for my stories."[42]

Another boatman, an old man like the first, moved Doppo especially. As he slowly poled his boat across the river he told Doppo of his earlier years in Nagasaki, where he had built "black ships."[43] Doppo commented, "I cannot forget this old man. This is because he has lived his life as a *soul* between heaven and earth. Even the life of an old man like this without question contains a profound story."[44] Anyone familiar with Doppo's works will have no trouble in finding in these words germs of his future masterpieces.[45]

Doppo had spent most of his boyhood in Yamaguchi Prefecture, where he certainly had many opportunities to admire natural scenery before he went to Tokyo at the age of sixteen, but four months after he left Saiki he recalled in his diary, "It was my life in Saiki that brought me close to nature."[46] Presumably what he meant was not that he had been unaware of the beauty of nature before living in Saiki, but that he had been unable to appreciate nature as it really is, as opposed to nature as depicted in paintings or described in countless poems. The change in attitude was brought about by Doppo's readings in Wordsworth, who taught him to look not only at conventionally admired sights but also at humble village houses, village people unnoticed by the world, and even beggars.

Perhaps the experience in Saiki that exercised the most important direct influence on Doppo's future writing was noticing the idiot boy Kishū, a beggar in a fishing village. He wrote,

> Yesterday at the waterfront I ran into the usual beggar. Just as reports have it, he was searching in the filthy things of a refuse heap, and when he found something he put it in his mouth. I had Shūji [Doppo's younger brother] give him a persimmon. I asked the boy, "Is it sour?" He answered, "It's sweet." His voice conveyed nothing but the fact of the flavor. His voice, his

tone, his manner all said merely "sweet." There was no overtone of gratitude, or shame, or joy, or disappointment or discontent—all he said was merely "sweet." He is to be pitied, I'm sure. I've heard from pupils at the school that this beggar is eighteen or nineteen. Last night I made further inquiries about him. People call him Kishū because he himself says he comes from Kishū, but nobody knows whether or not his parents are alive.[47]

A beggar who ate refuse from a garbage heap, if mentioned at all in earlier literature, would have been depicted in terms of revulsion, but Doppo seems drawn to Kishū. The boy's lack of responsiveness would provide the central theme of Doppo's first work of importance, the short story "Gen Oji" (Old Gen). It is likely that his interest in the young beggar was occasioned by his readings in Wordsworth, especially the poem "The Idiot Boy." The theme of Wordsworth's poem is mother-love at its most absolute: the mother of the idiot boy asks nothing in return for her love, and does not even perceive the pathos of loving a creature who is incapable of answering her simplest questions, let alone responding to her affection. This, combined with the boatman in whom Doppo sensed there must be a "story," provided all the materials he would need for his first work of fiction. Without Wordsworth, he would probably not have noticed either the boatman or the beggar in Saiki.

Thoughts about the love that the mother (or old Gen) lavished on an uncomprehending person may also have aroused in Doppo an awareness of how much he, too, wanted to be loved. He wrote in his diary, just three days after describing Kishū, "I want a lover. Without someone to love me, and someone for me to love, I feel the desolation of this life of travail. Holy incarnation of love, come and rescue me from this prison!"[48] A craving for *ren'ai*, a word invented to convey the Western meaning of "love," had marked the writings of the early Japanese Romantics and now found expression in Doppo's diary. A year and a half later he would indeed fall in love, as he craved, but his love for Sasaki Nobuko, the best-known episode of Doppo's life, brought him little happiness.

Doppo left Saiki on August 1, 1894. Not a word in his diary suggests he was sorry to leave behind the acquaintances he had made; whatever friendships he may have formed are not even mentioned. His last diary entry prior to leaving Saiki was typical of what had occupied his mind throughout his days there:

"Ah, I truly sympathize with all other creatures who live on the face of the globe. God! grant that I may find a vocation appropriate to this sympathy."[49]

From Saiki he traveled to Hiroshima and from there to Yanai in Yamaguchi Prefecture, which he considered to be his hometown. His diary entries continue in much the same philosophical vein, with hardly a mention of how he spent his time when he was not brooding over life, faith, God, and so on. Typical comments include: "How strange human life is, ah, how strange!" or "Ah, a man who has become an intellectual but who lacks faith is a cursed man."[50]

Doppo left Yamaguchi by steamship for Osaka, and from there continued his journey by train to Tokyo. Two days after his arrival he went to call on Tokutomi Sohō, but he was out and Doppo returned fruitlessly to his lodgings. His only comment was, "How strange human life is!"[51] Four days later, Tokutomi sent Doppo a telegram, asking him to meet that evening at the office of the newspaper *Kokumin Shimbun*. This led immediately to a dinner invitation at a Western restaurant together with the newspaper's other employees. On September 17, 1894, Doppo reported for work at the *Kokumin Shimbun*.[52]

Although Doppo hardly mentioned it in his diary, which is still crammed with exclamations concerning life and faith, war with China had broken out in July, just before Doppo left Saiki. However, Tokutomi and his colleagues, as professional journalists, impressed on Doppo at their dinner the great significance of this war. "They argued that the history of the entire world is bound up in this war between Japan and China, and they vowed to throw their full energies into their work."[53] Doppo was not unmoved. He wrote, "My blood has caught fire. The world is alive! The world is alive! Exactly the kind of world where a heroic man can display his prowess!"[54]

Doppo was suddenly stirred by patriotism, but he was not about to abandon his Wordsworthian dreams. On September 13 he wrote: "This morning, at the front gate of the palace, I reverently saw off the emperor, who is to assume personal command of the troops. The splendor of the monarch! I felt envious of Napoleon. Ah, the monarch! The monarch! I who envy him also envy life in the mountains and forests. What a strange mentality I have!"[55]

Doppo volunteered for service as a war reporter. He explained his decision in these terms:

"Why have I of my own free will volunteered to board a warship and rush headlong into the area between life and death? I answer: it is in order to regenerate myself amidst nature. Or, to put it in another way, it is so that I may become more and more of a sincere child of nature. Or, to use still other words, it is in order to cause my spiritual nature to advance another step."[56]

It is hard to doubt Doppo's sincerity, but if we accept this explanation of why he volunteered, he must surely have been the only reporter with such high ideals!

On October 16, as he noted in his diary, "I reported to imperial headquarters, and obtained authorization to take part in the campaign."[57] At first he served aboard the *Saikyō Maru*, but he later transferred to the warship *Chiyoda*. His experiences during the Sino-Japanese War would be described in his book *Aitei Tsūshin* (Letters to My Beloved Brother), but his diary gave his reactions more truthfully.

The tone of Doppo's account of the war, at first so cheerfully consecrated, totally changed once the *Chiyoda* entered Korean waters. For the first time, perhaps, the world of human endeavors seemed of importance to Doppo, and although there are still occasional exclamations in his usual, spiritual vein, most of the entries describe things he saw or actions he performed. The occasions for self-examination were furnished by the outer, rather than the inner, world.

Doppo went ashore on the first Korean island captured by the Japanese. The inhabitants had fled at the approach of the Japanese, who (for the fun of it) stole a pig, two ducks, and two pairs of women's shoes. Doppo confessed,

> I now cannot keep from regretting that I deliberately brought back with me a woman's shoe. What right had I to steal an article of these people's household pleasure? Regardless of what others might do, how could I, who embrace as an article of faith that these people must be thought of with a fraternal spirit, as being like ourselves the children of heaven, do such a thing? Perhaps it was no more than a sudden, mischievous impulse, but the fact is that I performed this harmful act without reflecting on it. I truly cannot stop regretting it.[58]

Doppo was shocked at his own action. He has also become aware that a man who is part of a group is apt to act differently from his normal behavior. After a week of life aboard ship, he wrote, "I have forgotten much about nature; I am almost completely given to self-indulgence. Although I am engaging in a war, I am almost without feeling . . . I have myself forgotten that I am in this heaven and earth. I have made myself small."[59]

This self-analysis, more than the accusations Doppo previously leveled at himself for insufficient faith or insufficient diligence, commands our respect. For the first time Doppo seems to be writing as a mature man, and subsequent entries are in the same vein: "Yesterday afternoon about two I went ashore and bought an ox and a pig. To tell the truth, it was half stealing. But the natives were not suspicious of me. When they accepted my demands they should also have thought of their own profit."[60] When he received a letter from Toku-tomi worrying about his safety, he wrote, "I am happy for your solicitude, but feel that I have somehow been coarsened. No, I have coarsened myself in front of other people. This is the kind of unmanly nature I have."[61] Such self-reflection carries greater conviction than any earlier entry.

Doppo was aware that he was disliked by others aboard the ship. Characteristically, he blamed this on himself: "I am someone who has no idea how to associate with worldly people other than my close friends and acquaintances. This is because I have too much self-respect and I look down on others."[62] At one stage his despair over his inability to get along with others even made him consider suicide: "It is not that I haven't thought of suicide. It's simply that my resolve is still weak."[63]

On November 21 Port Arthur fell to Japanese troops. Doppo went ashore three days later. He wrote, "I saw Chinese corpses for the first time. The sight is still graven vividly in my eyes. The actual observation of 'war dead' has made me intuit the profoundly serious meaning of the word 'war.'"[64]

In the meantime, Doppo's relations with the naval officers of the ship had considerably deteriorated. A certain lieutenant had declared in his presence that only stupid people believed in religion. Doppo demanded to know what right the officer had to insult "a young man who earnestly hopes to belong to heaven, to become a true child of nature, and to achieve freedom and liberty?"[65] In January 1895 Doppo quarreled with an Ensign Yamaji. According to Doppo, Yamaji roundly abused him. Yamaji was drunk, and this perhaps explained his insolence, but Doppo's judgment was severe: "He is a pleasant-enough fellow, but he is, in short, a fool who resembles a clever man."[66] It is refreshing that Doppo did not blame himself for Yamaji's behavior. In this, too, we sense a new maturity.

Doppo's first mention of the title he gave his diary does not occur until December 1894 while he was aboard the *Chiyoda*. He wrote, "Ever since I began to write 'An Undeceitful Account' I have felt a truly great number of things and have experienced a great number of struggles. However, my faith and knowledge are the same as before. I still go on talking of progress, always of progress. Where is the progress, I wonder? Would it not be more accurate to speak of retrogression?"[67] Despite his pessimism, Doppo had definitely made progress as a human being since starting the diary two years before. Although he still used the language of Romanticism, his despair no longer seemed the pose of an impressionable young man:

> Life is darkness. Human beings are infirm. I am in the process of sowing the seeds of infirmity and reaping a crop of despair ... Autumn of infirmity, come and kill me! Ghosts of paralysis, come and seize me! And yet, and yet, I shall not blindly follow the world and other people. Though starvation and penury afflict me, I vow that I will never lose my freedom, no matter what happens. I yearn to be buried on a desert island in some distant sea. But I shall maintain my freedom to the end. I have absolutely no dreams of achieving glory in Tokyo in the country of Japan.[68]

The Japanese fleet captured Wei-hai-wei at the end of February 1895, and early the next month the *Chiyoda* returned to Japan. Doppo landed at Kure and proceeded to Hiroshima, where he was met by eight newspaper acquaintances headed by Tokutomi Sohō. After various excursions, he returned to Tokyo and resumed his work at the *Kokumin Shimbun*. On April 17 he was named the editor of the magazine *Kokumin no Tomo* (The Nation's Friend), a magazine controlled by Tokutomi's political organization. The diary entries at this time are in the objective vein commenced during the war, though moments of self-examination and self-torment are not lacking: "Already twenty-five years old! It makes me want to weep. Just a student who'll never amount to anything! How shameful!"[69] His readings were still mainly of his old favorites, and he occasionally passed such judgments as: "Carlyle is greater than Hugo. There is truth and depth in him. Wordsworth was more of a prophet than Hugo."[70]

The diary entry for June 25 sounded a new note: "Of late, the hope has arisen within me that I might move to Hokkaidō, engage in agriculture, and lead a life of independence and self-reliance."[71] Doppo set about obtaining books describing Hokkaidō and also went to see people who were familiar with conditions there. He explained this sudden interest in terms of his desire to be completely independent of others: "An employed person, no matter what the pretexts or the appearances, cannot help but be more or less of a slave. He should instead fight with nature. He should choose hardships and obtain liberty."[72] The idea of "fighting with nature" (as opposed to the more common Japanese insistence on "having nature as one's friend") also stemmed from his readings in European literature. Hokkaidō was another realm where, unlike Japan with all its hampering restrictions, a man could live, according to his own principles, a life of freedom and faith in God. As usual with Doppo, he had second thoughts. He asked himself what he *really* was seeking in Hokkaidō.[73] Was he perhaps susceptible to the craving for wealth and fame, the reason some men went to Hokkaidō? But, after examining this unwelcome possibility, Doppo concluded, "I wonder if what I am seeking is not love?"[74]

Doppo did not leave immediately for Hokkaidō. On July 4 he recorded in his diary his new morning prayers: "I must record in this 'Undeceitful Record' the words of the first prayers I offer to God early every morning, before I get to work. This is because the written word is the impression of the heart."[75] The prayers, among other requests, ask God to make him stronger, juster, and purer.

In the entry for the following day he noted casually, "I visited Miss Sasaki." On the sixteenth he again visited her, and on this occasion he wrote merely, "Chatted with Nobuko."[76] On the twenty-ninth he was more expansive:

Yesterday morning Sasaki Nobuko came to see me. The hour and a half that we spent together passed like a second. She had gone out on an errand to her father's place in Kugimise, and had secretly stopped by on the way. In the end we came to have clandestine meetings. This was entirely the doing of her mother, Toyoju: it was her groundless suspicions of us that drove her daughter and me to this point. We were forced into a position where we had no choice but to fall in love. Her constraints actually were the helpers of love. The letter [Nobuko] sent me the night before last brought tears to my eyes. She is undergoing such agony that she is unable to sleep. God, lead us to the good. Lead us to a pure, lofty, profound, strong love![77]

Doppo's craving for love seems to have been answered in the most romantic terms. He wrote *Warera wa ren'ai no uchi ni ochiirinu* (We have fallen in love), a sentence that reads like a literal translation from English. On July 31 Nobuko visited him again. He wrote, "We share the same dream of living in Hokkaidō. We did not reach any definite commitment, but we promised that we would remain together for the rest of our lives."

The meetings between Nobuko and Doppo multiplied, though they still had to be kept secret due to her mother's opposition. Doppo was not discontent: "If one is in love, one must be ready to shed the hot blood of one's entire body and mind."[78] On August 6 he received a note from Nobuko that ended, "Remembrances of you do not leave me for an instant," and he commented, "Fair maiden, you too have at last fallen in love. Very well, if that is the case—let us dip together the inexhaustible springs of love!"[79]

Even amid this happiness, however, Doppo was subject to recurrent fits of doubt: "I have no faith that can give me peace. God's truth is still not clear to me. Why am I unable to kill myself?"[80] It is hard to believe that Doppo seriously contemplated suicide at this moment, but perhaps he was reading Goethe's *Werther*. "A knife has been prepared. Why do I hesitate?" What could be more romantic?

A few days later he and Nobuko again met secretly. He was determined to confess the love that was tormenting him. They strolled together. "Nobuko held tightly to my arm as we walked. I spoke slowly, one word at a time, and when I finally confessed that feelings had reached the point of love, my emotions were too much for me and I swallowed tears. She also swallowed her tears."[81] Nobuko told him that the rumors saying she was about to marry another man were false. She poured out words of love even more intense than his. He wrote, "We made a firm pledge that our love would remain unchanged *forever*."[82] Romantic love had triumphed.

The chief obstacle to the marriage of Doppo and Nobuko was the girl's mother. On August 14 Nobuko's father "called Nobuko and myself to a place where there was nobody else, and told us that he had agreed to our engagement."[83] The two young people were naturally overjoyed. They went for a walk together. "The two of us went hand-in-hand to the teahouse by the Gensammi Cave, and from there went up the mountain stream, crossed a bridge, and reached a lonely valley where we stopped. Autumn clarity and a dark ravine, sunset glow filling the mountains, human figures rare—at this time and in this place the two lovers walked hand-in-hand, morning joy enfolded in their breasts. What could be missing here? It was the paradise of a lifetime."[84]

A few days later Doppo left for Hokkaidō, unhappy over his parting from Nobuko, but confident of their love. After reaching Sapporo, he sent a telegram asking about the reactions of Nobuko's mother to their engagement, but there was no answer. Even amid Doppo's exclamations of joy over having found in the lonely regions of Hokkaidō a place where he would be able to perform work in consonance with his ideals, he worried over the reactions of Nobuko's family. A letter finally came from Nobuko reporting that her mother was furious with the young couple.[85] She had decided to send Nobuko to America in order to break up the affair.

Doppo returned to Tokyo in October. By the beginning of November he at last obtained permission to marry Nobuko, but only after agreeing to conditions laid down by her parents. On November 11 the wedding was performed by Uemura Masahisa. Doppo wrote in his diary, "This evening at seven o'clock Nobuko and I were married. My love has at last triumphed. I have at last triumphed. I have at last won Nobuko."[86]

Their happiness did not last long. In April 1896 Nobuko, on her way back home from church, disappeared. Doppo wrote on April 15,

"I am now sitting at my desk writing a biography of Lincoln. But I feel as if a leaden lump of grief has sunk and rolled to the bottom of my heart. My dear, my beloved Nobuko is no longer in my house. Her laughing voice no longer echoes here. Where is she now?. . . But I tell myself: Act like a man. Endure. Show your love in every act. Do not lose your temper."[87]

A few days later he learned that Nobuko wanted a divorce. Apparently the combination of parental opposition and Doppo's poverty had induced her to leave him, even though she was carrying his child. Friends tried to comfort Doppo, but to no avail: "My grief since Nobuko disappeared seems to have afflicted my spirit in some extraordinary manner. Life is earnest. Death is a fearsome voice."[88]

On April 22 he wrote Nobuko a long letter. It is beautifully expressed and should have melted her heart, but Nobuko was no longer to be swayed by Doppo. His diary entry for April 24 began, "Today is the last of the married life of Nobuko and myself. Yesterday I met Nobuko. I verified that Nobuko's heart is set on a divorce."[89] Tokutomi urged Doppo to go to Hawaii, and offered him a hundred yen for the journey. He urged Doppo to forget Nobuko who, he insisted, was not worth grieving over. He told Doppo's brother that Doppo should curse Nobuko as an evil spirit, called her a she-fox, and said Doppo should congratulate himself on having got rid of such a woman. He ended up by denouncing Nobuko as the kind of woman who was sure to commit adultery seven times.[90]

For comfort, Doppo read the Book of Job. The Christian leader Uchimura Kanzō (1861–1930) encouraged him to go to America, and urged Doppo to thank God for the ordeal that had made him a better man.[91] Doppo wrote in his diary, "I must go to America. God has granted me the mandate of an apostle. My sufferings are the work of providence; it is intended that I should save this degraded Japan."[92] But Doppo did not go to America. Instead, he threw himself into literary composition. The last entry in the diary, for May 18, 1897, states, "Today I sent 'Old Gen' to Mr. Ōta."[93] He had emerged from the ideal so painstakingly recorded in the diary and now would write not only for himself but also for the world.

Notes

1. *Kunikida Doppo Zenshū* (henceforth abbreviated *KDZ*), VI, p. 298.
2. *Ibid.*, p. 343.
3. *Ibid.*, p. 237. The Longfellow quotation is from "The Psalm of Life." Kunikida probably read this in English, but a Japanese translation was published as early as 1882 in *Shintaishi Shō*. See my *Dawn to the West*, II, pp. 194–95.
4. *KDZ*, VI, pp. 155–56.
5. *Ibid.*, p. 392.
6. *Ibid.*, VII, p. 44.
7. *Ibid.*, p. 49.
8. *Ibid.*, VI, p. 242.
9. *Ibid.*, p. 288.
10. *Ibid.*, p. 285.
11. *Ibid.*, p. 157.
12. *Ibid.*, p. 28.
13. *Ibid.*, pp. 28–29.
14. *Ibid.*, p. 117.
15. *Ibid.*, pp. 121–22.
16. *Ibid.*, p. 123.
17. *Yose* are theaters where storytellers recount *rakugo*, anecdotes of a humorous nature.
18. *Jōruri* often means the puppet theater today more commonly called Bunraku, but in Tokyo especially the singing of the texts without puppets was more popular.
19. *KDZ*, VI, p. 143.
20. *Ibid.*, p. 144.
21. *Ibid.*, p. 18.

22. *Ibid.*, p. 82.

23. *Ibid.*, p. 78.

24. *Ibid.*, p. 79.

25. *Ibid.*, VII, p. 29.

26. *Ibid.*, p. 83.

27. *Ibid.*, VI, p. 30.

28. The newspaper founded in 1882 by the Jiyūtō (Liberal Party).

29. *KDZ*, VI, p. 25.

30. *Ibid.*, p. 68.

31. *Ibid.*, p. 70.

32. *Ibid.*, p. 203.

33. *Ibid.*

34. This was Doppo's real name.

35. *KDZ.* VI, p. 296. The words in italics are in English in the original. They may be quoted from some work Doppo was reading at the time.

36. *Ibid.*, p. 300.

37. *Ibid.*, p. 301.

38. *Ibid.*, p. 303.

39. *Ibid.*, p. 312.

40. *Ibid.*, p. 327.

41. *Ibid.*, p. 328.

42. *Ibid.*, p. 331.

43. "Black ships" was a term used of Commodore Perry's fleet, and meant by extension any foreign-style ships.

44. *KDZ*, VI, p. 333.

45. For example, his first successful story, "Gen Oji" (Old Gen, 1897), is the tale of a boatman, and his "Wasureenu Hitobito" (Unforgettable People, 1899) similarly drew on his experiences in Saiki. For an account of these and other early stories by Doppo, see my *Dawn to the West*, I, pp. 232–34. For translations see Jay Rubin, "Five Stories by Kunikida Doppo."

46. *KDZ*, VII, p. 257.

47. *Ibid.*, VI, p. 349.

48. *Ibid.*, p. 351.

49. *Ibid.*, VII, p. 177.

50. *Ibid.*, pp. 189–90.

51. *Ibid.*, p. 207.

52. *Ibid.*, p. 217.

53. *Ibid.*, p. 210.

54. *Ibid.*

55. *Ibid.*, p. 213.

56. *Ibid.*, p. 237.

57. *Ibid.*, p. 238.

58. *Ibid.*, p. 242.

59. *Ibid.*, pp. 247–48.

60. *Ibid.*, p. 250.

61. *Ibid.*, p. 251.

62. *Ibid.*, p. 252.

63. *Ibid.*, p. 253.

64. *Ibid.*, p. 255.

65. *Ibid.*, p. 257.

66. *Ibid.*, p. 265.

67. *Ibid.*, p. 262.

68. *Ibid.*, p. 271.

69. *Ibid.*, p. 289.

70. *Ibid.*, p. 294.

71. *Ibid.*, p. 304.

72. *Ibid.*

73. The special meaning of Hokkaidō for Japanese of the Meiji era, especially for Arishima Takeo (see below, pp. 405–406), is discussed by Paul Anderer in his *Other Worlds*, pp. 19–40.

74. *KDZ*, VII, p. 306.

75. *Ibid.*, p. 308.

76. *Ibid.*, p. 317.

77. *Ibid.*, p. 320–21.

78. *Ibid.*, p. 323.

79. *Ibid.*, p. 328.

80. *Ibid.*, pp. 328–29.

81. *Ibid.*, p. 335.

82. *Ibid.*

83. *Ibid.*, p. 356.

84. *Ibid.*, p. 357.

85. *Ibid.*, p. 364.

86. *Ibid.*, p. 379.

87. *Ibid.*, p. 413.

88. *Ibid.*, p. 423.

89. *Ibid.*, p. 429.

90. *Ibid.*, p. 432.
91. *Ibid.*, p. 439.
92. *Ibid.*, pp. 446–47.
93. *Ibid.*, p. 547.

Bibliography

Anderer, Paul. *Other Worlds*. New York: Columbia University Press, 1984.

Keene, Donald. *Dawn to the West*, 2 vols. New York: Holt, Rinehart and Winston, 1984.

Rubin, Jay. "Five Stories by Kunikida Doppo," *Monumenta Nipponica* 28:3, 1972.

(*Teihon*) *Kunikida Doppo Zenshū*, VI and VII. Tokyo: Gakushū Kenkyū Sha, 1978.

The Diaries of
Masaoka Shiki

During the years following the Meiji Restoration of 1868, many traditions that originated in the remote Japanese past were attacked as being unsuited to the new Japan. Few traditions suffered worse treatment than those of poetry. Although many amateurs continued to compose waka (or tanka, as they came to be called at this time) and haiku on conventional subjects, using hackneyed poetic language, it seemed as though poets who had something to say and were not content with repeating clichés about the short-lived cherry blossoms or the reddening autumn leaves would surely abandon the traditional poetic forms in favor of the freer forms introduced from the West.

If any one person can be credited with having saved Japanese poetic tradition, it was probably Masaoka Shiki (1867–1902), though that was hardly the object of his early criticism. In 1898, he published a series of ten short essays in the form of letters to tanka poets, in which he made a number of controversial declarations. He wrote, for example, that the *Kokinshū*, the tenth-century anthology of poetry that had hitherto stood at the summit of waka composition, was a "bad collection" and its compiler, the revered Ki no Tsurayuki, "a bad poet." Such comments made Shiki many enemies among lovers of traditional poetry, who supposed that he aimed at nothing less than a total destruction of both the tanka and the haiku. But before long, Shiki took to composing both, attempting to infuse his poetry with a modern sensibility and to make the old verse forms vehicles for individual expression and not merely oft-repeated platitudes.

If, however, Shiki had not been afflicted by serious illness toward the end of his short life, his poetry might never have acquired the intensity necessary to inspire other poets. In 1888, when Shiki was twenty-one, he coughed blood, the first sign of the tuberculosis that took his life at thirty-five. Initially, this sign of a dreaded illness did not bother him. In 1895 he volunteered for service as a war correspondent during the Sino-Japanese War and endured the discomforts of military life. He returned from China so seriously ill that he was carried from the ship to a hospital and his family was summoned to witness his last moments, but he miraculously recovered. In 1900, he again coughed blood, and from that time he was confined to a sickbed.

Even during his last years, Shiki kept up his literary activity at an extraordinary pace. He not only composed large numbers of both tanka and haiku but was also a columnist for the newspaper *Nihon*; and, as a judge of new compositions, he read an astonishing number of poems submitted for his inspection. His chief activity, however, was the writing of two diaries that he published in *Nihon*: the first, *Bokuju Itteki* (A Drop of Ink), appeared from January to June 1901, and the other, *Byōshō Rokushaku* (My Six-Foot Sickbed), from May to September 1902. In addition to the published diaries, Shiki kept a private diary, largely concerned with his illness, called *Gyōga Manroku* (Stray Notes from a Supine Position), written from September 1901 to July 1902.

As we read the details of Shiki's illness in *Stray Notes*—how many times his bandages were changed, how much pain the slightest movement caused, how his illness provoked him into intemperate outbursts against his mother and sister who nursed him—we cannot but be astonished that he managed to keep writing so regularly for the newspaper and often so amusingly. *A Drop of Ink* appeared every day of the week. Sometimes the entries in this diary were only a few lines long, but others went on for pages. The editor of *Nihon* was obviously ready to print anything Shiki wrote. But where did he find the strength to write, when he could hardly move? Keeping the diaries must have seemed as important as life itself; they proved he was still alive, or, to use the phrase of Pascal, another writer who was confined to a sickbed, Shiki proved that, battered though he was by terrible illness, he was still a "thinking reed."

Probably Shiki wrote the published diaries because he needed the income, but the unpublished *Stray Notes* had special significance as a kind of self-attestation. At one point, after reading the diary of the haiku poet Ishii Rogetsu (1873–1928), he commented, "Read Rogetsu's diary. It says everything one needs to know about his life these days. I'd like to show my diary to Rogetsu."[1] Shiki's diaries were a testament to the world: his recompense for the physical effort it cost him each day to apply brush to paper was the knowledge that his private diary, no less than the published ones, would long outlive him. Surely he did not ask on his deathbed, as many other dying diarists have done, that his family burn his diaries. It has often been recounted that Shiki was disappointed when his senior disciple, Takahama Kyoshi (1874–1959), refused to be his successor and carry on his work. Shiki, not having any children, feared that his art might not be perpetuated. Of course, some of his poems would be remembered, but that was not enough. He wanted to live on as Masaoka Shiki—which is precisely what he achieved with his diaries.

Although all three of Shiki's diaries were composed under the same circumstances and were similar in many ways, the two he published serially in *Nihon* contain a much greater variety of subject matter than *Stray Notes*, and they are marked by the sense of humor that Shiki managed to retain even during his long and painful illness. The variety suggests the professional author's fear of boring his readers, but Shiki was never too professional to repeat, even in the published diaries, intimate details of his daily life. The entry in *A Drop of Ink* for January 23, 1901, though short, communicates both his pain (which kept him from even turning his head toward visitors) and his humor:

"Unable to endure the agony of my sickbed, I writhe and groan, feeling I simply can't go on. Two or three people are nearby. One of them says with a laugh, 'It's really peculiar when one goes on looking at nothing but a person's ears.' I realized for the first time that healthy people do such things as to stare at people's ears."[2]

In his diary entry for the next day Shiki explained why he felt compelled, despite the pain it cost him, to keep writing the diary:

> In addition to the pain I have felt in my groin for years, since last year the pain on the left side of my abdomen has become increasingly severe and has now reached a point at which I am unable to take up my brush and write. This means that I am so choked with things I want to express that even my mind has started to hurt. There's no point in going on if I have to live like this. But how am I going to distract myself from the boredom of my sickbed? While I was pondering this in a state of depression, I suddenly had an idea. It occurred to me I might write something called "A Drop of Ink." This would be no more than twenty lines for long entries, and ten, five, or even one or two lines for short entries. I would wait for moments of respite from my illness and use them to write whatever came into my head, no matter what it was. It would be better than not writing anything at all. But I would not publish such childish items in the hope that gentlemen with refined tastes would read them. All it would amount to was giving myself a bit of pleasure when I opened the newspaper each morning and saw the little piece I had written.[3]

Writing the diary—if diary is the right word for so unconventional a daily composition—was a distraction from the boredom of being confined to a sickbed. It was also an outlet for the thoughts that passed through his head as he stared at the ceiling during the long hours of wakefulness. The random thoughts of most people who spend months or even years in a sickbed are generally not worth preserving, but Shiki was no ordinary person. His thoughts had not only to be voiced in conversations with visitors but communicated in print as well. Only then could expression bring comfort.

Even though he was almost completely cut off from the world, he never lost his curiosity. On May 26, 1902, he wrote:

> It is already six or seven years since I was confined to a sickbed. I used to be taken out for a ride two or three times a year, but ever since the year before last this has been more than I can manage. All I know about the rapidly changing appearance of Tokyo is the little I read about it in the newspapers or hear from my visitors. No matter how badly I would like to see something, it is quite beyond my powers. But let me make a list of things I have never seen but would like to see:
>
> 1. Motion pictures
> 2. Bicycle races and stunts
> 3. Lions and ostriches in the zoo
> 4. The Asakusa aquarium
> 5. Baboons and otters in the Asakusa Garden
> 6. The sites of the dismantled approaches to the castle
> 7. The statue of Kusunoki Masashige in Marunouchi
> 8. Automatic telephones and red postboxes
> 9. A beer hall
> 10. Women fencers and Western-style theaters
> 11. An athletic meet of girl students in maroon skirts.
>
> But I haven't the time to enumerate them all.[4]

This delightful list is evidence of Shiki's vitality even during the worst of his illness. It also suggests how much he participated in the spirit of the Meiji era.

✦ ✦ ✦

Most diarists, after first carefully noting the weather of a particular day, describe how they spent that day, generally going somewhere, perhaps attending a party or the theater. But if the diarist is restricted to a sickbed and cannot make it even to the next room, what is he going to write about? In Shiki's case, these difficulties were compounded by the conviction that poetry, whether tanka or haiku, should be composed in accordance with the principle of *shasei*, the accurate depiction of nature. But how was Shiki to describe nature when all he could see of it was a small corner of the garden or the potted plants his visitors brought him? For Shiki, both as a poet and a diarist, to be imprisoned in a sickroom was the supreme test of his imaginative powers.

One possibility open to Shiki was to describe in his diary, as exactly as possible, what he could see from his pillow. He could do this only once, however, because (with the exception of seasonal flowers) nothing ever changed in his room. He must have saved this desperate expedient for a day when he really had nothing else to write about. His first extended description of his sickroom did not appear until the June 5, 1902, entry in *My Six-Foot Sickbed*:

> Today, just now (six o'clock on June 5), I tried making an inventory of the objects surrounding my bed. Apart from the things that have been here for any number of years, things I have been looking at for ages—a farmer's cape and rain hat, a plaque in Date Masamune's hand, a watercolor showing a late autumn scene at the Hyakkaen Garden in Mukōjima, a watercolor of a forest in the snow . . . and suchlike—I have:
>
> A stereoscope. This was a thoughtful present from Koshū. He gave it to me after I had said the previous day that I would like to see a motion picture. The cherry blossoms at Koganei, a moonlit night over the Sumida River, waves in the Bay of Tago, bush clover at Hyakkaen—everything seems three-

dimensional, stretching off into the distance. Some people might say that looking through a stereoscope is a childish pleasure, but it makes me so happy it's almost more than I can bear.

A lantern made of a blowfish . . . This hangs over my head. It is amusing how everybody who comes here mistakes it for a pig's bladder.

A Lamaist mandala. This is a piece of cloth about three feet by five feet that has been made into a wall hanging . . .

Scattered near my pillow are several dozen picture books and magazines. An alarm clock, a thermometer, an inkstone, writing brushes, a spittoon, a chamber pot, a bell, a back scratcher, handkerchiefs, and, conspicuous among such objects, a gaudy sateen blanket, a present from a friend on a warship.[5]

The full list contains many more items, especially botanical, and makes Shiki's sickroom seem like an exceptionally cluttered junk shop. It suggests not so much a collection of objects chosen with an eye to comforting a bedridden invalid as the odds and ends accumulated by an elderly eccentric. Yet each object tells us something about Shiki's exceptional range of interests.

The main problem for anyone confined to a sickbed, especially someone of Shiki's intelligence, is finding sources of distraction. Shiki could pass some time each day looking through the stereoscope, but the number of photographs was limited, and sooner or later this diversion was bound to pall. Until the last year or so of his life, he was able to read books, not only those published in Japan but even foreign ones. Despite his insistence (at various points of his diaries) on the inadequacy of his English, Shiki read the *Autobiography of Benjamin Franklin* in English, as we know from the diary entry for September 1, 1902, in *My Six-Foot Sickbed*, where he contrasted his present inability to read books with his much more bearable condition of a year before:

It keeps getting hotter and hotter. I haven't been able to read even the newspapers recently, and I can't manage a conversa-

tion. The inside of my head feels exactly as if it had become
hollow, and it has become difficult for me even to keep my
eyes open. This time last year I was reading Franklin's *Autobiography* as a daily task. It was especially difficult because I
wasn't accustomed to reading sidewise and the English was in
fine print. I would read three pages and stop, five pages and
stop. It was painful reading, but the pleasure I derived from it
was enormous. It was indescribably interesting to read how
Franklin, who might be called the founder of Philadelphia,
made plans for the city. At the same time, though he was an
extremely poor typesetter, he also made plans to advance his
own career, and he steadily advanced toward success despite
the adversity and failure surrounding him. This is a famous
book, and I imagine many people even in Japan have read it,
but I doubt anyone has been as profoundly impressed as myself.[6]

It is easy to imagine a bedridden intellectual turning to works of
philosophy or religion for comfort, but Shiki's mind was too down-
to-earth for speculation, and he preferred Franklin, a model with
whom a young man of the Meiji era could easily identify. Franklin's
Autobiography is the story of a man who overcame the obstacle of
poverty and, by dint of hard work and the use of his native intelligence, established himself as the "first civilized American." Shiki
may have found in Franklin a surrogate for himself. Unable to stir
from his bed, he could not emulate Franklin in his actions, but in
spirit he, like Franklin, belonged to an age when the watchword was
"Boys, be ambitious!"
As a boy, Shiki had in fact been exceptionally ambitious. In *Stray
Notes*, he says:

When I was sixteen or seventeen, my ambition was to become
the prime minister. It was only after going to Tokyo that I
heard about philosophy. I thought nothing was as noble as phi-

losophy and made up my mind to become a philosopher. Later, when I learned that literature, too, was not to be sneered at, I came to have literary aspirations, since I had an inborn taste for it. Moreover, though I have recently learned to look down on cabinet ministers, as a matter of principle, I still feel emotionally that being a cabinet minister is the most exalted of professions.[7]

Shiki's illness seems to have robbed him of such ambitions. He even wondered what he would do if, by some miracle, he regained his health. Writing was the obvious choice, but if he could not make a living by writing,

"I have thought that I would like to become a kindergarten teacher, but I couldn't do that unless I had a little money. Reforestation might be interesting, but I have never studied anything in that line, and I lack the qualifications for employment as a forestry expert. If I myself owned a mountain, planting trees would be all the more exciting, but not having the money to buy a mountain, what am I to do?"[8]

The bedridden Shiki could hope, at the most, that he would make up for his inability to move from his sickbed by the brilliance of his writings.

For a literary man, Shiki depended surprisingly little on books for relief from the tedium of his sickroom, True, he continued to read vast quantities of haiku that had been submitted to *Nihon* for publication in its haiku column. He complained in his diary that some people submitted as many as seventy haiku on each of the assigned topics; but he usually needed to read no more than four or five of the haiku a poet submitted to decide whether or not he had talent. "No," Shiki continued, "I can tell, even without reading one haiku, that none of them will be any good. If fifty or sixty can be tossed off on any subject whatsoever, they must be truly worthless things that anybody at all should be able to compose without effort. It would be better for people if, instead of attempting to learn how to compose anything as stupid as haiku, they learned how to grow loofahs."[9] Shiki could not have derived either pleasure or profit from most of the haiku he read at this time, but apart from the mention of Franklin's *Autobiography*, nothing indicates that he staved off boredom by reading sustained literary works. Probably even holding a book up over his eyes had become too great an effort for him.

In July 1902 he recorded in his diary that he was now asking his mother to read the news to him, suggesting that he could not lift even a newspaper, though reading the news each day had always been one of his chief pleasures:

"Of late I have been getting my old mother to read the newspapers aloud to me. I half listen, half not listen, my nerves calmed, as she reads, stumbling along with the aid of the *furigana*,[10] the transcript of the silly account of some professional storyteller, and I feel myself growing drowsy. This is the happiest time of the day."[11]

Relief from boredom came mainly from two sources: food and friends. *Stray Notes* regularly listed exactly what Shiki ate each day and in what quantities. Considering that he scarcely budged from one position in the course of a day, he maintained his appetite astonishingly well. It must have been a great burden for his mother and his sister, Ritsu, to prepare varied meals each day for a sick man who was likely to explode with annoyance if the food did not come up to his standards. Meals were usually the most important part of any day, but Shiki foresaw that even this pleasure might soon be taken from him:

"Thinking that the time when I can enjoy my meals is already running out, I often feel an impulse to eat now, while I can, everything I want to eat, and I order the people of my household to serve me an extravagant feast—for example, by having food brought in from a restaurant. That is why I feel a sudden need for more pocket money. I have pondered this over and over, but the only way I can think of raising money is to sell my books. The trouble is, I haven't any books that are worth selling."[12]

At times, Shiki declared that eating was his sole pleasure, but no sooner did he eat something than his stomach and intestines "began a strange motion" and the food would pass through him, undigested.[13] On October 27, 1901, the day before his birthday, he ordered two meals from an expensive Japanese restaurant to share with his mother and sister, "to thank them for their trouble in looking after me."[14] Shiki permitted himself this extravagance, the only one he was capable of enjoying, because he correctly foresaw that this would be the last "birthday party" he would know. (He died on September 19, 1902.) And, as he also foresaw, long before he died he had lost interest in food. He wrote in *My Six-Foot Sickbed*:

"The desire for food and drink, which I still felt up to last year as my only remaining pleasure, has now almost totally disappeared. It's not only that—whatever I eat or drink actually has a bad effect on my body and causes me to spend day and night writhing in pain, a not uncommon experience of late."[15]

One last pleasure was left to Shiki—the company of other people. He was blessed with a large number of disciples, many of whom remained faithful to the end, visiting his sickroom, bringing him presents of food, flowers, and whatever else might give him pleasure, and relaying odd bits of information about the outside world, especially developments that were unlikely to be reported in the newspapers. For example, in *My Six-Foot Sickbed* Shiki mentioned thirteen instances of "recent changes" in Negishi, the section of Tokyo where he lived, including these: "Ever since a telephone was installed at a certain villa, the crying of cranes can no longer be heard" and "A fan has been installed in the local beauty parlor."[16] Perhaps hearing about the fan in the beauty parlor inspired Shiki's craving for one. He wrote in his diary a few days later, "The heat these days has been so unbearable that I mentioned I wished I had some sort of machine to stir up a breeze. [Kawahigashi] Hekigotō was kind enough to make one himself and suspend it over my bed."[17] In this and similar ways the faithful disciples tried to alleviate their teacher's suffering.

Sometimes they tried to divert Shiki with inventions newly imported from the West. One day, a disciple brought something wrapped in a big *furoshiki* and asked Shiki, "Would you like to hear some music?" Shiki was rather suspicious about the contents of the cloth wrapper, but said he would indeed like to hear some music, whereupon the disciple produced a phonograph. This was Shiki's first experience of the instrument, and he was rather intimidated when the horn was trained on him. He recalled,

> Then he produced something that looked like a bamboo tube that had been cut six or seven inches long. It was made of wax, and the extremely fine lines carved into the surface of the wax were, I was told, what had been left by the recorded voices. When this cylinder was placed on the machine and the handle was turned, the machine began all by itself to emit the sound *buruburuburuburu* . . . He brought a total of eighteen of these things that looked like bamboo tubes and tried playing one after another, but since most of them were Western songs, we didn't really understand them. All the same, I thought they were interesting because there were more variations in rhythm than in Japanese songs . . . Among the Western songs was one called a "laughing song." I had no idea what the words meant, but the song was sung at a very fast tempo, and every so often it was interrupted by laughter. I was told that it had been recorded by a Western musician whose skill at laughing was famous. I tried imagining what the words of the song might be:
>
> > *Five or six blackbirds*
> > *Came flying along*
> > *And let go their droppings*
> > *On Gombei's head.*
> > *Ahhaha haha ahhahaha.*[18]

Such passages demonstrate that Shiki's sense of humor did not desert him even when beset by terrible illness. Another delightful interlude with his disciples took place at his birthday party in 1900. He invited four of them—Kawahigashi Hekigotō, Sakamoto Shihōda,

Takahama Kyoshi, and Samukawa Sokotsu—asking each to bring him a different present. A year later, at the lonely birthday party with his mother and sister described above, he recalled this happy occasion:

> Kyoshi was asked to bring something red, either food or a toy, and he brought a boiled egg that he had dyed a bright red. He said that this is what they do to eggs at the Nikolai Cathedral.[19] Sokotsu, asked to bring something green, brought an unripe tangerine. Shihōda, who was assigned yellow, brought a ripe tangerine and a papier-mâché tiger. Hekigotō got brown, and I got white, but I forget what we contributed. After dinner, the conversation really took off. It was so much fun that I forgot about the uncertainties and unpleasant things that had been bothering me earlier in the day. Thinking I would show them a cartoon of an elephant and a giraffe standing on their heads, I frantically thumbed through the pages of the magazine in which I had seen it while Shihōda, twisting upward the whiskers of the tiger he had brought, said, "This is the German kaiser!" The fun was almost too much for me.[20]

Shiki divined that this would be his last festive birthday party, but there is no suggestion of self-pity in his account. For a while he and his disciples had forgotten that his death was imminent.

Visitors were an absolutely necessary diversion for Shiki, and on days without them he sometimes fell into a state of depression or else lost his temper, as he mentioned in the entry for October 29, 1901: "No visitors. At night I felt a tantrum coming on."[21] It was only the diversion of having the quilts changed on his bed that spared the others in the house the effects of the tantrum. Six months later (in June 1902), he described himself in these terms:

"Here we have a sick man. His body hurts, and he is so weak that he is almost incapable of movement. His brain tends to be addled, and his eyes swim, making it impossible to read books or newspapers. It is even less possible for him to take up his pen and write something. Is there nobody by his side to look after him, no visitor with whom he can converse? How will he get through the day? How will he get through the day?"[22]

The next day's entry is even more heart-rending. It opens: "When I took to my sickbed, as long as I could still move I didn't find my sickness too hard to endure, and I lay there quite serenely. But when, as of late, I have become unable even to stir, I am prey to mental anguish, and almost every day I feel pain enough to drive me out of my mind."[23]

He tried to bear his affliction with fortitude:

"I have tried my utmost to bear it, but I have reached the point where I can endure no more, and my patience is at last exhausted. A person who gets into such a state is no use for anything. Screams. Howls. More screams, more howling. I have no way to describe the pain, the agony. I think it would be easier if I turned into a real lunatic, but I can't even do that. If I could only die, that would be more welcome than anything else."[24]

Day after day, especially when no visitors came to distract him, he wondered how he would get through that day: "Isn't there anyone to save me from this pain?" In fact, some people would have been glad to help Shiki—the Buddhist or Christian priests who attempted to impart their messages of comfort. But for Shiki, educated according to rationalist, Confucian principles, religion could bring no comfort.

He tried to amuse himself with his stereoscope, but the three-dimensional pictures had lost their interest, and he was left with a headache from having gazed too long through the lenses. The only distraction left was the visits of friends. Sometimes Shiki and his visitors ran out of things to talk about, and he was aware not only of his own suffering but also of the mental suffering of the visitors as they watched him. All the same, to have visitors and listen to what they

had to say, even when their only topics of conversations were subjects
unrelated to himself, was better than being alone.

As Shiki correctly guessed, his disciples found it painful to visit
his sickroom and see their teacher wasting away. They tried to divert
him with stories, and more often than not they succeeded because
Shiki was basically the same cheerful, fun-loving man they had
known when he had been well. The day after the bout of extreme depression described above, he listed recent presents from his disciples
that had comforted him: twenty colored pictures of fruit; a Ming
painting of the Eight Immortals in their cups (a copy); a sketch of
flowering plants by Aigai[25] (a copy); a landscape scroll by Wang Chi
(a copy); a landscape scroll by Tsao Chi-chun in the manner of the
"eighteen principles of painting" (a copy); a basket of cherries; a selection of pastries; and a lozenge-shaped kaleidoscope.[26]

At no point during the last two years of his illness did Shiki entertain the hope that he might somehow be miraculously cured. He
saw plainly that he was doomed to grow ever feebler and that each
day that passed would attenuate his hold on life. Not surprisingly, his
thoughts on occasion turned to suicide. He would have preferred to
die naturally, but he could not tell how long his agony was to be prolonged, and the possibility of putting an end to his misery was seduc-
tive. Perhaps the most poignant pages of his diary describe the
occasion when only his total helplessness prevented him from killing
himself. It is found in the *Stray Notes* entry for October 3, 1901:

> Today again my meals didn't taste any good. The weather im-
> proved somewhat after about two in the afternoon. Ritsu went
> out saying she was going to the public bath. My mother was
> sitting by my pillow without saying a word. Suddenly a pecu-
> liar agitation shattered my peace of mind. "I can't stand it, I
> can't stand it," I said. "What am I going to do?" I was suffer-
> ing physically, and I had also begun to feel mental torment. At
> the thought that I might be on the verge of one of my usual at-
> tacks, my feelings grew increasingly turbulent, and I kept re-

peating again and again, "I can't stand it. What am I going to do?" My mother said quietly, "It can't be helped." I was in such a state that I thought I would telephone somebody and ask him to come here, but there was no way for me to telephone.

Shiki's mother went out to send a telegram to his disciple Shihōda. Normally, either his mother or his sister would have remained near him, in case of a sudden crisis, but now Shiki was alone. He wrote in his diary,

The house had become silent. Now I was alone. Lying on my left side, I stared at the writing set before me. Four or five worn-out brushes and a thermometer and on top of them, lying quite exposed, a blunt little knife a couple of inches long and a two-inch eyeleteer. The suicidal feeling that sometimes sweeps over me even when I am not in such a state suddenly surged up. The thought had already flashed through my head while I was writing the telegram message to Shihōda. But I could hardly kill myself with that blunt little knife or the eyeleteer. I knew a razor was in the next room if I could only get there. Once I had the razor, cutting my throat would be no problem, but sad to say, I can't even crawl now. If no other way existed, cutting my windpipe with the little knife would not be impossible. Or I could pierce a hole in my heart with the eyeleteer. I could certainly kill myself in that way, but I wouldn't want a long-drawn-out and painful death. I wondered if I would die immediately if I drilled three or four holes. I thought over every possibility, but to tell the truth, fear won out, and in the end I couldn't bring myself to do it. I wasn't afraid of death, but of the pain. I thought that if I found the pain of my sickness unbearable, how much more horrible the pain would be if I botched my suicide. But that was not all.

When I looked at the knife, I felt something like a current of
fear flowing from it and welling up inside me.[27]

Shiki's agony of uncertainty was cut short by the unexpectedly
prompt return of his mother. In his diary, he drew pictures of the
knife and the eyeleteer as if to emphasize their reality. The passage
otherwise has a special immediacy because Shiki wrote it in the colloquial, rather than in the classical language of previous diary entries.
For a moment we seem to hear Shiki's voice directly, without any
suggestion of literary artifice. The next day's entry, describing how
Shihōda responded to the telegram and hurried to his bedside, is once
again in the classical language. Shihōda's conversation on this occasion consisted mainly of complaints about money matters. A few
hours earlier, Shiki had been ready to kill himself, and Shihōda said
nothing to reassure him, but the human contact had restored Shiki's
innately cheerful disposition, and the use of a classical style suggests
that he was again capable of viewing himself objectively.

The indescribable pain Shiki suffered at times made him extremely
short-tempered, especially toward his mother and sister. He recognized this failing in himself and was delighted to hear about people of
the past who had relieved their pain by complaining: "It seems, then,
that I am not the only one who has lashed out indiscriminately
against family members when in pain."[28] He gave some examples of
his irritable behavior: "When visitors looking at my face say, 'I'm surprised you're not thinner,' and similar things, I fly into a fury and I
stick out my leg, which has become as thin as a poker, and ask, 'This,
too?'"[29] Almost anything could irritate him when he was in pain, but
he was saved from becoming an intolerable burden on his family and
friends by his awareness that he was acting unreasonably. Even when
he was angriest, he might a few minutes later return to his normal
good humor.

Shiki's sister, Ritsu, undoubtedly bore the heaviest burden of his bad moods. She must have lived under extreme strain. Shiki could not be left alone because his illness might at any moment take a turn for the worse, and his bandages had to be changed every day. This was Ritsu's responsibility. The least roughness in her movements would cause him excruciating pain, and he could not stifle his screams. The sight of Shiki's body, running with pus, must have been revolting, no matter how much sympathy she felt for her brother. Among her more agreeable tasks was preparing three or four meals for Shiki each day. He rarely indicated in his diary any appreciation for the effort that went into planning and preparing his meals, but he was quick to complain if he did not like what was served. In *Stray Notes* he drew an unfairly harsh picture of Ritsu. Perhaps his comments were inspired by some intuitive sense that Ritsu lacked sympathy, but the language he used was unpleasant:

"Ritsu is a rationalistic woman. She seems to be made of wood or stone, without a trace of sympathy or understanding. She looks after the invalid dutifully, but she never attempts to comfort him with her sympathy."[30]

He complained of Ritsu's inability to take hints. No matter how often he might express a wish to eat, say, dumplings, she would never buy him any because, as he said, she lacked empathy, but if he ordered her to buy dumplings, she would comply. Still, for all her perceived faults, he could not help recognizing that if he were deprived of her care for even a single day, he would be dead. "Therefore, I always think it would be better for me to die than for her to fall ill."[31]

Even after admitting that he could not live without someone attending to his needs and that he could never have afforded to hire a professional nurse, his bitterness toward Ritsu would well up again:

"She is bad-tempered. She is obstinate. She is inconsiderate. She hates asking people things. She is extremely clumsy with her hands. Once she's made up her mind to anything, there's no changing it. Her faults are too numerous to mention. Sometimes I get so angry with her that I think of killing her."[32]

Such comments were followed by an unexpected conclusion: "But to tell the truth, I can't help loving her all the more because she is a spiritual cripple. It is because I can imagine how her failings will make her suffer if one day she should have to stand alone in the world that I keep trying always to correct her irritability. I wonder if, after she has lost me, she will remember my admonitions."[33]

At such times, their relationship is altered from that of a sick man who is totally dependent on his nurse to that of the kindly elder brother who worries about how his sister will fare when he can no longer give her advice. The contradiction—if it is one—seems to be evidence that Shiki really loved his sister, even though in moments of desperation he obscured this love with his intemperate criticism.

As we read Shiki's diaries we cannot help but feel extremely intimate with this poet. We would like to forgive this man who so mercilessly criticized the sister who served him like a slave, knowing that his short temper was caused by his suffering and that he himself was well aware of the immoderate nature of his demands. He wrote, "As the pains of my illness increase, I constantly lose my temper whenever anything is done that is not the way I want it, and I rail at people. The members of my family become afraid to come near me."[34]

We know from the diaries exactly what Shiki ate each day, how many times he had bowel movements, when his bandages were changed. We are told his opinions of each visitor, his criticisms of haiku, paintings, and other works of art. In addition he related, with no attempt to excuse his conduct, how he had cheated on the entrance examinations for the preparatory division of the university. We also know exactly how his illness first began. We may feel that Shiki has told us everything about himself, but on reflection, we may come to feel that at least in one sense we do not know as much about Shiki as we do about the court ladies of the Heian period, who kept diaries a thousand years earlier. Shiki died at the age of thirty-five. He was not so young that he could not have had one or two love affairs before he died, but he does not reveal any such occurrence in his diaries. The poets of the Japan of the past treated love as the most unforgettable of human experiences, but one does not find in Shiki's diary any expression of regret that he was fated to die without having once tasted the joys or sorrows of love. It is difficult to imagine that Shiki never experienced romantic feelings for anyone; I wonder if Confucian morality did not keep him from touching on this subject. Even when he seems to lay bare everything about himself, he preserves a strict silence about such matters. Death, rather than love, was his theme.

The diary *A Drop of Ink* contains an amusing scene in which Shiki pictures himself as appearing before Great King Enma, the ferocious divinity who presides over the afterworld. He announces himself as a sick person from Negishi and asks why nobody has come for him from Enma's office.

"Then Enma, without any show of annoyance, searched through the registers for 1901 and 1902 without finding any such name. Enma was getting more and more frantic, and great drops of sweat poured from his brow. At last he discovered that my name had already appeared in the register for 1897 but had been crossed out."

Enma summoned the Number Five Blue Demon and asked what had happened. The Number Five Blue Demon reported that he had gone to get Shiki, but that the streets in Negishi are so narrow and twisted that, unable to locate Shiki's house, he had returned empty-handed. The bodhisattva Jizō, hearing this, suggested to Enma that Shiki's life should be prolonged ten years, but Shiki objected: "Nobody would refuse if life could be prolonged for ten years without sickness. But if I must go on suffering the way I have, I would prefer it if you called for me as soon as possible." Enma asked if Shiki would like to be taken that night, but he answered, "I would prefer to have it happen unexpectedly."[35]

This dialogue is typical of Shiki's sense of humor, but it is rather strange all the same that he could have faced death not only with equanimity but also with amusement. The last entry in *My Six-Foot Sickbed* concludes with a comic waka composed by a friend, and his own last three haiku, written just before he died, which are in a wryly comic vein. As we read his diaries, we tend to think of Shiki as one of us, a modern man, but the wryly humorous ending to his life sets him a little apart. Perhaps he should be considered a last survivor of the *bunjin*, the men of letters of the previous era who rejoiced in the pleasures of life but were never guilty of the bad taste of regretting to leave it.

Notes

1. Masaoka Shiki, *Shiki Sandai Zuihitsu*, p. 360.
2. *Ibid.*, p. 10.
3. *Ibid.*, pp. 10–11.
4. *Ibid.*, pp. 175–76.
5. *Ibid.*, pp. 192–94.
6. *Ibid.*, p. 303.
7. *Ibid.*, p. 409. This is in the entry for October 19, 1901.
8. *Ibid.*, p. 410.
9. *Ibid.*, p. 123. Entry for June 4, 1901. *Hechima* is a type of gourd, used as a kind of washing sponge by the Japanese. The word is otherwise used in conversation to express contempt for something.
10. Phonetic pronunciations given alongside the Chinese characters.
11. Masaoka, *Shiki*, p. 265. Entry for July 31, 1902, in *Byōshō Rokushaku*.
12. *Ibid.*, p. 414. Entry for October 25, 1901.
13. *Ibid.*, p. 417. Entry for October 26, 1901.
14. Shiki ate one of the two dinners, his mother and sister the other one.
15. Masaoka, *Shiki*, p. 210. Entry for June 21, 1902.
16. *Ibid.*, pp. 238–39. Entry for June 11, 1902.
17. *Ibid.*, pp. 247–48. Entry for July 19, 1902. Kawahigashi Hekigotō (1873–1937) was one of Shiki's chief disciples.
18. *Ibid.*, p. 76. Entry for April 5, 1901. Shiki gave two other "interpretations" of the laughing song. I would guess that the record was of the celebrated laughing song from *Manon Lescaut* by Auber, which had been recorded by this date. It might also be the laughing song from *Die Fledermaus*. The use of cylinders for recordings preceded the flat disks, but survived past this time.

19. See p. 264, n. 8. The coloring of Easter eggs is still practiced, especially by Ukrainians.
20. Masaoka, *Shiki*, p. 419. Entry for October 27, 1901.
21. *Ibid.*, p. 411.
22. *Ibid.*, p. 208. Entry for June 19, 1902.
23. *Ibid.*, pp. 208–9.
24. *Ibid.*, p. 209.
25. Aigai was the professional name of Takahisa Chō (1796–1843). He painted in the *nanga*, or Southern Sung, style.
26. Masaoka, *Shiki*, p. 211. Entry for June 22, 1902.
27. *Ibid.*, pp. 400–402.
28. *Ibid.*, p. 179. Entry for May 28, 1902.
29. *Ibid.*
30. *Ibid.*, p. 361. Entry for September 20, 1901.
31. *Ibid.*, p. 365. Entry for September 21, 1901.
32. *Ibid.*, p. 364.
33. *Ibid.*, p. 366.
34. *Ibid.*
35. *Ibid.*, p. 113. Entry for May 21, 1901.

Bibliography

Beichman, Janine. *Masaoka Shiki*. Boston: Twayne Publishers, 1982.

Beichman-Yamamoto, Janine. "Masaoka Shiki's *A Drop of Ink*," *Monumenta Nipponica* 30:3, 1975.

Brower, Robert H. "Masaoka Shiki and Tanka Reform," in Donald H. Shively, *Tradition and Modernization in Japanese Culture*. Princeton, N.J.: Princeton University Press, 1971.

Keene, Donald. *Dawn to the West*, II. New York: Holt, Rinehart and Winston, 1984.

_____. "Shiki and Takuboku," in *Landscapes and Portraits: Appreciations of Japanese Culture*. Tokyo: Kōdansha International, 1971.

Masaoka Shiki. *Shiki Sandai Zuihitsu*, in Kōdansha Gakujutsu Bunko series. Tokyo: Kōdansha, 1986.

The Diaries
of Ishikawa Takuboku

The diaries of Ishikawa Takuboku (1886–1912) move me most of all the literary works of the Meiji period. This opinion is likely to surprise people who think of modern literature as being essentially the novel, or who are apt to think of Meiji literature in terms of the masterpieces of Mori Ōgai and Natsume Sōseki. Compared to these and other works of fiction of the period, Takuboku's diaries have been little read, though his poetry ranks among the most popular ever composed in Japan. The appeal of a diary is obviously not that of a novel if only because the diarist, unlike a novelist, is unable to control what will happen the next day, let alone months or years ahead. Again, unlike the hero of a modern novel, Takuboku's central character, himself, is not consistently drawn because the diaries were created not at a single time but over a period of years, and the opinions of the "I" vary wildly with the passing of time and the emergence of new problems in his life. Takuboku, unlike the author of a novel, was not free to enter into the thoughts of any other person in his work, and the motivations of other people are therefore apt to remain obscure to the end. There are also loose ends in the diary that a finicky novelist would not permit in his work and that readers would not readily accept.

These are all inherent limitations of the diary as a literary genre, but the diary also has advantages. If a writer has trouble structuring his work, the diary has a natural structure, imposed by the passage of the days. The writer who (like Takuboku) is apt to lose interest in the subject of a novel he has started will receive fresh stimulation to write each day, and if there are inconsistencies they will be accepted by readers as part of the natural process of growth and development.

The essential feature of any modern diary of literary significance is the believability and interest of the author's self-portrait. In reading diaries of, say, the Meiji period, we are sometimes moved and even delighted by a sudden, vivid insight into the character of the author, a moment when we feel that we have truly understood what he or she is like. But often there are blanks just when we think that some important truth is about to be revealed. At such times we may want to stop the author and ask, "But what did you *really* feel?" If we could get an answer from the world of the dead, it might be, "I wrote down exactly what I felt." In that case, we may conclude that the author does not fully belong to our world.

With Takuboku, however, there is no room for doubt: in all senses, bad as well as good, he is one of us. He is the first Japanese who strikes me as being a specifically modern man. Perhaps that is why I feel a bond between him and me as I read his diaries that I sense only intermittently when reading the diaries of earlier Meiji writers. This does not mean that I was insincere when I praised earlier diaries; it means, rather, that almost every sentence of Takuboku's diary not only moves me but makes me feel I know him as well as I have known any human being.

Takuboku began to keep a diary in 1902, when he was sixteen years old. He gave the first of his diaries a fancy title and a self-conscious preface, an indication that he intended from the start to make it a literary composition. The style is elaborate, reflecting a young man's delight in difficult expressions and especially in unusual Chinese characters. The diary opens as Takuboku, having been expelled from middle school in Morioka, is about to go to Tokyo for the first time. In the preface he stated the circumstances of his departure in these terms:

> It has been seventeen years [1] since as an infant I raised my first cries, and eight years since I left the knees of my father and mother to study in Morioka. What lies ahead is still shrouded in drifting clouds. This autumn, following the vicissitudes of the stream, wherever it may lead me, I have left school, bid farewell to my friends, separated from my parents, quit my native hills, and even parted from the fair visage of the girl I love, to wander off, a lonely traveler, to the Eastern Capital. Ah, who will recognize the music played on the strings of the heart of this voyager? [2]

If this could not be excused as the writing of a sixteen-year-old boy, the pretentiousness might well seem offensive. Takuboku seized every opportunity to display his erudition, especially his reading in the Chinese classics, by using, wherever possible, difficult terms to designate simple things. For example, instead of calling the city where he attended middle school Morioka, he referred to it as Toryō (Tu-ling), the name of an ancient Chinese city; instead of the plain "years" he wrote "stars and frosts"; and the last sentence refers to the story of a Chinese musician who broke the strings of his lute after his friend died, fearing that there was now no one to understand his music.

In the light of Takuboku's mature writings, this early composition seems an aberration; at the same time, it is hard not to be impressed that the boy who wrote this elaborate prose received his early education in a school in Shibutami, a village situated in a remote part of Iwate Prefecture, itself a backwater, far from the centers of culture of modern Japan. Takuboku, though he never graduated from middle school (his expulsion was for cheating on an examination), enjoyed reading the poetry of Po Chü-i and Tu Fu in the original, and even composed a few poems in classical Chinese. He read English, including fairly difficult works of criticism, with confidence and understanding. He also read *The Tale of Genji* and other Japanese classics for pleasure. Quite apart from his study of literature, he taught himself to play the violin and the organ and (unlike Masaoka Shiki) was deeply impressed by Western music, especially that of Wagner. After moving to Tokyo, he attended shows of modern painting at the museum in Ueno, and commented with a professional air on the works displayed. He read the newspapers diligently, making intelligent observations in his diary on such matters as the crisis in Morocco and the significance of unrest in the Balkan peninsula. I wonder if a poor boy of this time, living anywhere else in the world, could have received so good an education. There could hardly be a better demonstration of the effectiveness of the educational program instituted by the Meiji government.

It would be easy to attribute Takuboku's literary accomplishments to genius, but saying that explains little. He certainly had the typical failings of genius—an inability to complete most works that he started; a conspicuous unevenness in the quality of his poetry, ranging from superb to dreadful; an unbelievable sloppiness with respect to money; a marked inconsistency in his views on almost any subject. He also possessed the positive qualities of genius, but they revealed themselves not so much in his poetry or critical works, and certainly not in his fiction, as in his success in creating in his diary a fully rounded individual, the first in modern Japanese literature.

Takuboku may have begun in 1902 to keep a diary as part of his growing awareness of himself as a writer. In his diary for 1906, more simply titled *Shibutami Nikki* (Shibutami Diary), he expressed what had induced him to record events in such detail:

"Keeping a diary is extremely interesting. It is interesting while one is actually writing it, but I am sure that it will be far more interesting when, after some years have passed, I read it over again."[3]

As a matter of fact, Takuboku several times mentions having reread earlier entries, but his reactions were not those he predicted in *Shibutami Diary*. For example, on July 20, 1908, he wrote,

I took out my old diaries and read them while lying in bed. I had hardly read five or ten lines before I felt so choked with sadness that I threw down the diary and shut my eyes. What could be sadder? I read more, burst into tears, and after weeping, read some more. I told myself that I couldn't let this go on, got up, and sat at my desk. It didn't take long for my mind to black out. I threw down my pen, got back into bed, and read the diary. After I had repeated this process a number of times, I noticed it had grown dark. I have a body, a mind, but no idea of what to do with myself. I have the feeling I spend too much time toying with the idea of death, so I try as hard as I can not to listen to its whisperings; but sometimes, I can't say when, I can hear its gentle murmur behind my ears. I haven't tried anything as extreme as making preparations for suicide, but I feel somehow as if the only time I really feel at peace with the world is when I am listening to the whisperings of death.[4]

Takuboku does not say what in particular in his old diaries depressed him so much that he thought of suicide. Probably it was the contrast between the happiness of his days in Shibutami and the frustration and loneliness of his life in Tokyo two years later. Takuboku had mentioned in *Shibutami Diary* his joy at having found a sacred profession:

"I have discovered a new world, a place where all dissatisfaction, gloomy thoughts, and discontent are transcended. What, you may ask, is this place called? The sacred profession of teaching, that's what it is called . . . With tears in my eyes, I shout my joy."[5]

It is easy to imagine the effect produced on Takuboku when he read these words two years afterward: the teaching position that had so exhilarated him was terminated after he led a strike at the Shibutami elementary school, and he would never again experience such joy in his work.

Takuboku did not mention it, but he must have had another reason for keeping an extensive diary. As he undoubtedly was aware, a diary could be published. Takuboku rewrote one section of *Shibutami Diary*, giving it another name, and tried to get it published as his "confessions," but it did not appear in print until after his death.[6] Takuboku probably also planned to publish his diary for 1908. This opens on a bleak New Year's Day when Takuboku was absolutely penniless. After a week the diary entries became skimpy and finally broke off altogether; but Takuboku later rewrote the entire diary, presumably to enhance its literary appeal. He was unsuccessful also in his attempts to get this diary published, but it is of the greatest interest.

The most striking quality of Takuboku's diaries is the honesty with which he recorded his thoughts and experiences. He was aware, however, of the danger that his diary might be read by some other person, and this caused him at times to be less than completely frank, as we know from other sources. For example, his diary for 1907 mentions his reluctance to leave the school in Shibutami where he has been teaching, though he realizes that, for the sake of his career as a writer, he must go somewhere else to find greater intellectual stimulation. He narrates with evident satisfaction the performances of his pupils at the farewell party tendered him just before the end of the school year:

"How enchantingly my pupils behaved! Ah, isn't this further evidence that the year I have spent here has definitely not been meaningless?"[7]

A few days later Takuboku was urged by a man from the village office to remain in Shibutami as a teacher. The man asked the principal of the school to return Takuboku's letter of resignation. "My colleagues have unanimously urged me to stay," Takuboku noted in his diary. But on the next page we find the stark entry: "Account of the Strike." This is followed by some extremely terse entries for a week, concluding: "22nd. Official announcement of dismissal. 23rd. Farewell ceremony."[8] Probably Takuboku was too involved in the strike to keep a diary regularly, but it is strange that he at no point mentioned the cause of the strike or what happened. Perhaps he was afraid that if he described the strike in his diary it might be read and other teachers involved in the strike implicated.

A clearer case of Takuboku's reticence relates to his correspondence with Sugawara Yoshiko, a woman from Kyūshū whom he never actually met. He received a letter from her in July 1908, in which she described herself, her family, and her love of poetry. She wrote how much she desired to go to Tokyo and become his disciple.[9] This was all that was needed to stir romantic fantasies in the highly susceptible Takuboku; he mentions in his diary that he could think of nothing except Yoshiko. From then on there are brief mentions of his correspondence along the lines of: "A letter to Kyūshū. After finishing a long letter, I burned some mosquito-repellent incense and lay down to sleep."[10] He also made fair copies of Yoshiko's poems and passed them on to Yosano Tekkan (1873–1935), the editor of the literary magazine *Myōjō*, for possible publication. He also quoted scraps of the letters he received from Yoshiko, such as: "To Takuboku, my faraway big brother."[11] But nothing in the diary remotely suggests the actual tone of the letters he sent to Yoshiko. For example, his diary entry for August 24 says merely, "Wrote a letter to Kyūshū," but the letter he wrote (which has been preserved) contains such passages as:

> My dear, my sweetest dear, why is it not possible for us to see each other? That is the thought that has been tormenting me night after night, over and over, whenever I lie down to sleep. My dear, why can't I meet you? Why, when I love you so, can't I meet you and tell you what is in my heart? Why, when I love you so, can't I take your hand, your warm hand, in mine, and sniff the fragrance of your black tresses, and press my lips on your burning lips? And why, when my body and heart are burning like fire, can't I put my arms around your soft, pearly body, and intoxicate myself in a dream that knows no awakening by burying my head in your throbbing breast?[12]

Takuboku begged Yoshiko for a photograph, but she was strangely reluctant to comply. Finally, three months after their correspondence began, she sent one. He wrote in his diary, "A letter and a photograph from Kyūshū. Slanting eyes, a big mouth, not a beautiful woman."[13] His ardor was immediately cooled. The next day, when a friend, the poet Yoshii Isamu, visited, they both had "a big laugh over the woman from Kyūshū." If Yoshiko had not saved Takuboku's letters, the diary alone would have revealed extremely little about their passionate correspondence, an indication of the caution Takuboku sometimes took when writing his diary.

Takuboku's fears that his diary might be read by someone else were not without foundation. In August 1908 a woman of whom Takuboku had grown tired forced her way into his lodgings when he was out and stole the diary. He wrote,

"There was a note left lying on my desk. It said that if I wanted the diary back I should come and get it. I was boiling mad. Probably she riffled through my desk, read a couple of letters, then read the parts of this diary where I inveigh against her, which made her so angry she took the diary off with her!"[14]

Takuboku was unable to write his diary for twelve days. When the woman finally returned it, he discovered that she had torn out the page from the end of the entry for July 29 through the thirty-first, probably because he had written something disagreeable about her.[15]

His most serious fear, however, was that his wife might read the diary. Probably that is why his accounts of buying prostitutes in Asakusa are deliberately vague:

"About eight-thirty I set out in a hurry. The cold was enough to give me gooseflesh. There weren't many pleasure seekers in Asakusa either. Business is bad in the 'park,' and that's why the women grab so furiously at your sleeve. Kiyoko had gold teeth. She's a woman with dimples. Masako said she was just a simple girl. She had sticking plaster on her forehead.—I got back at midnight, feeling strangely chilled. I'm not going there again."[16]

Takuboku was torn between conflicting desires—to reveal himself nakedly and to keep others from knowing what he was really like. His frankest description of himself is found in his *Rōmaji Nikki* (Romaji Diary), or diary in roman letters. A revelatory passage occurs near the beginning:

"Why did I decide to keep this diary in roman letters? Why? I love my wife, and it's precisely because I love her that I don't want her to read this diary. No, that's a lie! It's true that I love her, and it's true that I don't want her to read this, but the two facts are not necessarily related."[17]

Takuboku explained his use of roman letters in terms of not wishing to wound his wife's feelings by allowing her to learn of his acts of infidelity. The matter is complicated by his tacit refusal to face the fact that his wife could probably read roman letters; her formal education was about as good as his own. Although the need to be absolutely truthful was strongly felt, he needed a sop to his conscience: if he wrote the diary in ordinary Japanese orthography he could not even pretend that his wife would be unable to read it.

This conflict affected the disposition of his diaries. After Takuboku died, his wife Setsuko recalled, "Takuboku told me to burn them, but my attachment wouldn't let me do that."[18] Years later (in 1926) Maruya Kiichi, a friend of Takuboku's last years, urged that the diaries be burned, insisting that Takuboku had told him, "When I am dead, some stupid guy may appear saying he wants to publish my diaries. But don't let him. Once I am dead, do me a favor and burn all my diaries."[19]

What did Takuboku fear? That his wife would learn he had bought prostitutes? But surely that was not unusual at the time. That his friends would learn that he had written ill of them? But he was hardly at pains to conceal his feelings in everyday association with other people. That the police would learn of the socialist leanings of his last years? But the bedridden man had committed no act that could incur the wrath of the authorities. Probably his reluctance came from a sense of shame at being seen naked, but it is precisely because of this nakedness that his diaries are so moving.

❖ ❖ ❖

Takuboku's diaries, though they provide splendid testimony to his growth as a human being, are surprisingly uninformative with respect to his career as a writer. Early in his life he sometimes expressed joy at being a poet: "Ah, when I have thought that I was born to be a poet, I have felt such heartfelt joy that it has made me weep."[20] But he never wrote in his diary (though he did elsewhere) why he chose to write tanka rather than more modern forms of poetry. He seems to have taken his poetic gifts for granted, and rarely expressed surprise or pleasure when his tanka were printed in poetry magazines. When one of his poems appeared at the head of the inaugural issue of a new poetry magazine, his diary is silent about his reaction, though he was at the time only twenty years old and as yet little known.[21]

On one occasion, probably to test whether his poems were being accepted because he had established something of a reputation or because they were really superior, he submitted poems under a pseudonym. Sixty of the seventy tanka were published in a leading literary magazine, but he expressed no satisfaction over this objective proof of their excellence.[22] Composing poetry was almost too easy. He wrote in June 1908, "My head has completely turned into poetry. Everything I see, everything I hear, becomes a poem. I composed 141 poems by two o'clock this morning. About 40 of the poems were about my parents. Composed in tears."[23] The tanka composed on this occasion included some of his best, but he did not quote them in the diary.

A month later he described in prosaic terms the process of composing tanka:

"For the past couple of days I seem to have stopped thinking about women. Instead, a weariness of life itself, a desire for death has occasionally risen up inside me. Composing poetry is exactly the same thing as smoking a cigarette. It's nothing more than that."[24]

He came to take it for granted that if he attended a poetry session at the house of some distinguished literary figure such as Mori Ōgai or Yosano Tekkan his poems would be judged the best, even though they were composed absolutely without effort. The only contribution to the art of the tanka in which Takuboku took any pride was his practice of writing his poems in three lines instead of the usual one.[25]

Takuboku often expressed his resolve to become a novelist. Before a summer vacation of the school where he taught in Shibutami, he had written in his diary that he intended to use the time to write a five-act play and three novels in the hope of winning one or more literary prizes. Needless to say, he did not write any of these projected masterpieces, but he never lost the ambition to write novels, which he evidently believed to be a more important form of literature than the poetry he wrote so easily. In 1906, during the two weeks when pupils were released from the school in Shibutami to help plant rice, Takuboku went to Tokyo and stayed with Yosano Tekkan and his wife, the celebrated poet Yosano Akiko. He decided afterward that Tokyo was nice for a visit, but he wouldn't want to live there:

"Tokyo is definitely not a place for anyone like me to live. There's no advantage to being there except for the convenience of all the books to read. The city has always been the grave of the spirit. I see now that the best thing for me is to stay in the country and make adequate preparation for the plans of my great revolution."[26]

Takuboku wrote that the only thing he brought back from Tokyo was the conviction that he must become a novelist. He wrote, "I have read most of the recently published novels. Natsume Sōseki and Shimazaki Tōson are both educated new novelists and they are the only ones worth considering. The rest are all hopeless. Natsume has remarkable literary talent, but there is no 'greatness' about him. We can expect much of Shimazaki. *The Broken Commandment* is outstanding. But he is not a genius. He is not a hero of the revolution."[27]

By implication, Takuboku was saying that he possessed the qualities of "greatness" and "genius" that Natsume Sōseki and Shimazaki Tōson (1872–1943) lacked, and that it was therefore incumbent on him to become a novelist. Whether or not this made sense, it is impressive that Takuboku had the critical acumen to choose the two best authors of the day, at a time when each had published only one book of importance.

The ability to recognize excellence in other writers did not enable Takuboku to write good novels himself. His first story, "Kumo wa Tensai de aru" (The Clouds Are Geniuses), started soon after his return to Shibutami from Tokyo, was probably his best work of fiction. He wrote about it in his diary,

"This is the story of a young man whose pent-up revolutionary spirit, still chaotic, whirls about his breast. Both the title and the structure are probably unprecedented. It is the bell at break of day proclaiming the great destruction of the revolution. The hero is myself, and all the rest of the characters are quite peculiar. Even as I write this, I feel strangely agitated."[28]

Despite the excitement he felt while writing this story, he broke it off to start work on another. It was typical of Takuboku to shift from one unfinished work to another; fragments of over forty abandoned stories are included in his complete works. Shifting the subject when one gets tired of it is normal if one is writing tanka, but a novelist must be more persistent than Takuboku.

Takuboku's longest work, the novel *Chōei* (Shadow of a Bird), was serialized in a Tokyo newspaper. Sixty episodes were printed, but the novel was left unfinished, and during his lifetime no one was willing to publish *Shadow of a Bird* in book form. It contains some brilliant episodes, but as a whole it is a failure. Takuboku did not devote much time or care to most of the daily installments, as we can infer from a passage in his diary: "While chatting I wrote the first section of Chapter 9 and sent it off."[29] Takuboku trusted that his natural abilities would carry him over the hurdles of a newspaper serial, but his genius, though amply revealed in his poetry and diaries, did not extend to the writing of fiction.

Although Takuboku would have liked to gain fame as a novelist (or possibly as a writer of modern poetry), he lacked the sense of structure necessary to keep a long work from becoming disjointed;

his gifts were those of an improviser, rather than of a skilled craftsman who polishes his work. A single brilliant perception is enough for a tanka, but a novel or a long poem requires a persistent devotion to craft that Takuboku lacked. It was only toward the end of his life that Takuboku recognized that the tanka was better suited to his poetic gifts than any longer form of poetry. In a story written in 1910 a man (presumably his alter ego) says,

> Some people say that the tanka is inconvenient because it's so short, but I think that being short is actually what makes it convenient. Don't you agree? Everybody experiences at all times an endless succession of emotional reactions, some originating inside, some outside, moments that are forgotten as soon as they have passed, or if not forgotten are never mentioned in the course of a whole lifetime for lack of any suitable occasion. Most people look down on these feelings ... But anyone who loves life cannot feel contempt for such feelings ... These are moments of life that will never return. I love each of those moments. I don't want to let them passed unnoticed. The most convenient way to capture such moments is with a tanka which, being small, does not require much time or trouble. That's what really makes it convenient. One of the few blessings that we Japanese have is the poetic form called the tanka.[30]

In an essay written in 1909 Takuboku recalled his experiences as a writer of poetry in modern forms: "My recollection of the time when I was composing modern poetry is that I went from yearning to sorrow and from sorrow to self-mockery."[31] This was an accurate description of most of his writings, but particularly of the poems. He concluded this section of the essay with an anecdote:

"The courteous old politician who had accompanied me to the newspaper office in Kushiro introduced me to somebody with the words, 'He writes modern poetry.' I have never felt so horribly insulted by a person's good intentions as I did at that moment."[32]

Elsewhere, Takuboku contrasted the spontaneity of the tanka with the exaggeration typical of a modern poem:

"Say I saw a tree about six feet high standing in a vacant lot and I felt something as I looked at the sun shining on it. Unless I turned the empty lot into a wilderness, the tree into a gigantic tree, the sun into either the rising or the setting sun and the person who saw this tree, myself, into a poet, a wanderer, a young man bowed down by grief, it wouldn't have accorded with the poetry being written at the time and I wouldn't have been satisfied with it myself."[33]

By contrast, the tanka could capture without exaggeration or undue artifice the momentary perception of even an unremarkable scene.

Takuboku possessed also a spontaneity of expression that is entirely appropriate in tanka composition and a source of his appeal to readers. On the infrequent occasions when Takuboku polished an earlier work, he generally made it worse. He was tough-minded by nature, but his ideas of what made for literary expression tended to sentimentalize his original perceptions when revising. For example, in his diary entry for March 7, 1906, he wrote,

"The day before yesterday, then yesterday, and then again today, the children in the upper division came to play with me. I imagine they will be coming every day from now on. It would seem that there's something in my nature that makes it easy for children to get along with me."[34]

When Takuboku rewrote sections of his *Shibutami Diary* for publication the passage was changed to read, "The day before yesterday and then yesterday, and then again today, the children came to play with me. I imagine they will be coming every day from now on. Their hands and feet are pitch black, and every time they come they shed fleas, but they are all my little brothers."[35] I find something unpleasantly condescending in the expression, as if Takuboku, by mentioning the dirty hands and feet and the lice, was congratulating himself on his egalitarian ways. The original version, like everything else in his diaries, is spontaneous, but the revised account sacrifices this quality to conventional literary appeal.

Takuboku's diaries at their best give the impression of having been written before his reactions to the events he describes had had time to cool; in this sense, they resemble his tanka. In a novel, at least the kind of novel that was being written in Takuboku's day, every passage had to be firmly linked to the rest of the book, and any marked change in outlook of a central character had to be explained. But in a diary changes in the author occur quite naturally, as he imperceptibly sloughs off his old skin and becomes a different person.

When Takuboku succeeded in marrying Setsuko, despite the opposition of her family, his joy was expressed in his diary in the form of the high-flown words he addressed her, describing her as "the source of unending bliss" which she poured into his heart, and invoking the Bible, "What God has joined together, let no man sunder."[36] Five years later, in the *Romaji Diary*, he wrote, "Am I a weakling then? No, my trouble comes entirely from the mistaken institution of marriage. Marriage! What an idiotic institution!"[37]

When reading Takuboku's diaries we experience no difficulty in accepting such contradictions in his opinions because we have followed day after day the little changes in his life that have accumulated until they constitute a total change in his attitudes. If the diaries were a novel, we would probably regret the loss of the youthful romanticism, but we cannot regret any development in the diary; whatever happens is inevitable.

Even Takuboku was aware of the changes in his beliefs. As tension mounted between Japan and Russia in 1904 he wrote in his diary, "War cannot be avoided. And because it cannot be avoided, I hope on the contrary that our great people will rise up as soon as possible."[38] When the war finally broke out Takuboku exulted in Japanese victories and wrote a series of patriotic articles which he published in a local newspaper. Two years later, while teaching school in Shibutami, he wrote in his diary, "I wonder what kind of human beings I am trying to create when I teach the children that the defeated Russians are more admirable than the victorious Japanese."[39] Another two years later, he wrote, "The Russo-Japanese War broke out in February. I, innocent subject that I was, or more exactly, innocent member of a militaristic people that I was, wrote a serial for twenty days under the title of 'Marginalia on the War Clouds' in which I casually discussed the war."[40]

His political views changed in a similar manner. While in Shibutami he wrote, "I value the rights of the individual too much ever to become a socialist. On the other hand, I am too prone to sympathy, too ready with tears, ever to subscribe to any theory of authoritarian self-interest. In short, I am, in a special sense, an individualist."[41]

At the time that he wrote these words he installed in his *tokonoma* (display alcove) a photograph of Richard Wagner. Wagner was his hero, in part because of his music (especially the pilgrims' chorus from *Tannhäuser*), but mainly because of his political activity. Takuboku wrote, "The mind of Richard Wagner, who cursed the three thousand years of European history and asserted that it was a record of nothing but retrogression, is to be cherished."[42] Any manifestation of defiance appealed to Takuboku, who hoped that an essay he contributed to the alumni magazine of his junior high school would prove to be "a bombshell launched at the Meiji educational system."[43]

Takuboku's diary for 1907 opens with an account of the New Year ceremonies at his school. As he sang *"Kimi ga Yo,"* the national anthem, with his pupils he thought of the millions of schoolchildren all over Japan who at that moment were singing the same words. "My chest suddenly expanded, and I felt as if tears would come . . . It is presumptuous of me to say it, but His Majesty Mutsuhito [Emperor Meiji] is really and truly a great monarch, head and shoulders above the great monarchs of past and present. Hearing the name of the emperor always makes me straighten my clothes in respect."[44] But, after expressing his gratitude for the privilege of having been born during the reign of Emperor Meiji, he added: "However, if anyone imagines that the greatness of his virtue makes for a heaven on earth, or supposes that everything of this Meiji culture deserves to be praised and exalted just as it is, this is truly a great mistake . . . There is only one way to live as a human being, and that is to have freedom of thought."[45]

The following year he wrote about Kigen-setsu, the traditional date of the founding of the Japanese empire,

"Today is the day on which we celebrate the invasion by a belligerent tribe called the Yamato people (who had moved their capital from Kyūshū to Yamato) of the territories of the Ainu people, their victory, and finally, after they had occupied the center of the island of Japan, the accession of their chieftain to the rank of emperor under the name of Jimmu. I had intended to attend the ceremony at the First School, but I overslept."[46]

Obviously, Takuboku's attitude toward the emperor had changed, but it was an organic evolution, rather than a sudden shift of ideology. With respect to socialism, too, his views evolved from an outright rejection of socialism because of his individualism, to a passive acceptance as "a part of my thought,"[47] to the wholehearted adoption of socialism of his last years. When reviewing the events of 1910, a year for which only a fragment of his diary survives, he wrote, "This was an important year as far as my thought is concerned. I discovered the key that brought together my character, my tastes, and my political tendencies. It was the question of socialism."[48]

Takuboku did not specify what had caused the change in his thought, but it is clear that the grand-treason trial of Kōtoku Shūsui was an important cause. New friends also influenced him. A few days before sentence was passed on Shūsui and the others who were accused of having plotted to assassinate Emperor Meiji, Takuboku was lent a work by the anarchist Prince Pyotr Kropotkin, and he was later lent a copy of Kropotkin's autobiography. He wrote in his diary on May 12, 1911,

"Today I felt something peculiar in my chest, and I spent almost the entire day in bed. But thanks to this indisposition, I read Kropotkin's autobiography from the time of his arrest to his escape and his going to England. It made me think of all kinds of things."[49]

Takuboku's last diary is called *Diary for 1912*. The fact that it is not dated according to the year of Meiji's reign is significant: Takuboku now seemed to be unwilling to accept the imperial chronology. This year opened with a strike of conductors and motormen on the Tokyo trams. Takuboku was pleased to learn about it: "I have the feeling somehow that this is a portent of all kinds of things occurring in Japan that won't please the conservatives."[50]

There were few reasons for Takuboku to rejoice in 1912. Apart from mention of buying Kropotkin's history of Russian literature, at a time when he desperately needed money to pay for the medicines consumed by his mother and himself, Takuboku was too ill and too feverish to give much serious thought to socialism. He was irritable, but so feeble that, when his wife annoyed him, "I felt that I had to say something or other to express my irritation. But at the time I was lying flat on my back, and I completely lacked even the strength to get angry."[51]

Although Takuboku's diaries are all of interest, there can be little doubt that the most memorable of his diaries is the one he kept in roman letters between April 7 and June 16 of 1909. A few entries in his previous diary were also in roman letters, but this diary is set off from the others not only by the script but by the extraordinary frankness with which Takuboku recorded all aspects of his life. He wrote as if he were using a code that would baffle other people, though any Japanese with even an elementary school education could unlock the mysteries of roman letters. Although he specifically mentioned that he did not wish his wife to read this diary, he wrote nothing disagreeable about her. Indeed, he praised her in these terms:

> Setsuko is really a good woman. Is there in all the world another such good, gentle, and at the same time reliable woman? I simply cannot imagine a better woman to have as a wife than Setsuko. I have been attracted by other women, and I have wanted to sleep with other women. Sometimes I have thought

such things even while I was actually sleeping with Setsuko.
And I have slept with them—I have slept with other women.
But what has that to do with Setsuko? I was not dissatisfied
with Setsuko. It is simply that people have complex desires.[52]

No doubt it would have been embarrassing if Setsuko had read
the diary, despite Takuboku's praise, but it would have been far more
embarrassing if the diary had been read by his friend, the linguist
Kindaichi Kyōsuke (1882–1971). Takuboku was in every way in-
debted to Kindaichi, and he more than once had the occasion to express his admiration, but in this diary he wrote with venom:

"There's no getting around the fact that Kindaichi is an extremely jealous, weak man. It's an indisputable fact that there are two
sides to each person's character. My friend has one side that is really
gentle, good-natured, affectionate, sympathetic; but, at the same
time, his other side is jealous, weak, conceited, effeminate."[53]

Takuboku seems to have felt while writing this diary that he was
obliged to reveal everything, without concealment. His attitude, however, did not resemble that of the naturalist writers who seemed eager
to expose their own contemptible selves. Takuboku was not confessing his sins, and he felt no guilt, even when he copied into his diary his
mother's pathetic letter begging for one yen, at a time when he was
spending far more money in Asakusa on his pleasures. Takuboku's
only interest was in telling the truth, as if he was tired of maintaining
even the small amount of decorum and reticence found in his earlier
diaries. He seems to be saying, "This is what I am really like!"

But whom is he addressing? Surely he could not have kept this
diary solely with the intention of rereading it some day, taking pleasure in the detailed descriptions of half-forgotten experiences. If his
diary was not for himself, it was certainly not for Setsuko or for his
small daughter. It can only have been written for us. Takuboku was
determined to defy convention by describing what his life was really
like, no matter how unfavorable a light this might cast on him.
Takuboku asked that his diaries be burned after his death, but some-

where within him there must have been the contradictory hope that people would read the diaries and understand that such a human being once existed.

As we read Takuboku's diaries we are likely to feel that we know him better than any previous Japanese writer. This is not simply because he reveals in unabashed details his sex life, but because each entry adds a significant touch to his self-portrait. It is true that he does not clarify the most intriguing of the mysteries surrounding him, how a young man with a limited education, who had received poor marks at school and was expelled for cheating, was able to write so many memorable tanka and to create in his diaries a monument of modern Japanese literature.

Takuboku does not mention any influences on his poetry, though at one point he acknowledged the important contribution made by the New Poetry Society, headed by the poet Yosano Tekkan, to the "revolution in the tanka." He also wrote that in modern poetry, too, Tekkan's encouragement had "given birth to Ishikawa Takuboku."[54] Whatever influence Tekkan may have exerted on Takuboku's early career, it did not last long. When Takuboku first went to Tokyo he was happy to be invited to Tekkan's house, and submitted poems for Tekkan's comments, but six years later, in 1908, when he was living in Tokyo and had frequent contacts with Tekkan, he had lost all respect for the man. He wrote, "This poet is old."[55] After showing his poems to Tekkan he wrote, "The poems of mine that Mr. Yosano corrected are all worse than they originally were." In the *Romaji Diary*, too, he wrote of Tekkan,

"I do not now have any special respect for Mr. Yosano. We are both writers, but I somehow feel that we are traveling different roads. I have no desire to be any closer to him, but at the same time I do not feel it is necessary to make a break. If an occasion comes, I should like to thank him for all he has done for me."[56]

His conclusion with respect to the other members of the New Poetry Society was: "If their so-called literature is the same thing as my literature, I will not hesitate to throw away my pen at any time what-soever."[57]

Undoubtedly, Takuboku was influenced by modern Japanese poets he admired (such as Kitahara Hakushū), and there was influence from English and American poets as well. He quoted such poems as Matthew Arnold's "Dover Beach," and he knew various works by Gorky, Maeterlinck, and Ibsen, writers who were all still alive when he first encountered their works. The time lag that had long existed between the creation of new literary works abroad (whether in China or the West) and their introduction to Japan had now virtually disappeared. In a real sense, and not only chronologically, Takuboku was the contemporary of the foreign writers he most admired.

The last year of Takuboku's life was spent in unspeakable gloom. He underwent operations for tuberculosis that did not remedy his sickness. His wife fell ill with pulmonary catarrh, and her slatternly appearance depressed him. His son Shin'ichi was born and died the same day. The doctor who examined his mother predicted that she would not last through the winter. There was no money to pay for doctors or medicine, so the clothes he redeemed from the pawnbroker with money raised by fellow employees of the *Asahi Shimbun* were returned to the pawnbroker after one night. The last part of the diary is painful to read, but it is not unworthy of what has preceded, the final touch given to the portrait of an unforgettable man.

Notes

1. Takuboku is counting his age by Japanese, rather than Western, reckoning. This adds one year to his age by the Western count.
2. *Takuboku Zenshū*, V, p. 5.
3. *Ibid.*, p. 99.
4. *Ibid.*, p. 305.
5. *Ibid.*, p. 98.

6. *Ibid.*, p. 117.

7. *Ibid.*, p. 147.

8. *Ibid.*, p. 148.

9. *Ibid.*, p. 295.

10. *Ibid.*, p. 306.

11. *Ibid.*, p. 320.

12. *Ibid.*, VII, p. 249.

13. *Ibid.*, V, p. 342.

14. *Ibid.*, p. 317.

15. *Ibid.*, p. 318.

16. *Ibid.*, p. 362.

17. *Ibid.*, VI, p. 54. Translation from my *Modern Japanese Literature*, p. 212. Another translation in Sanford Goldstein and Seishi Shinoda (trans.), *Romaji Diary and Sad Toys*, p. 62.

18. *Takuboku*, V, p. 406.

19. *Ibid.*, p. 408.

20. *Ibid.*, p. 91.

21. *Ibid.*, p. 90.

22. *Ibid.*, pp. 284, 291.

23. *Ibid.*, p. 287.

24. *Ibid.*, p. 303.

25. *Ibid.*, VI, p. 226.

26. *Ibid.*, V, p. 101.

27. *Ibid.*, p. 102.

28. *Ibid.*

29. *Ibid.*, p. 371.

30. *Ibid.*, IV, p. 284.

31. *Ibid.*, p. 209.

32. *Ibid.*

33. *Ibid.*, p. 208. Translation from Carl Sesar (trans.), *Poems to Eat*, pp. 15–16.

34. *Takuboku*, V, p. 66.

35. *Ibid.*, VI, p. 357.

36. *Ibid.*, V, p. 54.

37. *Ibid.*, VI, p. 54. Translation from Keene, *Modern*, p. 212. Another translation in Goldstein and Shinoda, *Romaji*, p. 62.

38. *Takuboku*, V, p. 37.

39. *Ibid.*, p. 118.

40. *Ibid.*, p. 334.
41. *Ibid.*, p. 79.
42. *Ibid.*, p. 87.
43. *Ibid.*, p. 114.
44. *Ibid.*, p. 130.
45. *Ibid.*
46. *Ibid.*, p. 217.
47. *Ibid.*, p. 184.
48. *Ibid.*, p. 226.
49. *Ibid.*, VI, p. 213.
50. *Ibid.*, p. 236.
51. *Ibid.*, p. 239.
52. *Ibid.*, p. 80. Translation from Keene, *Modern*, pp. 227–28. Another translation in Goldstein and Shinoda, *Romaji*, p. 85.
53. *Takuboku*, VI, p. 59.
54. *Ibid.*, V, p. 194.
55. *Ibid.*, p. 256.
56. *Ibid.*, VI, p. 74. Translation from Keene, *Modern*, pp. 224–25. Another translation by Goldstein and Shinoda, *Romaji*, p. 80.
57. *Ibid.*

Bibliography

Goldstein, Sanford, and Seishi Shinoda (trans.). *Romaji Diary and Sad Toys*. Tokyo: Tuttle, 1985.

Keene, Donald. *Modern Japanese Literature*. New York: Grove Press, 1956.

_____. "Shiki and Takuboku," in *Landscapes and Portraits: Appreciations of Japanese Culture*. Tokyo: Kōdansha International, 1971.

Sesar, Carl (trans.). *Poems to Eat*. Tokyo: Kōdansha International, 1966.

Takuboku Zenshū, 8 vols. Tokyo: Chikuma Shobō, 1967–68.

The
Early
Twentieth
Century

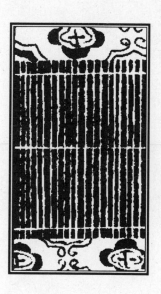

Record of Impressions

Arishima Takeo (1878–1923) grew up in a well-to-do household. A passage in his diary written at the end of 1898, when he was twenty years old, recalled his life up until this point. "My family—fortunately or unfortunately—had enough money for us never to be in want of anything."[1] His family life was happy: "In my whole life I have virtually never come in contact with anything that might be called tragic."[2] As a child, he received an internationally oriented education. His father, a man of samurai origins who had prospered after the Meiji Restoration, was convinced that the Japanese must learn Western customs and manners and sent his two older sons (Takeo being the oldest) to study with an American family resident in Yokohama. From the age of seven to ten Arishima attended a mission school, but his family transferred him afterward to the Peers' School. His perfect deportment and exceptional intelligence earned him the honor of being chosen as the companion for the crown prince, the future Emperor Taishō.

Arishima's earliest surviving diary, written in 1891, describes with boyish high spirits his life as a pupil at the Peers' School. A typical page contains this entry for October 8, 1891:

"Got up at 5:30 this morning. Her Majesty the empress dowager is leaving for Kyoto today, and that's why we had breakfast at 6:00. The pupils of the elementary school division (and only they) were lined up in formation, and at 6:30 we left the school gates and marched to the Aoyama Palace, where we stood by. Presently His Highness the crown prince arrived in his carriage. At 7:20 the empress dowager came out of the gate. We all saluted her. Afterward we went back to the dormitory."[3]

There was nothing remarkable about this day in the life of a pupil at the Peers' School, but it is startling to think that the boy who wrote these words would in the course of a short life acquire political convictions strikingly similar to those of Ishikawa Takuboku, who was born and lived his entire life in poverty.

Arishima recorded in his diary what seems to have been his first encounter with children who were less fortunate than himself. The description recalls how Shakyamuni Buddha, on leaving his palace, saw for the first time poverty, sickness, and death:

I went with Father to the duck-hunting grounds at Haneda in Ōmori. On the way I saw something peculiar. As we went along the Rokugō Embankment, we saw a great many dirty-looking children playing there. As soon as they saw us, they started shouting at us, "Get away from here!" and things like that. We continued on to the hunting grounds and took three ducks. On the way back, we passed by the same place as before, and this time there was a really big crowd of kids who chased after us, singing something like a song. It was so strange we asked the rickshaw man who they were. He said it is usual for people who have gone to worship at the Daishi-gawara Temple in Kawasaki to give small sums of money—two sen or so—to the children on the way back. He suggested that we give some money too. At last I understood what it all meant. Father threw them a few copper coins and they scrambled for them, overjoyed.[4]

Arishima was still too young at the time to make the obvious contrast between his own happy circumstances and the misery of children who had no choice but to be beggars, but this glimpse of a world remote from the Peers' School may have planted the first seeds of doubt concerning the propriety of one person living like an aristocrat while another was condemned to poverty.

Seven years later, when Arishima was a student in Sapporo, a teacher told him that no one could really sympathize with persons less fortunate than himself unless he himself had suffered. Arishima commented in his diary, "Ah, I have hardly ever experienced anything that might be called suffering. It was because I realized how difficult it was for someone who was a little more privileged than other people to express sympathy that I tried insofar as possible to listen to stories of those who really had suffered."[5] Still later in his life his feelings of guilt over the privileges he had enjoyed led Arishima to turn to socialism.

Arishima's principal diary is called *Kansōroku* (Record of Impressions). The title was well chosen. Unlike most diaries, it rarely gives more than brief notations on the weather, and little is said about Arishima's daily activities; but his thoughts are related in detail. He did not state why he kept a diary, but we can infer that he was attempting, at least unconsciously, to discover his individuality. Recording thoughts that he probably would not have expressed openly was one way of proving his distinctiveness as a human being.

The surviving diaries—it seems likely that parts of his diaries were either lost or destroyed—do not reveal all the important steps in the process of the formation of the individual we know as Arishima Takeo. There is a gap of six years between the diary he kept while at the Peers' School and the beginning of *Record of Impressions*, written while he was at the Imperial College of Agriculture in Sapporo. It was highly unusual for a graduate of the Peers' School to attend an agricultural school rather than a national university. We can infer it was because of the dissatisfaction Arishima felt with the world represented by the Peers' School that he decided to attempt to escape into a totally dissimilar society. Several years later, he recalled his feelings on arriving in Sapporo in these terms:

"I had always been as unstable as a chip of wood that, responding to repeated external stimuli, escapes from a whirlpool and buoyantly floats in place for a while, only to be caught up again in the whirlpool and end by rotating with it. But my thoughts at the time were extremely confused and extremely vague, no more than a dream within a dream. Embracing these vague thoughts—thoughts that, however, had continued to occupy me for a long time—I went to far-off Sapporo."[6]

Though Arishima had not anticipated it, he was greatly attracted to the scenery of Hokkaidō, so much more open and wild than the scenery elsewhere in Japan. He wrote in June 1897,

"Amid the brilliance of the fresh green fields cattle and horses play, and students, guiding their plows, cultivate the pasturage that bends like waves in the wind. The clean beauty makes a magnificent panorama that one could not find elsewhere in Japan, no matter where one looked."[7]

Probably Arishima was attracted also by the missionary spirit that had been imparted to the Imperial College of Agriculture by William Smith Clark (1826–1886), an American educator who not only taught agricultural techniques to the students but also converted many of them to Christianity. His farewell address to the students, pronounced in 1877 after a year at the school, included the celebrated injunction "Boys, be ambitious!" today graven in stone at Hokkaidō University, the successor to the agricultural school.

Clark's converts included two of the major leaders of Christianity in Japan, Uchimura Kanzō and Nitobe Inazō (1862–1933). It was with the Nitobe family that Arishima lived after arriving in Sapporo. The first time Nitobe met Arishima, he asked which subjects he liked best. Arishima truthfully replied, "Literature and history." "Then, you've come to the wrong school," said Nitobe with a laugh. As a matter of fact, Arishima seems to have spent very little time studying agriculture. His diary frequently mentions the Bible classes given by

Nitobe and other classes in English and German, but hardly a word is said about subjects that were in his ostensible field.

Nitobe's influence on Arishima was considerable. Arishima described one lecture Nitobe gave on ethics in these terms: "If I had to give a title to the lecture, it would be 'Dream Your Dreams!'"[8] People generally laughed at dreamers, but Nitobe insisted that the lack of dreams was what made contemporary education so unsatisfactory. Students were industrious, and eventually acquired enough knowledge to achieve worldly success, but there were no outstanding men. Nitobe continued, "The world of education today has reached so degenerate a state as to make it impossible for students to develop their talents to the full; instead, they are made to feel content with a paltry salary and a modicum of fame."[9] Nitobe's injunction to the students was: "Raise your ideals to the highest level you can possibly achieve." Such words, in the spirit of "Boys, be ambitious!" probably strengthened the resolve to lead his own life that Arishima had displayed when he defied the expectations of his family and chose to attend the Imperial College of Agriculture.

The most important influence Arishima received while in Sapporo (and perhaps during his whole lifetime) came from Morimoto Kōkichi (1878–1950), a fellow student. On June 15, 1897, the day of the festival of the Sapporo Shrine, Morimoto (who at this time was known as Masuyama) visited Arishima, and that afternoon Arishima returned the visit. He wrote in his diary,

"Today I had a talk with Masuyama that covered many subjects. He seems to have a really solid *foundation*.[10] He only discusses essentials. He is an unconditional believer in Christ. He explained to me how he had recently, after long efforts, managed to discern God. I felt I was really witnessing pure sincerity gush forth from him. He urged me again and again to study this religion."[11]

Arishima did not immediately respond. Perhaps under the influence of his grandmother, a devout Buddhist, he was sitting in Zen meditation almost every morning at a local temple; and when, at Nitobe's suggestion, he read Carlyle's *Sartor Resartus*, he commented in his diary, "There are points in his arguments that strikingly resemble Buddhism (especially Zen Buddhism). Many times I could not help but feel that the author must surely have read Buddhist books."[12] Arishima was not yet ready to abandon his faith.

On August 23 he and Morimoto went for a stroll in the country-side. They were caught in a sudden shower and took shelter in a sta-ble. There Morimoto addressed Arishima in formal language: "There is something I'd like to ask of you, with all due deference." Arishima asked what it was, and he received the following response:

> I have always desired nothing more than to find the God of the Cosmos. I have not been remiss in my devotions, not for a mo-ment, but I have never been able to approach Him. I am often depressed and unable to protect myself from gloom, but I have no friend to show me sympathy . . . It seems to me now that anyone who merits being called a friend after one's heart, or anything of the kind, must be someone who in Carlyle's words will stand shoulder-to-shoulder with one in face of danger and will join one in the pursuit of truth. I have great hopes for you. These days I feel more and more depressed, both mentally and physically, and I am prey to extreme uneasiness. If you have even a particle of feeling for me, promise me that you will join with me in advancing toward the truth, overcoming whatever obstacles lie in our path. Do you understand what I am trying to say?[13]

Arishima's response was instantaneous: he accepted Morimoto's invitation to share with him the pursuit of truth, and declared that having once given his word, he would never break it.

Arishima and Morimoto became inseparable companions. Some-times they behaved like other students: "Tonight Morimoto came to my room. We took off our clothes and tried arm wrestling, squat wrestling, finger wrestling, and every other test of strength. It bucked us up a lot."[14] But more often they plunged into desperately serious discussions of religion and philosophy. Arishima was deeply grateful to Morimoto for this inspiration, and from this time on always referred to him as *ani* (elder brother). "As the year draws to a close, I feel no hesitation to thank brother Morimoto from the bottom of my heart. The intensity of his efforts to guide me is truly immense."[15] Morimoto tried to convert Arishima to Christianity, but although Arishima recognized that Christianity was a religion worthy of belief, he was still convinced of the value of Buddhism. "If, even before I have been able to gauge the immutable value of Buddhism, I were suddenly to direct my heart toward Christianity, what would heaven say of me?"[16] It would take more than philosophical discussions to convert Arishima to Christianity.

In March 1898 Morimoto, out for a walk in the snow with Arishima, suddenly turned to him with a resolute expression on his face and declared,

> I am going to tell you a great secret. Hear me out, please. I have always been firmly convinced of the existence of God, and have applied myself to following the principles He laid down, but I have still not managed to make much progress. In the eyes of God, I am truly a sinner of the worst sort. I am by nature narrow-minded and deceitful. It makes me unbearably sad when I think of myself. Day after day, night after night, I have agonized over my predicament, but I have yet to come into contact with the voice or form of God. Sometimes I have all but wanted to take a gun and kill myself. There is only one course left to me now. It is to leave the agricultural school resolutely and, taking with me just a few religious books, give myself to study, in the hope of finding God. If my quest is successful, that will be fine, but if I am unsuccessful, the only choice left me will be death. What do you think of this?[17]

Arishima was astonished by this passionate outburst. His life had been tranquil, and he had never experienced anything resembling the torments that afflicted Morimoto. He was touched that Morimoto should have chosen him as the one person in whom he could confide, but he lacked the experience to offer advice. It was hard to be sure that Morimoto really intended to go through with his plan, but even if he was only one-tenth serious, it was imperative that he be dissuaded from leaving school and carrying out his dangerous experiment.

A few days later Arishima sent Morimoto a letter (which he copied into his diary). It opened: "To my revered and esteemed brother Morimoto."[18] He recalled how in September of the previous year they had gone for a long walk in the country and (though he was unworthy of it) he had been favored with Morimoto's friendship. He was sure that he was not Morimoto's equal, but he vowed in his heart to repay his friend's kindness one day, though he was aware that no amount of beating a slow nag (himself) could make it catch up to a peerless steed. These words may suggest that Arishima was trying to flatter Morimoto, or perhaps to encourage him by such praise and give him the strength to face the world, but Arishima was absolutely sincere, as his subsequent actions demonstrated. He genuinely admired Morimoto, and he was desperately attempting to save his life. The first paragraph of the letter concluded: "There is one thing I can swear before the world: I have been so inspired by your manly courage that I am ready to repay it with my life."

Arishima begged Morimoto to let him speak for the moment not as his friend but as a kind of devil's advocate. He proceeded to criticize Morimoto's rashness in threatening to commit suicide. He recalled Morimoto's words of the previous year: "I have come to know God. When I pray, I can hear His clear voice; when I meditate, I can dimly see His form. This joy will not leave me for a long time. It baffles me that you do not choose the same path."[19] Of late, however, Morimoto had said that he was unable to sleep at night because of his shame over his sins, and that he was considering shooting himself. But, Arishima insisted, faith can be gained only after repeated suffering. Suffering is not absolute but relative, and what seems today to be unendurable may tomorrow seem of small importance.

Arishima mentioned in the letter how envious he felt of Morimoto's faith, and reminded him of the words of advice he had given for acquiring faith. Arishima pointed out the disastrous effects on Morimoto's family if he yielded to his hasty decision and, after expressing confidence that Morimoto would contribute greatly to society, concluded his long letter with the declaration that if Morimoto changed his original intentions "in the middle of the journey," his life would be in Arishima's hands. "This, I believe, is the greatest gift I can offer you, my brother, to express my gratitude."[20]

Arishima's letter persuaded Morimoto not to make his dangerous wager with God, and the incident drew the two young men closer together than ever. Morimoto, apparently feeling that this new relationship compelled him to speak with complete frankness, began to criticize Arishima, who reported in his diary,

> He has given me many useful warnings. For example, he told me that I was excessively insensitive (this criticism really hit the mark, but such is my nature, and no matter how hard I try to correct it, I doubt it will have much effect). For one thing, I have the bad habit of attaching excessive importance to what other people think. He added, "Don't be afraid. If there is something to oppose, big or small, oppose it and make enemies. You'll never succeed in the struggles of your heart if you want to be loved by everybody."[21]

Arishima not only accepted this criticism but, infected by Morimoto's constant awareness of his burden of sins, Arishima also began to discover sins in his own past. When he was fourteen or fifteen and first began to reveal his superior intelligence, he was flattered by his classmates, and the flattery went to his head:

"At first, allowing my arrogance free rein, I looked down on others for no reason, but in the end my arrogance turned into servility, and servility into delinquency. I was dragged off into the ranks of the bad boys, and I wasted money on clothes, smoked, and lorded it over those with less strength than myself. When I recall how pleased I was with myself, I feel myself sweating with unbearable shame."[22]

This recitation of his sins indicates the degree to which Morimoto had come to influence Arishima, and when Morimoto reported with approval the criticism a classmate had made of Arishima's lack of zeal, he could not help but agree.

At a loss what to do to improve himself, Arishima visited a Buddhist temple, hoping to discuss his problems with the priest, but he was prevented from doing so by an old man who happened to be there and who monopolized the priest's attention. Arishima was enraged by the priest's willingness to listen to the chatter of the old man, and left. He wrote in his diary,

"At the thought that the typical Buddhist believer behaved like that old man, and the typical priest like Mokurai, I made up my mind that henceforth I would not depend on Buddhists, whether of the priesthood or the laity. At the same time, I could not suppress the feeling that it was because Buddhism itself was bad that it gave rise to such believers, and I all but lost hope in the efficacy of the perseverance I had hitherto practiced."[23]

Disappointed by this experience with Buddhism, Arishima fell increasingly under the spell of Morimoto's Christianity, but he was still unable to share Morimoto's obsession with sin: "Unlike Morimoto, who has deeply pondered what is sinful and has learned to recognize exactly what sin is, I (though I am aware of my many sins) have never reached the point where this knowledge takes possession of me truly and profoundly, nor have I experienced its terror. This is most unfortunate. Ah, true laughter comes only after tears, but I would like to laugh without having wept."

On December 29 he wrote in his diary, "Tonight during our silent meditation, for the first time I uttered aloud a prayer before Morimoto—no, it was the first time before anyone."[24] Arishima had taken the first, decisive step toward becoming a Christian, but on December 30, the day after he and Morimoto prayed together, Arishima wrote, "Last night was for both Morimoto and myself a truly extraor-dinary experience. I hate to mention even in my diary what happened. Ah, if only I were a man of normally firm disposition, I should certainly never have allowed Morimoto to resort to such behavior. In the final analysis, my sin of inadequate experience has involved even Morimoto. I feel terribly ashamed before this landscape of Jōzankei,[25] whose beauty should correct the heart of even the humblest man."

On January 5 he wrote in the same vein,

"Last night I again fell into grave error. Seeing how my own brothers are pursued night after night by undesirable love, I have often warned them about this, and had successfully controlled it. I had hoped that I myself would never be drawn into such emotions, but my feeble efforts did not suffice to overcome Morimoto's feelings. In fact, I succeeded only in arousing his passions all the more deeply."[26]

It is not clear exactly what took place between the two young men, but the tone indicates that Morimoto insisted on having sexual relations with Arishima. He at last had something about which to feel guilty, but the experience did not change his relationship with Morimoto. Arishima blamed himself for not having been firmer in his responses, and he kept wondering why he was so foolish and weak-willed.

Morimoto was frequently in tears, and was apt to cry out, "I am a sinner, and a useless idler. If I go on living in this world, is there anything I can contribute? Is there any need for me to go on living?"[27] Arishima, unable to comfort his friend, spent sleepless nights. Not long afterward Morimoto, his voice choked with tears, asked Arishima why he had not once visited him when he was ill. Arishima, unable to find anything to say in his defense, reproached himself in these terms: "I am the demon who has compounded his illness. I have been truly heartless to him." Only one solution suggested itself: "I thought then that the only way I could make amends to him was with my death."[28]

After leaving Morimoto's lodgings, Arishima went to the Shinto shrine in Maruyama and spent the night kneeling in prayer, which brought no relief:

"My mind was in a daze, like that of an idiot chasing after a dream, and I could not decide anything. The one clear thing was that I was unable to kill myself, but if I went on living I must find some other way to devote myself to him. I have a really inferior character, and I lack the faith that might adequately comfort him. This thought saddened me as I went home, uncomforted by prayers."[29]

On February 15 he again visited Morimoto who, as usual, looked extremely unhappy. He read to Arishima passages from Byron's *Manfred*, a suitably gloomy work. The tone of his conversation grew steadily more pessimistic. Arishima was at a loss what to do. "If I could really know God and could share with Morimoto the love that comes from God, perhaps I might be able to comfort him. No other means would suffice." In the end, he reached this conclusion: "The best plan for me now is to separate from Morimoto, my brother, by killing myself . . . If, by dying, I can really restore his spirits, what better plan could there be?"[30]

The diary entry for the following day opens, "Ah, longed-for death! You have at last become mine! Morimoto cannot be revived except with my lifeblood." Arishima had parents and brothers and sisters who awaited his return, but he wrote, "One must sacrifice even one's parents for the greater good." He was sure that if he could save Morimoto he would be accounted "a person who has done much in this world."[31] He had by now convinced himself that he had to die in order to save Morimoto and to atone for his good fortune in having been born in a happy family and having been blessed with many friends. He now felt sure that he could carry through his suicide despite his naturally timid nature: "My heart is weak, but is not my blood boiling like fire to carry out this deed?"[32]

Arishima planned to kill himself on February 18. The preceding night scenes from his childhood flashed before his eyes in his dreams. "My childhood days came back with astonishing vividness. I was standing in a flower garden, hand-in-hand with my little sister. She was lovely as a flower, and I was so happy, favored by heaven and earth . . . I had come with my parents, my younger brothers and sisters to a beautiful, joyous place that was like paradise." Into this dream his old friends suddenly appeared, and they shouted at him variously, "Be at peace!" "Suffer torments!" "You fool!" "What an honest man!" "A great man!" "A nonentity!"[33] Other, confused scenes followed kaleidoscopically. In the last one his grandmother was calling to him, "Look at the lamp, grandson! Look steadily, and don't turn your eyes away." At this point Arishima woke up with the realization, "Tomorrow I will know God. I am destined to kill myself."

The next afternoon he obtained a rifle, bathed to purify himself, and after completing the other necessary preparations for his suicide, went to Morimoto's lodgings to inform him of his decision. Morimoto refused to accept the arrangement. He said, "How could I go on living by myself after having made you a victim? I beg you, let me die first. You live on and do my share." Arishima commented,

> But I was resolved to be the victim, not somebody for whom another person became a victim. So I refused firmly. Then, after a long discussion, we decided to die together. We both felt that even if we went on living, we could not be sure of realizing our aspirations, and we made up our minds not to remain in this world. This resolve was definitely not anything reached after reasoned consideration. We were both aware that it was a cowardly impulse that stemmed from a lack of perseverance, but having come this far, there was nothing else we could do. We decided to leave the next day for Jōzankei and to make our escape from the floating world.[34]

Arishima and Morimoto agreed to set off the next morning together, but Morimoto was late. He had gone to the Sapporo Hospital for a medical examination. What could be more absurd—a man who expected to die the next day having a physical checkup! But neither Morimoto nor Arishima sensed the absurdity. They left Sapporo in the afternoon by sleigh and arrived at Jōzankei after dark. Arishima wrote in his diary, "At the thought that our graves would be here, we felt like criminals who have been led to the gallows, and we shook with fear."[35]

They had only one gun, making it almost impossible to die at the same moment. Morimoto was anxious that people in the future would know why they had killed themselves and asked Arishima to write a statement. This would take some time, so they decided not to set the hour of their final act.

February 20 dawned. Arishima wrote,

> At this point the conscience inside our hearts gradually raised its head, and the question welled up as to whether killing ourselves was something we were doing because we feared God, or whether indeed it was a rational act. Once again we had fallen, quite unexpectedly, into a labyrinth, and our thoughts wandered this way and that, as unstable as water weeds. The day came to a close without our having done anything and we went to bed, but by this time we had more or less decided that we would offer up ourselves to the service of God and brave once more the angry waves of the floating world.[36]

The next day, however, Morimoto was gloomy, and Arishima agreed to join him in death, but after more discussion they reached the decision not to kill themselves. Arishima insisted in his diary, "This was absolutely not because we were afraid to die." They now clearly saw the work before them: "We must do battle with the devil. We must do battle with death."[37]

Arishima, having passed through the ordeal, felt cheerful. The first step ahead was to write his family asking permission to become a Christian. This was his resolution:

"From now on I shall serve God, associate with Morimoto, revere my parents, brothers, and sisters, and destroy the devil. I must do all within my powers not to lose the resolve I feel today, no matter where it may lead me. God, I entrust my body and soul to you completely. I ask that you will vouchsafe to take into consideration my feelings and grant me manly courage and fortitude so that my purpose will be righteous and that I may struggle my life long with the enemy."[38]

Arishima's family was deeply distressed to receive the letter in which he announced his intention of becoming a Christian. He wrote, "Father considers that my plan to become a Christian is no more than a blind impulse provoked by some temporary cause. Mother considers that in joining a false religion I have abandoned my conscience and committed the sins of disloyalty and disrespect to my parents. Grandmother did not express any opinion, but in a note in which she merely asked about my health she enclosed some money. I wept most over Grandmother's letter."[39]

Arishima felt especially close to his grandmother, and the thought of the agony his decision must be causing her, a devout Buddhist, affected him more deeply than the rebukes of his parents. He wrote, "Christ said, 'If you intend to follow my way, be prepared to make even your father and your mother, your brothers and sisters, your enemies.' I understood this as soon as I heard it, and I must be ready to do exactly that. With respect to my parents, I am ready to twist my feelings and do battle with them, for the sake of truth. But if I heard that my grandmother was dying and grieving over me, my heart would surely falter."[40]

Despite his hesitation, Arishima's course had been set irrevocably. From this point on quotations from the New Testament occur frequently in his diary, but on April 4 he wrote, "I offer myself body and soul to God, but will God accept so defiled a body and soul?"[41] Morimoto was his guide and companion in his quest of God, and when they went for a walk in the country the beauty of the scenery seemed to them a manifestation of God before which to pray. Arishima wrote, "We went down to the riverbank, and for a while we were both plunged into solemn thoughts that could not be spoken. We spent a while in silent meditation. Then my brother prayed. I too prayed, from the depths of my heart."[42]

In the middle of May Arishima had word that his grandmother was dying. He rushed back to Tokyo and was relieved to find that she was still alive, though her condition was so grave that he spent whole days at her bedside. All the time he was back at home he kept waiting for his parents to bring up the subject of his conversion to Christianity, but it was not until five days later that his father broached the matter. He stated that he had not the slightest intention of reprimanding Arishima, and that his conversion would not affect their relations. "However," he added, "each country has its own particular customs and habits . . . Are you able to stand up to the customs of this country? Our family has an ancestral shrine. There are also the ancestors of the Imperial Household. A subject is obliged to revere them. Can you defy this?"

Arishima replied, "Your unworthy son knows none but the one and only God. I know of no others. For that reason, even if you, my father, command me to worship as gods the imperial ancestors or our own family ancestors, I cannot bring myself to do so. But what hesitation would I feel to offer my respects to the glorious achievements of the imperial ancestors or to the illustrious memory of our own ancestors?"[43]

Similar dialogues must have occurred many times in Meiji Japan. Shinto and Buddhism had coexisted for centuries, and belief in either religion was no impediment to belief in the other, contradictory though their doctrines often were. But the Christian could not worship other gods, and if a man's family opposed this religion, he had no choice but to disobey, distressing though this was, especially to someone whose education had been in accordance with traditional principles.

After Arishima had expressed his convictions to his father, he tried to defend Morimoto, but "Father interrupted me immediately. He said, 'When you visit this person after you go back to Hokkaidō, tell him that it was impertinent of him, a perfect stranger, to advise a son to say this or that to his father.' With these words he got up and left."[44]

With his grandmother, Arishima was gentle, trying to reassure her. He said, "The main teachings of Christianity by no means run counter to those of Buddhism. Up to a certain point they go absolutely side-by-side." It is not clear from his diary whether or not he succeeded in reassuring her. He wrote that her faith in Buddha was equaled only by Morimoto's faith in God.[45] It must have caused him great pain to think that his newfound faith would forever divide him from her in the world to come.

Arishima felt obliged to return to Sapporo after spending about two weeks by the bedside of his dying grandmother. Toward the middle of June he received word that she had died. He wrote, "That night I was assaulted by unmanly feelings and I wept fruitless tears, unaware of what I did. I haven't the courage even to describe it in my diary."[46] The last remark is strange: it suggests that he may have been thinking of his diary as a public document in which he was ashamed to record unseemly personal emotions. Later in the entry for the same day, by way of explaining why he was so attached to his grandmother, he gave a full account of the affection she had bestowed on him over the years, and how people had laughed at his exceptional devotion to her.[47] But why should he have included this information (about which he surely had no need to remind himself) in his diary unless he was planning to publish it? Or perhaps he thought of the diary as a confession to the world.

Some years later (in 1903) Arishima wrote, after he had neglected his diary for several weeks, "I had thought that I would confine myself to noting in my diary major events that had befallen me, but this policy seems not to have worked. To someone who is accustomed to keeping a diary, a failure to write an entry for even one day produces an effect of having subtracted a day from his whole life. For this reason, I think I will again begin keeping my diary every day."[48]

Undoubtedly, there were some important experiences he either passed over in silence or else alluded to only briefly, but these episodes were probably not of a romantic nature. He gave an account of a certain unfortunate woman whom Morimoto had helped and who subsequently had fallen in love with him. Morimoto felt compelled to reject her lest she endanger his great mission in life. Arishima shared Morimoto's attitude. He described his feelings about the woman:

"God, I beg you to make her happy. If I should ever feel anything toward this woman beyond the affection of a friend, I pray that you will use your powerful stick to knock that feeling from me. I am by no means made of wood or stone. I weep over her unhappy lot, and I feel intoxicated by her beauty. But I must absolutely, yes, absolutely not allow such turbulent thoughts to arise. I pray that you will wrench this affliction from my breast."[49]

Although Arishima would also fall in love with mature women, the most striking feature of his love life is what has been called his "Lolita complex." We have a first sounding of this theme in the entry for November 3, 1900: "This morning I got back home to find Mr. Uchida's fourteen-year-old daughter there. When I saw her sit up in bed to pray, the bedclothes still over her head, I was struck by an indescribable feeling of tenderness, and I thought that whatever prayer might issue from this innocent heart, God would surely grant it with a smile."[50] The great loves of his life, the American girl Fanny and the Swiss girl Tildi, were about the same age as Uchida's daughter, and the diary contains mentions of other "nymphets" who attracted him at least briefly.

Arishima claimed that until his marriage (at the age of thirty-one) he was a virgin, but there are entries in his diary that suggest he was not without sexual experience. In 1901 he wrote,

"On May 23 I myself, in the presence of God, forgetting that Christ understands everything about us, committed adultery. (I am not guilty of adultery in the sense that most people use the word.) Since then, I have not been able to offer prayers before God, and I have felt an emptiness I cannot remedy . . . I rise like other people, I work like other people, I sleep like other people, but ever since I lost the ability to pray, the whole of me no longer exists. That is why I have forsaken my diary."[51]

Whatever it was that happened on the fatal night of May 23, it seems to have inspired in him the feelings of guilt from which Morimoto habitually suffered. The next critical event of Arishima's life was his military service. He spent a little less than a year in the army, from December 1901 to November 1902. His only literary activity for this period was some poetry and a few pages of diary entries for the end of 1902. He explained, "I dislike the excessive ordinariness of my life so much that I decided to stop keeping a diary, but all the same I managed to scribble a few pages. This is a prodigy as far as I am concerned!"[52]

The importance to Arishima of his year as a soldier was that it implanted pacifist and antinationalist convictions that would last for the rest of his life. The first entry in the brief diary entitled "Remembrances of Army Life" opens, "On the first of December last year I entered the army and, after a year spent with an instrument for slaughter in my hands, here I am once again facing a desk, a sluggard."[53] The pacifist overtones of the words "an instrument for slaughter" (*sesshō no utsuwa*) may have had roots earlier than the year he spent in the army: Nitobe Inazō, a devout Quaker, may have transmitted to his students the pacifism that characterizes the sect. But it is from this time that Arishima's resolutely pacifist convictions become prominent in his diary.

Arishima hated every minute spent in the army. He wrote of his first day as a soldier, "I have this day entered a prison where I have been deprived of every freedom, and where I must drip unproductive sweat from my arms and legs. At a time when my schoolmates and, indeed, my contemporaries all over the world are using their full energies to advance in whatever direction they have chosen, I am in prison, my brains tied up and my heart condemned to chains. They say it is my duty to my country. What is a country? What do they mean by duty to country?"[54]

He felt envious of his classmates who were free to do as they pleased. His military experiences also inspired hatred of the state, which imposed this cruel punishment on its citizens. Soldiers were

constantly enjoined to be ready to throw away their lives for this en-
tity. Arishima continued,

> Surely, there is nothing vaguer in meaning than what is called
> a state (*kokka*). The so-called state, established in accordance
> with customs full of vanity and selfishness that go back to re-
> mote antiquity, still grips the whip of authority that inspires
> fear. Once the state lifts its hand, people with parents, with
> children, with friends, with God, topple by the dozens, by the
> thousands, like mowed stalks of rice. Moreover, this authority
> is what enables the state to maintain its existence, and the citi-
> zens of the state wildly rejoice when they see their kinsmen
> fall, smeared with blood, because they themselves have gained
> a secure existence; and they sing the praises of the graciousness
> of the state that protects them. That is why there has never
> been any solution to the conflicts between brother and brother
> on the face of this little globe. Human beings, who should be
> like affectionate children before God, sad to say grasp swords
> and rifles. If they meet, they kill one another; if they are sepa-
> rated, they curse one another. They never cease even for a mo-
> ment to emit the imprecations that tumble from their lips.[55]

Arishima's vehement expressions of hatred for the ideal of the
state is extraordinary for its time, especially if we remember that
Japanism (*Nippon shugi*) was at its height. It is not clear whether his
rejection of the state was inspired by his readings or if he formed his
views independently, but there can be no doubt of his intense sincerity when he cried, "What kind of authoritarian state are we living in
that we must suffer this way? Get thee gone, fiend! Destroyer of
mankind!"[56]

On January 5, 1903, Arishima went to visit Uchimura Kanzō, the
eminent Christian leader, for whom he had conceived such respect
that he was always paralyzed in his presence. He had gone to seek advice on the desirability of studying abroad. Uchimura expressed op-

position, to the disappointment of Arishima, who was most eager to see other countries. Uchimura spoke so strongly that he almost persuaded Arishima to give up his plans. He wrote, "By sheer force of willpower he turns even mistaken ideas into truth."[57] Two days later, Arishima went to see Nitobe Inazō who approved of his (and Morimoto's) proposed journey. He recommended that Arishima attend Haverford College, a small but excellent Quaker institution outside Philadelphia.

Arishima did not leave for America until the end of August that year. In the meantime he studied English with Mrs. Nitobe (who was an American), read various works of religion, literature, and history, attended lectures, visited the theater and art exhibitions held in Tokyo, and otherwise occupied himself with agonizing over his state of religious belief. Morimoto was studying in Sendai, but they corresponded frequently. Arishima could tell from even the most casual postcard that Morimoto was in his habitual state of misery: "I received a postcard from my brother. He did not say one word about it, but I knew how he was suffering in his loneliness."[58]

Arishima was still convinced that Morimoto was truly extraordinary: "Whether in grief or in joy, he always reaches a realm of profundity such that no one else can intrude, and that is why he never ceases to search for truths beyond the ken of other people."[59] He believed also that the highest purpose in his life was to aid Morimoto: "It is because of him that I have not forsaken the world. When I think of his suffering, I yearn for wisdom, I yearn for more subtle sympathy, I yearn for courage, I yearn to be strong, I yearn to live a long life. Lord, enable me to offer my most heartfelt prayers for him."[60]

During the next few years, however, the two men would drift apart. Less than two years later (in February 1905) Arishima would write in his diary (in English), "And the letter of Morimoto! We seem never come to the mutual agreement about the discussion of war and peace. The more I think of peace the intense my belief tends to it."[61] Morimoto apparently defended the waging of the Russo-Japanese War, which Arishima opposed. Morimoto's fiery idealism gradually

dwindled into ordinary faith and an ordinary desire for worldly comforts.

In April 1908 Arishima, back in Sapporo from America, would
write, "But M. himself seems to feed a feeling to direct his energy to
the worldly fortune in the bottom of his heart, but yet holds fast to his
old habit and what he thinks to have believed. How strongly the
outer world tempts!"[62]

A year later he wrote, "The distance between him and me on account of the building up character seems to get wider as time ad-
vances. I feel sorry that I am not able enough to stir up an interest in
him. But after all it might have been better to leave him remain in the
place where he now is. Dreadful it is to lose every sort of illusion."[63]

It is sad to think that Morimoto, whose impassioned beliefs had
stirred Arishima so powerfully, and for whom he had been willing to
die, had turned into a middle-of-the-road believer. His stay in America seems to have tamed rather than enhanced him. Perhaps that is
what Uchimura Kanzō feared when he advised young Japanese not
to study abroad. But this did not happen to Arishima, who continued
to grow, responding strongly to each new stimulus. It is hard to say
whether his stay in America was happy or unhappy, but it certainly
did much to form both Arishima the writer and Arishima the hu-
manitarian.

On August 25, 1903, Arishima sailed from Yokohama for America.
That night he wrote in his diary his thoughts on leaving Japan: "I feel
as though my ideas concerning my mother country have of late
changed considerably. I, like a child who has lived by his mother's
knee but never known her love, though I have lived in this splendid
country, feel extremely little affection for it. To tell the truth, I have
never understood the meaning of patriotism."[64]

On the way to Yokohama from Tokyo he had looked out of the
train window and seen farmers working in the rice fields. This sight,
combined with the proximity of his departure, inspired a new senti-

ment: "Nature here is beautiful. I wonder if I shall be able to see such beautiful scenery when I am abroad."[65] Yes, he conceded, there would probably be tall mountains and broad rivers in America, but they would not be as beautiful as those in Japan because they lack the human element that is so important a part of the Japanese landscape. "The farmers who engage in cultivating the land are in such harmony with nature that they almost seem to be part of it, and almost seem as if they cannot be separated from it. But a corrupt country tears the people from the land and leaves them no connection . . . I consider that the politics, industries, religion, and education being practiced in this country are a disgrace."[66] His mother had wept when they said goodbye at the family residence, but Arishima wrote, "I shed not one tear at the prospect of leaving my native country."[67]

Aboard ship Arishima read Goethe's *Sorrows of Young Werther*, a book he would not only read many times but would also consciously or unconsciously imitate in his life. He also read the poetry of Shimazaki Tōson and wept over the beauty of Japan in autumn. He pondered the nature of Japanese philosophical discourse. When he was told that a fellow passenger, a young man named Fujioka, was of a melancholy disposition and prone to depression, Arishima was naturally attracted: "When I looked at him, I could not keep myself from feeling sympathy. Ah, he too has arrived at the age of tasting the bitter cup of life."[68]

After an uneventful crossing of the Pacific, the ship called at Victoria in British Columbia. He noticed from the ship some Japanese standing on the pier. His reaction was somewhat surprising: "What a disappointment! There was something insignificant and at the same time servile about them. Not one of them looked like a gentleman. Ah, I should not hope to find a gentleman here!"[69]

Arishima landed at Seattle, the next port, and stayed at a hotel run by Japanese in a poor quarter of the city. Next to the hotel, he discovered, was a "den of shame," and the woman in the room next to his dressed herself up each night and went off to that den.[70] He boarded a train for Chicago on September 11. He had been sure that no scenery was comparable to that of Japan, but he was impressed all the same with the Rocky Mountains: "The majesty and magnificence of the scenery are incomparable. Truly, one could not imagine such grandeur and sublimity if one had not actually seen it."[71] But, no less than the scenery, he was taken with some little girls on the train, and he drew a picture of one of them in his diary.

The closer Arishima got to Chicago the less favorable his impressions of Americans became. He wrote on September 14, "If the people of this region are typical of the majority of the Americans, there is no country I hate as much as America. Its scenery is actually superior to Japan's, but the people possess only skin-deep politeness that operates solely on the surface."[72]

In Chicago Arishima met an old friend, Mori Hiroshi, and the day after his arrival heard from Mori about the tragedy of his life. Arishima was, in fact, expecting to hear this story. While still in Japan he had met the former wife of Kunikida Doppo, Sasaki Nobuko, and he knew that she had traveled to America with the expectation of marrying Mori. During the voyage across the Pacific, she had had an affair with the ship's purser, and when the ship reached Seattle she refused to go ashore. Mori, in tears as he related the story, said, "I am not saying that I would still like to marry her. But when we first became engaged, I was fully aware of her nature and behavior, and although I knew that all kinds of rumors were in circulation about her, it certainly did not pose any problem. I thought that we would learn to trust each other over the years."[73]

He had given her the benefit of every doubt, even when the evidence was overwhelming that she had deceived him. The realization that dragging out his unhappy relations with Nobuko could only cause pain to his parents and friends induced him in the end to send her a formal letter breaking off their engagement, but he still loved her. The story Arishima heard from Mori would be developed by him years later into his masterpiece, the novel *Aru Onna* (A Certain Woman).

While in Chicago Arishima visited the Art Institute. This was his first encounter with great works of European painting that he had previously known only from photographs, and he was delighted especially by the colors of the originals. His interest in art remained with him throughout his life, and his diary is graced with sketches made at various times. But European music made no impression on him. He wrote, "I haven't an ear for music."[74]

From Chicago he proceeded to New York, where he was met by friends. He visited an art gallery, the zoo, and Central Park:

> Toward dusk the three of us took a boat out on the lake. "Men of talent and beautiful women," I suppose one would call the people plying their boats, three here and five there, and there must have been many exchanges of soft words. Our boat was the only one that was different. Three young men with yellow faces and black hair regretted the darkening sky of an autumn sunset, and rowed against the wind for about half an hour. The maple leaves on both banks were turning yellow, and we saw how the grass had started to wither on the soaring green cliffs.[75]

The next day, when Arishima went to visit a friend who lived across the Hudson River in New Jersey, he described him as "another short, yellow-faced man." Racial differences of features, which he seems not to have noticed when he met missionaries in Japan, had acquired enough significance for him to mention them in his diary. As a member of a small minority in a foreign country he became aware of himself.

On September 24 Arishima arrived at his destination, Philadelphia. On the train from New York he mused, "From now on, for a whole year, I shall be living on American soil as a lonely Japanese."[76] Fortunately, he was wrong in this prediction. His year at Haverford seems to have been on the whole very happy, but his diary for this year has few entries. The one aspect of his life we know best is the love he conceived for Fanny, a girl of thirteen who was the sister of his friend Arthur Crowell. His diary is dotted with romantic exclamations: "Ah, ah, Fanny—the pure guiding spirit of my life!"[77] "Remembrances of Fanny give me life. Whenever I think of her, I feel a gentle, beautiful, faint sorrow welling up in the purest part of my heart. She is an angel who keeps temptation far from me."[78]

Arishima obtained a Master of Arts degree from Haverford after only one year of study. His thesis was entitled "Development of Japanese Civilization—from the Mythical Age to the Time of Decline of Shogunal Power." It was no small achievement for a Japanese who had never been abroad before to write a thesis in so short a time. No doubt somebody helped rewrite his English, which is conspicuously better than in the sections of his diary written in English, but he had used a wide variety of sources, including books about Japan by Europeans and Americans, and the thesis presented a view of Japanese society that is recognizably his own.

He spent the summer of 1904 working at an insane asylum run by the Quakers not far from Philadelphia. It was a strange choice of employment, as Arishima was aware. He wrote in his diary, "Why have I come to a place like this? Even I myself do not know the deeper implications . . . However, I can't doubt myself. God has led me here."[79] It seems likely that he was at least unconsciously following in the footsteps of Uchimura Kanzō, who had undergone a similar trial while in America.

Arishima worked fifteen hours a day, for which he was paid eighteen dollars a month in addition to room and board. The other male attendants at the asylum were unfriendly, and on the whole the experience was disagreeable for Arishima. The one redeeming feature was the presence of a beautiful girl of fifteen, the daughter of a supervisor there. Her name was Edith, which he misheard as Lily (suggesting that his ears were as yet not fully attuned to English). He continued to refer to her as Lily even after he had learned her correct name. At night he would pick flowers, which he left on the steps of her house. "Ah, I am afraid my feelings are rather too much like those of a little boy!" he noted.[80]

Arishima was popular among the patients because of his kindness and solicitude for their comfort. One patient, a Dr. Scott, whose mind had given way after the suicide of his younger brother, enjoyed Arishima's company so much that he spent hours conversing with him. Ten days after Arishima left the asylum in September in order to enter the graduate school at Harvard, he learned from a newspaper that Scott had committed suicide.[81] Arishima was horrified, but he expressed confidence that his shock over Scott's death would inspire him to even deeper faith. However, fifteen years later, when he wrote about the experience, he traced the beginning of his alienation from Christianity to the disillusion he felt over the inability of the religion to prevent a needless death.

Another source of disillusion at this time was the discovery that most of the Americans he met favored Russia in the Russo-Japanese War because the Japanese belonged to a different race and religion. This view, again, appears in a much later work than the diary, so it is difficult to be sure that these were actually his impressions at the time. It is clear, however, that Arishima opposed the war: "Is it not astounding that they use an average of 500,000 dollars a day in military expenditures? If they were to halt the fighting for two days they could build a great university with the money they saved. I don't know if the present conflict is necessary or not, but war itself is unnecessary."[82] Arishima's opposition was confirmed by reading an article by Tolstoy denouncing those of his countrymen who believed that the war was just.[83] Disgust with the war prepared Arishima for the next step in his intellectual development, the study of socialism.

Arishima's diary for the year he spent at Harvard is very spotty, with hardly a reference to classes he attended or people he met. He lived in the house of a man named F. W. Peabody who was separated from his wife and family. Arishima was shocked when Peabody brought home a woman who spent the night, and considered informing Mrs. Peabody of what had happened. In his diary he appealed to Fanny, the incarnation of purity, to protect him from this immorality.[84] But it was Peabody who introduced Arishima to the poetry of Whitman, an enthusiasm that remained with him the rest of his life.

The only Japanese student at Harvard mentioned in Arishima's diary was Kaneko Kiichi (1875–1909), a socialist who was outspoken in his anti-Christian views. At the time Arishima had come to believe that Christianity and socialism taught essentially the same principles, but Kaneko made him doubt their compatibility. While in Sapporo, Arishima had attended some socialist meetings, and he admired the writings of such Christian socialists as Kinoshita Naoe (1869–1937) and Abe Isoo (1865–1949), but socialism had seemed to him to be a means of putting into practice Christian beliefs, rather than a political philosophy that was antagonistic to organized religion. Under Kaneko's influence Arishima began to read such writers as Engels and Kautsky and, if we can trust his later recollections of this period of his life, he began moving away from Christianity.

Arishima's third year in America was spent mainly in Washington, where he studied at the Library of Congress. He read plays by Ibsen, Georg Brandes's studies of Ibsen and other Scandinavian dramatists, Dostoevsky's *Crime and Punishment*, and various works by Gorky, Turgenev, and Kropotkin. He was particularly impressed by Ibsen's unflinchingly honest portrayals of society, and this led him eventually to publish in Japan a study of Ibsen's *Brand*.

Arishima sailed from New York for Naples (where his younger brother Mibuma was studying art) on September 1, 1906. His diary for this period of his life is partly in English. It opens on August 30 with fourteen letters addressed to Fanny, though he clearly never intended to send them. The letters are filled with expressions of endearment and romantic fantasies:

"My dearest Fanny, the fondest creation of my dream! You are a creature who never breathed in the world. No mortal ever saw you but I, nay, not even I, but I when I am asleep. Still you are real, so real to me. I feel your hands round my neck, I feel your lips on my lips. I feel your heart beating against mine. O my! Is this dream? Is this fancy? Nay! Dreadful reality of the world! Dream exists, and you exist! And you exist, I love you madly!"[85]

The letters also include an appraisal, in English, of the importance to him of his stay of three years in America:

> I must say first of all that it was this country that made me to think myself, to speculate free. I have lived in this country as free as a child and done great deal in the formation of my self and principle . . . But Fanny, pity me, I have one thing still undone. I tried to be independent in framing my thought, but not my action. I am still a slave of conventionality and tradition . . . Fanny, whatever learned may say, I have realized firmly that there is no boundary whatever in human heart . . . When our soul takes away the clothes of tradition and flesh, then, then, we are one and same . . . "State must go" is the necessary conclusion of every progressive mind of this age. The only question is how and not why. Let America have the honor to solve it, and let history remember. her name on that account.[86]

If Arishima indeed learned all this in America, his stay was eminently worthwhile.

Arishima's travels in Europe took him from southern Italy to Switzerland and Germany, and finally to England. He traveled much of the time with his brother, and for a time they took turns writing a diary. Perhaps because this was open to his brother's inspection, Arishima wrote virtually nothing of a personal nature, and this part of the diary is of far less interest than earlier sections. He dutifully noted paintings he saw in the different museums. He had a natural gift for appreciating painting, as he revealed, say, in his praise for Vermeer's *View of Delft* in The Hague.[87]

There are many blank pages in the diary. Explaining why he had let a month go by without making a single entry, he wrote, "My little cosmos loses its order and discipline whenever I visit a big city."[88] Not a word in his diary describes his stay of over a month in England, though we know from other writings that his meeting with Prince Kropotkin in London was one of the memorable events of his life.

Arishima's diary from this point until 1919 is largely in English. He does not explain why he kept the diary in English, probably because he did not anticipate that readers might ask the question. It is not likely that he wrote in English in order to keep other people from reading the diary. Most likely, his main purpose was to retain his facility in writing the language. His English is always intelligible and often charming, the language of an educated but not native writer of English. Arishima often got his letters *l* and *r* mixed up, and he rarely heard a foreign place-name correctly. It nevertheless gave him pleasure to use not only English words but characteristically English (or, at any rate, un-Japanese) modes of expression: "No one can realize the beauty of stars unless he comes across the luxuriant lustre of tropical heaven. They sing & dance, and instead of gazing they smile."[89] Stars that sing and dance are not typical of English poetry, but it is easier to describe them in English than in Japanese.

The use of English unfortunately tended to restrict the content of the diary to things Arishima could easily express in what was, after all, a foreign language. Perhaps the effort of writing English was responsible for the frequent interruptions in the diary, though he usually attributed them to the dullness of his life. For example, in March 1916 he wrote, "From this day on I have decided again to write the diary, after a long interval. I thought, when I stopped writing, useless to jot down commonplace occurrences of my life having no other motive than that of jotting them down. Thus the days and years slipped from my memory irrecoverably."[90]

Arishima's diary after his return to Japan in April 1908 is intermittently of interest for what it tells us about the background of the events of his life. His apostasy from Christianity, his unhappy marriage, his associations with writers and his own nascent career as a writer, his decision to turn over to the tenants the land in Hokkaidō bought for him by his father, and his increasingly socialistic political convictions are all touched on, but not as fully or as significantly as in other writings. The last diary entry is dated September 23, 1922, soon after he met Hatano Akiko, the married woman with whom he committed suicide on June 8, 1923.

Arishima's diary was for years the outlet for his most deeply felt emotions, and was itself of literary importance, but after he became a professional writer it served the function mainly of reminding him of events in his life that might provide materials for works of literature.

Notes

1. *Arishima Takeo Zenshū* (henceforth abbreviated *ATZ*), X, p. 113.
2. *Ibid.*
3. *Ibid.*, pp. 8–9.
4. *Ibid.*, pp. 16–17.
5. *Ibid.*, pp. 98–99.
6. *Ibid.*, p. 111.
7. *Ibid.*, p. 45.
8. *Ibid.*, p. 31.
9. *Ibid.*, p. 32.
10. Words in italics are in English in the original.
11. *ATZ*, X, p. 44.
12. *Ibid.*, p. 39.
13. *Ibid.*, p. 66.
14. *Ibid.*, p. 79.
15. *Ibid.*, p. 84.
16. *Ibid.*
17. *Ibid.*, pp. 92–93.
18. *Ibid.*, p. 94.
19. *Ibid.*, p. 95.
20. *Ibid.*, p. 98.
21. *Ibid.*, p. 99.
22. *Ibid.*, p. 100.
23. *Ibid.*, p. 107.
24. *Ibid.*, p. 110.
25. A mountain gorge near Sapporo known for its scenic beauty and its hot springs.

26. *ATZ*, X, pp. 117–18.
27. *Ibid.*, p. 119.
28. *Ibid.*
29. *Ibid.*
30. *Ibid.*, p. 121.
31. *Ibid.*, p. 122.
32. *Ibid.*, p. 123.
33. *Ibid.*, p. 125.
34. *Ibid.*
35. *Ibid.*, p. 126.
36. *Ibid.*
37. *Ibid.*, p. 127.
38. *Ibid.*, pp. 127–28.
39. *Ibid.*, p. 130.
40. *Ibid.*
41. *Ibid.*, p. 135.
42. *Ibid.*, p. 138.
43. *Ibid.*, pp. 144–45.
44. *Ibid.*, p. 145.
45. *Ibid.*, p. 146.
46. *Ibid.*, p. 150.
47. *Ibid.*, p. 152.
48. *Ibid.*, p. 243.
49. *Ibid.*, p. 169.
50. *Ibid.*, p. 178.
51. *Ibid.*, pp. 198–99.
52. *Ibid.*, p. 222.
53. *Ibid.*
54. *Ibid.*, p. 223.
55. *Ibid.*
56. *Ibid.*, p. 224.
57. *Ibid.*, p. 233.
58. *Ibid.*, p. 327.
59. *Ibid.*, p. 336.
60. *Ibid.*
61. *Ibid.*, p. 524.
62. *Ibid.*, XI, p. 210.
63. *Ibid.*, XII, p. 42.

64. *Ibid.*, X, p. 419.
65. *Ibid.*, pp. 419–20.
66. *Ibid.*, p. 420.
67. *Ibid.*
68. *Ibid.*, p. 428.
69. *Ibid.*, p. 436.
70. *Ibid.*, pp. 437–38.
71. *Ibid.*, p. 439.
72. *Ibid.*, p. 440.
73. *Ibid.*, p. 441.
74. *Ibid.*, p. 444.
75. *Ibid.*, p. 448.
76. *Ibid.*, p. 450.
77. *Ibid.*, p. 472.
78. *Ibid.*, p. 489.
79. *Ibid.*, p. 459.
80. *Ibid.*, p. 468.
81. *Ibid.*, p. 507.
82. *Ibid.*, p. 475.
83. *Ibid.*, p. 496.
84. *Ibid.*, p. 521.
85. *Ibid.*, XI, p. 3.
86. *Ibid.*, pp. 4–6.
87. *Ibid.*, p. 111.
88. *Ibid.*, p. 121.
89. *Ibid.*, p. 137.
90. *Ibid.*, XII, pp. 54–55.

Bibliography

Arishima Takeo Zenshū, 15 vols. Tokyo: Chikuma Shobō, 1976–82.

The Diary of Kōtoku Shūsui

As we have seen, the direct cause of Ishikawa Takuboku's having turned to socialism was his indignation over the grand-treason trial of Kōtoku Shūsui (1871–1911). Arishima Takeo, before he went to America, attended a lecture given by Shūsui in Sapporo on socialism, an experience that did not directly convert Arishima to socialism, but strengthened his radical convictions, and may also explain why he was attracted to the anarchist ideas of Prince Kropotkin, There is no doubt that Shūsui was a seminal figure in the development of socialist thought in Japan.

Two of Shūsui's diaries have been preserved. The first, *Jishiroku* (An Up-to-Date Record), was kept from August to December 1899; the second, *Tobei Nikki* (American Diary), was devoted chiefly to his stay in America in 1905–6. These diaries have scant literary interest, but they provide unexpected sidelights on the thought of an unusually appealing man.

At the time that he wrote *An Up-to-Date Record*, Shūsei was working for the newspaper *Yorozu Chōhō*, and four times a month he also contributed a column of humorous writing to the magazine

Marumaru Chimbun. His income was meager, and this at times depressed him, but on the whole the diary is surprisingly cheerful. The friend whose name most often appears in its pages is not some political figure but the satirist Saitō Ryokuu (1867–1904). Ryokuu and Shūsei both hated contemporary Meiji society, but their reactions to it were different: Ryokuu, yearning for the past, found the manifestations of the new culture vulgar and ugly, but Shūsui, angered by the present, directed his thoughts toward the future.

In September 1899 Ryokuu took Shūsui to see the *hagi* (bush clover) at various temples and shrines. Shūsui wrote in his diary,

> We visited the Tenjin[1] Shrine at Kamedo. A great profusion of
> *hagi* was blossoming in the grounds. We went into the tea
> shop, where Ryokuu, leaning on the railing around the pond,
> said, "I'll show you what the struggle for existence means."
> Calling to the carp in the pond, he began to throw bits of
> bread[2] at them. "The carp here are something special—not to
> be compared in numbers or in size with those in Asakusa Park
> or at Kudan. They come so thick and fast the whole surface of
> the pond turns red. It's not true when the plum blossoms or
> the wisteria are in bloom, and they get more food than they
> can eat, but at this time of year there aren't many visitors, and
> the way they fight for the bread is something terrific. It really
> is a struggle for existence, and big though they are, they all en-
> gage in it." Like a child, he threw one piece of bread after an-
> other, until he had thrown all thirty-one pieces in the basket.
> The old lady in the tea shop was astonished.[3]

The struggle for existence is mentioned earlier in the diary. Shūsui had heard from the journalist and founder of the Japan Socialist Party, Sakai Toshihiko (1871–1933), that his child was in the hospital with a disease that was likely to prove fatal. Even if cured, the child would be left an imbecile. Shūsui thought that the best thing would be for the child to die quickly. He related also a conversation with Sakai in which Shūsui said,

"I remember you told me you thought it was not improper to suggest to a friend who was suffering from tuberculosis that he kill himself. If, as Kidd[4] claims, social progress depends on a natural process of selection that results from the fierce struggle for existence and the survival of the fittest, it would be desirable in the interests of the improvement of the race to weed out the sickly."[5]

Shūsui could not accept such reasoning with its brutally totalitarian overtones. He wrote, "This argument disregards humanity and love. Further observation should be made, taking these factors into consideration, before judgment is passed." This statement indicates that, despite his allegiance to newer thought, the Confucianism that Shūsui had learned as a youth still influenced his opinions.

At the Hagi Temple, which Ryokuu and Shūsui visited next, Ryokuu complained of the intrusion of the present on a traditional landscape: "Just look! Is it absolutely necessary for a city to be surrounded like that with nothing but chimneys?" Shūsui replied, "For all your complaints, you'll find, once you get accustomed to the chimneys, they're actually quite elegant. There are European oil paintings showing extremely beautiful scenes with just such chimneys." The difference in attitude was typical of the two men, but it did not prevent them from being friends.

Shūsui nowhere stated his reasons for keeping a diary. It is not difficult to surmise why he kept one describing his visit to America: a journey there was so memorable an event for a Japanese of the day as almost to require a record. But Shūsui offered no explanation of why he began in August 1899 to describe the events of each day during a period of his life of only average interest. There is strong reason to believe that the 1899 diary was not an independent work but part of a much longer diary that Shūsui had destroyed. A newspaper colleague of his, one Itō Gingetsu, recalled,

He [Shūsui] took out some volumes of his old diary and said he was burning them. He added, "I've consigned all the rest to the flames. These are the only ones left." Seeing what was happening, I said, "I realize that, not having been written to show to other people, the language isn't polished. One couldn't possibly find in them examples of your characteristically ringing style, Shūsui. But sometimes a carelessly dashed off composition contains more heartfelt expressions of truth and a livelier presentation of facts [than a polished work]." I insisted so strongly that he finally let me have one volume.[6]

Nothing special happened on August 17, 1899, the first day described in the surviving diary. That morning Shūsui called on an old friend named Sakurai Shin, who for years had insisted that liquor and good health were compatible, and the two men drank whiskey together in honor of the occasion. Shūsui's diary elsewhere contains mentions of heavy drinking and of returning home drunk.[7] He wrote interestingly about his profligate past:

"In the ardor of youth I used to go often to Yoshiwara and suchlike places, greatly enjoying the free and easy ways, and sometimes I would stay there for a day or two at a time. I later came to repent of this foolish indulgence, reminding myself I couldn't continue this dissipation forever, and I resolved before my marriage that I would never again set foot in the pleasure quarter. As a result, I have become terribly virtuous."[8]

His friends did not approve of this change and tried to tempt him into renewing his old acquaintances in Yoshiwara, but he insisted that his days of buying prostitutes were over, and even when the friends managed to inveigle him into going there, he refused to do more than chat with the women they summoned.[9] But it was obviously not in order to bare sins of the past that Shūsui kept the diary. Perhaps it was intended mainly to provide himself with materials for self-criticism.

The most moving part of this diary occurs near the end, the entry for December 23, He was to go to the funeral for Sakai Toshihiko's child the next day, so he decided to write a promised newspaper article a day earlier. But he kept being interrupted.

> Again, discussions about household finances. I haven't the courage to refuse firmly when my mother wants to bring up the matter, but nothing can be done about it. All I do is listen patiently, but such mundane matters absolutely paralyze my brain, and my thoughts on what I am to write scatter irretrievably in all directions. And when I try to force myself to find something interesting, it only makes me feel all the more upset. In the end, unable to write one line, I throw down my pen and swill a couple of pints of sake. Getting drunk brings no pleasure. A deep depression swells within me until I can't stand it any longer. I let my mother and my wife have a full blast of my bombast and lofty opinions, and storm out of the house. I am not in the least exhilarated, but I *am* extremely drunk, all but ready to keel over.
>
> I normally manage to forgive myself with a display of magnanimity. I tell myself that I am broad-minded enough to tolerate all sorts of behavior. But now I am ashamed. First, bothersome household matters, then I insisted on swilling down sake to dispel my irritation, and finally, instead of the sake cheering me, I give vent to a full range of drunken abuse. I really behaved like a monster.[10]
>
> I went to the newspaper office. I was still spilling forth my highfalutin language when I got to the editorial room. Everybody there, seeing how extremely drunk I was, showed me the greatest consideration, and Suzuki Shōgo sent me home in a rickshaw. I got back home after four. My mind was in such a daze that I hardly knew what was going on. Even after an hour or two had passed, I still had not sobered up. I went out again, dragging my wife with me. I staggered along drunkenly as far as the Kawashima in Hakkan-chō, where I drank

some more. After it grew dark, a gloomy rain started. When it got to be twelve, I walked home in the mud.

I have never known a day like this, when drunkenness made me behave like a madman. My mother must be furious. I must have been a nuisance to my wife. I have been an unfilial son and an inhumane husband. Is it possible not to be ashamed of myself?[11]

American Diary, which Shūsui kept from the time he boarded the *Iyo Maru* at Yokohama on October 17, 1905, until his return to Japan in June 1906, is by no means as interestingly written as the earlier diary. The entries for some days consist of no more than a single sentence, mentioning Shūsui's main activity on that day. However, careful reading of the diary, together with his letters written at the same time, suggests how he changed from a believer in parliamentary socialism into an advocate of violent change.

In a letter written on August 10, 1905, to the American anarchist Albert Johnson, Shūsui revealed why he had decided to make the journey to America. First of all, he said, it was "to learn to speak and write the foreign language that is most necessary to the activities of the international federation of communists or anarchists. (I can read English, but it is difficult for me to write or speak it.)"[12] While in America, Shūsui took English lessons for a time, but his principal activity was lecturing in Japanese to Japanese audiences, and it is unlikely his conversational English improved much during his stay.

Another reason Shūsui gave for his journey to America was more important: "It is to comment freely, in a foreign country to which the poisonous hand of the emperor does not reach, on the emperor himself, his political organization, and his economic system."[13] Shūsui had been imprisoned in February of that year for his responsibility as an editor of the *Heimin Shimbun* (Commoners' Newspaper), which had printed articles that were deemed subversive by the authorities.[14] The five months he spent in prison had seriously impaired his health, but he was determined to go to America, to learn from revolutionaries and to discuss crucial matters of principle without fear of police intervention.

The crossing of the Pacific was uneventful. The first port was Victoria in British Columbia. Shūsui noted laconically in his diary, "It's like a picture postcard."[15] He landed at Seattle, where he was met by several old friends. Two days later, on December 1, he gave a lecture to five hundred people at the auditorium of the Japanese Association. He commented, "Today was the first time I have broken my silence since February, and I felt as if I had somewhat cleared my chest."[16]

From Seattle he proceeded to San Francisco where he met the aged Johnson and some ten others. He was introduced to a Mrs. Fritz, a Russian woman, and her daughter, both revolutionaries, and to an American atheist. He later met various socialists, labor organizers and dissidents. In a letter written at this time he declared, "I still don't know anything about the middle or upper classes in America. They have already been sufficiently studied and described by earlier [Japanese] travelers. I intend instead to keep in contact with present tendencies in movements among the lower classes and in revolutionary movements."[17]

Shūsui rented a room in the house of Mrs. Fritz, and began to take English lessons from her daughter. Mrs. Fritz, he noted, "strongly insisted on the uselessness of ordinary elections."[18] She also advocated the assassination of rulers.[19] Shūsui made no comments on her opinions, but it is probably not a coincidence that he espoused very similar views after he returned to Japan.

Shūsui attended meetings in San Francisco where he joined in singing socialist songs. His emotions must have been rather like those of Japanese Christians who, after their arrival in America or Europe, joined with fellow Christians in singing hymns. The pleasure of fellowship might have been even greater in Shūsui's case. At that time religious freedom prevailed in Japan, and Christians could decorate their churches with religious paintings, but probably it was not until

Shūsui came to America that he could see on the walls photographs of Marx and Engels as he sang socialist rallying songs.

While living in the San Francisco area Shūsui delivered frequent lectures. Most were for the benefit of local Japanese, but he also took part in gatherings commemorating Red Sunday in Russia, in honor of Tom Paine, and in support of famine-relief efforts by the YMCA. He obtained a reader's card from the public library in order to investigate religious symbols: he had been much intrigued by an article by a certain professor who claimed that the cross was a phallic symbol.[20] Although he had not yet recovered completely from the effects of prison life, his health was sufficiently good for him to spend his time in research as he had planned.

Early on the morning of April 18, 1906, an earthquake shook San Francisco, causing immense damage. Shūsui's diary is, as usual, laconic: "There was an earthquake after five this morning."[21] The fires came close to the Heiminsha (Commoners' Society), the main Japanese socialist organization in the city, and the people living there fled to a vacant lot nearby. The members of the Fritz household also fled, but Shūsui and another Japanese remained behind. The next day, while fires were still burning, Shūsui went with some acquaintances to inspect the ruins. He stated in his diary, "An endless stream of people who have lost their homes goes by, wandering in search of safety. The destruction is indescribable. The authorities, for fear of explosions, have prohibited people from lighting lamps or burning fuel."[22]

Shūsui's letters are more expressive. He wrote, for example, "I have been staying in the front room in a three-story building that stands on high ground in a residential quarter. For this reason I have been able, day and night, a telescope in my hand, to witness this grand spectacle. Yes, it really is a grand spectacle. I believe that it is something that has rarely been seen in the course of history. Among the few comparable instances one might mention the torch of the man of Ch'u at the Hsien-yang Palace[23] or the spectacle of Rome burning in the fire set by Nero, the king."[24]

Shūsui, unlike most inhabitants of the stricken city, rejoiced in the effects of the earthquake. He wrote, "Ever since the eighteenth of the month, the whole city of San Francisco has been in a state of *Anarchist Communism*."[25] He spelled this out:

> At present there is no electricity or gas in the city, and it is completely forbidden to light lamps or burn fuel in one's house. At night one has no choice but to be in darkness. Martial law has been proclaimed, and anyone who uses fire in his house will be immediately shot by soldiers. There is no counting the number of prowlers, sneak thieves, and looters who have been killed. Ah, how delightful are the flames! In their path, there are no gods, no wealth, no authority of any kind. Of all the many imposing churches and towering municipal buildings, the many banks, the many fortunes, every last one fell in the rain of sparks.
>
> Do not say that because of this disaster cold and hunger will follow, that unemployment will follow. A hundred thousand poor people suffer together bitter distress—and the flames are not to blame; it is entirely the fault of the social structure.[26]

The earthquake provided Shūsui with an opportunity to see how Western people behaved during a crisis. He wrote,

"The white men pretend to be clever, but their unconstrained behavior is something that makes us orientals burst out laughing. When they meet up with some unexpected disaster, they are thrown into a panic, and don't know what to do with themselves. All they can do is to shriek, weep, or stand in dazed confusion. In extreme cases, quite a few of them crack up out of disappointment over having lost their wealth, or simply out of fear."[27]

Shūsui's words are understandable in terms of what he actually saw during his walks through San Francisco after the earthquake, but they are less appealing than the feelings of brotherhood he expressed for his fellow revolutionaries. I particularly like the poem in classical Chinese he addressed to Albert Johnson before leaving San Francisco for Japan. It is called "Twenty Rhymes on Bidding Farewell to the Venerable American Johnson" and relates how, even before they actually met, they had felt friendship, and how Johnson had gone to meet his ship: "When we caught sight of each other, we felt like flesh and blood."[28] Toward the end of the poem Shūsui used the familiar phrase, "Within the four seas all are brothers." It does not seem like mere rhetoric, but what he actually felt as he said goodbye to Johnson and the others who were, in a real sense, his comrades.

Notes

1. Tenjin was the name by which Sugawara no Michizane was known as a god. There are shrines sacred to Tenjin in many parts, notably in Kyoto and at the Dazaifu in Kyūshū.
2. Not really bread but *fu*, "wheat-gluten bread." It is still sold at booths near ponds to people who like to feed the carp.
3. Shioda Shōhei, *Kōtoku Shūsui no Nikki to Shokan*, p. 74.
4. Benjamin Kidd (1858–1916), a British social philosopher whose ideas were much in vogue at the turn of the century. A translation of writings by Kidd was published by Tsunoda Ryūsaku in 1899.
5. Shioda, *Kōtoku*, p. 64.
6. *Ibid*., p. 71. This description by Itō Gingetsu is included in Shūsui's diary *Jishiroku*, presumably inserted by Itō himself.
7. *Ibid*., pp. 69, 109.
8. *Ibid*., p. 68.
9. *Ibid*.
10. Shūsui used the word *shōjin*, which occurs in Confucian texts with the meaning of an unworthy, inferior person, the opposite of *kunshi*, or superior person.
11. Shioda, *Kōtoku*, pp. 123–24.
12. *Ibid*., p. 198.
13. *Ibid*.
14. Among the articles that had aroused the ire of the authorities was an editorial by Shūsui protesting an increase in taxes to pay for the expenses of the

Russo-Japanese War, and the first Japanese translation of the *Communist Manifesto* (in November 1904).

15. Shioda, *Kōtoku*, p. 133.
16. *Ibid.*, p. 134.
17. *Ibid.*, p. 218.
18. *Ibid.*, p. 136.
19. *Ibid.*, p. 137.
20. *Ibid.*, p. 142.
21. *Ibid.*
22. *Ibid.*, p. 143.
23. A reference to Hsiang Yü, from the state of Ch'u, who set fire to the palace of the first Ch'in emperor in 206 B.C.
24. Shioda, *Kōtoku*, pp. 234–35.
25. *Ibid.*, p. 236. The words "Anarchist Communism" are given in English after a Japanese translation of the term.
26. *Ibid.*, p. 235.
27. *Ibid.*
28. *Ibid.*, p. 144.

Bibliography

Shioda Shōhei. *Kōtoku Shūsui no Nikki to Shokan*. Tokyo: Miraisha, 1954.

The Diary of Tokutomi Roka

Various Japanese writers on their deathbeds asked that their diaries be destroyed. Fortunately for biographers, their wishes were usually ignored by their families, who could not bear to destroy documents that revealed the innermost thoughts of the husband or father who had died. Kōtoku Shūsui and Tokutomi Roka (1868–1927) are among the few authors who actually burned their own diaries. Roka apparently kept a diary from early youth, but in December 1905, when he was thirty-seven years old, he burned all of his diaries as part of what has been described as a "spiritual revolution."[1]

The year 1905 was particularly important for Roka. In February he wrote a friend that he was abandoning his artistic name (*gagō*) of Roka, and would henceforth sign his manuscripts Tokutomi Kenjirō, his real name, meaning perhaps that he had renounced the traditions of the *bunjin*, all of whom took artistic names, and would write as an ordinary member of society.[2] In April of that year he traveled to the Holy Land, and in June he went to Russia, where he visited Tolstoy at Yasnaya Polyana. He returned to Japan in August by way of Siberia. In December he founded the magazine *Kuroshio* (Black Current), which he intended to make an organ for his views, but it failed after two issues.

Roka's surviving diaries begin eight years later, in May 1914. It is not clear whether or not he kept a diary between 1905 and 1914. If such a diary existed, it would be of the utmost importance in understanding Roka's development as a man and social critic. In January 1911, outraged by the judicial decision after the trial of Kōtoku Shūsui and others for the alleged plot to kill Emperor Meiji, he addressed an open letter of remonstration to the emperor, and in February of that year delivered a lecture in which he eloquently defended Shūsui, who had been condemned to death. In 1913 a bitter quarrel erupted between Roka and his elder brother, the journalist Tokutomi Sohō, whom Roka did not see again until September 18, 1927, the day of his death, when the brothers were at last reconciled.

None of these events is described in the surviving diaries, though themes such as his hatred for Sohō, without explanation for its cause, appear on almost every page. For that matter, Roka nowhere stated his reasons for keeping a diary. Although it covers fewer than five years, it runs close to four thousand pages. For a considerable part of the years involved, keeping the diary was Roka's sole literary occupation. Each day's entry must have taken hours to write. Roka seems to have thought of the diaries as potential material for novels, and although each day's entry is very full, the diary is almost entirely restricted to personal experiences. There are, it is true, occasional sour comments on books or magazine articles he had read, but Roka hardly manifested a trace of interest in, say, the First World War. He regularly read the newspapers and must have known of the battles fought in France and Belgium, but he probably decided that these events could not figure in future novels and that there was accordingly no reason to mention them.

Roka's surviving diaries open on May 5, 1914. This was the twentieth anniversary of his marriage, and his wife had prepared dishes that were traditional at celebrations—red rice (*sekihan*) and *wakame* seaweed soup. But at the dinner table the wife had murmured to herself, "There's nobody here to congratulate us."[3] Despite the great love and desire for children shared by husband and wife, they had had none, and this misfortune is alluded to again and again in the course of the diaries. Tsuruko, the sixth daughter of Tokutomi Sohō, had been living with the couple. The girl, then eight years old, was the joy of their lives and they had unofficially adopted her; but on May 21 Roka suddenly decided to return Tsuruko to her parents. He seems to have wanted to wound Sohō's feelings, whatever the cost in pain to himself (and Tsuruko). On that day messengers came twice from Sohō to report that his and Roka's father was dying, and to ask that Roka come at once to see him before he died. Roka refused, unwilling to make a gesture that might be interpreted as a sign of reconciliation with his brother.

He wrote in his diary, "My parents, as far as I am concerned, are already dying. I too am already dying. I am prepared to be called unfilial, unbrotherly."[4] He explained his decision in terms of "It's fate, and it had to come sooner or later." This attitude upset his wife:

"My wife is unhappy over my attitude of pretending I don't see it when my father's death is before my eyes. But I swore to her that if she said even one word on the subject I would beat and drive her out of the house."[5] He added the comment, "I really meant it."

Roka's self-portrait in his diary is of a completely macho man. Again and again he describes his annoyance, anger, rage over some incident, however trivial. He characterizes most of the people who write to him as "fools" in such passages as the following:

"I hear that fool Ueda Misao has asked Keiseisha[6] to publish the book. The fool at Keiseisha says, 'We can't possibly publish a book with that title, etc.' In any event, Ueda is a fool and so is Bun."[7]

The diary frequently describes his sudden explosions of wrath when someone had annoyed him:

I said I was going to the bathhouse, but that cursed fool of an old woman stuck out her legs in my direction. When I returned home after having taken my bath, I admonished her a little, but the stupid old woman hardly even bowed her head and she didn't say a word of apology. The extremely bad humor I have been in since yesterday flared up. I pushed her over, forced her head (like the stump of a tree) down onto the tatami, and hit her again and again with my fists. The old hag farted. This time I pinched her legs. Mino[8] stared with wide-open eyes. My wife went over to the woman and admonished her. I kept at it. After sending the two young women to the bathhouse, I beat and kicked the old woman until she screamed that it hurt, and then I made her apologize.[9]

Such violence is shocking, especially in a writer who (in his own mind at least) was a devout Christian, but it is little short of astonishing that Roka should have recorded these incidents in such detail and clarity. Few diarists have been as uncompromisingly honest as Roka, and there is never any attempt made to justify his actions.

Roka's rage against his brother Sohō runs through the entire diary. Because he was not writing for anyone else's benefit, he never felt it necessary to explain why he hated his brother so much, but from time to time he recorded the ways in which the hatred exploded:

"That fool Sohō in the lecture he gave before the emperor said that people who deviate from the normal are generally people who come from unhappy homes. Of course that's true. It's because there are irresponsible elder brothers like you that there are unlucky people like me. Damned idiot! I'll club you to death."[10]

His hatred for Sohō extended to their parents, who lived in Sohō's house. Roka's violence, always on the point of exploding, directed itself at his father on one occasion:

First of all, I tore up a Yamaga fan[11] with "Tokutomi" written on it in red lacquer. Then, taking a "wilderness axe,"[12] I deliberately went out to the main gate and split up the doorplate with my name "Tokutomi Kenjirō." I further ripped up and crumpled four photographs of my father.[13] I threw the pieces into the garden and urinated on them, and then trampled them into the ground with my geta. In the afternoon I picked up the pieces and burned them. Having done even this much was probably a sin punishable by death.[14]

Roka could scarcely bear to mention his brother's name or even to refer to him as a brother; instead, he usually called him simply "Aoyama," this being the place where Sohō lived, as in the following:

"When I think about Aoyama or the attitude of the whole family, I feel as if I am going out of my mind. I would like to slit open my belly, pull out my entrails, and press them against their door. I want to kill someone. And as long as I am killing someone, I would like to thrust a dagger into my mother's chest. I would like to trample Aoyama's head to bits."[15]

I doubt that any other diarist has ever expressed the desire to stab his mother, but Roka repeatedly expressed violent hatred for her, and even denied that he was in fact her son. He had to admit, however, that he was his father's son:

My mother hates my father because of his sins, and she despises him because he is weak. My father is also slow when it comes to the workings of his brain, but my mother is comparatively sharp. I demonstrated a long time ago, at the age of five, that I was my father's son. That's why my mother abandoned me, as a reincarnation of my father. My life up to this point has been an alternation of remorse for my sins, efforts to make amends to my mother, and the desperation of failed hopes. That accounts for the plaintive strain always found in the things I have written. In the case of my wife too, my father welcomed her for my sake, my mother for the sake of the Tokutomi family, and my brother tried implicitly and explicitly to rob his younger brother of his wife. My brother—it goes without saying—and my many elder sisters, too, all take after their mother. Now, with the death of my father, I have become the only unfilial one, and that was because my mother, try as she might, was never able to love my father.[16]

Roka's feelings toward his parents were complicated. Although he urinated on his father's photographs, he had to admit that he resembled him, in his sins if not his virtues. This is the closest he comes to an explanation of why he could not restrain his desire to take into his arms any available young woman, especially maidservants. The first abortive romance described in the diary is with Okoto, the younger sister of his friend Ogasawara Zembei, who had committed suicide in 1908. Roka had used Zembei's unpublished manuscript when writing his own *Yadorigi* (Parasite Plant), and feelings of guilt apparently led him to take into his household Zembei's two sisters. Okoto attracted him, and he made passes at her from time to time. On July 18, 1914:

> After my bath, I took the right hand of Okoto, who was laying out the bedding, and (because the shutters were open) led her into the next room. I put my hand through her open sleeve and, hugging her sweaty back, kissed her. With the point of my tongue I forced open her teeth and rubbed her tongue with mine. And I embraced her fiercely. "Hold me tight!" I said. Okoto, her arms around me, said, "Father!" in a little voice. She's a clever little minx. That one word made me incapable of going any further. Much as it annoyed me, I released her from my embrace.[17]

It annoyed Roka to be called "father" because it emphasized the difference in their ages, but it may also have recalled to Roka his father's gross infidelity toward his wife, Roka's mother. He wrote in his diary the next day, "My late father slept with my mother on one side and his mistress on the other. I recalled how he took his pleasure with them by turns, even in broad daylight, and I thought that I would like to do the same."[18] If Roka really did remember this sight, the word "father" may well have inhibited him.

Roka's descriptions of his sexual life are undoubtedly the most interesting part of his diaries. Apart from professional libertines (such as Frank Harris), few diarists have been as explicit in their descriptions of their sexual behavior. He noted each occasion when he had intercourse with his wife, usually specifying the time and sometimes adding comments as to whether or not the experience was pleasurable. At the opening of the diary Roka was forty-six and his wife, Aiko, was forty. They had been married since 1894, twenty years earlier, but their mutual sexual pleasure showed no signs of abating. This did not prevent Roka from displaying interest in every female of even moderate attractiveness, but his cowardliness (to use his word) kept him from carrying out his fantasies. Sometimes he turned to pornographic books for sexual stimulation: "I want to read dirty books and look at dirty pictures."[19] But he could also be stimulated in the same way by works that were of great literary value: "Yesterday I read one of Tolstoy's posthumous works, the section of 'Father Sergius' describing how he committed fornication. I seem to be desperately eager to commit fornication myself."[20]

The first "romance" described in the diary was his unsuccessful attempt to seduce Okoto, in the manner related above. Again and again he returned to this failure, blaming himself for not having pursued Okoto more energetically. The night after her mention of "father" cooled his ardor, he wrote in his diary:

> Tonight is my only opportunity to take Okoto in my arms. Ever since she gave me the slip, by calling me "father," I have been suffering torment. I have waited for a chance to say, "I'm not your daddy. I'm in love with you. I absolutely must sleep with you." But the chance has never come. As usual, I've left things half done. It would have been better if I had raped her

once and for all. But once I learned, just as she said, she could only love me as a father and not as a man, I couldn't go through with raping her. All I can do is curse my years.

In 1928, the year after Roka's death, his wife appended her comment to this entry in the diary: "What a terrible way to defile his wife's birthday! The diary for this period is such that I feel like tearing it to pieces, burning it, and throwing it away, but I cannot find it in my heart to go so far as to destroy the pure soul hiding deep in his breast. I'll swallow my silent tears and allow it to live."[21]

Roka was aware of the danger that his wife might read his diary. (When his wife entered the hospital, he profited by her absence to read *her* diary.) About two months after writing the above entry, he wrote,

"Today I read over my diary since May. It is written in a very outspoken, or even exaggerated way. I can imagine how much it would pain my wife if she read such accounts of lascivious behavior. At the thought, I wondered if it would not be best to burn such a thing. However, even if I burn the diary, the facts obviously will continue to exist. No, the best thing is probably not to burn it."[22]

Roka had no illusions about the figure he cut in the eyes of the young woman he hoped to rape:

When I sit on the table in the eight-mat room, a naked man is reflected in the full-length mirror. He is a big man, with wide shoulders, and his breasts hang flaccidly. The lower part of his abdomen, where the hair grows, resembles the belly of a woman in the last months of pregnancy. On his close-cropped head, set on a thick neck, he wears glasses with gold rims and sports a coarse-looking mustache trimmed short. Who might this man be? The pimply boy of forty years ago? The slender, handsome, fair-skinned young man of thirty years ago? Who is this man with such an opaque, fleshy face, this fat, hairy man?[23]

A photograph of Roka, taken at the time, shows him clad only in a loincloth, practicing archery as his wife gazes on. The man in the mirror must have looked just like him.

Roka's most ardent lovemaking was directed at a servant. The occasion for the attempted seduction was the hospitalization of his wife, who remained there, at first in grave condition, from February until the end of June 1915. During this time Roka's sexual cravings gradually increased. He realized the danger from the start. He wrote on February 27,

"Last night I dreamed I embraced a girl of seventeen, and was severely scolded by my mother. I have such dreams because my libido has lately been aroused. If things go on this way, my wife may die, for all I know. Sexual desire is something dreadful. It may seem cowardly of me, but I pray for heavenly guidance."[24]

It did not take long for a sexual object to appear in his field of vision, the maid Kiyo. At the time, Roka was forty-seven and she was seventeen. On March 6 he wrote in his diary, "Last night Kiyo was brimming with sexiness. I held back, but toward dawn I had a dream that made my heart pound a bit. It's spring, I'm lonely, and I am a weak animal—I must watch my step, taking strength from a great love. In any case, imprudence is a formidable enemy."[25]

Ten days later the peril had become even more apparent: "When I was about to go to bed, Kiyo came to wipe my back. She couldn't be more sexy, and she seemed to be deliberately touching my body with her hands and legs. Each time it happened my heart throbbed. I think of her as a stupid girl, but all the same, I was intimidated by the power a young girl possesses. What a poor wretch I am! A man like me is really in danger."[26]

Roka regularly visited his wife in the hospital and fervently prayed for her recovery. He decided to build a coffin big enough for two and put it in his garden. If he died first, the wife could be placed in the coffin later on.[27] He was determined to remain by her side in death as well as in life. At the same time, he felt increasingly the claims of the flesh. Kiyo appeared before him every day, and whatever she did aroused him sexually. He began to respond to her: "She shaved me . . . then, after I got back, she patted me on the back, the way one might with a child. But she's a sexy girl of seventeen. Danger! Danger! She has been sent here as a messenger to test me."[28]

He tried to distract himself from thoughts of sex by going to see Kabuki, but the comment in his diary after attending a performance of *Kanjinchō* was: "My lust is easily aroused. I must make an effort to get rid of Kiyo."[29] But, after a night of disagreeable dreams about his brother in which he also beat his wife, Roka made his first pass at Kiyo: "My head still in a dazed condition, I grabbed Kiyo's arm, took her in mine, and lowered her to the floor of the veranda. I wonder just how far I was intending to go."[30] At the same time, he began to think guiltily that each lustful thought or action threatened his wife's life.

Once his self-imposed resistance to Kiyo wavered, his actions became overtly sexual: "Every morning I have her put on my *tabi*.[31] I often pat her shoulders or her hair. I stroke her back . . . She's a silly girl of seventeen, but she couldn't be sexier. Today again, when she passed behind my back in the corridor, I grabbed her hand. I have considerably aroused her lascivious feelings."[32]

His actions became bolder: "This morning, as usual, I rested my feet on Kiyo's lap. Then I threw my arms around her waist and lifted her up in the air."[33] On May 5, his twenty-first wedding anniversary, he wrote,

"The sexual passion that has been gathering inside me for some days keeps accelerating. This morning I embraced Kiyo twice. Sitting on a chair, I probed the upper part of her thigh with the point of my foot as she was putting on my *tabi*, and in the end I held her tightly around the waist. The knot I felt on her buttocks was probably a menstruation belt. Somehow I couldn't help feeling disgust, pity, sympathy."[34]

Roka went further with Kiyo and doubtless would have gone even further had his wife not returned from the hospital. His tone in painstakingly recording every detail of his lovemaking is not one of confession but of immense fascination with himself. He tried to understand his contradictory impulses. He declared that he loved his wife, wanted an absolute monopoly of her affection, and yet at times wished she were dead.

"I often think I will kill her. But my central element is love, is light, and I can't kill her . . . In the final analysis, I love my wife. The god in my heart is pledged to the god in her heart."[35]

After making this affirmation, he proceeded to describe that day's activities with Kiyo:

"Today too I played with Kiyo, that stupid girl. I embraced her around the hips, I pressed my belly against hers. You might say it was all but the same thing as sexual intercourse. And gradually I became more self-possessed, bolder, and I did it unconcernedly before a photograph of my wife and me, inside glass doors."[36]

To make love to another woman—a woman for whom he manifested only contempt—before the photograph of his wife no doubt gave him a special thrill compounded of pleasure and fear. The thrill was heightened as he described his actions in his diary, all but inviting his wife and perhaps future generations to observe him. Occasionally he expressed apprehension concerning the "evidence" recorded in the diary, but he always ended up by decided not to destroy it:

"I've been looking at the unseemly, scandalous diary I've kept since last year. I wonder if I should burn the diary. But one can't become an artist unless one can look squarely at anything, no matter what. I've decided not to burn it."[37]

Roka was convinced that he was destined to be an artist, and he was able to find a prototype for himself in the literature of the past: "I am a latter-day Genji, who, even while loving Murasaki, could love other women and who after Murasaki's death could not break off his relations with women."[38]

Sometimes Roka attempted to analyze what made him pursue Kiyo, a woman he did not love, and why, when he held her in his arms, he held back from raping her:

"What makes me want to violate this stupid girl? Flesh tries to *assert* itself. Flesh cannot stop until it has released every last seed of flesh. Because my wife is not here, I want to give my seed to a girl who happens to be close at hand. Then why have I not gone through with it? Because I am a coward. Because my eyes can see. Because I love my wife."[39]

Kiyo would probably not have resisted if Roka had attempted to have sexual intercourse. It would have given her special claims on him, especially if she bore a child to this childless man. But Roka feared the financial consequences. At one point, debating whether or not to buy some rosebushes from a catalogue, he wrote, "Shall I violate Kiyo or shall I buy the roses? The roses would be cheaper. I'm stingy, so I'll take the course of stinginess."[40]

Whatever affection Roka may have felt for Kiyo evaporated as soon as his wife returned from the hospital. His diary entry for June 27, 1915, concludes:

"Husband and wife hung the white mosquito netting and lay down in the double bed. The moon was white. My wife is still thin after her illness. We lay down side by side, each somewhat reserved. 'Hold me,' my wife murmured. And, in response to her words, I had sexual intercourse for the first time in 140 days—in the space of a dream."[41]

Roka's attitude toward his servants, earlier revealed in his account of how he beat an old woman who seemed insufficiently deferential, was even more unattractively displayed in his treatment of Kiyo. Once Roka's wife returned from the hospital he ceased to fondle Kiyo. He had never thought of her as anything but a "stupid girl," but one might have expected that memories of their daily embraces would have induced him to act gently even after he no longer needed her body. Instead, he acted with a brutality that is astonishing, even in this aggressively masculine man. Shortly before his wife returned home he recorded in his diary a first flare-up of anger with Kiyo:

Kiyo didn't answer me, so I lost my temper and screamed at her, "I'm the master here!" I hit the back of a bench and shouted, "I'll split your head in two!" And I hit a bucket with my walking stick hard enough to drive a dent into the rim. "When a teacher calls a pupil, is it all right for the pupil not to respond? When a parent calls a child, is it all right for the child not to answer?" But even as I was scolding her, I remembered all at once how I myself had not gone to my parents even when they called me twice. My recent fatigue, my jealousy toward young people, and my reluctance to let go of a young girl were all mixed in.[42]

His fit of anger on August 6 was even more unreasonable: "I sent Kiyo to the market to buy a watermelon. The taste was good, but the skin was unusually thick. I told Kiyo that the next time she went she should ask the man to come down a little on the price. She answered something to the effect that she didn't want to because the man was a relative. This irritated me and I gave her a long dressing down, in which my wife joined."[43]

Four days later, he wrote, "This morning Kiyo did precisely the opposite of what I had ordered her. I lost my temper at such extreme lack of attention. I hit her head with my fist and pulled her by the hair."[44]

Soon after this incident Kiyo went home, temporarily, Roka supposed. On August 16 he wrote, "Today I thought that Kiyo would come back with a watermelon so I didn't buy one myself, but she still hasn't come back. I became absolutely furious at the thought that she was following Mino's example, and I swore that if she came back I would trample her to death, I would beat her so hard the eyes would pop out of her head."[45]

On the following day he became apoplectic at the thought of all the suffering he had been caused by the inefficiency of Kiyo, Mino, and the nurse who had attended his wife in the hospital: "I was boiling and writhing with rage against them, and felt I was going mad."[46]

It is not surprising that Kiyo never went back to the Tokutomi household. Mino, who remained, endured similar abuse. One night when tempura was served for dinner, Roka became thirsty:

I was gulping down barley water. The barley water ran out. My wife rebuked Mino, "That's why I asked you a while ago, didn't I, to have a kettle ready." Mino at once filled a teapot. The contents had a pale color like tea. I was provoked into cursing Mino. I screamed at her, "You cretin! Haven't you the sense to realize that on a hot day like this we might want to drink barley water?" She continued to dilly-dally, and I finally pushed her over and pressed her head against the tatami. Mino let out a shriek and escaped me. She jumped, barefoot, into the garden. Thinking there would be hell to pay if she threw herself into the well, I jumped down into the garden after her. I caught up to her at the gate. I screamed at her. I imagine that Shiota and Kuramoto[47] were probably listening, but I couldn't check myself. I dragged Mino to her feet and grasped her hands. Then I took her to the three-mat room next to the dining room, and had her sit there. My wife, saying she would wash her feet, dashed a bucket of water from the bath over Mino's feet. She shrieked, "It's hot!" Now I screamed at my wife . . . I turned my attention back to Mino and screamed at her for having been disobedient toward my wife, and for unkindness in not having reported Kiyo's intention of leaving us. Mino tried to get out of this by saying that she thought Kiyo-chan[48] was only joking. I cursed her some more, then once again pushed her down to the tatami. I pulled her ears. And I made her apologize, first to me, then to the lady of the house. After all this, dinner was dismal.[49]

Even taking into account the severe discipline that employers of the Meiji period were likely to impose on their servants, Roka's behavior seems not merely brutal but demented. Most puzzling of all is his absolutely faithful reporting in his diary of events that most people would prefer to obliterate from their memories. There is no suggestion that Roka was confessing misdeeds of which he now felt ashamed. He did not doubt his special importance as a creative artist nor the justice of his every action. His unrelenting hatred directed at his brother and mother and his brutal treatment of women servants represented two aspects of his supreme self-importance.

Roka's uninhibited accounts of his sexual relations with his wife and his equally frank descriptions of erotic dreams lend considerable piquance to his diary, but the reader is apt to feel disappointed when reading the successive volumes of the diary. Roka's daily routine for months at a time consisted of reading the newspaper, writing his diary, and conversing with his wife. He occasionally pruned trees and otherwise cultivated his garden, and from time to time he read works of Japanese or foreign literature. This was a gentlemanly life; however, knowing Roka's earlier activities, one expects more excitement from him.

Roka kept reminding himself that he should be working: "I think I'll write something. I still haven't found what. I'd like to write something agreeable. But I can't find a title."[50] At times he even doubted that it was still in him to write anything:

> Why should I go on writing when I have no original inventions or discoveries that I must write about, no special authority? I am often puzzled as to why people feel they must write. In theory, every single person is absolutely unique in the universe, and this should mean that each person possesses something that he cannot leave to anyone else to describe; it is proper that he write about it, and he must write about it. But

regardless of the theory, it seems improbable that there is really anything that nobody but myself can do."[51]

Roka seems not to have considered that keeping a detailed diary was in effect a substitute for writing the kind of novel he vaguely hoped to write. The novel he had in mind would be a sequel to his *Kuroi Me to Chairo no Me* (Black Eyes and Brown Eyes, 1914), the autobiographical work in which he described his relations while at Dōshisha University with his teacher, the black-eyed Niijima Jō, and his first, unhappy love affair with a brown-eyed young woman. Roka had written this work very quickly, as we know from an entry in his diary for October 17, 1914:

"During the past weeks I have not even read my mail, let alone the newspaper, so intent have I been on *Black Eyes and Brown Eyes*, but I was determined to finish it today, and worked on it with absolutely undivided attention from morning on. For dinner I had some rice balls, eaten while still seated at my desk. I didn't take a bath. I finally finished it at one-thirty in the morning. Today I wrote about seventy pages of manuscript."[52]

The reception of the novel was disappointing, and Roka, like most authors, blamed the failure of the book on the publishers, vowing never to give them another manuscript. He managed to survive financially by borrowing money from other prospective publishers, but from time to time he reminded himself that he was a writer and really should be writing. On December 11, 1915, he wrote in his diary:

"It's just a year since the publication of *Black Eyes and Brown Eyes*. The months and days of the twenty-eight years since I broke loose from convention in Kyoto have also come back to me with immediacy. I would like to try looking back on my *history* since *Black Eyes* in as great detail as possible. First I will write an outline, and use it as material for self-examination."[53]

A few days later he wrote in his diary, "I began today to write the outline, notes, and topics for the history of my dissolute life since breaking away from Kyoto on February 16, 1887. I will not omit even the most depraved actions, and I don't know what sort of things will be included. I don't intend to dispose of them in any conventional way."[54]

Although there are repeated mentions in the diary of writing an outline of his "dissolute life," he seems not to have made much progress in writing a new book, as we can gather from the entry for January 24, 1916:

"Thinking of what I am to write, I set down various titles side-by-side. What am I going to write about this time? It seems likely that the final result will be something on the order of a sequel to *Mimizu*.[55] The fact is that the materials for writing about my life are still too raw to be made artistic. I must leave them to ferment a while longer. But my feelings are gradually becoming unified in the direction of writing a novel. I'm not going to rush it, nor will I neglect it."[56]

Roka was mistaken: he was not coming much closer to writing a new novel. *Fuji*, the autobiographical novel he was planning at this time, would not be serialized until 1925, and for most of the period covered by his diary Roka wrote very little else.

Roka's inability to write a novel may partly have been due to the hours he spent each day over his diary, but he may also have been too contented with his way of life to feel an urgent need to write. His satisfaction with himself was punctuated from time to time by sudden irruptions of violent anger, directed against his brother, his mother, and the many other people whom he labeled as "stupid," but on the whole his days were pleasantly uneventful, and his love for his wife is a constant theme.

There is no reason to begrudge Roka his happiness, but it is disappointing that the man who had so courageously defended Kōtoku Shūsui seems to have lost his social consciousness. In November 1915 he learned that the novelist Mushakōji Saneatsu was protesting the imminent execution of 903 Taiwanese who in July of that year had participated in an anti-Japanese uprising.[57] He wrote,

Mushakōji of the Shirakaba school[58] is protesting against the death sentences passed on the Taiwanese. I should really agree with a like spirit, but I feel myself filling with hatred whenever I can't have my own way, and this in fact makes me sympathize with the proud *authorities*, so I am in the awkward position of not being able to agree willingly. To return violence with violence—that's idiotic ... When one protests against evil, one ends by becoming a devil oneself. One has to stand on a higher plane.[59]

The next day, after reading an article on the subject by Mushakōji, Roka wrote, "He has done what I should have done."[60] But this is as far as his sense of social responsibility went. He was too busy analyzing his sexual drives (and also too busy tending his garden) to concern himself with other people. Late in November, in connection with the coronation of Emperor Taishō, there was an amnesty. Roka commented in his diary, "Nine-tenths of the eight hundred Taiwanese sentenced to death have had their sentences reduced by the amnesty issued for the coronation. That, as far as it goes, is fine."[61] One does not sense great relief or, for that matter, regret that not all the Taiwanese benefited by the amnesty.

Roka closely followed in the newspapers the coronation ceremonies in Kyoto. On the evening of November 9, as he was passing a rice paddy on his way home after doing some shopping,

To the east, black clouds like smoke or like devil's hands streamed forth and gathered in the Tokyo sky, only in a few moments to join hands over my head and make a huge black wreath. I felt extremely unpleasant. A frightening *symbol*—it brought to mind the writing on the wall in Nineveh. It seemed to me that some loathsome thing was casting an evil spell on the coronation. I felt painfully aware of the isolation of His Majesty Yoshihito.[62] Everybody thinks only of himself, and I doubt that there is a man who really is "faithful to his lord and devoted to his country."[63] I am sorry that hitherto I have taken such matters lightly and have been in a position of irresponsibility. I would like to pray with my wife for His Majesty, for Japan, and ultimately for all of humankind.[64]

Only in the last prayer does one catch a glimpse of the man who traveled to Yasnaya Polyana to meet Tolstoy. Perhaps the most puzzling aspect of Roka's diary during this period of his life is his indifference to the terrible war that was being waged in Europe. Once in a great while he alluded to the war, usually in almost farcical terms:

"A cabled report to the effect that the German kaiser is seriously ill with a throat ailment and that the crown prince and other princes have been summoned back. I don't know if this is true or false, but I think it would be a good thing if the German kaiser died."[65]

Most surprising is the minimal reaction Roka showed to the ending of a war in which ten million soldiers had died. His diary entry for November 12, 1918, mentions that on that day he studied German as usual, that he had only ten yen with which to pay the rice and charcoal merchants, that there was a major earthquake in Nagano, and that he and his wife dug sweet potatoes, peanuts, and winter potatoes.[66] There is not a word about the ending of the war. The next day's entry mentions the flight of the kaiser to Holland, followed by the comment:

"All absolutism has been overthrown by freedom; it is a judgment that the gods have won and the devils have lost. The aristocracies of Russia, Germany, and Austria have yielded to democracy, men have yielded to women. Brute force and arrogance have bowed their heads. It was a painful trial, but the world has surely been much purified by having passed through this purgatory."[67]

The tone is unpleasantly complacent. This surely was a moment for more serious reflection. Perhaps the central element in Roka's expression was the statement that "men have yielded to women." More and more the world had come to consist of only two people, Roka and the wife he devotedly served.

The most lasting impression one is likely to obtain from Roka's diary is not an appreciation of the literary talent that enabled his books to rank among the most popular of the Meiji era, nor an understanding of the fierce integrity that caused him to oppose authority, nor even of the pride that kept him from a reconciliation with his mother and brother, but of his abiding love for his wife, Aiko. This overall impression could not be foreseen at the opening of the diary, when he threatened to beat her and drive her from their home at the time of his father's death.

Even much later, he recalled in his diary, "Last autumn when we were on a trip, I looked at the back of my wife's head. She was riding in the rickshaw ahead of mine, and I can't remember how many times I cursed her and prayed in my heart she would die. It was because of her that I was suffering. Will she kill me? If not, I'll kill her."[68] Similar expressions of hatred recur, and sometimes he admitted that he had deliberately tormented her.[69]

Yet, in the end, he wanted to be only with her. Although admirers of Roka's writings constantly visited his house, hoping to meet the great man or at least to have a glimpse of his garden, he protected himself by putting up signs that he was in mourning (after his father's death), or notices such as "Indisposed. Absolutely No Visitors."[70] Roka's refusal to meet visitors meant that he and his wife spent much time alone. In the evenings they would listen to records of *jōruri*,[71] play games such as *sugoroku*,[72] paste picture postcards in albums,[73] and sing hymns together.[74] Aiko read aloud to Roka almost every evening. These quiet pleasures were enlivened by those of the bed. He had come to realize his great good fortune and was thankful: "It is a fact that recently my private life has been increasingly filled with light."[75]

Roka, at the time he wrote these words, seemed to have lost the passion that had inspired his novels and his commitment to social action, but he was joyful, and the cause of his joy was the wife to whom he had so often been unfaithful in spirit, if not quite in the flesh.

Notes

1. *Roka Nikki*, I, p. 529.
2. I have continued to call him Roka because, whatever his own wishes may have been, this is the name by which he is known to most people today.
3. *Roka*, I, p. 3.
4. *Ibid.*, p. 15.
5. *Ibid.*
6. A publishing firm that from the end of the Meiji period specialized in works by Christians. It published many of Tokutomi Roka's works, despite these harsh comments.
7. *Roka*, I, p. 229. Bun seems to have been the nickname for the editor at Kei-seisha.
8. A servant.
9. *Roka*, I, p. 227.
10. *Ibid.*, p. 403.
11. This is a round, Chinese-style fan (*uchiwa*), as opposed to the Japanese-style folding fan (*ōgi*). Yamaga is a place in Kyūshū, famous for various other things but not for its fans.
12. *Kaikon nata*, the kind of axe used in clearing forests.
13. Roka used the word *son'ō*, which is normally a term of respect for someone else's father, but context indicates it must be his own father, probably used sardonically.
14. *Roka*, I, p. 52. This violence, though unexplained, was occasioned by hatred of Sohō so intense that he hated anything connected with his brother, even his own name and their father.
15. *Ibid.*, p. 36.
16. *Ibid.*, p. 23.
17. *Ibid.*, pp. 65–66.
18. *Ibid.*, p. 68.

19. *Ibid.*, p. 501.

20. *Ibid.*, p. 422. The work by Tolstoy is "Otets Sergy" (Father Sergius).

21. *Ibid.*, p. 66.

22. *Ibid.*, p. 132.

23. *Ibid.*, p. 74.

24. *Ibid.*, p. 330.

25. *Ibid.*, p. 345.

26. *Ibid.*, p. 364.

27. *Ibid.*, p. 389.

28. *Ibid.*, p. 396.

29. *Ibid.*, p. 400.

30. *Ibid.*, p. 403.

31. Linen socks worn with a kimono.

32. *Roka*, I, p. 423.

33. *Ibid.*, p. 437.

34. *Ibid.*, p. 438.

35. *Ibid.*, p. 448.

36. *Ibid.*

37. *Ibid.*, p. 460.

38. *Ibid.*, p. 461.

39. *Ibid.*, p. 475.

40. *Ibid.*, p. 473.

41. *Ibid.*, p. 522.

42. *Ibid.*, p. 505.

43. *Ibid.*, II, p. 29.

44. *Ibid.*, p. 31.

45. *Ibid.*, p. 35.

46. *Ibid.*

47. The neighbors.

48. Kiyo-chan is a diminutive or affectionate way of referring to Kiyo.

49. *Roka*, II, pp. 66–67.

50. *Ibid.*, p. 92.

51. *Ibid.*, p. 144.

52. *Ibid.*, I, p. 176. Roka wrote seventy pages of *genkō yōshi*, or manuscript paper with space for four hundred characters. Ten pages a day is a more usual number for most Japanese writers.

53. *Ibid.*, II, p. 205. The word "history" is in English in the original.

54. *Ibid.*, p. 209.

55. A collection of essays entitled *Mimizu no Tawagoto* (Silly Talk of an Earthworm) was published in 1913.
56. *Roka*, II, pp. 302–3.
57. Japan seized possession of Taiwan after victory in the Sino-Japanese War of 1894–95.
58. The Shirakaba school was a group of writers, mainly graduates of the Peers' School, who stood for humanism and idealism. For an account of their activities, see my *Dawn to the West*, I, pp. 441–500.
59. *Roka*, II, p. 133. The original text gives *authority* in English, but I have made the word plural to agree with normal usage.
60. *Ibid.*, p. 134.
61. *Ibid.*, p. 148.
62. Yoshihito was the personal name of Emperor Taishō. "His Majesty Yoshihito" is something of an overtranslation for *Yoshihito no kimi*.
63. The formula in Japanese is *chūkun aikoku*.
64. *Roka*, II, p. 136.
65. *Ibid.*, p. 231.
66. *Ibid.*, VII, p. 365.
67. *Ibid.*, p. 366.
68. *Ibid.*, I, p. 73.
69. *Ibid.*, p. 307.
70. *Ibid.*, II, p. 88.
71. See *ibid.*, pp. 155, 266.
72. Something like backgammon.
73. *Roka*, II, p. 176.
74. *Ibid.*, p. 128.
75. *Ibid.*, p. 287.

Bibliography

Keene, Donald. *Dawn to the West*, 2 vols. New York: Holt, Rinehart and Winston, 1984.
Roka Nikki, 7 vols. Tokyo: Chikuma Shobō, 1985–86.

The Diaries of
Kinoshita Mokutarō

The diaries of Kinoshita Mokutarō[1] (1885–1945), like those of Tokutomi Roka, are incomplete. Although the early years of his life are so amply described that we are likely to feel we know him well, there follows a gap of some years, and when the diary resumes Mokutarō seems like a different man, leaving us to wonder what had caused the change.

The first diary opens on July 13, 1901. Mokutarō was only sixteen at the time, but he wrote with precocious maturity. He had been studying in Tokyo and was about to return for the summer to his home at Itō on the Izu Peninsula. He normally took a train as far as Kōzu, then a steamship to Itō, but this time he arrived too late for the boat and had to walk most of the way home. The only interest of this brief diary is his awareness, expressed here and there, that he has changed in some way from the boy who used to make the same journey. When he finally returned home, he did not feel quite as excited as he had expected,

"If I had been writing about this place last year or the year before, I would have written in terms of unbearable joy, and I would have buried this diary under an avalanche of adjectives, but having become more accustomed to the world, I have lost the pure thoughts of the past. That is unfortunate if one chooses to regard it so, but it is what people call wisdom."[2]

Mokutarō's first sustained diary, begun in 1903, is called *Kōshin Nikki* (Kōshin Diary).[3] Its conscious literary intent is revealed in the opening words:

"I know not whence I have come, nor how it was I was born, but this is where I am, and the universe stretches out before me. And is it not plain what it is incumbent on me to do in this situation?"[4]

The tone is painfully earnest, in the manner of the young Kunikida Doppo (and no doubt the young Tokutomi Roka in the diaries he destroyed). The diary is marked by bouts of self-examination and by exhortations to himself:

"I have had a self-awakening now. I have sworn in my heart. Oh, what manner of person am I? Am I not a miserable weakling? But here am I. And here is the universe. How could there not be a connection between the universe and myself? I pray that I may leave my footprints, however faintly, in one corner of it."[5]

Mokutarō goes on to state his reasons for keeping this record of his life and his anticipation of reading the diary on the last day of the year, when he will address it in this fashion: "My diary! When, for example, my voice has echoed in the mountains at dusk, it seems to rebound from you, speaking to me sadly, frighteningly, strengthlessly. Or, when on a bright morning a song has escaped my lips, you send back the song so powerfully it is unrecognizable as my voice. Diary, you are a strange echo. What I have written is myself, and at the same time, you are my judge."[6]

Mokutarō also considered the appropriate manner and content for his diary:

"This morning I spent at home. I took out the diaries I have kept up till now, wrapped them in paper, and put them in a wooden box. Then I considered what kind of diary I should write in this notebook. My conclusion was that I should not write it too carefully—that is, if I am excessively concerned with form and fear to smudge the writing, the diary will at once bog down. The most important thing is not to deceive myself, and to write down without fail the title of a book and my impressions after having read it."[7]

Throughout the early diaries Mokutarō displayed an intense self-absorption that may at times strike contemporary readers as comic, but there is no mistaking the desperate seriousness of this young man. His main problem at this time (and until much later in life) was his choice of profession. He was studying medicine in Tokyo, but it gave him no pleasure and he even doubted its worth:

"What is the value of medicine, the career on which I am now embarked? Death is eternal and cannot be held back by the physician's hands. People cannot obtain peace of mind from a physician."[8]

At times he thought he wanted to become an artist, at other times a literary career appealed even more, but in the end he yielded to his family's wishes and became a doctor. One can easily imagine such scenes being reenacted today in Japan and in many other countries, but Mokutarō differed from most young men who reluctantly follow a career that their natural inclinations make them resist. He had a distinguished career as a doctor—and was also an accomplished poet, playwright, and essayist.

By way of preparing for a career as a physician, Mokutarō was sent to a middle school where he learned German from the age of thirteen. A love for the German language and German literature remained with him throughout his life. German was, of course, highly useful to anyone studying medicine, but Mokutarō's diary seldom mentions medical books. Instead, one finds such entries as one written in February 1904, when he was at the German High School: "If when studying German, I read, for example, *Werthers Leiden* or *Hermann & Dorothea etc.*, it makes me rather happy, but when I get to zoology and mathematics, the happiness goes away at once."[9] As early as February 1905 he wrote entire entries in German, and as his knowledge of the language improved, the German entries became longer. By the end of 1909 more of the diary entries are in German than Japanese. Mokutarō also knew English, and studied French diligently in 1910 when he recorded such polyglot entries as: "*Kai ni wa Fujishima Takeji shi kuru. L'Expression des yeux ga etwas Europaeisch.*" (Mr. Fujishima Takeji came to the meeting. The expression in his eyes is somehow European.) The first sentence is in Japanese. The second begins in French, but includes the Japanese subject particle *ga*, then ends in German.[10]

Mokutarō's use of foreign words was probably not intended to prevent other people from reading his diary; the sentiments expressed in German were no more secret than those in Japanese. Under the date February 8, 1905, he wrote an entry that begins: "I had my hair cut at the school barbershop for four sen. In the noon recess I went to Baigetsu. That was because Professor Natsume [Sōseki] was not teaching today." After a few more lines in a similarly low-keyed vein there is a blank space followed by:

> To tell the truth, the above was written on the evening of Saturday, March 4. I did it after reading a book that had strongly moved me. My diary has fallen a month behind the date mentioned and that is why up to now I have always written it from notes, recalling what had happened without much excitement. I would like as soon as possible to write the diary on the date given. I must also mention that hitherto I have kept certain things secret from my diary and I have ornamented other things, just as if I were taking necessary precautions before showing the diary to other people. But nothing could be more stupid. I intend, beginning on one day in March 1905, to write the truth, just as it is. It may happen that a diary written in this manner will become a description of my crimes, but is not the truth absolute? But this cannot be done until my diary and the date are in agreement.[11]

But even when his diary had caught up with the date, he was still dissatisfied with its style: "Is it that I intend to show this diary to other people? How else to explain the many things I have hidden, the enormous number of decorations of the facts? Even though you may hide things before other people or yourself, what is there to hide before the Absolute?"[12]

Probably Mokutarō originally decided to write parts of his diary in German in order to improve his proficiency in the language, but he gave another reason immediately following a lengthy entry in German that described leaving home by ship on his way to Tokyo:

"With these thoughts in mind, I watched as the ship left behind the coast of my native place. I decided that, rather than describe in excessively clear Japanese how the sight was reflected in other people's eyes and in my own, I would describe it in the unfamiliar language of a distant country. Even while I was busy writing in this manner, the ship arrived in Ajiro."[13]

The use of a foreign language enabled Mokutarō to maintain a distance between himself and the raw emotions aroused by parting. Anyone who has learned a foreign language well has surely found it easier—or, at any event, more appropriate—at times to express certain thoughts in that language, not because his own lacks sufficient vocabulary, but because the language of everyday speech seems somehow inadequate to describe special experiences. Mokutarō's choice of German was natural in view of his schooling, but German was also the special language of elite students at that time and even much later. Almost everyone who had attended middle school knew at least a little English, but German was learned as a second foreign language, just at the time when students were likely to be first awakening to the beauty of literature. Medical students are always kept busy with required courses, but Mokutarō found the time to attend lectures on German literature, and often mentioned works he was currently reading. These works surely influenced the style and even the content of his diary.

Although Mokutarō insisted that he meant his diary to be unadulterated truth and not a literary work, a literary bias is apparent in his descriptions of, say, nature as he observed it during the walking tours of Izu and the Bōshū Peninsula. At first he seems to have traveled in the manner of those in the past who had gone from one *utamakura*[14] to the next, but his first visit to Bōshū disillusioned him; he soon discovered that nothing in the landscape recalled Bakin's *Satomi Hakkenden*,[15] the best-known literary work set in that region. He wrote,

> It was difficult for me to recover the emotions aroused by *Hakkenden* in what I had seen of Bōshū. Yesterday I thought that the *naiveté* of the past still lingered, but today, having become accustomed to the place, I doubted even that much is left. Or rather, I thought that it was an even more superficial canvas than the city. I have obtained nothing at all from this journey.
>
> Tomi-san is an absolutely ordinary mountain. There is not a trace of mystery in its appearance ... There are no descriptions of scenery in *Hakkenden*. I wonder if Bakin ever actually saw Bōshū.[16]

Mokutarō soon changed his mind about Bōshū. Probably the happiest of his many journeys was the one he took to Chōshi on the Bōshū coast in August 1905. His account, though recorded in the manner of a diary, consists of nineteen numbered sections, suggesting that he thought of each as a prose poem with its own theme. Mokutarō, after considerable hesitation, had decided to visit his friend Ishizu Hiroshi who lived in Chōshi. When once he had made up his mind to go, he was filled with joy:

> I have made up my mind at last. What good would it do me to spend a day over an introduction to philosophy? I decided not to go hear *Tannhäuser*, which is to be performed tonight at Hibiya Hall. I will go straight off to see my friend ... I put on an unlined *kasuri* kimono[17] and a *hakama*. I don't like the regulation student's cap, so I wore a funny-looking "wood-shaving" hat. On the way I stopped the rickshaw and bought a box of

sponge cake at Okano . . . The whole world had become beautiful in my eyes, and it also looked brand-new. I felt sorry for
the rickshaw man, sweating in the morning sunlight, and I
gave him a couple of sen extra.[18]

Mokutarō described what he saw, what he did, and even what he
wore with a precision rare in diaries of the time. Most Meiji diarists
tended instead to devote their attention to what they thought or felt,
but Mokutarō, as a gifted amateur painter, never ignored the visual
aspect of his experiences. The train journey to Chōshi itself was not
especially interesting:

"The scenery of this whole region consists of nothing but unbroken expanses of green fields, and the roofs of the villages glimpsed
through breaks in the rows of oaks. The sky is simply blue, the clouds
are simply white. I was glad that I had brought with me a copy of Turgenev's prose poems, and thought I would break the monotony by
reading. The first work in the collection portrays the peaceful countryside at harvest time. I read it with the deepest of pleasure."[19]

Mokutarō was able to transcend the actual experience of the
monotonous landscape of the Bōshū Peninsula by visualizing it in
terms of what Turgenev had written. This pleased him, though his
impatience to see his friend again may have made the landscape seem
drearier than it was in reality.

The boring journey was forgotten as soon as Mokutarō reached
Chōshi: "I arrived at the long-awaited Chōshi station. The time was a
little before three in the afternoon. Ah, was this not the town where
my dear friend was born?"[20]

He found his way to the friend's house with the aid of directions
from a policeman, but was informed that Ishizu had gone fishing and
had not yet returned. But Ishizu's father soon appeared. This first
meeting was a tense occasion for Mokutarō:

"I made my greeting to the master of the house on the occasion of
our first meeting. What did I say? How did I bow? (My elder brother
has frequently taken me to task for my bad manners.) I was thanked

by the master of the house for having shared a room with my friend and for having looked after him when he was ill, and he told me he felt we were traveling together on the same path through the world. In response to this, I said a number of times that I had not been able to do all I should, and apologized."[21]

This quite ordinary scene must have taken place many thousands of times in Japan during 1905, but its very ordinariness gives it charm. We can all but see the boy bowing and reciting the formulas of Japanese daily etiquette, leading up to an apology—an apology always made, regardless of the circumstances—for not having done enough for his friend. The entry continues:

> My friend's mother brought tea and I was greeted by her. Both of them are quite different from what I had imagined. I noted from the first brief glance the black hair of his father and his mother's gentle features. I had imagined that his father would be a very big, rather bald man . . . I sensed something stern behind the kindly face of the master of the house, and it made me feel rather ill at ease, but as the conversation proceeded, I could tell how much the father loved his son, and I couldn't keep a smile from crossing my face. I was able to understand completely all the points in my friend's makeup that had eluded me before.[22]

Ishizu's younger sister appeared with a *yukata* and informed Mokutarō that the bath was now free. He relates, "Wanting to wait until my friend returned, I declined, and remained in the room. My friend's mother, opening the shoji behind me, urged me not to wait. When she called me, instead of using 'Ōta-san,' she said 'Masao-san,' making me feel extremely happy, as if I had heard music from the past."[23]

Ishizu returned later from fishing. He had not been informed of Mokutarō's arrival, and the latter waited impatiently for him.

"It was dusk and the lamps had already been lit when my friend came in after his bath. He was sunburned, and his body, red from the bath, was wrapped in a boldly striped *yukata*. He greeted me casually in a voice that was almost too loud for the room. We did nothing but laugh—there were no words."[24]

The joy of the two friends is well conveyed, and the reader gets a vivid impression of Ishizu from his loud, unceremonious greetings and even from the bold stripes of his *yukata*. The scene is given poignance if read in conjunction with diary entries written six months later, when a rift occurred between the two young men, who were then sharing a house with two other students. Ishizu finally walked out, arousing this reaction from Mokutarō: "It was extremely unpleasant. Why it happened, I have no idea. All I know is that it started with Ishizu's leaving. His every action, his every word, and even his apologies were infuriating."[25]

Apparently, Ishizu's lack of consideration for the others in the house disillusioned Mokutarō. This possibility could not have been foreseen by the two young men as they hiked through the country-side around Chōshi. They climbed a hill overlooking the town, and Mokutarō recalled:

"I have heard that whenever Goethe on his Italian journey arrived at a town, he always climbed to the top of a tower. That was in an old country, celebrated for its arts; this is nothing more that a town on the seacoast, but the best way to see the whole and to obtain a rounded impression is to climb to a high place and to look below."[26]

Mokutarō had frequently boasted to his friends about the beauty of his native Itō, but having seen the beauty of Chōshi, he was now at a loss for words to praise Itō. He also reflected as he looked down from the heights, "If, standing here, I should jump, even if the wind did not erase my footprints, my body would never be discovered by human eyes. In peaceful Itō, when I searched in fun for a place where someone could kill himself, I never succeeded in finding one. I could not now keep from smiling."[27]

❖   ❖   ❖

It is hard not to be attracted to the Mokutarō of the early diaries. He was perhaps a bit too earnest, but if this is a fault, it is easily forgiven, and Japanese today who are the age he was when he wrote the diary may feel nostalgic for a time when students read Goethe and searched in their souls for confirmation of his every opinion. Less admirable, perhaps, was Mokutarō's unspoken conviction that he belonged to a superior class of human beings. On August 15, 1905, for example, he wrote a friend,

> I read yesterday afternoon your most recent letter. As soon as I finished reading it, I wanted to reply at once, while I was still under its spell, but a meeting of the "Itō Society of Local Friends" prevented this.
>
> Cursed be the "Itō Society of Local Friends"! Over twenty people assembled, all of them born in the same town and most of them graduates of the same school. What does it mean not to have even one friend with whom to "unbosom oneself" and beyond that, to converse about matters from the depths of one's *Herz*? At the meeting, believe it or not, they choose the "Three Champions"; the latest sleeper, the biggest womanizer, the man fondest of geishas! And they themselves don't feel in the slightest ashamed of taking part in such nonsense. Ah, to what should I, who do not believe in any god, swear—that from now on I will open a path for myself through *Alltagmenschen*.[28]

Such utterances make Mokutarō seem rather a prig, but as anyone knows who has attended a similar gathering, the intellectual level is deplorable, and deserving of this criticism. But five years later Mokutarō would of his own free will be attending meetings of the *Pan no Kai* (Devotees of Pan), at which boasting of one's exploits with women was normal. The difference Mokutarō seems to have found between the Itō Society of Local Friends and the Devotees of Pan was probably not so much in the subjects of conversation or their intellectual level as in the elite composition of the latter—all men known in the world of literature and the arts.

Mokutarō's transition from a serious student to a Devotee of Pan took place between 1906 and 1909. His diary for 1906 breaks off on August 2, and the next diary opens on January 1, 1909. During the three years between the two diaries, Mokutarō began his career as a writer; met Mori Ōgai, who would greatly influence him; and first associated with the members of the Devotees of Pan as well as with the editors of the literary magazines *Myōjō* and *Subaru*.

Even once the diary was resumed the entries are terse, more like memos to himself than the literary compositions of his earlier diaries. On January 9, for example, the entire entry consists of these sentences:

"Went to the Devotees of Pan. At seven o'clock I finished with that and went to the poetry meeting at Mr. Mori's Kanchōrō. It was snowing. Returned after ten."[29] On January 17, he wrote, "This afternoon about two I went to Ishikawa Takuboku's lodgings. Yoshii was there."[30] What I would not give for a lengthy description of Mokutarō's impressions of Takuboku! His fullest account of Takuboku is contained in the entry for April 4: "In the afternoon Ishikawa Takuboku came. He seemed to be suffering a bit from *Geldmangel*. [31] I lent him one [yen?]. We went out together to Hongō-dōri."

He noted in the margin, "Lent Oskar Wilde to Ishikawa."[32] His descriptions of meetings with other famous men are even briefer: "I visited Mr. Mori. He laughed ha-ha-ha-ha-ha."[33] Mokutarō writes as casually about Mori Ōgai as about any drinking partner at the Devotees of Pan, even when the matter is of importance to the historian of literature: "In the evening I visited Dr. Mori, and received a manuscript. It is called 'Half a Day.'"[34]

Mokutarō seems to have become a different person between 1906 and 1909, but some of the entries in German (as when he described finding Ishizu in a drunken state)[35] indicate that somewhere within, perhaps accessible only through the medium of a foreign language, the Mokutarō of the earlier diaries lingered.

❖ ❖ ❖

On May 27, 1921, Ōta Masao, professor of medicine at the Tokyo Imperial University, set sail from Yokohama. His destination was Paris,
but he was going by way of America. In addition to his regular diary,
which at this time consisted mainly of terse mentions of people with
whom he had dinner or meetings he attended, he began to keep another with the title *Ōbei Nikki* (Europe and America Diary). Perhaps
he expected that this diary, because of its unusual setting, would be as
literary as the diaries he had kept as a young man. The entries are in
fact more detailed and more revealing of his personality than in his
diaries of the previous dozen years, but he was not only older but also
less impressionable than in the past, as the opening entry reveals:

"After four or five tempestuously busy days, today at last I am to
depart. Rain started in the morning. Even as I looked from the train
window at the senior acquaintances, friends, loved ones, women, and
suchlike people who had come to see me off, I was not much stirred,
no doubt because I have become accustomed to travel."[36]

In the other diary he kept at the time he mentioned the names of
the people who had seen him off. Some, judging from their names
and professions, had said goodbye to Professor Ōta, but the friends
from the literary world and the "women" (identified by names that
indicate they were geishas) were probably taking leave of Kinoshita
Mokutarō, the celebrated poet and dramatist.

It is disappointing that Mokutarō did not feel greater excitement at
the prospect of visiting America and Europe but, as he wrote, he was
already much traveled, not only in Japan but also in Korea and China.
In 1916 he had been appointed professor and director of the dermato-
logical department of the South Manchuria Medical School in Muk-
den. During his stay in China he studied Buddhist and other Chinese
art, but the only items of interest in the diary he kept at this time (written almost entirely in German) are his sketches of scenery and people.
He later wrote essays describing the places he had visited, but the diary
was not the medium he chose for expressing his most personal or liter-

ary reflections. Only occasionally does one find fragmentary statements that are suggestive of his state of mind, as in the entry for April 21, 1921, written in a mixture of Japanese and French: "*Le sentiment de solitude*. A fate of going from one journey to another."[37]

The diary kept aboard ship on the way to America was in what had become his accustomed manner—notations that seem to have been intended to remind him of experiences or conversations that he did not feel like recording in full. However, he mentioned what he ate and drank each day, and such diversions as sketching the other passengers. He landed in Seattle and traveled by rail to San Francisco, where he dutifully attended a museum. He also had a Japanese meal at the Japanese Club. Readers who remember how desperately the first Japanese visitors to San Francisco yearned for Japanese food would no doubt welcome some comment from Mokutarō about what he ate, or even a word to suggest he was glad sashimi was available so far from home, but he passes over the meal in silence. When he stopped in Los Angeles, he ate lunch in a cafeteria, and this is described in detail, including his comment, "For us it was shaming to have to carry the trays ourselves."[38]

Mokutarō visited various American cities on his journey across the continent. His diary rarely suggests he was interested in anything he saw. Even Niagara Falls failed to elicit a comment. One is apt to conclude that although Mokutarō was only thirty-six, he had waited too long to travel to the West.

Mokutarō found nothing to admire in Boston, and the day he reached New York (July 5) it was so hot that the city seemed to him "exactly like hell."[39] One gets the impression that he was, in any case, resolved not to like anything; he had apparently lost interest in the industrialized countries of the West.

From New York he sailed to Havana. His only shipboard comment was: "Spanish sounds like the beating of a drum or, rather, a banging on a piece of corrugated iron, *geräusch*, or sometimes like lisping. (The accent rather resembles Korean. Can't understand it.)"[40]

The tropical vegetation of Cuba produced a more favorable impression, and Havana under the summer sun recalled the poetry of José María de Heredia, a French poet who was born in Cuba.

"The afternoon streets presented an appearance reminiscent of the violence and, at the same time, the stillness found in lines of José María de Heredia's poetry. The strength of the sun overpowers the yellowish buildings and streets, and is so awesome that not a single thing makes a noise."[41]

These lines provide proof that Mokutarō was capable of evincing interest in his surroundings, providing they were sufficiently exotic. If his *Europe and America Diary* were entirely in this style, it would be of literary merit, but such passages are rare.

Mokutarō reached Paris, his destination, on October 26, 1921, and remained in Europe, mainly in Paris, for almost three years. He wrote little in his diary about his studies, though he does mention the books he read to improve his French, the museums he visited, the performances he saw at the Opéra and at the Folies Bergère, the concerts and plays he attended. He attended a mass at the Madeleine, and heard lectures at the Sorbonne on the history of Japanese literature.[42] He ate at several expensive restaurants. In short, he did everything one would expect of an intelligent visitor to Paris. The only thing missing from his diaries is enthusiasm.

Mokutarō made a mistake when he decided to study in Paris. Vienna (which he liked) or some other German-speaking city would have been more suited to tastes formed in his boyhood days. But perhaps coming to Europe had been a mistake from the start. In a letter included in the diary entry for July 9, 1923, he wrote,

> To the young person who spends four or five days in Paris after a stay in Europe, it seems to be an absolutely marvelous place. But to tell the truth, I am tired of Europe. Especially of Paris. I thought I would try with all my strength—rather like clinging with great effort to a slippery rock—to enter the life

here (mainly the world of natural sciences), but whenever I thought I had achieved some little success, the waves came and made my hands slip from the rock. I am tired of making such efforts and when presently I leave, the others, who think of me as a completely unnecessary foreign object, will probably be much as they were before I came.

French culture is completely self-sufficient. This point is truly remarkable. And it is for this reason that the French are indifferent to every other culture . . . Foreign culture, as far as they are concerned, is a *curiosité*. Not long ago there was an exhibition here of Japanese art that created quite a sensation, but to these gourmets it was no more than a mere *curiosité*.[43]

Again, he writes,

I became fond of Western literature rather early, but now that I am at its source, I feel how extremely oriental I am . . . It sometimes happens that friends of mine in Japan who are younger than I write me letters couched in terms of how much they envy my being in Paris. Paris! Paris where more than 130 young painters, living in a state of ecstasy, converse about painting and women! Try to imagine someone in Paris who trudges through the streets, a morose look always on his unprepossessing, yellow face . . . A floppy overcoat long enough to conceal his ankles—a face broader than his shoulders—and (even more prominent) cheekbones that jut from his face—and little eyes, which, if you look at them carefully, seem even more cunning than those of a Japanese sparrow . . . Eyes mainly searching either for some hidden, easy-to-imitate originality—or else for somewhere to find a woman, one or the other—the yellowish brown of a drunken jaundice patient—left shoulder raised, back bent, protruding front teeth, Tom Thumb.[44]

This expression of self-hatred, or, at any rate, hatred for the Japanese abroad, recalls passages in Natsume Sōseki's diary or the poem *Netsuke no Kuni* (The Land of Netsuke) by Takamura Kōtarō.[45] I recall also Arthur Koestler's *The Lotus and the Robot*, an account of his travels in India and Japan, that concluded with the observation that the journey, far from being enriching, had impoverished him. Kinoshita Mokutarō seems to have reached the same conclusion.

Notes

1. He was also widely known by his real name, Ōta Masao.
2. Ōta Masao, *Kinoshita Mokutarō Nikki*, I, p. 4.
3. *Kōshin* was the cyclical designation for the year 1903.
4. Ōta, *Kinoshita*, I, p. 17.
5. *Ibid.*
6. *Ibid.*, pp. 17–18.
7. *Ibid.*, p. 18.
8. *Ibid.*, p. 36.
9. *Ibid.*, p. 49.
10. *Ibid.*, II, p. 3.
11. *Ibid.*, I, pp. 137–38.
12. *Ibid.*, p. 152.
13. *Ibid.*, p. 231.
14. A site celebrated in poetry.
15. An extremely long romance written between 1814 and 1842 by Takizawa Bakin (1767–1848). The title means literally, "Biographies of the Eight Dogs of Satomi." The "eight dogs" are men whose surnames begin with the word *inu* (dog) and who are descendants of the same noble dog.
16. Ōta, *Kinoshita*, I, p. 163.
17. *Kasuri* is a kind of cloth, typically of hemp or cotton, with patterns of reserved white against a dark blue ground. It was often used for *yukata*, the summer kimono.
18. Ōta, *Kinoshita*, I, p. 237.
19. *Ibid.*, p. 238.

20. *Ibid.*

21. *Ibid.*, p. 240.

22. *Ibid.*

23. *Ibid.*, p. 242. It would be normal to call a young man of Mokutarō's age by his surname. Ishizu's mother calls him instead by his personal name, a privilege reserved for someone who has known him from childhood. Mokutarō used the word *kyūon* (old music). This word may have been of his invention, referring to the well-known Chinese story of the man who broke his lute when his friend died, because he was sure nobody would now be able to understand his music.

24. *Ibid.*

25. *Ibid.*, p. 330.

26. *Ibid.*, p. 248.

27. *Ibid.*, p. 250.

28. *Ibid.*, p. 259.

29. *Ibid.*, p. 364. Kanchōrō was the name Mori Ōgai gave to his house, where he regularly held meetings to compose poetry.

30. *Ibid.*, p. 366. Yoshii Isamu (1886–1960) was a well-known tanka poet.

31. A farcical name for the sickness called lack of money.

32. Ōta, *Kinoshita*, I, p. 376.

33. *Ibid.*, p. 366.

34. *Ibid.*, p. 369. The story, "Hannichi," treats the strained relations betwen Ōgai's mother and wife. The latter prevented the story from being published until 1951. See above, p. 313; also, my *Dawn to the West*, I, p. 358–59.

35. Ōta, *Kinoshita*, I, p. 398.

36. *Ibid.*, II, p. 329.

37. *Ibid.*, p. 292.

38. *Ibid.*, p. 333.

39. *Ibid.*, p. 335.

40. *Ibid.*, p. 313.

41. *Ibid.*, p. 338.

42. *Ibid.*, p. 367. The lectures were given by Michel Revon, known especially for his *Anthologie de la littérature japonaise des origines au XXème siècle* (1910).

43. *Ibid.*, p. 409.

44. *Ibid.*, pp. 410–11. In this translation the ellipses and dashes do not indicate omissions but follow the original text. "Tom Thumb" is a translation of *issun bōshi*.

45. Translated in my *Modern Japanese Literature*, p. 206.

Bibliography

Keene, Donald. *Dawn to the West*, 2 vols. New York: Holt, Rinehart and Winston, 1984.

_____. Modern Japanese Literature. New York: Grove Press, 1956.

Ōta Masao. *Kinoshita Mokutarō Nikki*, 5 vols. Tokyo: Iwanami Shoten, 1979–80.

The Diaries of Nagai Kafū

Seiyū Nisshi Shō (Selections from the Diary of a Journey to the West) consists of extracts made by Nagai Kafū from the diary he kept between September 1903 and March 1908. It opens as Kafū (1879–1959) was about to board ship for America. He was bound for Tacoma in the state of Washington, where his father, a banker, had a business acquaintance with whom Kafū was to stay. Kafū's overpowering love for French literature had impelled him to beg his father to send him to France, but the father, fearful that the temptations of Paris might confirm Kafū in his dissolute ways, insisted he go to America instead. Kafū reluctantly obeyed, hoping that he might be able to go on to France from there.

Tacoma proved to be a pleasant little city. Kafū wrote in his diary, "The quiet of the town pleases me especially." He took walks in a park where he caught glimpses of Mount Rainier. "The local Japanese call it Tacoma Fuji. It rises through the clouds, capped with snow. The scenery here is extremely beautiful."[1] When he went by train to Seattle a week later, he reported, "The scenery along the way was lovely enough to make one forget the loneliness of travel."

Nothing in the diary indicates that Kafū had already commenced making the survey of Japanese society in America that would take artistic form in his *Amerika Monogatari* (Tales of America, 1908). The literary experiences recorded in the diary are confined to mentions of his readings (in English) of various now-forgotten novels. He confessed his desire to write a romance (*denki shōsetsu*) and expressed dissatisfaction with the colloquial style he had used in his Naturalist writings. He declared, "Perhaps it is because I am now living abroad that of late I have somehow found it hard to stop thinking about the special flavor of the old writings, so rich in artistic effect. I take from my suitcase such works as *The Tale of the Heike* and *A Tale of Flowering Fortunes* and read them at night by the fire."[2] His nostalgia for Japan did not take the usual form of missing friends or longing for Japanese food but instead of yearning for the beauty of the old literature.

Kafū referred to Japan only occasionally in this diary. He noted, for example, the outbreak of the Russo-Japanese War, but without comment. He wrote with greater feeling about the death of Saitō Ryokuu in April 1904, no doubt because it seemed to signify the end of an epoch:

"The newspapers and magazines I have been sent from Japan all report the death of Saitō Ryokuu. As I read the accounts I felt a sadness that was definitely not that of a total stranger—sadness that Ryokuu's life had been a tragedy created by his own character. Ah, I thought, the last man to delight in the Edo pleasure quarters as a connoisseur of their charms had in the end been unable to survive the struggle for existence of twentieth-century society."[3]

In October 1904 Kafū traveled to St. Louis with some other Japanese to see the fair. He wrote not one word about what he saw, possibly because the long train journey had exhausted him, but more likely because he was more attracted to the past than to the vision of the future presented by the fair. He stayed for a while in a village some fifteen miles from St. Louis, where he wrote, "The mooing of the cows and the crowing of roosters are extremely peaceful. For no particular reason, I enjoy hearing these sounds."[4] For the city-bred Kafū even the mooing of cows seemed agreeably exotic.

Kafū had intended to go from St. Louis to New Orleans: "I have always loved southern ways, and that is why I wanted to go south, following the flow of the Mississippi River. I planned to enter Louisiana University. When I heard that even now there are many French people living there, and that they use the French language in their daily conversations, I was extremely eager to go, but people warned me not to, saying the climate was unhealthy. I had no choice but to head north instead."[5]

Kafū ended up in Kalamazoo, Michigan, where he studied at the local college for about six months. At first he was appalled by the cold, but after he gradually grew accustomed to the rigors of the northern winter, he wrote in his diary, "The dream of a beautiful, fragrant, fan-shaped city has at last faded from my heart, and I have come to enjoy instead a snowbound life of absolute tranquillity."[6]

For a brief interval in a life otherwise spent in great cities, Kafū felt the quiet charm of a small town. He would lovingly describe it in his *Tales of America*.

Kafū left Kalamazoo in June 1905 with lingering affection for the town. From there he traveled to various places where he had acquaintances in the eastern part of the United States, including New York, where he placed an advertisement in a newspaper announcing that he was looking for work.[7] He had no luck there, but negotiations to end the Russo-Japanese War were about to begin, and the Japanese Legation in Washington needed help. He eventually found a job there as an errand boy. Kafū wanted more than ever to go to France, but his father continued to disapprove. Despairing of ever winning his father's consent, he wrote,

"Ah, nothing can be agreed on between my father and myself. Why should I, who have grown accustomed to failure and disappointment, be surprised or lament at this late date? Sooner or later I shall leave Washington and hide myself in some alley in New York, never to return to Japan again."[8]

One evening while he was still in Washington, feeling sorry for himself, he went to a bar. As he sat at a table drinking a cocktail, the woman sitting next to him struck up a conversation, and before long they were strolling together along the Potomac. Then, "at her invitation, I went to her house."[9] This was the beginning of Kafū's affair with a prostitute named Edyth. She fell genuinely in love with him, and it was with regret that he left Washington when, the peace treaty with Russia having been signed, the legation no longer needed his services. He related in his diary how he broke the news to Edyth:

> I suggested we go into the park. As we walked along a deserted path, the moonlight filtering through treetops that had begun to lose their leaves was misted over. There was no wind that night, and the strong fragrance of the cosmetics she wore made me think I was in a garden where roses bloomed on a spring night. When presently I informed her that I would be leaving the city and going to New York, she said nothing for a while, but merely kicked angrily and noisily with the point of her narrow shoes at the leaves that had fallen and accumulated. Suddenly she threw her arms around me and, embracing me tightly, said in a voice clouded with tears, "Then you must come to my place every night from tonight on. I probably won't be able to follow you, much as I'd like to, but please come to see me every day without fail until the day we must part." So saying, she pressed her face closely against my chest.[10]

Kafū added the comment, "Ah, there is nothing harder to predict than a person's fate." Neither he nor Edyth foresaw that they would ever meet again. Kafū intended to get a job as a live-in servant in New York and save enough money to travel to France, but after various disappointments while job-hunting, he received a letter from his father informing him that he had arranged a job for Kafū as a probationary office worker at the New York branch of the Yokohama Specie Bank. Kafū's first thought was that it would be easy to travel from New York to Washington to see Edyth: "We will be able to meet again and get drunk on hot kisses."[11] His next thought, however, was that working in a bank might take him away from a literary career. He made this resolve: "Literature is my life. Even though I have no choice, for family reasons, but to be employed in a bank, I must devote every possible moment to the study of literature." He added, "When I think that for a time I have been obliged to separate myself from literature, I feel as if I have committed some sort of sin, as if I have sunk into an abyss of deep degradation. There is not a ray of light in my heart."

Kafū did not foresee that his experiences in America, even those at furthest remove from literature, would provide him with the materials for his first masterpiece, *Tales of America*.

The day after he arrived in New York, Kafū went to the opera. At the time there were two major opera houses in New York, the Metropolitan and the Manhattan, and Kafū regularly attended performances at both. This was the golden age of opera in New York, when great singers, including the immortal Caruso, sang every night. Kafū wrote little about most of the performances he heard, but he was evidently impressed by *Tristan und Isolde*: "Today Wagner's *Tristan* was performed. I rushed there from the bank as soon as I could. I was deeply moved, and I felt as if I had been able to intuit some of what Wagner had meant by his profound ideal of capturing in music the highest beauty of poetry. Enveloped in boundless joy and hope, I returned to my humble lodgings."[12] *Tristan* is not easy to appreciate on first hearing, but Kafū's comment demonstrates how responsive he was to this magnificent music-drama.

Kafū was fortunate also in having been able to see Sarah Bernhardt perform in New York. He recorded in his diary, "Posters announcing the forthcoming American tour of the celebrated French actress Sarah Bernhardt have driven me wild with excitement a week before the actual performances."[13] He saw Bernhardt first in *Phèdre*, then a week later in Sardou's *Sorcière*. He wrote,

"When I first conceived the idea of going abroad, it was because I wanted to see Western plays performed. Comments on the theater that are based (like the empty theories of certain persons) exclusively on books are of no use whatsoever. Ah, I have been fortunate enough to have been able to see with my own eyes the artistry of the greatest *Tragédienne* in the world. My aim in making the long voyage has been realized."[14]

In January 1906 Edyth wrote from Washington that she would visit him the following week in New York. Kafū noted in his diary, "Edyth is a Washington prostitute. Last summer when I was living in that city, we accidentally became acquainted, and since then we have frequently exchanged letters." It is curious that Kafū found it necessary to remind himself who Edyth was. Or was he already planning to publish the diary? In any case, he and Edyth did not meet again until July. She wrote him that she intended to move to New York and wanted to live with him. Kafū was torn by conflicting emotions:

I feel as if I have become exactly like a character in a French novel. I all but weep out of happiness and gratitude, but at the same time, when I think of how much sadder the second parting will be when, inevitably, it presently comes, it seems that the best thing would be to make a clean break now. Mulling over such thoughts keeps me from sleeping. A fierce struggle in my breast between love and my artistic dreams is about to be proclaimed. Should I stay permanently in New York with Edyth and become an American? If so, when will I be able to visit Paris, for which I have longed all these months and years? Recalling the sadness of Tannhäuser who, sated with the love of a voluptuous goddess, attempted to escape from her grotto, I despondently looked at her as she slept. Ah, nothing is so sinful as a man![15]

When Edyth left New York to return to her place of business in Washington, Kafū accompanied her as far as the other side of the Hudson River. He wrote in his diary,

"On the way she kissed me again and again, inside the carriage, then on the ferryboat. As the time for the train to depart approached, she threw from the train window the rose she wore at her throat, as a keepsake until we should meet again. I suddenly felt that I could not abandon her, no matter what sacrifices this might involve."[16]

Kafū looked forward to his future life as a "menial in a brothel," and was delighted when he received from Edyth a cigarette case inscribed, "Love is everything." He had also become so fond of America that he was sure he could never leave. He told himself, "Never say it is because of a woman. Consider how dear to you now are the landscapes, the vegetation, everything of America."[17] But it did not take long for his dreams of France to revive, and he could not renounce his deepest desire, to become a writer, meaning that he would have to return to the only country where Japanese is read. When his father arranged for him to be transferred to the Lyons branch of the bank, he did not hesitate. Edyth promised to visit him in Lyons, but (as he confessed in his diary), "Already there is nothing left in my heart except my artistic ambitions. I listened absentmindedly to Edyth's complaints, delivered in tears."[18]

The diary includes the period when Kafū worked in Lyons, but it contains surprisingly little about his life in France. Working in a Japanese bank, even in France, clearly had not fulfilled his dreams of Paris. The diary concludes, "I arrived in Paris at midnight. I spent one night in the hotel before the station, but tomorrow I intend to move to the Latin Quarter."[19]

Kafū's *Shinkichōsha Nikki* (Diary of One Recently Returned to His Country), published in 1909, is not a diary in the sense that the earlier diary is one. The entries are dated by month and day, but not by year, rather in the manner of a diary of the Heian period. There are also unmistakable elements of fiction in the portrait Kafū gives of the diarist. For example, if this were a diary in the normal sense of the word, he would not have pretended to be the son of a viscount, an accomplished pianist who had spent eight years studying music in Paris and America. Again, the account of the unspoken love felt by the diarist for a beautiful Japanese lady who speaks perfect French does not tally with what we know about Kafū's romantic involvements after he returned to Japan. The work is unquestionably a work of fiction cast in the diary form; but the opinions expressed by the diarist so closely reflect Kafū's at this time that the work can be read as a diary, at least in the sense that we read the diaries of the Heian court ladies or Bashō's *Narrow Road of Oku*.

The diary opens late in November, about six months after the diarist's return to Japan. He recalls the sweltering heat of summers in New York, a city made of steel and stone, but also the steam heating that made the coldest winter days bearable.[20] He follows these recollections with the first of many generalizations about contemporary Japanese:

"It has been a long time now since first we heard ineffectual voices calling for improvements in clothing, in housing, in absolutely everything. But as a matter of fact, the Japanese will probably go on forever living in their inadequate houses. The cold wind blowing outside comes in from everywhere, through cracks in the tatami, through cracks in the shoji."[21]

He describes a naked Indian he saw sitting under a palm tree who passively accepted the changes of the seasons without stirring from his hut:

"This was the essence of the peculiarly oriental way of life. Ever since returning to Japan the only thing I have felt afresh is this invisible oriental atmosphere . . . Japan, following the wise planning of the architects of the Restoration, has attempted every day, from morning to night, to lead a modern life of the kind one sees in Europe. But I wonder if this attempt possesses the characteristics necessary to win a final victory on oriental soil where the sound of the bell tolling the impermanence of all things is still heard."[22]

Throughout this diary we hear Kafū's voice complaining again and again about the pretentiousness and hypocrisy of Meiji Japan. It is the same voice we hear in such works as *Tales of America* or *Furansu Monogatari* (Tales of France). Whatever was genuine and admirable in the old Japanese culture has been overwhelmed by cheap imitations of the West. The diarist's return to Japan, far from being an occasion for rejoicing, had made it painfully clear that what he learned abroad disqualified him as a member of Japanese society.

He is asked to play the piano at a benefit concert, but as his fingers produce notes composed by Chopin, he feels despair:

"It was not simply because the ancient piano installed in a Japanese sitting room was horribly out of tune. Nor was it because my playing was still immature. It was that the whole feeling of a Japanese room simply did not match this kind of music. In a Japanese room where the ceiling, the walls, the pillars, the *fusuma*, the shoji, the tatami each bared its particular, unpleasantly soiled color, not only was there a lack of harmony in the colors, there was not even a boundary between interior and exterior."[23]

Kafū, speaking through the diarist, harshly appraised Japanese architecture, not only because it failed to provide a congenial setting for European music but also because it lacked the elegance of upper-class houses he had visited abroad. He could not have foreseen that the aspects of a Japanese house he particularly condemned, such as the uninterrupted flow of space from the interior to the exterior, would one day be admired and imitated by architects in the West.

Kafū constantly complained in the diary about the falseness and vanity of the imitation of the West by Japanese of the Meiji era. It is easy to imagine that a nationalist would deplore external influences that had corrupted Japanese traditions, but Kafū was far from being a nationalist who insisted on the superiority of native Japanese ways to those imported from the West. Rather, he believed that if the Japanese could truly absorb European culture (as he himself had absorbed it), they might be able to make Japan into a decent place for cultivated people to live. But, he insisted, the Japanese were too intent on profits ever to do more than imitate the externals of European culture:

> Commonsensical Japanese are always preoccupied exclusively with actual profit and loss, and that is why there is absolutely no likelihood they will ever develop into an ideally great people ... Japanese who have been abroad are convinced that if they succeed in borrowing solely the external methods of foreign industry or politics or whatever it may be, they will create a splendid civilization. But if they take over only the forms and there is no content, what can they achieve? This is the state of Japanese civilization today. Because they do not examine, do not understand, do not feel the contents of real civilization, the Japanese importation of European civilization has become something of a truly repellent nature.[24]

A haiku poet called Uda Ryūsui, a friend of the diarist, also expresses contempt for Meiji culture. He believes that the literature of the Tokugawa period was vastly superior to the Naturalism which, in his opinion, had destroyed pure Japanese literature by the beginning of the twentieth century.[25] The Naturalist authors deliberately wrote flat, unornamented prose, in the belief that the elegance of style of earlier writers was false and frivolous, but Ryūsui was convinced that literature consists essentially of two elements—untruths and play. Kafū himself had begun his career by writing novels under the direct influence of French Naturalism, but by this time he had abandoned this style. The diarist does not agree with everything Ryūsui says, but the two men (like Kōtoku Shūsui and Saitō Ryokuu) joined in expressing distaste for the new, "enlightened" régime.

The diarist explains his return to Japan in terms of a false alarm concerning his father's health. He had returned to Japan at once, only to discover that his father had already recovered from the allegedly fatal illness, leading him to suppose that the real reason he had been summoned home was that his family feared he might marry a foreign woman.[26] As a matter of fact, there had been no such woman in his life, but the diarist admits that he had considered never returning to Japan. Even as a boy he had been fascinated by the West:

"Ah, what strange magic there was in the call of the West. I have never forgotten it. From the time when I was still an innocent school-boy I believed that imported wares—whether pens or ink or books or anything else—were superior to Japanese ones. 'Made in Japan' conveyed immediately the sense of crude and inferior merchandise."[27]

He was not alone in these beliefs. At the time, he recalls, admission to Japanese universities depended not on the student's ability in Japanese literature or classical Chinese but on his mastery of foreign languages. Although the diarist opined that the only way to achieve a truly modern culture in Japan was to abandon completely the traditional culture and to learn exclusively from the West, Kafū himself did not wish to see a total abandonment of Japanese traditions; but Japanese patriots infuriated him, and this led him to make extreme statements rejecting whatever they admired. He disliked in particular class reunions at which the past is fondly recalled:

"Recollections of the past have exactly the opposite effect on me—they bring back memories of endless pains and indignation . . . I feel as if my life first began the day I set foot on the soil of the American continent, and I would like to forget memories of the past in Japan as if they were nothing more than a dream."[28]

The diarist represents an extreme case of a phenomenon not uncommon even in our own day. During his stay abroad he had never felt an urge to return to Japan, and even Japanese scenery, which almost invariably stirs the heart of a Japanese who returns home, produced no impression:

"The wilderness of North America fascinated me with its grand sorrow and loneliness. It induced me to sink into philosophical contemplation. Nature in my native land, even though it was the same season of year—winter—produced almost no emotional reaction whatsoever in me. This was not simply a matter of the difference between big and small."[29]

He was dismayed especially by the manners of fellow passengers on the train: "Two or three passengers, lucky enough to find empty seats, had already sprawled out over them in their underwear, exposing their hairy shins."[30]

He could not help contrasting this and similar instances of Japanese behavior with the decorum that prevails in public places in Europe, and came to the conclusion that in Japan there was no distinction between "private life" and "public life." A friend suggested to the narrator, "The Japanese are a people living in Utopia. It's a sin to teach them the agony of new ideas." Kafū, like many foreigners resident in Japan at the time, seems to have decided that the Japanese tended to behave either like children or else like happy savages. The narrator did not hesitate to refer to Japan as "an uncivilized country" (yabankoku).[31]

The closest friends of the diarist once he returned to Japan were the books he had brought back from Europe; with few exceptions, these were the only friends he could trust in a country whose sole morality was that of a profit-hungry tradesman:

> Frankness and sincerity have fled completely from the Meiji era; apparently somebody decided that frankness and sincerity do not accord with the Meiji era. It is true that in certain respects European and American society are even more conspicuously corrupt than Japan, but unshakable traditions still exist, and on a number of points one can confidently trust in them. In Japan almost nothing, from the usual public enterprises down to the most insignificant article of merchandise, fails to arouse the suspicion that it is pretending to be better that it actually is.[32]

The "half-European" lady to whom the narrator is attracted expresses views similar to his own. She is baffled by the interest in

Japanese art expressed by the American couple with whom she is studying English conversation. The narrator summarizes her views in this fashion: "We yearn for the West, but people in the West have arbitrarily decided that Japan is a country of incomparably beautiful dreams. I wonder if there isn't something in human nature that makes people love things that are far away." He quotes her letter: "I won't feel particularly sorry even if I never see Matsushima, Itsukushima, and Ama no Hashidate, the Three Great Sights of Japan that people have praised so much all these years, but having been born as a human being, I want somehow to find a way to see the Alps and the color of the water of the Mediterranean."[33] Most Japanese young men of the time would have found such a woman pretentious, even if she expressed these views with complete sincerity, but Kafū's diarist was delighted to have found someone whose tastes so exactly corresponded to his own.

As one reads Kafū's harsh criticism of Meiji Japan, one wonders how he managed to survive in so uncongenial an atmosphere. He recognized, of course, that he and like-minded Japanese were no more than a tiny minority. When his friend, the haiku poet Ryūsui, asked him, "Do you suppose any Japanese is truly satisfied with the situation today?" he replied, "I'm sure there must be some. There simply have to be some people who, to exactly the degree that we find conditions intolerably disagreeable, are desperately eager to take advantage of opportunities. The various phenomena of society, the tendencies in the times, are manifestations of the psychology of the majority of the citizens. This means that the outward appearance of our cities, the proof that care has been devoted only to externals must, if we extend the parallel to the life of an individual, be considered a frightening example of a decay in morals."[34]

Most Japanese were pleased with the false fronts of the shops along the Ginza, but Kafū felt only hatred for these examples of the architecture of a new Japan that seemed symbolic of the culture—a superficial imitation of the West that revealed its shallowness as soon as one looked behind the fancy exterior. He commented, "Meiji is a truly innocent, comic, fraudulent era."[35]

The diarist, when his friend praised the impressive appearance of the new Tokyo, said, "Every last building, from the Imperial Palace on down, was erected by the people of Edo."[36] In later years Kafū would be known as an antiquarian who searched for traces of the old Edo in the rapidly changing Tokyo, especially in the pleasure quarters, a bastion of the old culture. At the time he wrote *Diary of One Recently Returned to His Country*, however, these views were attributed to Ryūsui; the narrator, rather than attempt to return to Edo, favored a genuine adoption of Western culture, as opposed to a hypocritical veneer of foreign influence on a basically unchanged feudal system. He opined, "I would like to see the matter happily settled one way or the other. If it is to be barbarism, let it be barbarism. If it is to be civilization, let it be civilization."[37]

Listing the many changes that had been trumpeted in recent years, he asked cynically, "I wonder why Japanese have never, to this day, clamored for a reform of the color of their skin or of their eyes."[38] As he listened to the street noises—a man singing some vulgar popular song following on the heels of someone singing a *jōruri* work, he mused, "These pathetic sounds of things and human voices, heard of a winter night, vividly brought to mind, as if I saw it with my own eyes, the content of the chaotic, disordered present, when the orderly Tokugawa culture has been destroyed and the new Meiji culture has yet to come into existence."[39]

Although Kafū retained his love for the West throughout his life, his rejection of the vulgar present came increasingly to take the form of nostalgia for the vanishing Edo. In time, when far less congenial ways than those he criticized in this diary had come to dominate in Tokyo, Kafū expressed affection even for the disappearing Meiji-period buildings he had once despised as shallow imitations of the West. He turned increasingly from admiration for the triumphs of European civilization to affectionate remembrances of the frivolous pleasures of the Tokugawa era. In the short story "Hanabi" (Fire-works), published in 1919, Kafū attributed the change in his attitudes to an incident that he had witnessed in 1911:

> While I was going to Keiō University, I often saw on my way a line of five or six horse-drawn police wagons heading along the street through Ichigaya in the direction of the law court in Hibiya. Of all the worldly incidents I have ever seen or heard about, none had ever inspired such unspeakable disgust as this one. As a writer, I should not have kept silent about this question of ideology. Was not the novelist Zola forced to become an exile because he had cried out for justice in the Dreyfus case? But I, like the other writers of the day, did not say one word. I was assailed by unbearable pangs of conscience. I felt extremely ashamed to be a writer. I reasoned with myself that from then on the best thing for me to do would be to lower the level of my art to that of the Edo *gesaku* writers.[40] From that time on I wore a tobacco pouch, collected ukiyo-e prints, and began to play the samisen.[41]

Kafū was probably referring here to the Kōtoku Shūsui trial and execution. Although he had never previously displayed any interest in politics, the sight of police vans bearing the condemned men to their deaths horrified him. His escape into the world of *gesaku* fiction was probably the safest retreat he could have found, short of going abroad and never returning to Japan.

Many Japanese who spend months or years abroad find it difficult to adjust to life after their return to Japan. They grow accustomed to societies in which relationships are less strongly felt than in Japan, and they find the constant pressure of obligations in their own country constricting. They may pass from exasperation over their particular situation to generalization about what makes the Japanese unlike other peoples. Kafū in *Diary of One Recently Returned to His Country* voiced many such statements as:

"I felt as if I had discovered a frightening trait in the Japanese character—the delight taken in pointing out the faults of other people. The attitude of the Japanese press—exposing, in the name of justice, the private conduct of people—was not the result of any decline in social morality, but was undoubtedly the product of the general national character that makes such actions inevitable."[42]

When the narrator of the diary hears that Haruko, the beautiful "half-European," intends to marry an American, he is at first deeply disappointed that he cannot have her for his own bride, but he is relieved that she has chosen to marry a foreigner:

"Ah, Haruko in the end could not be satisfied with Japan. She did not wish to become a tortured and humiliated Japanese wife and mother. I decided I would do everything in my power to ensure that this marriage would take place."[43]

Perhaps if Kafū had lived abroad longer and become more familiar with the attitudes displayed by members of American and European families when discussing their relatives and friends, he might not have reached the conclusion that pointing out flaws in others is a peculiarly Japanese characteristic. As an outsider in a society in which he lived for a relatively short time, he was able to see some aspects of that society more clearly than its members, but his knowledge of it was never as deep as his knowledge of Japan. He chose to praise the West and belittle Japan. More Japanese who have traveled abroad have done the opposite, expressing relief to be home after years spent among strangers whose ways they never could understand.

If Kafū had been a musician, he might have remained abroad indefinitely, like those Japanese who today are members of European and American symphony orchestras. A painter might also find it possible to live abroad without thought of returning to Japan, satisfied that the company of fellow artists provides stimulation he cannot get at home. But a writer cannot remain an expatriate unless he is willing to give up his most precious possession, his mastery of his mother tongue. Kafū deliberately made the narrator of this diary a musician, perhaps because he believed that music is the universal language—but the music of Europe is so unlike that of Japan that a Japanese composer cannot be satisfied (unless he delights in superficial exoticism) with merely adding Japanese coloration to a fundamentally European piece of music. The narrator plans to write an opera based on the Nō play *Sumidagawa* (Sumida River), but Kafū wrote a quite different *Sumidagawa*, the superb story of a boy who wishes to play the samisen and sing traditional *tokiwazu* music but is forced by his ambitious mother to study mathematics and science.

In later years Kafū wrote an extremely detailed diary called *Danchōtei Nichijō*[44] in which he traced day-by-day the changes in the world around him. This diary often gives the impression of bitterness, but Kafū's diaries of the Meiji era are more cheerful even when his criticism is most pointed, suggesting the complex emotions aroused in Japanese when, in the early years of the twentieth century, they faced a new world.

Notes

1. *Nagai Kafū Shū*, I, p. 322.
2. *Ibid*. The two works of classical literature he mentions are *Heike Monogatari* and *Eiga Monogatari*. Both have been successfully translated into English.
3. *Ibid*., p. 323.
4. *Ibid*.
5. *Ibid*. The warning not to go to New Orleans and the suggestion that he study instead in Michigan were probably made by some Japanese he met in St. Louis, including the painter Shirataki Ikunosuke (1873–1960). See Hiraiwa Shōzō, *Seiyū Nisshi Shō no Sekai*, pp. 202–3.
6. *Nagai*, I, p. 324.
7. The advertisement appeared in the July 9, 1905, *New York Herald*. It stated: "Japanese general houseworker wants position in small family. Nagai, 17 Concord, Brooklyn." See Hiraiwa, *Seiyū*, p. 210.
8. *Nagai, I,* p. 326.
9. *Ibid*.

10. *Ibid.*
11. *Ibid.*, p. 327.
12. *Ibid.*, p. 328.
13. *Ibid.*, p. 327.
14. *Ibid.*, p. 328.
15. *Ibid.*, p. 332.
16. *Ibid.*
17. *Ibid.*, p. 333.
18. *Ibid.*, p. 337.
19. *Ibid.*, p. 340.
20. *Ibid.*, p. 202.
21. *Ibid.*
22. *Ibid.* The "sound of the bell tolling the impermanence of all things" seems to be a reference to the celebrated opening of *The Tale of the Heike*.
23. *Ibid.*, p. 203.
24. *Ibid.*, p. 210.
25. *Ibid.*, p. 209.
26. *Ibid.*, p. 202.
27. *Ibid.*, p. 205.
28. *Ibid.*, p. 206.
29. *Ibid.*, p. 207.
30. *Ibid.*
31. *Ibid.*, p. 220.
32. *Ibid.*, p. 214.
33. *Ibid.*, p. 218.
34. *Ibid.*, p. 219.
35. *Ibid.*, p. 218.
36. *Ibid.*, p. 219.
37. *Ibid.*, p. 221.
38. *Ibid.*, p. 215.
39. *Ibid.*, p. 213.
40. The *gesaku* writers maintained an air of detachment from their works, pretending to have no loftier ambition than to entertain the public, though some *gesaku* compositions were in fact quite serious.
41. *Nagai*, I, p. 319. The tobacco pouch (*tabako-ire*) was by this time, when people of Kafū's world normally smoked cigarettes, an anachronism.
42. *Ibid.*, p. 220.
43. *Ibid.*, p. 221.

44. Danchōtei was the name Kafū gave to his residence in Tokyo. *Nichijō*, a rather unusual word for "diary," had been used by Narushima Ryūhoku.

Bibliography

Hiraiwa Shōzō. *Seiyū Nisshi Shō no Sekai*. Tokyo: Rokkō Shuppan, 1983.
Nagai Kafū Shū, I, in Gendai Nihon Bungaku Taikei series. Tokyo: Chikuma Shobō, 1969–70.

Conclusion

In *Travelers of a Hundred Ages*, my earlier book on Japanese diaries, I discussed one thousand years of diaries. The present volume covers only about sixty years, but even so, I have not been able to treat all the important diaries of the period. Modern diaries are not only far more numerous than those surviving from the past, but each diary is generally many times the length of those composed in Japanese during the preceding millennium. It is true that some very long diaries were written in Chinese during the Heian period and later, but their contents are of interest mainly to specialists in the history of the time, and they do not often provide enlightenment on what interested me most, the Japanese as revealed in their diaries. The diaries of the present series sometimes run to thousands of pages and, in the best, almost everything is worth reading.

These diaries have a general theme: the experiences of Japanese who came into contact with non-Japanese after the end of the more than two hundred years during which the country was closed to the rest of the world. The non-Japanese included the Okinawans and the Ainu who now form a part of the Japanese population, but also Chinese, Europeans of various nationalities, and Americans. I was not always successful in my search for diaries that would convey the different facets of Japanese experiences abroad. I tried, for example, to find an interesting diary that related the experiences of a Japanese in Korea, but to the end I was unsuccessful, though undoubtedly such diaries exist.

Not all of the diaries were kept by people who traveled abroad. Several of the most accomplished diarists of the modern period, including Masaoka Shiki and Ishikawa Takuboku, never left Japan, but even they were deeply affected by intellectual influences emanating from the West, and their unconventional attitudes concerning Japanese tradition indicate that they too belonged to a brave new generation of Japanese.

Diarists who went abroad are divided between those whose irritation with foreign ways made them eager to get back to Japan as soon as possible, and those who, even after they returned to Japan, retained affectionate remembrances of foreign landscapes and people. One finds both varieties in the first diaries in this book: Muragaki, the governor of Awaji, had not one word of praise or even of surprise for what he observed abroad, but Kimura, the governor of Settsu, who traveled at exactly the same time, left his American friends with regret. The last two diaries present a similar contrast: Kinoshita Mokutarō's irritation with life in France made him long to return to Japan, but Nagai Kafū could scarcely tear himself away from France. Perhaps there will always be this division of opinion. Fortunately so—how dreary it would be if all Japanese displayed the same reactions to foreign countries and peoples!

The new generation of travelers journeyed much farther than the Heian court ladies, Bashō, or even the monks who made the perilous voyage to China. They not only saw distant countries but were seen and, especially in the 1860s, were welcomed by huge crowds eager to have a look at the Japanese. As time passed and the Japanese became less of a curiosity, the crowds diminished, but almost every diarist who went abroad had at least a few happy memories to take home. Though these memories were intangible, they usually made the hardships of travel—seasickness, unfamiliar food, deceitful merchants, and the rest—seem of small consequence. The diarists brought back to Japan souvenirs they had purchased and gifts that had been bestowed on them, but more precious than these mementoes were the diaries in which they recorded for the edification of their families or for the world in general impressions of their experiences that still have the power to move us now. Though their experiences differed greatly from those of earlier Japanese diarists, they too form a part of the long line of travelers of a hundred ages.

Index

Abe Isoo, 430

Account of Ezo People in Recent Times (Kinsei Ezo Jimbutsu Shi) (Matsuura Takeshirō), 155–60, 161

Account of My Hut (Hōjōki) (Kamo no Chōmei), 275–76

Acrobats, Japanese, performing in Europe, 86

Adams, Captain, 19

Additional Account of Northern Ezo (Kita Ezo Yoshi) (Matsuura Takeshirō), 150–51

Aden:
  Ichikawa's visit to, 49
  Shibusawa's visit to, 83

Ainu, 19, 393
  ancient Japanese culture preserved by, 157
  bear hunting of, 151–52
  Bird's description of, 160–61
  food of, 153, 154
  Japanese exploitation of, 155–56, 157–58
  Matsuura's admiration for, 154–55, 156, 157, 161

  in Matsuura's party, 150, 151–55
  music of, 155
  Okinawans compared to, 181–82
  physical appearance and demeanor of, 160
  unpleasant aspects of life among, 158
  yukari (epic poems) of, 157

Aitei Tsūshin (Letters to My Beloved Brother) (Kunikida Doppo), 343

Albert, prince consort, 68

Alcock, Sir Rutherford, 50, 57, 61, 62, 87

Alexander II, czar of Russia, 85

Alzire (Voltaire), 156

Amami Ōshima, 173

America, 90

American Diary (Tobei Nikki) (Kōtoku Shūsui), 436, 438, 441–45

Amerika Monogatari (Tales of America) (Nagai Kafū), 489, 490, 492, 496

Analects (Confucius), 335

Andō Tarō, 127

Aoki Shūzō, 195

architecture:
  Japanese vs. Western, 496
  of Meiji period, 500–501
Arishima Mibuma, 430, 431
Arishima Takeo, 403–33
  alienated from Christianity, 429, 430
  art as interest of, 426–27, 431
  childhood and early education of,
    403–6
  as college student, 405–19
  converted to Christianity, 406–12,
    416–19
  on departure from Japan, 424–25
  diary viewed as public document by,
    419
  English–language writings of, 428,
    432
  in Europe, 431–32
  family background of, 403
  in first encounter with less fortu-
    nate, 404–5
  grandmother's relationship with,
    417, 418, 419
  interruptions in diary of, 431–32
  love life of, 420–21, 427–28, 430
  military service of, 421–22
  Morimoto's relationship with,
    407–18, 423–24
  motives of, for keeping diary, 405
  Nitobe's influence on, 407–8
  political convictions of, 404, 405,
    421–22, 423, 429, 430, 431, 436
  possible homosexual experience of,
    413
  after return to Japan, 432–33
  self-criticism of, 411–12
  studying in America, 422–23,
    424–31
  suicide contemplated by, 413–16
  working at insane asylum, 428–29
Arnold, Matthew, 397
Art Institute of Chicago, 426–27
Arts:
  Arishima's interest in, 426–27, 431
  Christian scenes in, 107–8, 109

  and European imitation of Japanese
    traditions, 105–6
  government protection of, 105
  Kume's observations on, 104–8
  nudes in, 107
  realism in, 53, 106–7
  see also Japanese wares
Aru Onna (A Certain Woman) (Ar-
    ishima Takeo), 426
Asahi Shimbun, 397
Asia:
  Matsuura's travels in, 148–61
  Ōgai's travels in, 192–93
  Ryūhoku's travels in, 121–24
  Sasamori's travels in, 164–82
  Shibusawa's travels in, 77–84
  Sōseki's travels in, 216
  Takezoe's travels in, 135–46
  see also specific countries and cities
Autobiography of Benjamin Franklin,
    361–62, 364
Azamukazaru no Ki (An Undeceitful
    Record) (Kunikida Doppo),
    329–54

Baba Kochō, 284
Bashō, 136–37, 143, 495, 508
Beggars:
  Arishima's first exposure to, 404–5
  Takezoe's encounter with, 137
Beiō Kairan Jikki (True Account of a
    Tour of America and Europe)
    (Kume Kunitake), 90–115
  essays scattered throughout, 91–92,
    94–96
  literary quality of, 98, 99
  official purpose of, 91
  stylistic complications in, 99
Belgium:
  Ichikawa's travels in, 48
  Kume's admiration for, 114
Berlin:
  first Japanese embassy in, 46–47, 59,
    60
  Ōgai's visit to, 206

Bernhardt, Sarah, 492–93
Bible, 124, 256
    Kume's observations on, 108–9
    Niijima's encounters with, 238, 243
    Ryūhoku's use of images from, 121
Bible Society (New York), 108
Bird, Isabella, 142–43, 144, 160–61
Biyō Ōkō Manroku (Leisurely Account
    of the Journey to Europe of a
    Fly on a Horse's Tail)
    (Ichikawa Wataru), 44–54
Black Eyes and Brown Eyes (Kuroi Me
    to Chairo no Me) (Tokutomi
    Roka), 462
Bois de Boulogne (Paris), 125–26
Bokuju Itteki (A Drop of Ink)
    (Masaoka Shiki), 356, 357–59,
    366, 374
Bōshū Peninsula, Mokutarō's travels
    in, 474–78
Boston:
    Arishima's studies in, 429–30
    Niijima's stay in, 242–43, 249
Bowing, Japanese-style, 193–94
Brand (Ibsen), 430
Brandes, Georg, 430
British Museum (London), 102–3
Broken Commandments, The (Shi-
    mazaki Tōson), 387
Brooke, John M., 33, 37, 40*n*–41*n*
Brutus, Decimus Junius, 128
Buchanan, James, 22–23, 24
Buddha, 145, 208, 404
Buddhism, 84, 208, 227, 228, 261, 418,
    419
    Arishima's acceptance of, 407–8,
        409, 412
    in Ceylon, 82–83
    Christian missionaries' views on, 225
    Kume's views on, 108, 109, 110
Bungakkai, 297, 300
Bunjin, 131*n*
Burials at sea, 19–20
"Buried Life, A" (Umoregi) (Higuchi
    Ichiyō), 297

Burns, Robert, 335, 336, 338, 339
Byōshō Rokushaku (My Six-Foot
    Sickbed) (Masaoka Shiki),
    356–62, 365, 374–75

Caesar, Julius, 128
Carlyle, Thomas, 330, 335, 346, 407,
    408
Caruso, Enrico, 492
Catholicism, 108, 110. *See also* Chris-
    tianity
Censorship, 255–56
Certain Woman, A (Aru Onna) (Ar-
    ishima Takeo), 426
Ceylon:
    Fuchibe's visit to, 59
    Kume's description of, 98–99
    Ōgai's visit to, 192–93
    Ryūhoku's visit to, 122, 124
    Shibata's visit to, 75
    Shibusawa's visit to, 82–83
    Sōseki's visit to, 216
Chance Meetings with Beautiful Women
    (Kajin no Kigū) (Tōkai San-
    shi), 205
Chang Chun, 139
Chanoine, Charles, 127
Ch'en Hsi-ch'ang, 146
Ch'eng-tu, 145–46
Chia Tao, 136, 137
Chicago, Arishima's visit to, 425–27
Chih-hsin, 136
Ch-in Kuei, 139
China, 83
    beggars in, 137
    decline of, 79–80
    food in, 137, 141, 145
    hardships of travel in, 137–42
    inns in, 138, 140, 141–42, 145
    Mokutarō's visit to, 481
    monuments and mementoes of past
        in, 138–40
    Okinawan culture influenced by,
        169–70
    Okinawans' allegiance to, 173, 178

China (*cont'd*)
  opium consumption in, 140–41
  Ryūkyū Islands claimed by, 166,
    170–71
  samurai culture linked to, 135
  sandō and mountain scenery in,
    143–45
  Shibusawa's travels in, 78–81
  Takezoe's travels in, 135–46
  toilets in, 141–42
  see also Sino-Japanese War
Chiyoda, 343–46
Chōei (Shadow of a Bird) (Ishikawa
    Takuboku), 388
Christ, 109
  crucified, depictions of, 108, 109
Christianity, 53
  anti-Christian riots in Chungking
    and, 146
  Arishima's alienation from, 429, 430
  arts and, 107–8, 109
  compatibility of socialism and, 430
  diarists' responses to great churches
    of, 108, 110, 124, 309–10
  Japanese converts to, 225–26,
    227–28, 406–12, 416–19
  Kume's disdain for, 107–11
  and religious freedom in Japan,
    442
  Ueki influenced by, 256–57
  worship of imperial ancestors incon-
    sistent with, 418
  zealotry and, 109–10
  see also Bible
Chronicles of Japan (Nihongi), 290
Chuang Tzu, 335
Chungking, anti-Christian riots in, 146
Clark, William Smith, 406
"Clouds Are Geniuses, The" (Kumo
    wa Tensai de aru) (Ishikawa
    Takuboku), 388
"Concerning Equal Rights for Men
    and Women" (Danjo Dōken ni
    tsukite no koto) (Ueki Emori),
    260–61

Confucianism, 156, 227, 228, 256, 261,
    438
  Kume and, 91, 109, 110, 111
  in Okinawa, 169–70
Confucius, 228, 335, 336
Congress, U.S., 25
Constitution, Japanese, 263
Constitutional monarchies, in Europe,
    92
Cooper, James Fenimore, 156
Craig, William J., 221
Crime and Punishment (Dostoyevsky),
    290
Crowell, Fanny, 420, 427–28, 429,
    430–31
Cuba, Mokutarō's visit to, 482–83
Cunningham, Commodore, 38
Curtius, Jan Hendrik Donker, 50, 60

Daily Record of Shiribeshi (Shiribeshi
    Nisshi) (Matsuura Takeshirō),
    151–52
Danchōtei Nichijō (Nagai Kafū), 504
Dancing, 53
  in America, 24–25, 39
  Fuchibe's description of, 58
  at Rokumeikan in Tokyo, 24,
    213–14, 269
"Dancing Girl, The" (Mori Ōgai), 204
"Danjo Dōken ni tsukite no koto"
    (Concerning Equal Rights for
    Men and Women) (Ueki
    Emori), 260–61
Date Munenari, 88n
De Long, Charles E., 93
De Long, Mrs., 305
De Witt, John, 325
Democracy:
  in America, 23–24, 25, 92
  in France, 67
Denmark, Kume's admiration for, 114
Devotees of Pan (Pan no Kai), 479–80
Diaries:
  appeal of novels vs., 377–78
  fabrication in, 1–2

general theme of, 507

Heian, 2, 287–89, 290, 310, 495, 507

length of, 507

literary importance of, 223

purposes served by, 2–4

see also specific diarists

Diary for 1912 (Ishikawa Takuboku), 394

Diary of a Journey to Europe (Ōkō Nikki) (Fuchibe Tokuzō), 57–62

Diary of a Member of the Japanese Embassy to Europe (Biyō Ōkō Manroku) (Ichikawa Wataru), 44–54

Diary of a Voyage (Kōkai Nikki) (Muragaki Norimasa), 10–28

Diary of a Voyage (Kōkai Nikki) (Niijima Jō), 242–43

Diary of a Voyage to the West (Kōsai Nikki) (Mori Ōgai), 190–93

Diary of Bridges in the Clouds, Rain in the Gorges (San'un Kyōu Nikki) (Takezoe Shin'ichirō), 135–46

Diary of His Excellency's Stay in Paris (Pari Gozaikan Nikki) (Shibusawa Eiichi), 87

Diary of One Recently Returned to His Country (Shinkichōsha Nikki) (Nagai Kafū), 494–504

Doitsu Nikki (German Diary) (Mori Ōgai), 190, 193–210

originally composed in classical Chinese, 196

publishing of, 204

Doppo. See Kunikida Doppo

Dōshisha University (Kyoto), 249

Dostoyevsky, Fyodor, 290, 430

"Dover Beach" (Arnold), 397

Drop of Ink, A (Bokuju Itteki) (Masaoka Shiki), 356, 357–59, 366, 374

Dutch Reformed Church, 91

Edo. See Tokyo

Education:

under Meiji government, 378–80

political purpose of, 178

in Ryūkyūs, 177–78

Egawa Tarōzaemon, 251

Egypt:

Fukuzawa's visit to, 65–66

Ichikawa's visit to, 49

Shibusawa's visit to, 83–84

Emerson, Ralph Waldo, 330, 332, 334, 335

Emma, queen of Hawaii, 16

Engels, Friedrich, 430, 443

England:

America contrasted with, 113

Arishima's travels in, 431–32

artistry in, 104–5

dirty atmosphere of, 130, 218–19

first Japanese embassy in, 43–44, 46, 48, 51, 53, 61, 62, 67–68

Hong Kong and, 81, 192

as imperialist power, 81, 82, 83, 112–13, 192

Kume's travels in, 100, 101–3, 108, 114

literary knowledge among inhabitants of, 219–21

rumored conflicts beteen Japan and, 62, 240, 274

Ryūhoku's travels in, 129–30

Shibata's travels in, 73–75

Sōseki's travels in, 215, 217–23

treatment accorded to women in, 100–101

Umeko's travels in, 308–10, 311

Enma, Great King, 374

Etiquette, 477

American informality and, 17–18, 20–25

in Germany, 193–94, 197–98

Western, accepted in late-nineteenth-century Japan, 213–14

Etorofu, 149

Eugénie, empress of France, 71, 252

Europe:
    Arishima's travels in, 431–32
    artistic traditions of, 104–8
    Christianity in, 107–11
    churches in, 108, 110, 124, 309–10
    constitutional monarchies in, 92
    extraordinary welcomes for
        Japanese in, 46–47, 60
    first Meiji mission to (1871), 100–115
    gaudy tastes ascribed to, 59
    greed for material things in, 111–12
    Japanese acrobatic troupes in, 86
    Japanese embassy of 1862 to, 43–72,
        85
    Japanese embassy of 1865 to, 73–75
    Japanese embassy of 1867 to, 77–87
    Japanese language studied in, 50–51
    Japanese visitors' lack of knowledge
        about, 139
    Japanese wares in, 51, 60, 61, 62,
        67–68, 86, 103–4, 105–6
    Kume's travels in, 98, 100–115
    Mokutarō's travels in, 481–82,
        483–85
    museums in, 52, 53, 58, 101–8
    Ryūhoku's travels in, 120, 121–22,
        124–30
    Shibusawa's travels in, 84–87
    Sōseki's travels in, 213–23
    treatment accorded to women in,
        100–101
    young Japanese illegally traveling to,
        189–90
    see also specific countries and cities
Europe and America Diary (Kinoshita
    Mokutarō), 481–85
Europe and America Diary (Ōbei Nikki)
    (Ōta Masao), 481
Exposed in the Fields (Nozarashi Kikō)
    (Bashō), 136–37
Ezo. See Hokkaidō

Fan Ch'eng-ta, 136
"Fireworks" (Hanabi) (Nagai Kafū),
    502

Florence, Ryūhoku's visit to, 124,
    128–29
Food:
    of Ainu, 153, 154
    in China, 137, 141, 145
    Japanese, travelers' longing for, 15,
        34, 59, 69, 71
    in Okinawa, 168–69
    Western, diarists' experiences with,
        37, 59, 78, 121–22, 125, 307
France:
    artistry in, 104–5, 106
    as Catholic country, 108
    first Japanese embassy in, 43–44,
        45–46, 48, 50, 51, 53–54, 58–60,
        62, 66–67, 70
    Indochina and, 81, 85
    Japanese people compared with in-
        habitants of, 114
    Kafū's stay in, 494
    Ryūhoku's travels in, 122, 124,
        125–28, 129
    Shibata's visit to, 73–75
    Shibusawa's visit to, 85–87
    see also Paris
Franklin, Benjamin, 361–62, 364
Fritz, Mrs., 442
Fuchibe Tokuzō, 57–62, 68
    able to adapt to European life, 59–
        60
    European landscapes appreciated by,
        58–59
    in France, 58–60
    in Holland, 60, 61, 62
    Japanese wares and, 61, 86
    in Lisbon, 62
    as painter, 57–58
    shogunate's seclusion policy criti-
        cized by, 60–61
Fuji (Tokutomi Roka), 463
Fujiya Unokichi, 234
Fukuzawa Yukichi, 64–72, 231, 255
    in America, 45, 64, 65
    in Egypt, 65–66
    in England, 67–68

in Holland, 68–69
impersonality of diaries of, 44, 71–72
in Lisbon, 70
memorandum book containing various observations of, 71
in Paris, 66–67, 70
in St. Petersburg, 69–70
on voyage abroad *Kanrin Maru,* 33
Fuller, Loie, 34
Furansu Monogatari (Tales of France) (Nagai Kafū), 496
"Futsueikō" (Journey to France and England) (Shibata Takenaka), 73–75

Garibaldi, Giuseppe, 84, 89*n*, 110
Gennyo, 120, 124, 129
"Gen Oji" (Old Gen) (Kunikida Doppo), 341, 351, 352*n*
German Diary (Mori Ōgai). *See Doitsu Nikki*
Germany:
    etiquette in, 193–94, 197–98
    first Japanese embassy in, 46–47, 59, 60
    Kume's observations on, 100–101, 114
    Ōgai's stay in, 193–210, 213–14, 219, 223
    Ōgai's voyage to, 190–93
    treatment accorded to women in, 100–101
Gesaku fiction, 502, 505n
Gobelin, 105
Goethe, Johann Wolfgang von, 335, 336, 338, 339, 348, 425, 478, 479
Gorky, Maxim, 397, 430
Gossamer Years, The, 287
"Governments that Make Men into Monkeys" (Hito wo Saru ni suru Seifu) (Ueki Emori), 255–56
Grand Hotel (San Francisco), 93–94
Great Britain. *See* England
"Growing Up" (Takekurabe) (Higuchi Ichiyō), 285, 300–301

Gyōga Manroku (Stray Notes from a Supine Position) (Masaoka Shiki), 356–57, 362–63, 364, 366–73

Hakodate (Hokkaidō):
    Niijima's stay in, 228–35
    Russian hospital in, 233
Hakodate Kikō (Journey to Hakodate) (Niijima Jō), 229–31
"Half a Day" (Hannichi) (Mori Ōgai), 313, 318, 480
Hamlet (Shakespeare), 315
Han Wei-kung, 138–39
"Hanabi" (Fireworks) (Nagai Kafū), 502
"Hannichi" (Half a Day) (Mori Ōgai), 313, 318, 480
Harada Naojirō, 202, 203
"Hard Road to Shu" (Li T'ai-po), 97
Hardy, Alpheus, 226, 242–43, 250, 306
Hardy, Mrs. Alpheus, 226, 243–44, 250, 306
Harris, Townsend, 22
Haruko, 499–500, 503
Harvard, Arishima's studies at, 429–30
Hashimoto Tsunazune, 193, 195
Hatano Akiko, 433
Hawaii, 64
    Muragaki's visit to, 14–16
Hayashi Shihei, 190–91
Heco, Joseph, 10
Heian literature, 2, 310, 495, 507
    Ichiyō's writings and, 287–89, 290
Heimin Shimbun (Commoners' Newspaper), 441
Heredia, José María de, 483
Hidden, Miss, 243–44
Higuchi Ichiyō, 284–301, 313
    archaic diction of, 287–89
    calligraphy of, 288
    diary's contribution to legend of, 285
    doubts about credibility of diary of, 284, 286–87

Higuchi Ichiyō (cont'd)
  education of, 288, 292, 299–300
  family shop and, 298–99, 300
  father's death and, 292–93, 298
  as fiction writer, 285, 290, 291, 297,
    300–301
  last days of, 301
  literary interests of, 289–90
  literary quality of diary of, 284–85,
    288
  on love, 295
  Mineko compared to, 314–15
  motives of, for keeping diary, 287,
    288
  private nature of diary of, 285, 291,
    299
  as samurai daughter, 293, 298, 302n
  scholars' reproofs of character of,
    285–86
  supposed deathbed request of, 285
  titles of diaries of, 291–92
  Tōsui's relationship with, 286–87,
    292, 293–97, 298
Higuchi Kuniko, 285, 291, 293
Hirata Atsutane, 261
Hirata Kiichi (Hirata Tokuboku),
    297–98, 300
"Hito wo Saru ni suru Seifu" (Gover-
    ments that Make Men into
    Monkeys) (Ueki Emori),
    255–56
Hoffmann, Franz, 195
Hoffmann, Johann Joseph, 50, 55n
Hōjōki (Account of My Hut) (Kamo no
    Chōmei), 275–76
Hokkaidō (Ezo), 19, 148
  ancient Japanese culture preserved
    in, 157
  Arishima's student days in, 405–17
  Bird's description of, 160–61
  bitter water in, 154
  difficulties of travel in, 158–59
  Doppo's desire for independent life
    in, 347, 348, 349
  indigenous people of. See Ainu

  Japanese exploitation of Ainu in,
    155–56, 157–58
  Matsuura's travels in, 149, 150–60,
    161
  naming of, 161
  Niijima's travels in, 228–35
  Russians in, 232–34
  unpleasant aspects of life in, 158
Holland:
  first Japanese embassy in, 46, 47, 51,
    60, 61, 62, 68–69
  as imperialist power, 112–13
  Japanese artworks in, 105, 106
Holy Man Nichiren's Sermons at the
    Crossroads, The (Nichiren
    Shōnin Tsuji Seppō) (Mori
    Ōgai), 317
Hong Kong:
  Fuchibe's visit to, 59
  Ichikawa's visit to, 45, 48, 49–50
  Ōgai's visit to, 192
  Ryūhoku's visit to, 121, 123, 192
  Shibusawa's visit to, 81
  Sōseki's visit to, 216
Hōshi Meriken Kikō (Journey to Am-
    erica in His Excellency's Ser-
    vice) (Kimura Yoshitake), 31–
    40
Hugo, Victor, 335, 346

Ibsen, Henrik, 397, 430
Ichikawa Wataru, 44–54
  in Belgium, 48
  concerned about presentation of
    Japanese culture to West,
    51–52
  in England, 46, 48, 51, 53
  European civilization as viewed by,
    52–53
  Europeans who had studied
    Japanese met by, 50
  on extraordinary welcomes for
    Japanese visitors, 46–47
  in France, 45–46, 48, 50, 51, 53–54
  in Hong Kong, 45, 48, 49–50

non-European foreigners disdained by, 49

surroundings described in detail by, 45–46

Ichiyō. *See* Higuchi Ichiyō

"Idiot Boy, The" (Wordsworth), 341

Ienaga Saburō, 256

Ihara Saikaku, 290

Ijichi, Captain, 200

Ike no Taiga, 271

Imai Tadaharu, 331–32

I-men-chen, *sandō* at, 143–44

Imperial College of Agriculture (Sapporo), 405–7

Imperialism:

    Kume's views on, 112–13

    Russian, in northern Japan, 149–50, 157, 231, 233

    Shibusawa's depictions of, 79–83, 85

In the Shade of Spring Leaves (Wakaba Kage) (Higuchi Ichiyō), 292–301

India, 83, 113

Inoue Kaoru, 164

Inoue Tetsujirō, 206

Internment camps, 325–26

Iriomote, 175–77

Ise, Great Shrine of, 149

Ishigaki, 174–75, 177, 179

Ishii Rogetsu, 357

Ishikawa Setsuko, 384, 385, 391, 394–95, 397

Ishikawa Takuboku, 377–97, 404, 436, 480, 508

    audience envisioned for diaries of, 395–96

    burning of diaries requested by, 385, 395

    changes in, reflected in diaries, 391–93

    earlier works revised by, 382, 390–91

    education of, 378–80, 396

    fearful that wife would read his diaries, 384, 385, 394

    genius of, 380, 387

    last year in life of, 397

    literary influences on, 396–97

    literary style of, 378–79

    marriage of, 391

    motives of, for keeping diary, 2–3, 380–82

    moving nature of diaries of, 377, 378, 385

    as novelist, 387–89

    occasional reticence of, 382–85

    as poet, 386–87, 389–90, 391, 396–97

    political convictions of, 385, 391–94

    preface to first diary of, 378, 379

    prostitutes frequented by, 384, 385

    publishing of diaries intended by, 3, 382

    reading and cultural pursuits of, 379–80

    roman letters used by, 385

    romantic affairs of, 383–84

    structural weaknesses in works of, 388–89

    as teacher, 381, 382–83, 391–92

    on Tokyo, 387

    works abandoned before completion by, 388

Ishizu Hiroshi, 475–78

Itagaki Taisuke, 256

Italy:

    Kume's travels in, 104

    Ryūhoku's travels in, 121–22, 124–25, 128–29

    Shibusawa's reportage on, 84, 89*n*

    Sōseki's travels in, 216–17

Itō Gingetsu, 438–39, 445*n*

Itō Hirobumi, 90

"Itō Society of Local Friends," 479–80

Iwakura, Prince, 305

Iwakura Tomomi, 85, 90, 93, 127, 269

Iyo Maru, 441

Izumi Kyōka, 301

Japanese language:

    Europeans' study of, 50–51

    Okinawan dialect and, 166–67, 183*n*

Japanese wares:
  displayed in Europe, 51, 60, 61, 62, 67–68, 86, 103–4
  European imitations of, 105–6
  Fuchibe's dismay at quality of, 61, 86
Jimmu, emperor of Japan, 259, 393
Jishiroku (An Up-to-Date Record) (Kōtoku Shūsui), 436–41
  as part of larger diary, 438–39
Jiyū Shimbun (The Liberal Newspaper), 337
"Jiyū wa Senketsu wo mote Kawazaru Bekarazaru Ron" (Why Liberty Must Be Bought with Fresh Blood) (Ueki Emori), 256
Johnson, Albert, 441, 442, 445
Journal of a Voyage to the West (Kōsei Nichijō) (Narushima Ryūhoku), 120–31
Journey to America in His Excellency's Service (Hōshi Meriken Kikō) (Kimura Yoshitake), 31–40
"Journey to France and England" (Futsueikō) (Shibata Takenaka), 73–75
Journey to Hakodate (Hakodate Kikō) (Niijima Jō), 229–31
Journey to the West (Seikōki) (Fukuzawa Yukichi), 64–72

Kafū. See Nagai Kafū
Kagetsu Sōshi (A Tale of Flowers and the Moon), 290
Kaifū Maru, Niijima's journeys aboard, 227, 228–31
Kaikoku Heidan (Military Talks for a Naval Country) (Mori Ōgai), 190–91
Kainan Shigaku (Tokyo), 254
Kajin no Kigū (Chance Meetings with Beautiful Women) (Tōkai Sanshi), 205
Kakehashi (narrow "bridges" along cliffs), 143

Kamehameha IV, king of Hawaii, 15–16
Kamo no Chōmei, 275–76
Kaneko Kiichi, 430
Kanrin Maru, 44
  American assistance to, 32–33, 35, 37, 38–39
  Kimura's voyages on, 31–40
  Muragaki's mission and, 12, 14, 17, 31
  preparations for voyage of, 33–34
Kansōroku (Record of Impressions) (Arishima Takeo), 405
Kao Tsung, emperor of China, 139
Karafuto. See Sakhalin
Katsu Kaishū, 12, 31, 33
Katsura Kogorō. See Kido Takayoshi
Kautsky, Karl, 430
Kawahigashi Hekigotō, 365, 366–67
Kawai Baisho, 271, 272–73, 274, 275, 280
Kawai Koume, 270–82
  continuity of woman's occupation depicted by, 271, 277
  education of, 271
  motives of, for keeping diary, 272
  opening to West and, 270–71, 273–78
  as painter, 271–72, 273, 280
  prodigies described by, 278–80
  sake consumed in household of, 272–73
  on Satsuma Rebellion, 280–82
  violence and danger of time recorded by, 275–77
  waka composed by, 271, 274–75, 276–77
Kawai Yūsuke, 274, 280
Kawakami Otojirō, 317, 319n
Keiō University, 255
Kenkō, 298
Ker, William P., 214
Ki no Tsurayuki, 355–56
Kidd, Benjamin, 438, 445n
Kido Takayoshi (also known as Katsura Kogorō), 90, 127, 249–52

background of, 251
dull writing style of, 252
human interest lacking in diary of, 250–52
on Niijima, 249–50
Kigen-setsu, 393
Kimbara Meizen, 165
Kimura Yoshitake, 31–40, 508
friendships between Americans and, 37–38, 39–40
Muragaki compared to, 31–32, 34, 36–37, 39
ocean crossings of, 35–36, 40
promotion bestowed on, 34
in San Francisco, 36–40
Kindaichi Kyōsuke, 395
Kinoshita Mokutarō, 470–85, 508
America and Europe visited by, 481–85
on appropriate manner and content for diary, 471–72, 473–74
foreign languages spoken by, 472–73, 474, 480, 483
gap in diaries of, 470, 480
Izu and Bōshū Peninsula toured by, 474–78
medical career of, 472
motives of, for keeping diary, 471
precision of descriptions by, 476
superiority feelings of, 479–80
terseness of later diaries by, 480, 482
Kinoshita Naoe, 430
Kinsei Ezo Jimbutsu Shi (Account of Ezo People in Recent Times) (Matsuura Takeshirō), 155–60, 161
Kishū (beggar), 340–41
Kita Ezo Yoshi (Additional Account of Northern Ezo) (Matsuura Takeshirō), 150–51
Kitahara Hakushū, 397
Kitashirakawa, Prince, 171–72
Kiyo (maid), 455, 456–60
Koch, Robert, 195, 206
Kōchi Shimbun, 259

Kōda Rohan, 290, 297, 301
Kōdayū, 10
Koestler, Arthur, 485
Ko-Imari ceramics, 105
Kojiki (Record of Ancient Matters), 233
Kōkai Nikki (Diary of a Voyage) (Muragaki Norimasa), 10–28
Kōkai Nikki (Diary of a Voyage) (Niijima Jō), 242–43
Kokinshū, 355–56
Kokumin no Tomo (The Nation's Friend), 346
Kokumin Shimbun, 342, 346
Komi village (Iriomote), 176–77
Kondō Morishige, 157
Kosa Fuku Kaza (A Wind Blows the Northern Desert) (Nakarai Tōsui), 296–97
Kōsai Nikki (Diary of a Voyage to the West) (Mori Ōgai), 190–93
Kōsai Nikki (Voyage to the West) (Shibusawa Eiichi), 77–89
Asian travels in, 77–84
European travels in, 84–87
writing of, 88n
Kōsei Nichijō (Journal of a Voyage to the West) (Narushima Ryūhoku), 120–31
Kōshin Nikki (Kōshin Diary) (Kinoshita Mokutarō), 471–72
Kōtoku Shūsui, 436–45, 497
in America, 436, 438, 441–45
diary volumes likely destroyed by, 438–39, 447
drunken episodes of, 439, 440–41
English studied by, 441, 442
imprisonment of, 441–42, 443
motives of, for keeping diary, 438, 439
poem addressed to Johnson by, 445
political convictions of, 436, 441–43, 445n–46n
profligate past of, 439
trial and execution of, 393, 436, 448, 463, 502
Koume. See Kawai Koume

Kropotkin, Prince Pyotr, 393, 394, 430, 432, 436
Kuang-hsū, emperor of China, 259
Kume Kunitake, 90–115, 121, 124, 127, 130, 252
  on American character, 91–92
  in Ceylon, 98–99
  Christianity disliked by, 107–11
  as Confucian scholar, 91, 109
  on differences among nations of West, 113
  on differences between orientals and occidentals, 94–96, 111–12
  in England, 100, 101–3, 108
  in France, 114
  on imperialism, 112–13
  literary appeal of writings of, 98, 99
  museums and art galleries visited by, 101–8
  ocean voyage of, 90–91, 92–93
  progress as viewed by, 102–4
  in Russia, 114–15
  in San Francisco, 93–97, 99–100
  sensitive to scenic beauty, 97–99
  on treatment accorded to Western women, 99–101
"Kumo wa Tensai de aru" (The Clouds Are Geniuses) (Ishikawa Takuboku), 388
Kunashiri, 149
Kunigami region (Okinawa), 173
Kunikada Shūji, 339, 340, 350
Kunikida Doppo, 329–54, 471
  career plans of, 336–38
  divorce of, 350
  drinking episode and, 334–35
  earnestness of, 331
  as fiction writer, 341, 351, 352n
  high-flown ideals of, 330, 332–33, 337, 343
  independent life in Hokkaidō sought by, 347, 348, 349
  inspired by ordinary people of Saiki, 339–41, 352n
  internal nature of diary of, 329–30

  as journalist, 337, 338, 342–45, 346
  love craved by, 341–42, 347, 348
  marriage of, 349–50
  maturation of, 344–45
  morning prayers of, 347
  Nobuko's affair with, 342, 347–50
  occasional childishness of, 331, 332
  political ambitions of, 336–37
  readings of, 335–36, 346
  on role of poet, 335–36
  self-examinations of, 330, 332–35, 336–37, 338, 344–45, 346
  seriousness seen as virtue by, 330
  sex life of, 333–34
  Sino-Japanese War and, 342–45, 346
  as teacher, 329, 337, 338, 339
  Western influences on, 330–31, 332, 334, 335, 336, 338, 339, 340, 341, 346, 347
  world of nature and, 338, 340, 343
Kuril Islands, 148, 164
  Matsuura's journey to, 149
Kuroda Kiyotaka, Count, 304
Kuroi Me to Chairo no Me (Black Eyes and Brown Eyes) (Tokutomi Roka), 462
Kuroshio (Black Current), 447–48
Kuroyanagi Shōha, 215
Kusaka, 286
Kusamakura (The Three-Cornered World) (Natsume Sōseki), 219, 222, 224n
Kyoto:
  movement of capital to Edo from, 251
  Ueki's visits to, 257–58

Land of Netsuke, The (Netsuke no Kuni) (Takamura Kōtaro), 485
Lanman, Mr., 308
Lauer, Gustav von, 198
Legge, James, 50, 55n
Leisurely Account of the Journey to Europe of a Fly on a Horse's Tail (Biyō Ōkō Manroku) (Ichikawa Wataru), 44–54

Lepers, 173–74
Letters on Commonplace Matters (Tsu-
kinami Shōsoku), 290
Letters to My Beloved Brother (Aitei
Tsūshin) (Kunikida Doppo),
343
Li T'ai-po, 97, 98
Lincoln, Abraham, 24
Lisbon, first Japanese embassy in, 62, 70
London, 114
first Japanese embassy in, 51, 53, 61,
67–68
Japanese wares in, 51, 61, 67–68
pollution in, 130
Sōseki's stay in, 217–23
Umeko's visits to, 308–9
Longfellow, Henry Wadsworth, 330
Lotus and the Robot, The (Koestler), 485
Lu Yu, 136
Ludwig II, king of Bavaria, 206–7
Lu-sheng (Rosei), 138

Macbeth (Shakespeare), 290
Mackey, Captain, 37, 38, 39
Malaria, 165, 175, 181
Mamiya Rinzō, 10, 148, 157
Manjirō, John, 10
Marie Antoinette, queen of France, 126
Marseilles:
first Japanese embassy in, 46, 66
Ryūhoku's visit to, 125
Marumaru Chimbun, 437
Maruya Kiichi, 385
Marx, Karl, 443
Masaoka Ritsu, 356, 364, 365, 367, 371,
372–73
Masaoka Shiki, 1–2, 355–75, 380, 508
afterworld scene envisioned by, 374
birthday parties of, 365, 366–67
curiosity about outside world pre-
served by, 359
disciples' visits to, 365–67, 368–69,
371
early critical essays by, 355–56
food as interest of, 364–65

inventions presented to, 365–66
irritable behavior of, 367, 371–73
as judge of new poetic compositions,
356, 363–64
love affairs not revealed by, 373–74
motives of, for keeping diary, 357,
358–59
as poet, 356, 360
readings of, 361–62, 363, 364
sense of humor of, 357, 366–67,
374–75
sickroom described by, 360–61
sister as depicted by, 372–73
struck with tuberculosis, 356
suffering of, 367–68, 369–73
suicide contemplated by, 369–71
youthful ambitions of, 362–63
Materialism, Kume's views on, 111–12
Mathilde, princess of France, 86
Matsudaira Yasunao, 44–45
Matsuura Takeshirō, 148–61
Ainu admired by, 154–55, 156, 157,
161
at Ainu feast, 160–61
background of, 148
bear episode described by, 151–52
countrymen harshly described by,
155–56
on difficulties of travel in north,
158–59
equipment and clothing carried by,
150–51
foods described by, 151–54
Russian encroachments and, 149–50,
157
Sakhalin visited by, 149, 150–51, 155
unpleasant aspects of life among
Ainu, 158
as Zen priest, 149
Maximilian, emperor of Mexico, 85
Meiji, emperor of Japan (Mutsuhito),
120, 392–93, 448, 450
Meiji period:
abandonment of traditional poetic
forms in, 355

Meiji period (*cont'd*)
 first mission sent to West in, 90–115
 foreign influences in, 269–71, 277–78
 Kafū's critiques of, 495–504
 Nō theater and, 85
 persistence of woman's occupation
  in, 271, 277
Meiji Restoration, 87, 114, 251, 280
 Koume's depiction of time of,
  270–82
Meiroku Zasshi, 255, 261
Mi no Furugoromo (Higuchi Ichiyō),
 291–92
Military Talks for a Naval Country
 (Kaikoku Heidan) (Mori
 Ōgai), 190–91
Mill, John Stuart, 255
Milton, John, 335
Minamoto Tametomo, 178, 179, 180
Mineko. *See* Mori Mineko
Minidoka, Idaho, internment camp in,
 325–26
Mino (maid), 459–60
Miyako Island, 177, 183*n*
Mizutani Makuma, 333–34
Mogami Tokunai, 10, 157
Mokutarō. *See* Kinoshita Mokutarō
Mori Arinori, 136, 249, 264*n*
Mori Hiroshi, 426
Mori Mariko, 316, 318
Mori Mineko, 313–19
 daughter-in-law's strained relations
  with, 313, 318
 familiar with Western tastes and
  culture, 315
 Ichiyō compared to, 314–15
 on interment of mother's ashes,
  315–16
 modern language and literary tastes
  of, 315
 motives of, for keeping diary,
  313–14
 theater attended by, 315, 317
 thoughts and emotions concealed by,
  313, 314, 316–17

Mori Ōgai, 190–210, 315, 317, 377, 386,
 480
 birthday party for, 199–200
 civilian clothes worn by, 194
 course of study of, 195
 "The Dancing Girl" by, 204
 faces described by, 196
 farewell party for, 200
 German etiquette mastered by,
  193–94, 197–98
 German women admired by, 201–2
 German women's relations with,
  202, 203–4
 homesickness of, 205
 hostile attitudes encountered by, 201,
  207–8
 Japanese companions of, 205, 206
 on Japanese men's relations with
  European women, 202–3
 kanshi composed by, 190–92
 letters of, 314
 literary interests of, 205
 Ludwig II's death and, 206–7
 mission of, 190, 195
 mistaken for another Japanese,
  200–201
 mother's diary and, 313–14, 318–19
 on Naumann's address, 207–8
 participation of, in German life, 195,
  196–200, 208–9
 popular with fellow students,
  194–95, 209
 proficient in German, 193, 195, 198
 on prostitution, 202
 return of, from war, 318
 Sōseki compared to, 213–14, 219,
  223
 talk delivered in German by, 198–99
 uninterested in scenery or natural
  beauty, 196
 various nationalities encountered by,
  198
 voyage of, 190–91
 wartime diaries of, 314
Mori Shigeko, 313, 314, 318

Morimoto Kōkichi, 407, 408–17, 419–20, 421, 423–24
   Arishima converted to Christianity by, 406–12, 416–17, 418
   Arishima's suicide pact with, 415–16
   cooling of Arishima's relationship with, 424
   possible sexual relations between Arishima and, 413
Moriyama Takichirō, 57
Morley, John, 335–36
Moxa, 51
Muragaki Norimasa, 10–28, 74, 161, 199, 231, 508
   banquet attended by, 17–18
   career of, 10–11
   and customs relating to food, 15, 34
   in Hawaii, 14–16
   on informality of Americans, 17–18, 20–25
   informed of mission to America, 11
   Kimura compared to, 31–32, 34, 36–37, 39
   motives of, for keeping diary, 27
   in New York, 26–27
   ocean voyages of, 13–15, 16–17, 27
   Panama isthmus crossed by, 18–19
   poems composed by, 10, 12–13, 14, 16, 19, 23
   in San Francisco, 16–18
   skeptical about American democracy, 23–24, 25
   in Washington, D.C., 20–26
Murasaki Shikibu, 288, 289, 301
Museums, 52, 53, 58
   Japanese wares in, 103–4, 105, 106
   Kume's visits to, 101–8
   lacked by Japan, 102, 103
   progress and, 102–4
Mushakōji Saneatsu, 463–64
Music:
   of Ainu, 155
   Western, 13, 14, 16, 25, 36, 38, 39, 53, 58, 207, 380, 392, 492

Mutsuhito (Emperor Meiji), 120, 392–93, 448, 450
My Six-Foot Sickbed (Byōshō Rokushaku) (Masaoka Shiki), 356–62, 365, 374–75
Myōjō, 383, 480

Nabeshima, Prince, 250
Nagai Kafū, 2, 488–504, 508
   in America, 488–94, 498
   on American vs. Japanese scenery, 498–99
   as antiquarian, 501–2
   Bernhardt performance seen by, 492–93
   fascinated by West, 498
   fictional elements in diary of, 495
   in France, 494
   literary career pursued by, 492, 494
   literary style of, 497
   Meiji Japan criticized by, 495–504
   opera attended by, 492
   portrayed as pianist in diary, 495, 496, 504
   prostitute's affair with, 491, 492, 493–94
   return of, to Japan, 497–98
   travel to France as goal of, 488, 490, 491, 494
Nakahama Manjirō, 229, 244n–45n
Nakajima Utako, 292
Nakamura Keiu, 255
Nakarai Tōsui, 292, 293–97
   failings of, as writer, 294, 296–97
   Ichiyō's decision to break with, 286, 295, 298
   Ichiyō's description of, 293–94
   Ichiyō's feelings for, 295, 296
   Ichiyō's first meeting with, 286–87, 293–94
Naples, Sōseki's visit to, 216–17
Napoleon I (Bonaparte), emperor of France, 85, 242
Napoleon III, emperor of France, 70, 71, 128, 252

Narrow Road of Oku (Bashō), 495

Narushima Ryūhoku, 119–31, 172, 256
 adventurous eating of, 121–22, 125
 antiquities as interest of, 124–25
 Asian people derided by, 123–24
 Asian travels of, 121–24
 churches visited by, 124
 daughter's death and, 129
 difficult voyage of, 120–21
 in England, 129–30
 fall of shogunate and, 120, 127, 128
 foreign languages spoken by, 120, 122, 126
 foreigners' friendships with, 122, 127
 in France, 122, 124, 125–28, 129
 in Hong Kong, 121, 123, 192
 in Italy, 121–22, 124–25, 128–29
 kanshi by, 120–21, 122, 123–24, 125, 128, 130
 open to new experiences, 122–23
 posts held by, 119–20
 theater and opera attended by, 126

Natsume Sōseki, 213–23, 377, 387–88, 485
 brevity of diary entries of, 214
 depressed mood of, 214, 221–23
 indifferent to scenery, 216–17
 in Italy, 216–17
 Japanese and English people contrasted by, 218, 222
 at ladies' teas, 221–22
 in London, 217–23
 as novelist, 219
 Ōgai compared with, 213–14, 219, 223
 in Paris, 217
 on pollution in England, 218–19
 racial differences noted by, 219
 as scholar of English literature, 219–21
 voyage of, 214–17
 Westerners disdained by, 215–16, 221–22

Naturalism, 497

Naumann, Edmund, 207–8

Navy, Japanese:
 first ship of, 31; *see also Kanrin Maru*
 signal flag first raised by, 36

Netsuke no Kuni (The Land of Netsuke) (Takamura Kōtaro), 485

New Account of Yanagibashi (Ryūkō Shinshi) (Narushima Ryūhoku), 119

New Poetry Society, 396–97

New Year's Day celebrations, 196–97, 205

New York:
 Arishima's visit to, 427
 Kafū's visits to, 490, 491–94
 Muragaki's mission in, 26–27

Newspapers, Western, 52–53, 87

Nichiren Shōnin Tsuji Seppō (The Holy Man Nichiren's Sermons at the Crossroads) (Mori Ōgai), 317

Nihon:
 poetry submitted to, 356, 363–64
 Shiki's writings for, 356, 357–62

Nihongi (Chronicles of Japan), 290

Niijima Jō, 225–44, 306, 462
 American benefactor of, 242–43
 Amherst College attended by, 244
 background of, 226
 in Boston, 242–43, 249
 as convert to Christianity, 225–26, 227–28, 238, 240, 241, 243
 diary vs. later memoir of, 240, 241
 Dutch warships seen by, 226
 foreign travel as desire of, 227, 228–29, 234–35
 Hakodate visited by, 228–35
 Kido's mentions of, 249–50
 language studies of, 226, 231–32, 236, 237, 243
 menial tasks performed by, 236
 name of, 226, 239, 242, 244n
 parting of, from family, 228–30
 poems composed by, 230, 235, 241–42
 poor eyesight of, 232–33

samurai identity of, 226, 236, 237–38, 239, 240, 241
smuggled aboard American ship, 234–37
voyage to America of, 234–42
Western-style haircut of, 238
Nikolai (Russian priest), 232, 233–34
"Ningen Isshō no Gotoshi" (A Person's Life Is Like a Flower) (Ueki Emori), 261
Nitobe Inazō, 406–8, 421, 423
Nō drama, 85, 126
Nonomiya Kikuko, 287
Noro Kaiseki, 271
Nozarashi Kikō (Exposed in the Fields) (Bashō), 136–37

Ōbei Nikki (Europe and America Diary) (Ōta Masao), 481
Odin, 64–65
Ōgai. See Mori Ōgai
Ogasawara Okoto, 452–54
Ogasawara Zembei, 452
Ogata Kōan, 68, 231
Ogata Korenao, 203
Oka Takayoshi, 255–56
Okinawa:
    Ainu compared to inhabitants of, 181–82
    Confucian culture in, 169–70
    education in, 177
    food in, 168–69
    health problems in, 173–74
    heat in, 167–68
    inhabitants of, viewed as Japanese, 166, 167, 173, 178–79, 182
    Japanese viewed as intruders in, 172–73
    language of, 166–67
    marriages between Japanese men and women of, 180
    poisonous snakes in, 182
    Prince Kitashirakawa's state visit to, 171–72

Sasamori's adoption of local way of life in, 167, 168
Sasamori's mission to, 164–74, 177–82
sugar production in, 164–65
see also Ryūkyū Islands
Ōkō Nikki (Diary of a Journey to Europe) (Fuchibe Tokuzō), 57–62
Ōkubo Toshimichi, 90, 91, 127
Ōkuma Shigenobu, 91
"Old Gen" (Gen Oji) (Kunikida Doppo), 341, 351, 352n
On Heroes (Carlyle), 330
On Liberty (Mill), 255
Ono Azusa, 261
Opium, 140–41
Order of the Rising Sun, 207
Ōshima, 274
Ōta Masao, 481
Otokichi, 65
Ōyama Iwao, 196
Ozaki Kōyō, 290, 295

Pacific War (1941–45). See World War II
Pan no Kai (Devotees of Pan), 479–80
Parasite Plant (Yadorigi) (Tokutomi Roka), 452
Pari Gozaikan Nikki (Diary of His Excellency's Stay in Paris) (Shibusawa Eiichi), 87
Paris:
    brothels in, 101
    first Japanese embassy in, 45–46, 50, 51, 53–54, 59–60, 66–67, 70
    Kume's visit to, 114
    Mokutarō's visit to, 483–85
    Ryūhoku's visit to, 122, 124, 125–28, 129
    Shibusawa's visit to, 85–87
    Sōseki's visit to, 217
    teaching of Japanese language in, 51
Paris Exposition (1867), 77, 85–86, 87
Peabody, F. W., 429
Pearl Harbor, 323–24

Peers' School (Yokohama), 403–4, 405–6

Peking, British and French troops' capture of, 111

Perry, Matthew Calbraith, 19, 26, 189, 273–76

Perry, Mrs. Matthew, 26–27

"Person's Life Is Like a Flower, A" (Ningen Isshō no Gotoshi) (Ueki Emori), 261

Pettenkofer, Max von, 195

Philadelphia:
  Arishima as student in, 423, 427–28
  Muragaki's visit to, 26

Pillow Book of Sei Shōnagon, The, 289

Pinakothek (Munich), 106

Po Chü-i, 379

Poetry:
  abandonment of traditional forms in, 355
  epic, of Ainu (yukari), 157
  Shiki's early critical essays on, 355–56
  see also Tanka; specific diarists

Politicians, diaries by, 247–64

Pompeii, Kume's visit to, 104

Portugal:
  first Japanese embassy in, 62, 70
  as imperialist power, 112–13

Powhattan, 38, 44, 189
  Muragaki's mission and, 12–19, 31

Prodigies, Koume's descriptions of, 278–80

Progress:
  Christian fervor and, 109
  Kume's views on, 102–4

Prostitution:
  abolishing of, 262, 263
  in China, 80
  in Europe, 101, 114, 126, 202
  Kume's disapproval of, 101
  Niijima's comments on, 227, 230
  Takuboku and, 384, 385
  Ueki and, 257–63

Protestantism, 108, 110. See also Christianity

Racial differences, 219, 427

Ranke, Johannes, 201

Realism, European painting and, 53, 106–7

"Record of Foam on the Water, A" (Utakata no Ki) (Mori Ōgai), 207

Record of Impressions (Kansōroku) (Arishima Takeo), 405

Red Sea, 124

"Resolution and Independence" (Wordsworth), 336

Roanoke, 19–20

Robinson Crusoe, 227, 228, 242, 244n

Rocky Mountains, 426

Roka. See Tokutomi Roka

Rokumeikan (Tokyo), 24, 213–14, 269

Rōmaji Nikki (Romaji Diary) (Ishikawa Takuboku), 385, 391, 396

Rome, Ryūhoku's visit to, 121–22, 124–25, 128, 129

Roosevelt, Franklin D., 325

Rosei (Lu-sheng), 138

Rosny, Léon de, 51, 67, 70

Roth, Wilhelm, 199–200, 208

Rousseau, Jean-Jacques, 335

Russia:
  first Japanese embassy in, 47, 58, 59, 69–70
  frontier between Japan and, 43
  Kume's writings on, 111–12, 114–15
  shipwrecked Japanese fishermen in, 9–10

Russian Orthodox Christianity, 108

Russians:
  Niijima's experiences with, 232–34
  in northern Japan, 149–50, 157, 231, 233

Russo-Japanese War (1904-5), 314, 318, 321, 391–92, 446n, 489, 490, 491
  Arishima's opposition to, 423, 429

Ryojō (Travel Sadness) (Yokomitsu Ri-
    ichi), 108
Ryōhoku. *See* Narushima Ryūhoku
Ryūkō Shinshi (New Account of Yana-
    gibashi) (Narushima Ryūh-
    oku), 119
Ryūkyō Islands, 148
    Chinese claims to, 166, 170–71
    cold-heartedness ascribed to people
        of, 179–80
    dialect spoken in, 166–67, 183*n*
    education in, 177–78
    misery of life in, 166, 173–77, 178,
        181
    outer islands of, 167, 174–77, 181
    people of, 166, 167, 173, 178–79,
        182
    ruling family of, 171, 172, 173
    Sasamori's mission to, 164–82
    see also Okinawa

Sacramento, Kume's visit to, 97
Sada Yacco, 34
Saigō Takamori, 251
Saigon:
    Ōgai's visit to, 192
    Ryūhoku's visit to, 123
    Shibusawa's visit to, 81–82
Saikaku, 301
Saikyō Maru, 343
St. Petersburg, first Japanese embassy
    in, 47, 59, 69–70
Saitō Ryokuu, 437, 438, 489, 497
Saitō Tomezō, 35
Sakai Kiyoshi, 271
Sakai Toshihiko, 437–38, 439–40
Sakamoto Shihōda, 366–67, 370, 371
Sakhalin (Karafuto):
    Japanese-Russian frontier on, 43
    Matsuura's journeys to, 149, 150–51,
        155
    Russian encroachments in, 149–
        50
Sakurai Shin, 439
Samukawa Sokotsu, 367

Samurai:
    in administration of Ryūkyūs, 175, 177
    appeal of China among, 135
    unequal foot sizes of, 127
San Francisco:
    earthquake in (1906), 443–45
    Grand Hotel in, 93–94
    Kimura's visit to, 32, 36–40
    Kume's visit to, 93–97, 99–100
    Mokutarō's visit to, 482
    Muragaki's visit to, 16–18
    Shūsui's visit to, 442–45
Sandō (narrow "bridges" along cliffs),
    143–45
San'un Kyōu Nikki (Diary of Bridges in
    the Clouds, Rain in the Gorges)
    (Takezoe Shin'ichirō), 135–46
Sartor Resartus (Carlyle), 407
Sasaki Nobuko, 342, 347–50, 426
Sasamori Gisuke, 164–82
    background of, 164
    on Chinese influence in Okinawa,
        169–70
    on dangers of mission, 165
    on education in southern islands,
        177–78
    heat's effects on, 167–68
    language difficulties of, 166–67
    local customs followed by, 167, 168
    on misery of life in Ryūkyūs, 166,
        173–77, 178, 181
    Okinawan meal described by,
        168–69
    Okinawans and Ainu compared by,
        181–82
    on Okinawans' attachment to old
        régime, 171, 172, 173
    people of southern islands viewed as
        Japanese by, 166, 167, 173,
        178–79, 182
    on poor relations between Japanese
        and inhabitants of Ryūkyūs,
        179–80
    on Prince Kitashirakawa's state
        visit, 171–72

Sasamori Gisuke (*cont'd*)
publishing of diary and, 165–66
village officials' interviews with,
180–81
Sashida Rinzō, 35
Satomi Hakkenden (Takizawa Bakin),
475
Satsuma clan, 173, 251
Satsuma Rebellion (1877), 280–82
Savory, Captain, 234–35, 236–37, 238
Schiller, Johann Christoph Friedrich
von, 290
School for Scandal (Sheridan), 218
Scotland, Kume's travels in, 108
Scott, Dr., 429
Seclusion policy, 60–61
Sei Shōnagon, 288, 289
Seikōki (Journey to the West)
(Fukuzawa Yukichi), 64–72
Seiyū Nisshi Shō (Selections from the
Diary of a Journey to the West)
(Nagai Kafū), 488–94
"Self-Reliance" (Emerson), 332
Sesson Yūbai, 136
Sèvres, 105
Shadow of a Bird (Chōei) (Ishikawa
Takuboku), 388
Shakespeare, William, 335, 336
Shakyamuni Buddha, 404
Shanghai, Shibusawa's visit to, 78–81
Sheridan, Richard Brinsley, 218
Shibata Takenaka, 73–75, 124
Shibusawa Eiichi, 77–89, 96
in Aden, 83
in Ceylon, 82–83
European imperialism and, 79–83,
85
on Garibaldi, 84, 89n
in Hong Kong, 81
ocean voyage of, 77–78
in Paris, 85–87
in Saigon, 81–82
in Shanghai, 78–81
in Singapore, 82
West praised by, 81, 82, 83–84

Shibutami Nikki (Shibutami Diary)
(Ishikawa Takuboku), 380–82
revision of, 382, 390–91
Shiki. *See* Masaoka Shiki
Shikotan, 149
Shimazaki Tōson, 387–88, 425
Shimmi Masaoki, 22
Shimomura Toku, 321–26
arranged marriage of, 321–22
background of, 321
hardships recounted by, 323
on Pearl Harbor attack, 323–24
sent to internment camp, 325–26
voyage of, 322
Shinkichōsha Nikki (Diary of One Re-
cently Returned to His Coun-
try) (Nagai Kafū), 494–504
Shinto, 157, 418
Shipwrecked Japanese sailors, 9–10, 16,
65
Shiretoko Nikki (Shiretoko Diary)
(Matsuura Takeshirō), 159
Shiribeshi Nisshi (Daily Record of
Shiribeshi) (Matsuura Take-
shirō), 151–52
Shō Tai, 171, 172
Shō Ten, 172
Shuri Castle (Okinawa), 169
Shūsui. *See* Kōtoku Shūsui
Siebold, Philipp Franz von, 106
Sierra Nevada, Kume's descriptions of,
97
Singapore, 59
Ichikawa's visit to, 49
Ōgai's visit to, 192
Ryūhoku's visit to, 123–24
Shibusawa's visit to, 82
Sōseki's visit to, 216
Sino-Japanese War (1894–95), 171, 306,
310
Doppo's experiences during, 342–45,
346
Shiki's service in, 356
"Snowy Day, A" (Yuki no Hi)
(Higuchi Ichiyō), 297

Socialism:
  Arishima's espousal of, 405, 429, 430, 436
  compatibility of Christianity and, 430
  Shūsui and, 436, 441, 442–43
  Takuboku's views on, 385, 392, 393, 394
Socrates, 262
Sorrows of Young Werther (Goethe), 425
Sōseki. See Natsume Sōseki
Spain, as imperialist power, 112–13
Spencer, Herbert, 260
Stray Notes from a Supine Position (Gyōga Manroku) (Masaoka Shiki), 356–57, 362–63, 364, 366–73
Subaru, 318, 480
Suez Canal, 67, 83–84
Sugawara Yoshiko, 383–84
Sugiura Aizan, 88n
Sumidagawa (Sumida River) (Nagai Kafū), 504
Suzuki Sjōgo, 440
Sweden, copies of Japanese wares in, 105
Szechuan:
  sandō in, 143–45
  Takezoe's travels in, 136–46

Tachibana Kōsai, 69
Taiping Rebellion, 65
Taira, 178–79
Taishō, emperor of Japan, 403, 404, 464
Takahama Kyoshi, 357, 367
Takai Kitō, 215
Takamura Kōtaro, 485
Takeda Ayasaburō, 231, 232
"Takekurabe" (Growing Up) (Higuchi Ichiyō), 285, 300–301
Takenouchi Yasunori, 44
Takezoe Shin'ichirō, 135–46, 158
  background of, 136
  Bird's impressions compared to, 142–43
  difficult journey of, 137–42

monuments and mementoes of past visited by, 138–40
mountain scenery described by, 143–45
posts held by, 136
sorry state of Chinese society noted by, 137–38, 140–42
Takizawa Bakin, 475
Takuboku. See Ishikawa Takuboku
Tale of Flowers and the Moon, A (Kagetsu Sōshi), 290
Tale of Genji, The, 290, 380
Tales of America (Amerika Monogatari) (Nagai Kafū), 489, 490, 492, 496
Tales of France (Furansu Monogatari) (Nagai Kafū), 496
Tamashima, Niijima's visit to, 227, 228
Tanabe Kaho, 286, 293
Tanaka Fujimaro, 249, 250
T'ang-yin-hsien, 139
Tanka, 388
  advantages of form, 389, 390
  by Takuboku, 386–87, 389–90, 391, 396
Tasan Barrier, 144
Taylor, Captain, 238–41
Teahouses:
  in Japan, 87
  at Paris Exposition, 85–86
Thousand Buddha Cliff (Szechuan), 145
Three-Cornered World, The (Kusamakura) (Natsume Sōseki), 219, 222, 224n
Tobei Nikki (American Diary) (Kōtoku Shūsui), 436, 438, 441–45
Toilets:
  of Ainu, 158
  in China, 141–42
Tōkai Sanshi, 205
Toku. See Shimomura Toku
Tokugawa Akitake, 77, 87
Tokugawa Ieyoshi, 274
Tokugawa Jikki (True Record of the Tokugawas), 119

Tokugawa period:
    end of, 87, 120, 127, 128
    missions sent to West in, 10–89
    Nō theater associated with, 85
    seclusion policy in, 60–61
Tokugawa Yoshinobu, 77, 87, 88n, 280
Tokutomi Aiko, 450, 451, 459, 460, 461,
        465
    comment appended to Roka's diary
        by, 454
    hospitalization of, 454, 455–56, 458
    Roka's expressions of hatred for, 457,
        466
    Roka's love for, 457, 458, 463, 466
    Roka's sexual drives and, 452–58
    Roka's sexual relations with, 453, 458
    twentieth wedding anniversary of,
        448–49
Tokutomi Roka, 447–66
    animosity between brother and,
        448–52, 456, 463, 467n
    artistic name abandoned by, 447
    brutality of, 449–50, 458–61
    childlessness of, 449
    daily routine of, 461
    diaries destroyed by, 447, 470, 471
    enraged over trivial incidents,
        449–50
    fearful of wife reading his diary, 454
    hatred for parents expressed by,
        450–53, 463
    indifferent to World War I, 448, 465
    motives of, for keeping diary, 448
    sexual drives of, 452–58, 464
    social consciousness abandoned by,
        463–64
    twentieth wedding anniversary of,
        448–49
    visitors discouraged by, 466
    as writer, 461–63, 468n
Tokutomi Sohō, 335, 338, 342, 344–45,
        346, 350, 448–52, 456, 463, 467n
Tokutomi Tsuruko, 449
Tokyo (Edo):
    Kafū's views on, 501

movement of capital from Kyoto to,
        251
    Takuboku's visit to, 387
    Ueki's first visit to, 254–56
Tokyo University, 207
Tolstoy, Count Leo, 335, 429, 447, 465
Tōsui. See Nakarai Tōsui
Trade, Japanese indifference to, 61, 95
Train journeys, 19, 66
Travel Sadness (Ryojō) (Yokomitsu Ri-
        ichi), 108
Tristan und Isolde (Wagner), 492
True Account of a Tour of America and
        Europe (Kume Kunitake). See
        Beiō Kairan Jikki
True Record of the Tokugawas (Toku-
        gawa Jikki), 119
Tso Chuan, 256
Tsuda Mamichi, 261
Tsuda Seiichi, 136
Tsuda Sen, 304, 308
Tsuda Umeko, 304–11
    on American food, 307
    as Christian, 309–10
    in England, 308–10, 311
    English-language writings of, 304,
        306, 307, 308
    first American clothes obtained by, 305
    Japan and Western nations com-
        pared by, 308, 309
    language skills of, 306–7
    letters of, 308
    occasional depressed moods of, 310,
        311
    received by empress, 305
    sent to study abroad, 304–8
    susceptible to neither loneliness nor
        homesickness, 311
Tsukinami Shōsoku (Letters on Com-
        monplace Matters), 290
Tu Fu, 379
Turgenev, Ivan S., 430, 476
"Twenty Rhymes on Bidding Farewell
        to the Venerable American
        Johnson" (Kōtoku Shūsui), 445

Uchimura Kanzo, 350, 406, 422–23, 424, 428
Uda Ryūsui, 497, 500, 501
Ueda Misao, 449
Ueki Emori, 254–64
  abolishing of prostitution advocated by, 262, 263
  antimonarchical sentiments of, 259–60
  background of, 254
  Christian thought as influence on, 256–57
  dating system of, 259
  dreams of, 258, 260, 263–64
  equal rights for women advocated by, 260–61, 262
  geishas frequented by, 257–63
  imprisonment of, 255–56
  Kyoto visited by, 257–58
  marriage of, 263
  police interrogations and surveillance of, 257
  referring to himself as "emperor," 258–60
  on sexual desire, 261
  Tokyo first visited by, 254–56
Uemura Masahisa, 338, 349
Uffizi (Florence), 104
Umeko. See Tsuda Umeko
"Umoregi" (A Buried Life) (Higuchi Ichiyō), 297
Undeceitful Record, An (Azamukazaru no Ki) (Kunikida Doppo), 329–54
"Unforgettable People" (Wasureenu Hitobito) (Kunikida Doppo), 352n
United States, 43–44, 114
  Arishima's studies in, 422–23, 424–31
  banquets in, 17–18, 36
  dancing in, 24–25, 39
  democracy in, 23–24, 25, 92
  England contrasted with, 113
  first Japanese mission to, 10–28, 45, 64, 65

Japanese emigrés to, 321–26
Kafū's travels to, 488–94, 498
Kimura's mission to, 31–40
Kume's account of mission to, 90–97, 99–100, 108
Mokutarō's travels in, 481–82
Niijima's sojourn in, 242–44, 249–50
Niijima's voyage to, 234–42
opening of relations with, 11, 22–23, 61
Shōsui's travels in, 436, 438, 441–45
Umeko's travels in, 304–8, 309, 311
women in, 17, 22–26, 36, 99–101
young Japanese illegally traveling to, 189–90
Up-to-Date Record, An (Kōtoku Shōsui). See Jishiroku
"Utakata no Ki" (A Record of Foam on the Water) (Mori Ōgai), 207

Verbeck, Guido, 91
Vermeer, Jan, 431
Versailles, 58–59, 126
Victoria, queen of England, 68, 86, 100
Vienna Exposition, 105, 107
Voltaire, 156
Voyage to the West (Shibusawa Eiichi). See Kōsai Nikki

Wada Yoshie, 286
Wagner, Richard, 207, 380, 392, 492
Wakaba Kage (In the Shade of Spring Leaves) (Higuchi Ichiyō), 292–301
Wang Yang-ming, 335, 336
Washington, D.C.:
  Arishima's studies in, 430
  Muragaki's visit to, 20–26
Washington, George, 92
"Wasureenu Hitobito" (Unforgettable People) (Kunikida Doppo), 352n
Werther (Goethe), 348
Whitman, Walt, 27, 429

"Why Liberty Must Be Bought with Fresh Blood" (Jiyū wa Senketsu wo mote Kawazaru Bekarazaru Ron) (Ueki Emori), 256
Wild Rover, The, 239–42
Wilde, Oscar, 480
Willem II, king of Holland, 61
Wind Blows the Northern Desert, A (Kosa Fuku Kaza) (Nakarai Tōsui), 296–97
Windsor Castle, 130
Women:
    American, diarists' impressions of, 17, 22–26, 36, 99–101
    continuity in lives of, despite opening to West, 271, 277
    diaries by, 267–326
    diaries of men vs., 269–71
    equal rights for, 100, 260–61, 262
    formal dress for, 101
    at Japanese teahouses, 85–86, 87
    oriental, first to travel to West, 86
    Western, Kume's account of treatment accorded to, 99–101

Wordsworth, William, 334, 335, 336, 338, 339, 340, 341, 346
World War I, 311, 448, 465
World War II, 323–26
    internment camps in, 325–26
    Pearl Harbor attack in, 323–24

Yadorigi (Parasite Plant) (Tokutomi Roka), 452
Yamaji, Ensign, 345
Yamato Club (Berlin), 206
Yamato people, 393
Yamawaki Kamejo, 263
Yokomitsu Riichi, 108
Yorozu Chōhō, 436
Yosano Akiko, 387
Yosano Tekkan, 383, 387, 396
Yoshida Shōin, 189, 251
Yoshii Isamu, 384, 480
Yūbin Hōchi, 255–56
Yüeh Fei, 139
Yukari (epic poems), 157
"Yuki no Hi" (A Snowy Day) (Higuchi Ichiyō), 297

Zola, Emile, 502